Praise for The Leaders of Their Own Learning Co

"In a world of accelerating novelty and complexity, helping young people develop agency—the ability to manage their attention and their learning—may be the most important gift we can give them. *The Leaders of their Own Learning Companion* is full of tips and tools that equip teacher teams to help students gain a clear sense of what they do well, what they need to work on, and how to improve.

—Tom Vander Ark, CEO of Getting Smart;
former executive director of education,
Bill & Melinda Gates Foundation

"As a follow-up to their excellent book, *Leaders of Their Own Learning*, EL Education offers eminently practical advice to help teachers define clear and assessable learning targets, provide learners with on-going, descriptive feedback, offer models of excellence to inspire craftsmanship, and engage students in reflective self-assessment and personalized goal setting. I recommend this book as a 'must read' for all educators!"

—Jay McTighe, educational author and consultant,
coauthor of the Understanding by Design® series

"*The Leaders of Their Own Learning Companion* is a practical and useful guide for educators and educational leaders who seek to make a difference where it matters most: improving the learning outcomes of students. Written in an accessible style with lots of useful examples, this book is an insightful and invaluable resource."

—Pedro A. Noguera, PhD, distinguished professor of education,
faculty director, Center for the Transformation of Schools,
UCLA Graduate School of Education & Information Studies

"Once again, another book from EL Education that reminds us what engagement and student ownership of learning can really mean."

—Larry Rosenstock, founder and CEO, High Tech High

"A new vision for 21st century education requires a new posture for students: to be in the lead. This message was so powerfully captured by the groundbreaking book: *Leaders of Their Own Learning*. This vision also requires a new role for teachers as the guides of self-directed learning. There has been a tremendous void in the literature on this point, until now. The companion to *The Leaders of Their Own Learning Companion* will become the teacher's holy grail for the student-led classroom."

—Ken Kay, CEO, Edleader21, co-founder of the Partnership for
21st Century Skills and coauthor of *The Leader's Guide to
21st Century Education: 7 Steps for Schools and Districts.*

"EL Education made a huge impact on teachers and students across the country with *Leaders of Their Own Learning*. The sequel, *The Leaders of Their Own Learning Companion*, builds on this success with concrete and simple—yet powerful—strategies teachers can use to make high quality student-engaged assessment come alive in their classrooms. Ron Berger's work has been inspiring me since he was an award-winning project-based learning classroom teacher—with *The Leaders of Their Own Learning Companion*, Berger and his colleagues at EL Education will inspire and support hundreds of thousands more educators."

—Bob Lenz, CEO, PBL Works, Buck Institute for Education

"A playbook for student-centered teaching and learning! *The Leaders of Their Own Learning Companion* is a seminal guide for school leaders and teachers eager to overcome the challenges of implementing student-engaged assessment. This book provides practical strategies and tips on how to deepen learning targets, engage students in reflection and improve the quality of student work. With inspiring stories, quick-wins and lesson for leaders, this book will shortly become your dog-eared guide for changing your practice and transforming your school."

—Laura McBain, K12 Lab Director of Community & Implementation, Hasso Plattner Institute of Design, Stanford University

"Learning cannot be done to us. We must empower our children to be able to lead their own lives successfully. *Leaders of Their Own Learning* and this new *Companion* provide a much-needed foundation that enables and empowers learners to step inside their learning and take the lead."

—Paul Taylor, principal, Banora Point Primary School, Banora Point, New South Wales, Australia

THE LEADERS OF THEIR OWN LEARNING COMPANION

THE LEADERS OF THEIR OWN LEARNING COMPANION

New Tools and Tips for Tackling the Common Challenges of Student-Engaged Assessment

Ron Berger
Anne Vilen
Libby Woodfin

JB JOSSEY-BASS™
A Wiley Brand

A Wiley Brand
535 Mission St, 14th Floor, San Francisco, CA 94105
www.josseybass.com

Library of Congress Cataloging-in-Publication Data is available:

ISBN 9781119596721 (Paperback)
ISBN 9781119596752 (ePDF)
ISBN 9781119596745 (ePub)

Cover Design: Wiley
Cover Image: @ EL Education

Printed in the United States of America
FIRST EDITION
PB Printing V10013399_082719

Contents in Brief

About the Authors   xxi

About EL Education   xxiii

Acknowledgments   xxv

Foreword   xxvii

Preface   xxxi

Introduction   **1**

Chapter 1   **Learning Targets**   **5**

Chapter 2   **Checking for Understanding during Daily Lessons**   **45**

Chapter 3   **Using Data with Students**   **85**

Chapter 4   **Models, Critique, and Descriptive Feedback**   **117**

Chapter 5   **Student-Led Conferences**   **155**

Chapter 6   **Celebrations of Learning**   **193**

Chapter 7   **Passage Presentations with Portfolios**   **231**

Chapter 8   **Standards-Based Grading**   **271**

Appendix: What's in the Online Toolbox?   311

References   315

Index   317

Detailed Contents

About the Authors   xxi

About EL Education   xxiii

Acknowledgments   xxv

Foreword   xxvii

Preface   xxxi

Introduction   **1**

Chapter 1   **Learning Targets**   **5**

Pre-Assessment: Track Your Progress: Chapter 1   8

Learning Target 1: I can craft high-quality learning targets   9

Challenge #1: My students are working hard and generally doing what
I've asked them to do, but they aren't always learning what they need to learn   9

Challenge #2: I'm in a rut with my learning targets. I need help varying
them more and making them more interesting for my students   14

Learning Target 2: I can use learning targets throughout a lesson to
build students' understanding and ownership of their learning   19

Challenge #3: I feel okay about writing learning targets, but I'm in a
rut about how to use them. I always introduce them and unpack them
in the same way   19

Challenge #4: I teach young children. Learning targets are really
abstract for them. How can I help my students understand and own them?   24

Challenge #5: I have a high percentage of English language learners in
my class. I'm never sure how much the learning targets help them stay
focused on their learning because of language barriers   26

Challenge #6: I'm good at introducing the learning targets for every lesson,
but I'm not so sure what I should do after that. How do I return to them
throughout the course of a lesson?   27

Challenge #7: I post my learning targets on the board or on chart paper,
but as soon as students leave the room or move on to the next
learning target, they forget what work relates to what learning target   31

Challenge #8: I know that learning targets for character are a good idea, but I don't take them as seriously as academic learning targets, and therefore, I don't take the time to really focus on them with my students   33

Learning Target 3: I can create sets of learning targets that ensure my students are aiming for grade-level standards   36

Challenge #9: I'm struggling to translate standards into learning targets. I have so many standards to cover. Should there be a learning target for every standard? Is it a one-to-one relationship?   36

Challenge #10: I'm pretty good at writing learning targets, but I struggle to choose or craft assessments that clearly demonstrate that my students have met a target (and are therefore on their way to meeting required standards)   40

Lessons for Leaders: Chapter 1   42

Post-Assessment: Track Your Progress: Chapter 1   44

Chapter 2   **Checking for Understanding during Daily Lessons**   45

Pre-Assessment: Track Your Progress: Chapter 2   49

Learning Target 1: I can build a culture of trust, growth, and collaboration in my classroom so that students can honestly assess their progress   50

Challenge #1: I haven't developed enough of a positive culture in my classroom and, as a result, my students are afraid to accurately assess their understanding in front of other students   50

Challenge #2: My students don't view learning as a collaborative effort. They don't want to share their work or talk with other students about what they know   53

Learning Target 2: I can use checking-for-understanding techniques that help students assess their progress toward learning targets and allow me to monitor their progress   60

Challenge #3: I'm having a hard time finding checking-for-understanding techniques that give me the information I need (and I don't want to spend a lot of time teaching new techniques to my students)   60

Challenge #4: I'm never sure when to use which technique during the course of a lesson. I want to be judicious and efficient and not wear my students out checking for understanding too frequently   62

Challenge #5: I struggle to efficiently track student progress while I'm observing them at work or engaged in discussions   67

Learning Target 3: I can use questions effectively to check for understanding   71

Challenge #6: I ask lots of questions, but they don't elicit rich or engaging classroom discourse   71

Challenge #7: It's one thing to check for understanding on low-level questions, but I need new strategies for asking questions with a higher cognitive demand so that I can check for a deeper level of understanding   73

Learning Target 4: I can plan effective debriefs — 79

    Challenge #8: I always run out of time for the debrief at the end of my lessons. I struggle to prioritize it even though I know it's important — 79

    Challenge #9: When debriefing a lesson, I'll have students turn and talk or reflect with a peer, but I'm not capturing what they've learned — 80

Lessons for Leaders: Chapter 2 — 82

Post-Assessment: Track Your Progress: Chapter 2 — 84

Chapter 3   **Using Data with Students** — **85**

Pre-Assessment: Track Your Progress: Chapter 3 — 88

Learning Target 1: I can create a data-informed culture in my classroom — 89

    Challenge #1: My students and their families have a rigid idea of what data is. How do I help them see the bigger picture? — 89

    Challenge #2: My students don't get excited about academic data. They don't see it as useful or meaningful — 91

    Challenge #3: Looking at the data feels like another thing to do. How do I make time? — 95

Learning Target 2: I can teach students to use data to evaluate their progress in relation to a learning target — 97

    Challenge #4: With so many students, it's impossible for me to keep track of each student's data on a daily basis. How can I enlist students in organizing, tracking, and storing their own data effectively? — 97

    Challenge #5: My students don't see illuminating trends that can motivate them to persist in their learning. How do I get them to analyze data more effectively? — 103

Learning Target 3: I can support students to set meaningful and effective goals — 107

    Challenge #6: My students learn "in the moment." How do I help them see the big picture and use today's learning to set goals for tomorrow? — 107

Lessons for Leaders: Chapter 3 — 113

Post-Assessment: Track Your Progress: Chapter 3 — 115

Chapter 4   **Models, Critique, and Descriptive Feedback** — **117**

Pre-Assessment: Track Your Progress: Chapter 4 — 120

Learning Target 1: I can distinguish between assignments that should be revised and polished into quality final drafts and those that can be just practice and reflection — 121

    Challenge #1: There's so much to do in my curriculum. I don't have time for my students to critique and revise their work — 121

    Challenge #2: It's hard to predict how long it will take for students to refine their work. How do I create a plan that supports students to do quality work? — 122

Learning Target 2: I can choose engaging and effective models to help students understand what "good" looks like in that genre of work ... 126

Challenge #3: I'm not sure what good work looks like ... 126

Challenge #4: I don't know where to find good models for my students. Where do I look? What do I look for? ... 128

Learning Target 3: I can conduct a critique lesson that motivates students and gives them concrete takeaways they can use in their work ... 136

Challenge #5: I am not sure where to begin with a critique lesson ... 136

Challenge #6: My students do their work for the most part, but they don't take much ownership of it ... 137

Learning Target 4: I can structure descriptive feedback so that it helps students see their strengths and how to improve their work ... 140

Challenge # 7: Giving students feedback takes too much time ... 140

Challenge #8: I give verbal and written feedback to students all the time, and they don't seem to learn from it. They continue to have the same weaknesses in their work ... 141

Challenge #9: Peer conferencing feels like a waste of time. How do I help my students give and get high-quality feedback? ... 143

Lessons for Leaders: Chapter 4 ... 152

Post-Assessment: Track Your Progress: Chapter 4 ... 154

Chapter 5   **Student-Led Conferences** ... **155**

Pre-Assessment: Track Your Progress: Chapter 5 ... 158

Learning Target 1: I can collaborate with my colleagues to build a schoolwide system for effective student-led conferences ... 159

Challenge #1: Just scheduling all those conferences is a challenge! ... 159

Challenge # 2: Our families can't come to conferences during the school day and many don't speak English ... 163

Learning Target 2: I can structure portfolios and conference agendas so that families get the information they need and want ... 165

Challenge #3: Students want to share their best and favorite work, but families want and need to know the full story of how their children are doing, even if they are struggling ... 165

Challenge #4: My students have trouble finding, organizing, and reflecting meaningfully on their work ... 169

Learning Target 3: I can ensure that students are prepared to lead a conference with a high-quality presentation ... 172

Challenge #5: My students have good portfolios, but their presentations are weak ... 172

Challenge #6: Students are too focused on what they did and not on what they learned ... 179

Learning Target 4: I can prepare families to engage meaningfully
in their student's conference   181

   Challenge #7: This is new for families. How do I help them let go
   of old assumptions about conferences?   181

   Challenge #8: Families don't understand their role in the conference.
   They take over instead of letting the student lead the dialogue   182

   Challenge #9: Families feel frustrated when they don't get a full picture
   of their child's learning   186

Lessons for Leaders: Chapter 5   189

Post-Assessment: Track Your Progress: Chapter 5   191

Chapter 6   **Celebrations of Learning**   **193**

Pre-Assessment: Track Your Progress: Chapter 6   196

Learning Target 1: I can choreograph the details of a celebration of learning   197

   Challenge #1: There are so many details! How do I get it all done
   while I'm teaching?   197

   Challenge #2: We are disappointed with the level of family and community
   attendance   200

Learning Target 2: I can support students to produce original, high-quality
work for an authentic audience   203

   Challenge #3: My students' work is too similar; if you've seen
   one example, you've seen them all   203

   Challenge #4: Students and community members are excited about
   the celebration, but the quality of student work is not as strong as
   it could be   204

Learning Target 3: I can display student work with power and purpose   206

   Challenge #5: Students' individual work is high quality, but our display
   doesn't do it justice   206

Learning Target 4: I can prepare students to tell the story of their learning
in a way that informs, enlightens, and moves the audience   215

   Challenge #6: Students talk about what the work is, rather than
   what they learned from doing it   215

   Challenge #7: Students don't have enough to do during the celebration   218

Learning Target 5: I can structure celebrations of learning so that families
and community members can participate meaningfully   223

   Challenge #8: Family members and guests show up to look, but
   don't know what else to do   223

   Challenge #9: I'm not sure how to include the community members
   and experts who don't have children at the school   225

Lessons for Leaders: Chapter 6   227

Post-Assessment: Track Your Progress: Chapter 6   229

Chapter 7   **Passage Presentations with Portfolios**   **231**

Pre-Assessment: Track Your Progress: Chapter 7   234

Learning Target 1: I can communicate the purpose and audience for passage
presentations   235

Challenge #1: I am not clear on the purpose and value of passage
presentations   235

Challenge #2: I haven't yet figured out how to turn passage
presentations into a tradition that really matters to students
and families, rather than just another event   237

Learning Target 2: I can support students to create multi-year portfolios
with reflections   243

Challenge #3: I have student work everywhere! I need clear systems for
saving, storing, and managing students' portfolios over multiple years   243

Challenge #4: I'm not sure what students should include in the
passage portfolio   245

Challenge #5: My students can't find or don't have academic work
from multiple years   246

Challenge #6: My students are focused on what they can do now.
They have difficulty seeing their growth over multiple years   248

Learning Target 3: I can ensure that students are prepared to lead
passage presentations with professionalism   254

Challenge #7: My Students have strong portfolios, but their
presentation skills are weak   254

Challenge #8: My students falter when they have to think on their feet   259

Learning Target 4: I can prepare families and community members for
the important roles they play in passage presentations   262

Challenge #9: I am not sure how to build the panels for passages and
what the role of panelists should be   262

Challenge #10: Family and community members don't understand
their roles in passage presentations   264

Challenge #11: Panelists listen to students but don't give
meaningful feedback   264

Lessons for Leaders: Chapter 7   268

Post-Assessment: Track Your Progress: Chapter 7   270

Chapter 8   **Standards-Based Grading**   **271**

Pre-Assessment: Track Your Progress: Chapter 8   274

Learning Target 1: I can help families and students understand the
"why" behind standards-based grading   275

Challenge #1: How will I explain standards-based grading to students
and families if I don't fully understand it myself?   275

Challenge #2: Students and families are used to traditional grading. How do I help them understand how standards-based grading supports students? 279

Learning Target 2: I can effectively implement standards-based grading in my classroom, school, or district 286

Challenge #3: I have so many standards and learning targets. Which ones should count toward grades? 286

Challenge #4: I'm still not sure how to set up my grade book or how to calculate grades 287

Challenge #5: How do I empower ALL students to track their progress toward standards-based grades? 289

Learning Target 3: I can assess my students' work habits 297

Challenge #6: How do I measure learning behaviors that develop slowly over time? 297

Challenge #7: I don't have time to assess work habits regularly and consistently 297

Challenge #8: What are my options for communicating grades for work habits on a report card so that they mean something and don't make the report card too long? 302

Challenge #9: Our required report card format doesn't include work habits. What are other ways I can use to communicate a work habits grade to students and families? 303

Challenge #10: Families and students discount work habit grades because they don't "count" on official transcripts 304

Lessons for Leaders: Chapter 8 307

Post-Assessment: Track Your Progress: Chapter 8 309

Appendix: What's in the Online Toolbox? 311
References 315
Index 317

Video Contents

Chapter 1 **Learning Targets**
Video Spotlight 1.1: Unpacking a Learning Target to Clarify Terms and Concepts
https://vimeo.com/313842309 23
Video Spotlight 1.2: Scaffolding Discussion Skills with a Socratic Circle
https://www.edutopia.org/video/scaffolding-discussion-skills-socratic-circle 31
Video Spotlight 1.3: Leading Professional Learning on Student-Engaged Assessment
https://vimeo.com/286915631 42

Chapter 2 **Checking for Understanding during Daily Lessons**
Video Spotlight 2.1: Redirecting a Lesson with Exemplars
https://vimeo.com/121494565 48
Video Spotlight 2.2: a: Creating Class Norms
https://vimeo.com/124448656 50
b: Fostering Belonging with Classroom Norms
https://www.edutopia.org/video/fostering-belonging-classroom-norms 50
Video Spotlight 2.3: Classroom Protocols in Action: Back-to-Back and Face-to-Face
https://vimeo.com/164447189 54
Video Spotlight 2.4: Reading and Thinking Like Scientists, Day 1:
Strategies for Making Meaning from Complex Scientific Text
https://vimeo.com/117019945 66
Video Spotlight 2.5: Teaching Students to Prove Their Mathematical Thinking
through Questions, Charts, and Discourse
https://vimeo.com/123960860 76

Chapter 3 **Using Data with Students**
Video Spotlight 3.1: Knowing Every Child through Index Card Rosters
https://www.edutopia.org/video/knowing-every-child-through-index-card-rosters 90
Video Spotlight 3.2: Students Own Their Progress
https://vimeo.com/43990523 96
Video Spotlight 3.3: Paper Management
https://vimeo.com/124448650 97

Video Spotlight 3.4: Menu Math at Odyssey School of Denver
https://vimeo.com/108609925   103

Video Spotlight 3.5: K–2 Skills Block: End of Cycle Assessments
https://vimeo.com/159828967   112

Chapter 4   **Models, Critique, and Descriptive Feedback**

Video Spotlight 4.1: Using a Flow Chart to Keep Student on Track
https://vimeo.com/313436214   125

Video Spotlight 4.2: What Does Good Work Look Like?
https://vimeo.com/313883577   127

Video Spotlight 4.3: Inspiring Passion-Driven Education with
Yo-Yo Ma and Ron Berger
https://vimeo.com/313883577   130

Video Spotlight 4.4: Using a Problem-Based Task with Fourth-Graders
to Create Deep Engagement in Math
https://vimeo.com/117861347   134

Video Spotlight 4.5: Inspiring Excellence Part 4: Using Models and
Critiques to Create Works of Quality
https://vimeo.com/85779855   136

Video Spotlight 4.6: a: A Group Critique Lesson
https://vimeo.com/44053703   138

b: Ron Berger: Teachers as Learners
https://www.youtube.com/watch?v=
ulG65R6hH6Y&app=desktop   138

Video Spotlight 4.7: Scaffolding Research-Based Writing with Sixth-Graders,
Part 2: Staying on Track and on Target
https://vimeo.com/127193596   140

Video Spotlight 4.8: a: Praise, Question, Suggestion
https://vimeo.com/84899365   145

b: Using a Speed Dating Protocol to Think Critically
about Writing
https://vimeo.com/124633818   145

Chapter 5   **Student-Led Conferences**

Video Spotlight 5.1: Station-Based Student-Led Conferences
in Kindergarten
https://vimeo.com/291520157   161

Video Spotlight 5.2: a: Kindergarten Student-Led Conference
https://vimeo.com/49170218   172

b: Middle School Student-Led Conference
https://vimeo.com/41363907   172

c: High School Student-Led Conference
https://vimeo.com/43992567   172

Video Spotlight 5.3: Developing Agency with Student-Led Conferences

https://www.edutopia.org/video/developing-agency-student-led-conferences 185

Video Spotlight 5.4: Schoolwide Structures for Student-Led Conferences

https://vimeo.com/58187029 189

Chapter 6 **Celebrations of Learning**

Video Spotlight 6.1: Fox Creek Elementary Celebration of Learning

https://vimeo.com/313905677 197

Video Spotlight 6.2: Inspiring Excellence Part 1: Overview

https://vimeo.com/85779604 204

Video Spotlight 6.3: Inspiring Excellence Part 6: Writing and

Speaking with Power

https://vimeo.com/85789701 205

Video Spotlight 6.4: School as a Living Museum

https://www.teachingchannel.org/video/make-student-work-public-hth 206

Video Spotlight 6.5: Kindergarteners as Experts

https://vimeo.com/69120172 219

Video Spotlight 6.6: a: Students Share Work That Matters with an

Authentic Audience

https://vimeo.com/48803088 226

b: Community Faces: Humanizing the Immigrant Label

https://vimeo.com/276987940 226

Chapter 7 **Passage Presentations with Portfolios**

Video Spotlight 7.1: Portfolio Presentations from Ron Berger's Classroom

https://vimeo.com/313907607 235

Video Spotlight 7.2: Passage Presentations in Secondary Schools

https://vimeo.com/68481107 236

Video Spotlight 7.3: Third-Grade Passage Presentation at

Tahoe Expedition Academy

https://vimeo.com/312847213 236

Video Spotlight 7.4: a: Elevating Student Voice through Senior Talks

https://www.edutopia.org/video/elevating-

student-voice-through-senior-talks 238

b: Edward's Senior Talk

https://vimeo.com/81527464 238

Video Spotlight 7.5: Reflecting on Work Habits Fosters Growth

https://vimeo.com/313899543 251

Video Spotlight 7.6: Prompting Students to Reflect during Passage Presentations

https://vimeo.com/313894664 260

Chapter 8 **Standards-Based Grading**

Video Spotlight 8.1: Why Use a Standards-Based Grading System?
https://vimeo.com/43992307   279

Video Spotlight 8.2: Understanding Grades in a Standards-Based System
https://vimeo.com/43990524   288

Video Spotlight 8.3: Descriptive Feedback Helps All Students Reach Proficiency
https://vimeo.com/43992570   290

About the Authors

Ron Berger is chief academic officer for EL Education, overseeing resources and professional learning for schools nationally. Berger works closely with the Harvard Graduate School of Education, where he did his graduate work and teaches a course that uses exemplary student work to improve teaching and learning. He founded the open website Models of Excellence (https://modelsofexcellence.eleducation .org), the world's largest collection of high-quality student work. Berger is an Annenberg Foundation Teacher Scholar and received the Autodesk Foundation National Teacher of the Year award. His previous books include *An Ethic of Excellence, A Culture of Quality, Leaders of Their Own Learning: Transforming Schools through Student-Engaged Assessment, Transformational Literacy: Making the Common Core Shift with Work That Matters, Management in the Active Classroom,* and *Learning That Lasts: Challenging, Engaging, and Empowering Students with Deeper Instruction.* Berger's writing and speaking center on inspiring quality and character in students, specifically through project-based learning, original scientific and historical research, service learning, and the infusion of arts. He works with the national character education movement to embed character values into the core of academic work. Prior to his work with EL Education and Harvard, Berger was a public school teacher and master carpenter in rural Massachusetts for more than twenty-five years.

Anne Vilen is senior writer and project manager for EL Education. She taught English Language Arts in secondary and middle school for many years and then served as the director of program and professional development at an EL Education mentor school. She joined EL Education in 2011, first as a school coach and then as a staff writer. Her previous books include *Learning That Lasts: Challenging, Engaging, and Empowering Students with Deeper Instruction* and *Transformational Literacy: Making the Common Core Shift with Work That Matters.* In addition, she has published dozens of poems, essays, and articles on the topics of teaching, learning, parenting, feminism, and the natural world.

Libby Woodfin is director of publications for EL Education. Woodfin started her career as a fifth- and sixth-grade teacher at the original lab school for the Responsive Classroom in Greenfield, Massachusetts, and went on to become a counselor at a large comprehensive high school. Woodfin started with EL Education in 2007 while completing graduate work at the Harvard Graduate School of Education. Throughout her career, Woodfin has written articles, chapters, and books about important issues in education. Her books include *Familiar Ground: Traditions That Build School Community, Leaders of Their Own Learning: Transforming Schools through Student-Engaged Assessment, Transformational Literacy: Making the Common Core Shift with Work That Matters, Management in the Active Classroom, Learning That Lasts: Challenging, Engaging, and Empowering Students with Deeper Instruction*, and *Your Curriculum Companion: The Essential Guide to Teaching the EL Education K–5 Language Arts Curriculum*.

About EL Education

EL Education is redefining student achievement in diverse communities across the country, ensuring that all students master rigorous content, develop positive character, and produce high-quality work. By creating great public schools where they are needed most, EL Education inspires teachers and students to achieve more than they thought possible.

EL Education's portfolio of instructional materials and coaching services draws on decades of deep partnership with schools and districts in its national school network (those implementing its school model) and in its family of literacy partners (those implementing its Language Arts curriculum).

Based on its founding principles of meaningful work, character, and respect for teachers, EL Education's offerings transform teaching and learning to promote habits of scholarship and character that lead to high student achievement. In addition to success on standardized tests, EL Education students demonstrate critical thinking, intellectual courage, and emotional resilience; they possess the passion and the capacity to contribute to a better world.

EL Education's professional books, including *Leaders of Their Own Learning*, have reached over 100,000 teachers and school leaders and impacted millions of students across the country and internationally. The books' accompanying videos, available for free at ELeducation.org/resources/collections, have been viewed millions of times.

EL Education, a 501c(3) nonprofit, was founded in 1992 by Outward Bound USA in collaboration with the Harvard Graduate School of Education.

For more information, visit ELeducation.org.

Acknowledgments

Writing a book like this is deeply collaborative work. This book in particular was born out of conversation with school coaches, leaders, and teachers in schools around the country who were using our first book, *Leaders of Their Own Learning*. We are abundantly grateful for their ideas, suggestions, and feedback. Their contributions of real-world documents, tools, and examples are the backbone of this book. In the service of students in classrooms across the nation, we are honored to acknowledge the many talented and generous educators who made this book possible.

We offer particular thanks to Katie Schneider, Rosa Gaia, and David Grant for creating the videos featured in this book. Their work makes the practices come alive.

And, our profound gratitude to Leah Rugen, our coauthor for the original *Leaders of Their Own Learning*. Leah was not a coauthor for this *Companion;* nonetheless, we stood on her shoulders to write this book.

EL Education staff
Cyndi Gueswel

Jenny Henderson

Aurora Kushner

David Manning

Dave Manzella

Martha Martin

Katie Shenk

Anna Switzer

Heather White

Emily Williams

Teachers and leaders from the following schools and districts (alphabetically)
ANSER Charter School in Boise, Idaho

Banora Point Primary School in Banora Point, New South Wales, Australia

Beaverton School District in Beaverton, Oregon

Capital City Public Charter School in Washington, DC

Casco Bay High School in Portland, Maine

Codman Academy in Boston, Massachusetts

Conservatory Lab Charter School in Boston, Massachusetts

Conway Elementary in Escondido, California
Delaware Ridge Elementary School in Kansas City, Kansas
Florence City Schools in Alabama
Evergreen Community Charter School in Asheville, North Carolina
Fox Creek Elementary School in Littleton, Colorado
Genesee Community Charter School in Rochester, New York
Gilbert High School in Gilbert, South Carolina
Harborside Academy in Kenosha, Wisconsin
Harvard Graduate School of Education in Cambridge, Massachusetts
High Tech High in San Diego, California
Interdistrict School for Arts and Communication (ISAAC) in New London, Connecticut
Irving A. Robbins Middle School in Farmington, Connecticut
King Middle School in Portland, Maine
Kuumba Academy Charter School in Wilmington, Delaware
Metropolitan Expeditionary Learning School in New York City
Oakhurst Elementary School in Decatur, Georgia
Open World Learning Community in St. Paul, Minnesota
Pike Road Elementary School in Pike Road, Alabama
Polaris Charter Academy in Chicago, Illinois
Pottenger Elementary School in Springfield, Massachusetts
Presumpscot Elementary School in Portland, Maine
River Bluff High School in Lexington, South Carolina
Tahoe Expedition Academy in Truckee, California
Tapestry Charter School in Buffalo, New York
The Franklin School of Innovation in Asheville, North Carolina
The Noah Wallace School in Farmington, Connecticut
The Odyssey School of Denver in Denver, Colorado
Shutesbury Elementary School in Shutesbury, Massachusetts
The Springfield Renaissance School in Springfield, Massachusetts
World of Inquiry School #58 in Rochester, New York
Thomaston Grammar School in Thomaston, Maine
University Park Campus School in Worcester, Massachusetts
Two Rivers Public Charter School in Washington, DC
Washington Heights Expeditionary Learning School in New York City

Foreword

Walk into any school in Alabama and chances are you'll find evidence of student-engaged assessment in action. And, if you look closely, you'll find copies of *Leaders of Their Own Learning* in nearly every classroom.

For almost five years, the Alabama Best Practices Center has used *Leaders of Their Own Learning* (LOTOL) as one of our primary guiding texts in our statewide learning networks. The clear and compelling writing – rich with examples and scenarios – and the featured videos bring student-engaged assessment to life for teachers and leaders. Read on and you will understand our excitement about the arrival of another powerful professional learning tool, *The Leaders of Their Own Learning Companion*.

Making Students Leaders of Their Own Learning

Perhaps the most best way to understand the impact of LOTOL-inspired, student-engaged assessment is to see and hear students in action at some of our participating schools. For example, visit Weeden Elementary in Florence, Alabama, a high-poverty school where more than a third of students are English language learners, and students will show you their data notebooks. They'll explain where they stand on a particular learning target. And, you'll hear the pride in their voices as they note their progress.

Or, perhaps in the spring, head to rural Isabella High, a K–12 school in Chilton County – home to most of Alabama's peach production – and you'll enjoy a picnic in the school's sloping backyard, where students are sharing their academic progress with their parents through student-led conferences. "From the moment we began the book study of *Leaders of Their Own Learning*, I fell in love," Principal Sue Ellen Gilliland told me recently. "We are using these strategies with all students, including students with special needs, and I have personally witnessed their power in unleashing student ownership of their education."

Or, go to Pike Road Elementary School near Alabama's state capital, where regularly you see celebrations of learning with students showcasing artifacts of their learning. During my last visit, two students showed videos of their project to demonstrate motion and friction. And another fourth-grader proudly shared his "menu math" project, noting that he was learning fifth- and sixth-grade standards. You can view the videos of the projects here: https://bit.ly/2WCn75s.

There are many other examples of schools – Rock Quarry Elementary in Tuscaloosa and all of Oxford City Schools, as well as schools in Athens, Alabama – in which you can see student-engaged assessment in action. Alabama students are more engaged and learning more because of the commitment to making students leaders of their own learning.

Teaching and Learning in Alabama Is Transforming

In addition to the examples from schools just cited, there are a few key practices from *Leaders of Their Own Learning* that are worth highlighting for their transformative impact on schools throughout Alabama.

Going Deeper with Learning Targets

Since the introduction of Alabama's college-and-career standards, we've focused the professional learning we provide for our networks of schools and leaders on key aspects of standards-based instruction. After unwrapping the standard, teachers create learning targets. For many, that's where the challenges begin. In the early stages of this collaboration, some teachers felt that creating learning targets was just one more thing to do. Others would tell us they were already using learning targets (often laminated and ordered from a website). It became clear that we needed to step back and spend more time building teachers' knowledge and skills about the effective use of learning targets in everyday classroom instruction.

With *Leaders of Their Own Learning*, teachers can see, firsthand, what the use of student-friendly learning targets "looks like." The online videos and the suggestions in the book help teachers understand how to bring a learning target to life by dialoguing with their students to ensure that they understand the embedded words, concepts, and skills. This gives teachers the confidence to shift from simply posting the words on the wall to making the target the cornerstone for each day's learning, enabling both students and teachers to understand and monitor their progress.

By reading and watching the videos that accompany *LOTOL*, educators in our networks – teachers, instructional coaches, and administrators – have discovered how to use learning targets as a driver for student motivation and academic progress.

Engaging Students with More Frequent Checks for Understanding

Checking for understanding, the second component of student-engaged assessment, also becomes clearer to teachers as they deepen their understanding of target-driven learning. *LOTOL*'s video examples help teachers consider the rich variety of checks for understanding we can tap into, as well as how to use the checks to adjust instruction.

At our network sessions, teachers have at times made the connection to video games, where students receive instant feedback and adjust their strategies accordingly. It only makes sense, they said, to use the same strategies in the classroom.

Inspiring Quality Work with Models and Critiques

Another key aspect of student-engaged assessment that promotes excellence is the use of models, critiques, and descriptive feedback. *LOTOL* has helped teachers gain a deeper understanding of the importance of exposing students to exemplary student work. Teachers love the ability to tap into EL Education's online curated supply of outstanding student work for all grade levels and all subjects (modelsofexcellence.eleducation.org). They know that when students examine and critique great work, they can understand what it means to become better writers, mathematicians, scientists, and historians.

Why *The Leaders of Their Own Learning Companion* Matters

As you have learned here, the insights found in *Leaders of Their Own Learning* have been real "change drivers" for educators collaborating with the Alabama Best Practices Center. When teachers start implementing student-engaged assessment, they usually have questions and often face challenges that arise when professionals make significant changes in practice.

Our networks can help teachers grapple with these challenges. Network members can call or email each other with questions or can visit one another's classrooms or schools (and they often do). They also know that they can contact us for help. We often dip back into the book for answers, and we have invited Ron Berger to Alabama several times to work with teachers throughout the state.

Now, we have another option – one that can be at every teacher's fingertips: *The Leaders of Their Own Learning Companion.*

Ron, Anne, and Libby graciously allowed some Alabama teachers to "test-drive" the first two chapters of this new book, which feature learning targets and checking for understanding. They sought Alabama teachers' input – and the input of other teachers across the country – to refine the chapters and ensure the *Companion* sufficiently addresses common challenges faced by teachers as they pursue this work.

I love the way the chapters are organized and worded in the *Companion.* After a brief definition of the specific student-engaged assessment component, each chapter identifies learning targets related to that component. Also embedded in each chapter are common dilemmas and detailed suggestions for addressing them.

The wording is clear and personal and puts the reader at ease. Then comes my favorite part: each of the challenges is accompanied by a "Try This" section that offers suggestions about how to work through the challenge. It's like a virtual "help desk" available whenever a teacher needs it. You can be sure that we will use this valuable resource and encourage its spread within our networks. That certainly will not be a challenge. The teachers who previewed the manuscript have been clamoring for this *Companion* ever since!

It's Not Just about School, It's about Life

One of the things I most appreciate about EL Education is their commitment to helping educators develop good people. They understand that student-engaged assessment is not only about content knowledge and academic skills. It's about character development and nurturing a love of learning that lasts a lifetime. This new addition to the EL Education library will be another valuable resource for educators as they help students find the path that leads to self-assurance and self-worth.

Cathy W. Gassenheimer
Executive Vice President for the Alabama Best Practices Center, A+ Education Partnership
Montgomery, Alabama
April, 2019

Preface

When Ron Berger, Leah Rugen, and Libby Woodfin wrote *Leaders of Their Own Learning* in 2014, EL Education (then Expeditionary Learning) was in the early stages of building our library of high-quality books for educators. We have since published five additional books, with two more on the way in 2020, and they have been transformational for schools within and beyond our network.

All of our books have made an impact in schools; however, none have influenced teaching and learning more than *Leaders of Their Own Learning*. More than a million students have been taught by teachers who have read *Leaders of Their Own Learning* and who are bringing student-engaged assessment practices into their classrooms and schools. And, our viral video—Austin's Butterfly—which we made to accompany the book and that demonstrates the power of models and critique, has been viewed millions of times across the world and is a staple in teacher education and professional learning.

What is it about *Leaders of Their Own Learning* that has struck such a chord with educators around the country and around the world? We think there are two primary reasons for its success. First, it's a practical book and there are multiple entry points. Busy teachers and school leaders don't need to read it cover to cover but, rather, can pick it up and dig into the practices that their school community needs at any given point in time, whether that's learning targets, student-led conferences, or celebrations of learning. And second, it speaks to novice and veteran teachers in any setting and at any grade level. Whether you are in an urban, suburban, or rural setting, a district, charter, or independent school, *Leaders of Their Own Learning* can improve teaching and learning in your classroom and school.

Through all of this success with *Leaders of Their Own Learning*, we have learned that student-engaged assessment is a difference maker for students, but also that these practices, like many pedagogical practices, are hard. That's why EL Education decided to turn its attention to collecting the craft knowledge of teachers who have been successfully implementing student-engaged assessment practices since *Leaders of Their Own Learning* was first published. And now we are putting their practical wisdom into your hands.

The lessons and advice from teachers that you will find in this new book, *The Leaders of Their Own Learning Companion*, will accelerate and deepen your practice. Recognizing that the work is hard, but definitely worth it, this book provides *new* tools, resources, and videos to support you in this worthy work.

As one of our school coaches said when reviewing an early draft, this book has everything in it that she usually says out loud to teachers she's working with to hone these practices. If you can't have a coach beside you, we hope you'll keep this book open on your desk to provide you with the support and encouragement you need.

Scott Hartl
President and CEO, EL Education
New York, NY
April, 2019

THE LEADERS
OF THEIR OWN
LEARNING
COMPANION

Introduction

In January of 2018, I traveled to Wichita for the Kansas Learning Forward Conference, where I was fortunate to be able to dig into *Leaders of Their Own Learning* with teachers from across the state. It was a cold mid-winter day outdoors, the wind howling across the Arkansas River, but indoors the feeling was warm and excited. Teachers and school and district leaders were grabbing me ahead of time to say how transformational student-engaged assessment had been in their schools. I began my keynote address, as I always do, acknowledging the limits of my perspective. Though I have been an educator for over 40 years—over 25 years as a public school teacher—my understanding of their work and their lives was constrained by my identity and my narrow experience. I am a white man, and I was older than almost everyone at the conference. I live in New England and probably differed with many in the audience on certain issues in politics and culture. I absolutely differed when it came to sports, because when I mentioned rooting for the Patriots and the Red Sox, the entire audience booed and jeered. I wanted to be clear that our differences were real and I imagine some were deep. But there was also a common bond in the room: everyone present was an educator who had the courage to try out new ideas to elevate the thinking and voices of students. I admired them all.

I asked the audience to step up and challenge me if they felt my framing of the work did not resonate with their experience so that we could find common ground or at least understand our differences. Right away a gentleman stood up in the back of the ballroom and said, "We tried this in our district and it didn't work. It didn't work at all." I smiled and thanked him for his courage to stand up. I was curious: what exactly didn't work? He explained that teachers in his district "couldn't write good learning targets," and "students were not ready to lead their own conferences."

I told him he was not the only educator who felt this way. The practices in our book *Leaders of Their Own Learning* are not silver bullets that will "fix" a school, and they are not simple. It takes a great deal of faculty learning, collaboration, trials, and revision to make these practices work. Many schools and districts work on them deliberately for years. And I shared that we have been listening closely to educators who are using the book over the last five years to find out how we could have been clearer and more helpful. I explained that we were working right then on *The Leaders of Their Own Learning Companion,* naming the challenges and sharing strategies and resources that we have seen to be effective.

I have had similar experiences to this one in Kansas all over the country. At a statewide conference in rural Alabama, held in a barnlike building up in the western hills, a school leader explained to me that her staff has been working steadily over five years with the book, one chapter per year, and it was the best thing that ever happened to the school community. Minutes later, a different principal confessed that his teachers were struggling to implement the practices well. In West Virginia, California, Connecticut, South Carolina, Colorado, and Maine, there was tremendous excitement about how these practices had energized students and families and had transformed and improved schools. And there were also many educators who felt overwhelmed with implementing these practices and said they needed more help.

This book is our attempt to provide more help. It's not a solution: the practices of student-engaged assessment cannot be plugged in and turned on. Using these practices well demands a growth mindset and the courage to take risks, a professional culture of collaboration and support, and a commitment to working together over time to customize these practices to work in your setting. Here we offer tips and resources gleaned from schools across the country who are in this work with you. And we know that it can be very powerful when you get it right.

In the words of a teacher from Virginia who attended the statewide ASCD Conference on this topic in 2018, "[I learned] the most important assessment that takes place in my classroom on any given day is the assessment that's going on all block long inside the minds of my students: 'Is this good enough to submit? Am I on the right track? Am I the only one who doesn't understand this concept? Is this right/wrong?' . . . I want my students to gain a clear sense of what they do well, what they need to work on, and how to improve."

Ron Berger
February, 2019

How to Use This Book

Since *Leaders of Their Own Learning* was published in 2014, teachers and leaders like those described in the previous pages have shared with us not just the challenges of implementing these practices but also new and helpful tools and structures – variations on our advice and concrete customized examples of documents and resources related to the practices in the book – that work well in their classrooms. We have taken many of those tools and resources, and created some of our own, to help you tackle the common challenges of student-engaged assessment. What you will find in *The Leaders of Their Own Learning Companion* is the accumulated wisdom of practicing teachers and school leaders from across the United States.

When we first began drafting this new companion to *Leaders of Their Own Learning,* we worked with a focus group of teachers in Montgomery, Alabama, who reviewed the first two chapters and gave us detailed feedback. These teachers know the original book as well as any teachers we've met, and they were able to sum up the difference between old and new simply and beautifully. They decided that the original is the "why" of student-engaged assessment and this new companion is the "how." They felt that you could get by with just the how, but it's deeper and richer when you know the why that sits underneath. If you have already read *Leaders of Their Own Learning,* this new book will truly be a companion, building on what you already know about student-engaged assessment practices to deepen your practice. If you have never read the original, this book will be a practical stand-alone resource that you can use immediately in your classroom and school.

Use It as a Companion

If you have already read or worked with *Leaders of Their Own Learning* on your own or in professional learning at your school, we encourage you to use the *Companion* to revisit the challenges you have come up against while putting these practices to work in your classroom. You'll find fresh perspectives, new tools, and more detailed examples here to energize your efforts. And, if you are a teacher leader helping colleagues implement these practices across your team or in their own classrooms, these resources will provide tools and models for teaching teachers as well as working with students.

Use It as a Stand-Alone Guide

If you haven't read *Leaders of Their Own Learning* yet, you can use this book as a stand-alone guide – a "try this" approach to fast-tracking these practices in your classroom. Each chapter is anchored by three to five learning targets, which will support you to learn about each new practice. Within each learning target we have identified common challenges and then suggested practical "Try This" approaches to tackling each challenge. No doubt you will find that the challenges you face in your classroom are common for other teachers as well. You will also find URLs linking you to videos and printable versions of many of the tools. After reading all or parts of *The Leaders of Their Own Learning Companion,* you may find yourself ready to go back to the original book to read more about the "why" of these practices in order to anchor your learning about that practice and the big picture of student-engaged assessment in general.

Use It to Change Your School

Each chapter of *The Leaders of Their Own Learning Companion* ends with Lessons for Leaders, a section designed especially for school leaders – principals, instructional coaches, mentor teachers, and others who are leading professional learning, serving on school leadership teams, or helping to guide school-wide instructional consistencies. The work leaders do to drive the conversation and decision making behind "how we do school" shapes the culture and learning environment that students engage with each day. We hear frequently from school leaders who use *Leaders of Their Own Learning* as an anchor text to guide professional development throughout the school year; they view student-engaged assessment as an inspiring and effective entry point for school transformation.

You'll see one of these school leaders, Cherise Campbell, principal at Amana Academy in Alpharetta, Georgia, leading a learning walk with her staff in the video "Leading Professional Learning on Student-Engaged Assessment." Following the learning walk, teachers on her staff revisit *Leaders of Their Own Learning* while discussing student-engaged assessment strategies they plan to implement in their classrooms. This video, which accompanies the Lessons for Leaders section of Chapter 1 is a powerful illustration of how aligning teaching practices with progress monitoring, leadership decisions, and ongoing professional learning can transform teaching and learning across a school.

In the five years since we published *Leaders of Their Own Learning,* we have seen student-engaged assessment practices flourish in schools around the country. Many teachers are masterful practitioners; however, most will tell you that though they may be very strong in some areas (e.g., writing and using learning targets) they still lack confidence in other areas (e.g., running critique lessons). Student-engaged assessment is layered and nuanced and there is always room to hone one's craft. There is something for every teacher in this book – novice and veteran – no matter your experience with student-engaged assessment. There is always more to learn. We hope that in another five years we will have a new batch of tools and resources gathered from classrooms where teachers have continued to learn and iterate on the good work of those who have contributed to both of these books.

Learning Targets

Checking for Understanding during Daily Lessons

Using Data with Students

Learning Targets

Models, Critique, and Descriptive Feedback

STUDENT-ENGAGED ASSESSMENT

Student-engaged assessment is a system of interrelated practices that positions students as leaders of their own learning.

Standards-Based Grading

Student-Led Conferences

Passage Presentations with Portfolios

Celebrations of Learning

What Are Learning Targets?

Learning targets are goals for lessons, projects, units, and courses. They are derived from standards and used to assess growth and achievement. They are written in concrete, student-friendly language (beginning with the stem "I can"), shared with students, posted in the classroom, and tracked carefully by students and teachers during the process of learning. Students spend a good deal of time discussing and analyzing them and may be involved in modifying or creating them.

After reading *Leaders of Their Own Learning*, you may have charged enthusiastically into using learning targets, only to discover that it's harder than you thought to craft high-quality learning targets and use them well. You may be struggling to write learning targets that focus students effectively on the intended learning, or you write them on the board but students don't really engage with them. These are common challenges.

Learning targets are the foundation of a student-engaged assessment system. Yet many teachers find that it takes two or three years, or longer, to master the use of them. We have found that it is most helpful to think of learning targets as a strategy that one never gets perfect. Instead, creating and using learning targets artfully and effectively can become a core part of your practice that is continually improving every year. Your hard work and persistence will be worthwhile! When students really know what they are trying to learn, can see a pathway to success, and can monitor their progress along the way, they are more engaged and motivated to work hard and grapple with challenges.

In this chapter we will build on the techniques offered in *Leaders of Their Own Learning* to help you meet three learning targets. Along the way we'll give you an opportunity to explore solutions to the common challenges many teachers face when working toward each learning target.

> The moment my eighth-grade year [in an EL Education network school] ended, I became nervous to leave the world of learning targets behind. . . . [In my traditional public high school] I got really nervous because without a target, I had no purpose, no clarity, and no direction. . . . So I wrote targets for myself every single day in every single class.[1]
>
> —*Elena Fulton, graduate of The Odyssey School of Denver*

Learning Targets for Chapter 1

1. I can craft high-quality learning targets.
2. I can use learning targets throughout a lesson to build students' understanding and ownership of their learning.
3. I can create sets of learning targets that ensure my students are aiming for grade-level standards.

---

[1] You can see Elena Fulton giving a speech about her experience using learning targets at: https://eleducation.org/resources/elnc25-plenaries-elena-fultons-speech

Before we dive in, take a moment to assess yourself on each of the learning targets for this chapter. In Table 1.1, circle or place an X along the continuum from Beginning to Exceeding: **How would you rate your progress toward each learning target** *at this point in time?*

We'll give you a chance to assess yourself again at the end of the chapter.

Table 1.1 Chapter 1 learning target tracker

Learning Target 1: *I can craft high-quality learning targets.*
Beginning-------------------------------Developing-------------------------------Meeting-------------------------------Exceeding
Notes:

Learning Target 2: *I can use learning targets throughout a lesson to build students' understanding and ownership of their learning.*
Beginning-------------------------------Developing-------------------------------Meeting-------------------------------Exceeding
Notes:

Learning Target 3: *I can create sets of learning targets that ensure my students are aiming for grade-level standards.*
Beginning-------------------------------Developing-------------------------------Meeting-------------------------------Exceeding
Notes:

Learning Target 1: I can craft high-quality learning targets.

 Challenge #1: My students are working hard and generally doing what I've asked them to do, but they aren't always learning what they need to learn.

TRY THIS: GET *REALLY* CLEAR ABOUT WHAT YOU WANT STUDENTS TO LEARN *BEFORE* YOU WRITE LEARNING TARGETS

It may seem obvious, but it's important for you, as a teacher, to be really clear about what you want your students to learn before you start writing learning targets. It's easy to get caught in a trap of writing learning targets that map onto the basic *logistics* of a lesson, but fail to adequately target the intended *learning*.

For example, if students are going to create clay replicas of bird beaks during a lesson, you might be tempted to write a target something like this: *I can use clay to create an accurate replica of my chosen bird's beak.* However, if you pause to think about what you want students to learn during the lesson, you may realize that the learning target isn't quite right. Unless you are teaching an art lesson, the intended learning probably isn't about using clay. Perhaps the intended learning is actually about the purposes of different kinds of beaks (e.g., cracking seeds and nuts, probing for insects). A target that takes aim more directly at this might be something like: *I can use my clay bird beak model to explain how the beak shape helps my bird survive.*

Before writing your learning target(s) for any given lesson, it may help to write down or articulate to someone else your answers to two important questions:

1. What do I want students to learn in this lesson?

2. What do I want students to do in this lesson?

TRY THIS: USE PRECISE AND HELPFUL VERBS

When it comes to writing learning targets, the verbs are critical. They identify for students what they are supposed to do and, for both teachers and students, they give an indication of how progress will be assessed. Knowing, for example, that they will be *identifying* versus *describing* is good information for students – it helps them take greater ownership of their learning. If the verb isn't precise, things can go off track quickly. Consider, for example, a verb commonly misused in learning targets: *understand*. It's fair to identify understanding as a goal for your students, but as a target, it's not very helpful for students or for you because you can't directly see or measure understanding. Table 1.2 compares learning targets and assesses how precise and helpful their verbs are.

Figure 1.1 offers you a chance to take a stand. Are the verbs in the learning targets precise and helpful? Why or why not? If the learning target needs improvement, write a new version of it in the right-hand column: focus on precise and helpful verbs.

Table 1.2 Assessing learning targets for precise and helpful verbs

Learning Target	Precise and Helpful for Students?	Precise and Helpful for Teachers?
1.a. *I can understand the difference between living and nonliving things.*	No. There's no action for students to take. It will be difficult for many of them to know if they've met the target or not. This may undermine students' ability to be truly engaged in the assessment process.	No. Because there's no action for students to take, there's no way for teachers to assess their progress. How can understanding be assessed? This question should lead teachers to a more precise and helpful verb.
1.b. *I can explain the difference between living and nonliving things.*	Yes. Students know that in order to meet the target they will need to explain these differences. They must *show* their understanding somehow. What would be even more helpful to them would be an indication of what shape that explanation will take (e.g., . . . by participating in a Back-to-Back and Face-to-Face protocol; . . . by writing a paragraph that describes three differences).	Yes. Teachers can assess explanations, whether provided orally or in writing.
2.a. *I can read about the antecedents to World War II.*	No. This learning target doesn't make clear to students what the intended learning is. Since this is a high school learning target, it is unlikely that the intended learning is the skill of reading, which is what this target suggests.	No. Teachers won't be able to assess what students are learning.
2.b. *I can determine the most important antecedents to World War II.*	Yes. It should be clear to students that, as they read, they will need to evaluate what's most important. An additional learning target, such as "I can defend my reasoning about the most important antecedents to World War II in a five-paragraph essay," could be the learning target for the following lesson.	Yes. The intended learning is clear—determining what's important from what's not. The follow-up learning target also makes it clear how students will convey this learning—a persuasive essay.

Figure 1.1 Test yourself: Assessing learning targets for precise and helpful verbs
SOURCE: This document is available in the online toolbox at http://www.wiley.com/go/lotolcompanion.

Learning Target	Is the Verb Precise and Helpful? Why or Why Not?	If Necessary, How Would You Improve the Learning Target?
I can demonstrate understanding of whole class and individual data.		
I can cite evidence from the text to support my inferences.		
I can summarize a scientific journal article.		
I can create an accurate scale model.		
I can make sense of problems.		
I can think critically about current events.		

TRY THIS: FOCUS ON ONE THING AT A TIME

A learning target with more than one verb is usually going to be a problem, for you and your students. When a target demands multiple tasks, it is hard for students to know what to focus on. Many will struggle knowing where to start. And for teachers, it is difficult to assess progress because a student may succeed at one task and not another within a single learning target.

What follows are several sample learning targets. Consider what challenges each presents when it comes time for you and your students to assess progress:

1. I can read, analyze, and summarize the author's argument.

2. I can describe, compare, and represent my scientific thinking in pictures and words.

3. I can draw and calculate the surface area and volume of rectangular prisms.

It is important to emphasize that a lesson need not have only one learning target. There's no need to squeeze too many tasks together in one target. Two or three learning targets, with one verb each, will support students to focus on the task at hand and effectively monitor their progress. Remember, the whole point of the book *Leaders of Their Own Learning* is to engage students in the assessment process. One verb at a time helps them to know exactly what the intended learning is and to identify when they can say "I can."

What follows are the same learning targets, broken into multiple targets. Each set of learning targets may be introduced throughout the course of one lesson or span multiple days:

1. I can read, analyze, and summarize the author's argument.
   a. I can analyze the author's argument on pages xx of (text name).
   b. I can summarize the author's argument on pages xx of (text name).

2. I can describe, compare, and represent my scientific thinking in pictures and words.
   a. I can describe the science behind _____ during the Science Talk protocol.
   b. I can represent this scientific phenomenon in a scientific drawing with a caption and labels.
   c. I can compare my scientific drawing to my peers' during our Gallery Walk.

3. I can draw and calculate the surface area and volume of rectangular prisms.
   a. I can use a ruler to create 3-D labeled drawings of rectangular prisms.
   b. I can calculate the surface area of rectangular prisms.
   c. I can calculate the volume of rectangular prisms.

TRY THIS: WRITE LEARNING TARGETS THAT ARE FOCUSED ON THE *LEARNING*, NOT THE *DOING*

Since writing *Leaders of Their Own Learning* and working with teachers around the country who are implementing student-engaged assessment practices, we have found that understanding the difference between *learning* targets and *doing* targets is a key to success. This is an area in which many teachers struggle. If this is also true for you, know that you are not alone!

We offer an example in *Leaders of Their Own Learning* that is illuminating and helpful for many:

- *Doing target*: I can make a poster about the ideal habitat for a polar bear.

- *Learning target*: I can describe the ideal habitat for a polar bear in a poster format.

The first target suggests that all students need to do to be successful is make the poster. The second helps them understand the key learning in the lesson. Students often perceive "doing" targets as boxes to be checked off. They can be red herrings for students because they suggest that if they complete the task they will have met the target. For example, the learning target *I can complete two geometric proofs before the end of class* suggests that the goal is simply to complete the problems, not to learn the concept. A *learning* target here instead would be: *I can explain my geometric proof to another student.*

Sometimes examples are the best way to see the difference. Here are a few more:

- *Doing target*: I can complete my physics lab on force and motion.
- *Learning target*: I can use the data from my physics lab to demonstrate one of Newton's Laws.

- *Doing target*: I can create an interactive neighborhood map.
- *Learning target*: I can use eSpatial software to create an interactive map that shows demographic trends in my neighborhood.

- *Doing target*: I can finish my math problems before recess.
- *Learning target*: I can demonstrate two strategies for accurate double-digit addition.

- *Doing target*: I can read the text in English.
- *Learning target*: I can identify the new English vocabulary in our reading.

The key, as we have emphasized previously in this chapter, is to be clear on the intended learning for students. From there, write learning targets that take aim at that learning, rather than the way that students will demonstrate the learning (e.g., essays, drawings).

Just to make things a little more confusing, we would be remiss if we didn't point out that sometimes *doing* targets are entirely appropriate. If crafting a persuasive five-paragraph essay, accurately representing something in a scientific drawing, or creating a high-quality poster really is the goal for students, then the learning target can and should reflect that. Often such a *doing* target will come at the end of a set of related learning targets. For example:

- I can describe the ideal habitat for a polar bear.
- I can determine the top three threats to polar bears' survival.
- I can make a poster that includes full-color drawings and factual information that persuades people to protect polar bear habitat.

  or

- I can identify the new English vocabulary in our reading.
- I can grapple with the sentences to make meaning.
- I can write sentences that use at least three new vocabulary words.

These sets of learning targets suggest pathways for students – the poster and the sentences are final products, but the learning students need to do to create these products is clear and achievable for them.

TRY THIS: CONTEXTUALIZE THE LEARNING TARGETS

As we point out in *Leaders of Their Own Learning*, it's easy to make targets too broad or too narrow. A target like "I can analyze scientific text" is hard for students to take ownership of because it feels like what they do every day in science class. While this target might accurately reflect a scientific literacy standard, it doesn't lend itself to a single lesson or even a series of two or three lessons. The best daily targets are *contextualized* in the topic, text, and task that students are engaged with, so that students can ground their learning in the specifics of the lesson. Table 1.3 shows four different ways that you can contextualize your learning targets.

Notice that the contextualized learning targets often include words that describe the *quality* of the work, as well as the way in which students will demonstrate the learning. Such learning targets go a long way to supporting students in producing high-quality work. Toward that end, consider using the same language in your learning targets and the criteria list or rubric for a product. Taking the first learning target from Table 1.3 as an example – *accurate* and *detailed* would be excellent words to use in the rubric for a high-quality scientific diagram. Figure 1.2 shows a sample set of learning targets and a criteria list for a healthy habitat. Notice how the learning targets and the criteria list for this product match.

Table 1.3 Strategies for contextualizing learning targets

Strategy	Noncontextualized Target	Contextualized Target
Reference the specific topic of the learning.	*I can create a scientific diagram.*	*I can create an accurate and detailed diagram for a healthy habitat for our land snails.*
Use the discipline-specific vocabulary you want students to learn.	*I can explain figurative language.*	*I can write a poem that compares two things using a metaphor.*
Reference something or someone specific to your students or community in the target.	*I can solve quadratic equations.*	*I can use Keisha's method for solving quadratic equations.*
Include the assessment in the target, so that students know what to expect.	*I can summarize the main ideas in a text.*	*I can summarize the main ideas in Chapter 5 in preparation for the upcoming unit test.*

Figure 1.2 Sample first-grade learning targets and criteria list

Learning Targets
- I can persevere to record in my science notebook every day.
- I can use my scientist's eye to notice patterns and details.
- I can use our science vocabulary to describe our snails and their world.
- I can create an accurate and detailed diagram for a healthy habitat for our land snails.

Criteria List
- My notebook is complete, with all pages filled in.
- My illustrations show patterns and details.
- My descriptions use our science vocabulary words correctly.
- My diagram is accurate and detailed, with all parts labeled neatly.

Challenge #2: I'm in a rut with my learning targets. I need help varying them more and making them more interesting for my students.

TRY THIS: VARY THE COGNITIVE DEMAND REQUIRED TO MEET EACH LEARNING TARGET

Just like in life, variety gives learning targets some spice, and one of the best ways to vary learning targets is to pay close attention to the cognitive work students will need to do to meet them. Learning targets that require students to use different cognitive processes or skills as they move through their days and weeks in school give their brains a more well-rounded workout. It's like the difference between going to the gym every day and working only on your biceps, versus doing a daily circuit of all the weight machines in the gym – biceps, triceps, quads, hamstrings, etc.

We want students to use *all* of their brains, not just parts of them. Variety ensures that they have the best opportunity to develop their strengths. Imagine day after day of learning targets that ask you to read something or listen to a lecture and then restate what you read or heard by completing quizzes or short answers. Tasks like this fall into the *Knowledge* category of the Knowledge, Reasoning, and Skills framework and the *Remember* or *Understanding* level of Bloom's Revised Taxonomy. Unfortunately, this is a common scenario in classrooms – the cognitive demand of tasks doesn't vary much.

It's important to note that we are not preferencing one kind of cognitive work over another. It's neither good nor bad to ask students to recall information on a quiz. It's neither good nor bad to ask students to analyze two arguments in a persuasive essay or create a model of a plant cell.

Bloom's Revised Taxonomy (remembering, understanding, applying, analyzing, evaluating, creating) can be very useful, but it can also be harmful if it is seen as a rigid hierarchy in ways that don't always match the reality of the learning process. For example, sometimes truly understanding something is more challenging than evaluating. And sometimes understanding is actually built from students creating things; creating things shouldn't always be seen as the *end* point, as the graphics used to portray the taxonomy may suggest. These cognitive processes aren't discreet and hierarchical. What's important to consider when teaching – what we do *strongly* preference – is variety. And one of the best ways to ensure variety is to write learning targets for an arc of lessons – perhaps even a whole unit – and analyze the cognitive work they will require of students using available tools.

In *Leaders of Their Own Learning* we reference two tools for varying the cognitive demand of learning targets:

- The Knowledge, Reasoning, and Skills Framework, based on the work of Stiggins, Arter, Chappuis, and Chappuis (2006).

- The Hess Cognitive Rigor matrix, created by Karen Hess, based on Bloom's Revised Taxonomy and Webb's Depth-of-Knowledge Levels.

The Knowledge, Reasoning, and Skills Framework

As a refresher on the Knowledge, Reasoning, and Skills Framework, Table 1.4 shows how the verbs associated with each of the cognitive processes identified in the framework can be applied to sample learning targets.

Table 1.4 The Knowledge, Reasoning, and Skills Framework

Cognitive Process	Sample Verbs	Sample Standard	Sample Learning Target
Knowledge	explain, describe, identify, tell, name, list, define, label, match, choose, recall, recognize, select	**Third-grade social studies:** Discuss the lives of Americans who expanded people's rights and freedoms in a democracy.	*I can **describe** Susan B. Anthony's role in the women's suffrage movement.*
Reasoning	analyze, compare and contrast, synthesize, classify, infer, evaluate	**High school physics:** Understand the wave model and particle model for electromagnetic radiation.	*I can **compare and contrast** the wave model and particle model for electromagnetic radiation.* *I can evaluate which model is most useful for particular situations.*
Skill	observe, listen, perform, conduct, read, speak, write, assemble, operate, use, demonstrate, measure, model, collect, dramatize	**Seventh-grade ELA:** Use technology, including the internet, to produce and publish writing and link to and cite sources as well as to interact and collaborate with others, including linking to and citing sources.	*I can **write** an essay in Google Docs.* *I can use Google Docs to respond to suggestions and comments on my draft.* *I can use EasyBib to generate my bibliography in MLA style.*

The Knowledge, Reasoning, and Skills Framework + Bloom's Revised Taxonomy

Table 1.5 maps Bloom's Revised Taxonomy onto the Knowledge, Reasoning, and Skills Framework and identifies a sequence of learning targets that give students a full-brain workout in their study of insects. While a content standard for the study might be something like: "Given several pictures of adult organisms, identify and explain which organisms are insects and which are not," this standard can and should be mapped with literacy standards that are a good fit. In this case, students will be writing informative paragraphs and creating a scientific drawing for a class field guide. (We'll cover bundling standards in this way more thoroughly later in this chapter.)

Table 1.5 is copied in Figure 1.3, but this time the learning targets column is not filled in. We encourage you to print out Figure 1.3 and consider an arc of lessons you have planned for approximately one to two weeks. If you have already crafted the learning targets for these lessons, fill them into the table in the appropriate row. Do they leverage the full range of the Knowledge, Reasoning, and Skills Framework and Bloom's Revised Taxonomy? If not, how can you adjust them so that you are varying the cognitive demand of the tasks you are asking students to do? If you haven't yet created learning targets, do so with variety in mind – fill in most or all of the rows of the table with at least one learning target.

Bloom's Revised Taxonomy + Webb's Depth-of-Knowledge Levels = Hess's Cognitive Rigor Matrix

In Chapter 1 of *Leaders of Their Own Learning*, we provide a version of Hess's Cognitive Rigor Matrix (p. 39), which offers sample tasks for students mapped onto both Bloom's Taxonomy and Webb's Depth-of-Knowledge Levels. Hess's website[2] offers more detailed matrices specific to content areas:

- Close Reading
- Math-Science
- Written and Oral Communication
- World Languages
- Social Studies and Humanities
- Fine Arts
- Health and Physical Education
- Career and Technical Education

---

[2] http://www.karin-hess.com

Table 1.5 The Knowledge, Reasoning, and Skills Framework + Bloom's Revised Taxonomy

Knowledge, Reasoning, Skills Framework	Bloom's Revised Taxonomy	Sample Verbs	Sample Learning Targets
Knowledge Facts and concepts to be learned outright or retrieved using reference materials	**Remembering**	name, match, select, choose, order, label, list, arrange, identity, locate, define, duplicated, memorize, recognize, relate, recall, repeat. . .	*I can name the main body parts of an insect.*
	Understanding	tell, describe, explain, discuss, express, report, restate, review, translate, paraphrase. . .	*I can describe what makes an insect different from other bugs.*
Reasoning Using knowledge to solve a problem, make a decision, plan, etc.	**Applying**	use, draw, sort, write, solve, demonstrate, infer, dramatize, employ, interpret, operate, practice, schedule. . .	*I can sort insects from non-insects.*
	Analyzing	question, infer, test, experiment, compare, contrast, analyze, calculate, categorize, criticize, differentiate, discriminate, distinguish, examine	*I can examine a specimen collected during fieldwork and determine whether or not it is an insect.*
	Evaluating	argue, assess, choose, compare, defend, estimate, judge, predict, rate, select, support, value, evaluate, appraise. . .	*I can assess whether a specimen should be included in our class's insect field guide based on the following criteria. . .*
Skills Using knowledge and reasoning to perform skillfully	**Creating**	create, do, perform, read, speak, operate, model, dramatize, measure, collect, compose, construct, design, develop, formulate, manage, organize, plan, assemble prepare, propose, arrange, write. . .	*I can write an informative paragraph on insect identification for our class field guide.* *I can create a scientific drawing of an insect for our class field guide.*

Figure 1.3 Map your own learning targets onto the Knowledge, Reasoning, and Skills Framework + Bloom's Revised Taxonomy

SOURCE: This document is available in the online toolbox at http://www.wiley.com/go/lotolcompanion.

Knowledge, Reasoning, Skills Framework	Bloom's Revised Taxonomy	Sample Verbs	Your Learning Targets
Knowledge Facts and concepts to be learned outright or retrieved using reference materials	**Remembering**	name, match, select, choose, order, label, list, arrange, identity, locate, define, duplicated, memorize, recognize, relate, recall, repeat. . .	
	Understanding	tell, describe, explain, discuss, express, report, restate, review, translate, paraphrase. . .	
Reasoning Using knowledge to solve a problem, make a decision, plan, etc.	**Applying**	use, draw, sort, write, solve, demonstrate, infer, dramatize, employ, interpret, operate, practice, schedule. . .	
	Analyzing	question, infer, test, experiment, compare, contrast, analyze, calculate, categorize, criticize, differentiate, discriminate, distinguish, examine	
	Evaluating	argue, assess, choose, compare, defend, estimate, judge, predict, rate, select, support, value, evaluate, appraise. . .	
Skills Using knowledge and reasoning to perform skillfully	**Creating**	create, do, perform, read, speak, operate, model, dramatize, measure, collect, compose, construct, design, develop, formulate, manage, organize, plan, assemble prepare, propose, arrange, write. . .	

We urge you to familiarize yourself with the matrices that are most relevant to you and to use them as planning tools. Consider printing out the relevant matrix for an upcoming arc of lessons and map your learning targets onto it. Strive for learning targets that fit in boxes all over the matrix. Figure 1.4 shows an example of this mapping using the learning targets about insects featured in Table 1.5. The boxes that represent the cognitive process of each learning target are circled.

TRY THIS: DON'T BE AFRAID TO BE PLAYFUL

If your learning targets are boring (i.e., very much the same from day to day; only using dry, academic language), your students are likely to get bored or tune them out. Don't be afraid to surprise your students with playful learning targets. Keep everything else we've talked about regarding writing high-quality learning targets in mind, but throw in a little spice. See Table 1.6 for a few examples.

Table 1.6 Playful learning targets

Playful Option	Less Playful Option
I can earn a chili pepper cheer for juicy word choice in my story.	I can use strong verbs and interesting nouns in my story.
I can describe conditions that will keep our milkweed bugs living a cushy, cozy life.	I can describe the ideal conditions for a milkweed bug to thrive.
I can compose a rap about reconstruction that uses no swears and that will make me rich and famous.	I can summarize the main events of the reconstruction period in a rap format.
I can create an Olympic tumbling routine using the skills I know.	I can link together the tumbling skills we learned.
I can write a high-five solution to this week's mathemagical wizard stump-the-chump story problem.	I can solve mathematical story problems.
I can be a word detective by using context clues to identify parts of speech.	I can identify the parts of speech in our language dive sentence.
I can paint so my images pop and my colors capture your heart.	I can paint with vivid style.

Check Yourself Checklist

Crafting High-Quality Learning Targets Checklist

For each learning target, check all that apply:

- ❏ The learning target begins with "I can."
- ❏ The verb in the learning target makes clear to students the intended *learning*.
- ❏ The learning target contains only one verb. If students need to focus on more than one thing during a lesson, there is more than one learning target, each with only one verb.
- ❏ The target is a *learning* target, not a *doing* target (unless the learning target is purposefully written to take aim at a craftsmanship skill).
- ❏ The learning target is contextualized to the specific topic, text, or task in the lesson—it is not a general learning target that could be used for any old lesson.
- ❏ Multiple learning targets during a lesson or across more than one day fall into a variety of categories on a cognitive rigor tool (e.g., the Knowledge, Reasoning, and Skills Framework; Bloom's Revised Taxonomy; Hess's Cognitive Rigor Matrix).
- ❏ When appropriate, the learning target uses playful, engaging language.

(This checklist is available in the online toolbox at http://www.wiley.com/go/lotolcompanion.)

Figure 1.4 Hess's Cognitive Rigor Matrix with sample annotations

HESS COGNITIVE RIGOR MATRIX (MATH-SCIENCE CRM):
Applying Webb's Depth-of-knowledge Levels to Bloom's Cognitive Process Dimensions

TOOL 2

Use these Hess CRM curricular examples with most mathematics or science assignments or assessments.

Revised Bloom's Taxonomy	Webb's DOK Level 1 Recall & Reproduction	Webb's DOK Level 2 Skills & Concepts	Webb's DOK Level 3 Strategic Thinking/Reasoning	Webb's DOK Level 4 Extended Thinking
Remember Retrieve knowledge from long-term memory, recognize, recall, locate, identify	• Recall, observe, & recognize facts, principles, properties • Recall/identify conversions among representations or numbers (e.g., customary and metric measures)			
Understand Construct meaning, clarify, paraphrase, represent, translate, illustrate, give examples, classify, categorize, summarize, generalize, infer a logical conclusion), predict, compare/contrast, match like ideas, explain, construct models	• Evaluate an expression • Locate points on a grid or number on number line • Solve a one-step problem • Represent math relationships in words, pictures, or symbols • Read, write, compare decimals in scientific notation	• Specify and explain relationships (e.g., non-examples/examples; cause-effect) • Make and record observations • Explain steps followed • Summarize results or concepts • Make basic inferences or logical predictions from data/observations • Use models/diagrams to represent or explain mathematical concepts • Make and explain estimates	• Use concepts to solve non-routine problems • Explain, generalize, or connect ideas using supporting evidence • Make and justify conjectures • Explain thinking/reasoning when more than one solution or approach is possible • Explain phenomena in terms of concepts	• Relate mathematical or scientific concepts to other content areas, other domains, or other concepts • Develop generalizations of the results obtained and the strategies used (from investigation or readings) and apply them to new problem situations
Apply Carry out or use a procedure in a given situation; carry out (apply to a familiar task), or use (apply) to an unfamiliar task	• Follow simple procedures (recipe-type directions) • Calculate, measure, apply a rule (e.g., rounding) • Apply algorithm or formula (e.g., area, perimeter) • Solve linear equations • Make conversions among representations or numbers, or within and between customary and metric measures	• Select a procedure according to criteria and perform it • Solve routine problem applying multiple concepts or decision points • Retrieve information from a table, graph, or figure and use it solve a problem requiring multiple steps • Translate between tables, graphs, words, and symbolic notations (e.g., graph data from a table) • Construct models given criteria	• Design investigation for a specific purpose or research question • Conduct a designed investigation • Use concepts to solve non-routine problems • Use & show reasoning, planning, and evidence • Translate between problem & symbolic notation when not a direct translation	• Select or devise approach among many alternatives to solve a problem • Conduct a project that specifies a problem, identifies solution paths, solves the problem, and reports results
Analyze Break into constituent parts, determine how parts relate, differentiate between relevant-irrelevant, distinguish, focus, select, organize, outline, find coherence, deconstruct	• Retrieve information from a table or graph to answer a question • Identify whether specific information is contained in graphic representations (e.g., table, graph, T-chart, diagram) • Identify a pattern/trend	• Categorize, classify materials, data, figures based on characteristics • Organize or order data • Compare/contrast figures or data • Select appropriate graph and organize & display data • Interpret data from a simple graph • Extend a pattern	• Compare information within or across data sets or texts • Analyze and draw conclusions from data, citing evidence • Generalize a pattern • Interpret data from complex graph • Analyze similarities/differences between procedures or solutions	• Analyze multiple sources of evidence • Analyze complex/abstract themes • Gather, analyze, and evaluate information
Evaluate Make judgments based on criteria, check, detect inconsistencies or fallacies, judge, critique		"UG" = unsubstantiated generalizations = stating an opinion without providing any support for it!	• Cite evidence and develop a logical argument for concepts or solutions • Describe, compare, and contrast solution methods • Verify reasonableness of results	• Gather, analyze, & evaluate information to draw conclusions • Apply understanding in a novel way, provide argument or justification for the application
Create Reorganize elements into new patterns/structures, generate, hypothesize, design, plan, produce		• Brainstorm ideas, concepts, or perspectives related to a topic	• Generate conjectures or hypotheses based on observations or prior knowledge and experience	• Synthesize information within one data set, source, or text • Formulate an original problem given a situation • Develop a scientific/mathematical model for a complex situation	• Synthesize information across multiple sources or texts • Design a mathematical model to inform and solve a practical or abstract situation

Learning Target 2: I can use learning targets throughout a lesson to build students' understanding and ownership of their learning.

 Challenge #3: I feel okay about writing learning targets, but I'm in a rut about how to use them. I always introduce them and unpack them in the same way.

TRY THIS: PLAN AHEAD

Writing high-quality learning targets is important work for teachers, but it's really just the tip of the iceberg. Learning targets must be also be *used* effectively in order to truly empower students to be leaders of their own learning. They can't just be written on the board or mentioned once and then forgotten. But, how exactly should they be used? Should you introduce all of the learning targets for a lesson at the very start of the lesson? Should you introduce them one at a time for each chunk of the lesson? Should students grapple with a problem or text prior to introducing learning targets?

The reality is that there is no one right way to introduce learning targets to your students. What's more important than having a set structure for the practice is that you have a strategy and a plan. In order to motivate students to take ownership of their learning and help them understand not only where they're going, but how they are progressing, they need to truly *engage* with the learning targets. That means that first they need to understand what the target means (we'll get to that in the next section), and then they need to see how they can take aim at it. Helping students connect any given learning target with what they already know and what they'll need to know in order to make progress is a key consideration for when to introduce each target.

There is a strong example of a strategic approach to introducing learning targets in the case study on page 28 of *Leaders of Their Own Learning*. Because it's still a strong and useful example, we have included it here for you as well. The teacher in this case study activates students' prior knowledge by giving them an engaging problem to grapple with. By the time she introduces the learning target, students are fully engaged in why that learning target makes sense in the lesson. They are hooked because they now care about meeting the target and can see their way forward with it.

Case Study

Finding the Right Time to Introduce a Daily Learning Target in an Algebra II Class at The Springfield Renaissance School in Springfield, Massachusetts

Just as they do every day, students in Hilary Ducharme's eleventh-grade Algebra II class come into the room and get right to work grappling with new problems, which are written on the board. Today Ducharme has asked her students to FOIL a series of problems, multiplying terms within parentheses in a particular order (first, outer, inner, last). A quiet hum settles on the room. Students are working together in groups while Ducharme walks around taking attendance and checking in with individual students. As students finish, several of them walk to the board and write their solutions.

Students pull out their homework, a problem set with one of four long-term learning targets for the semester written at the top: *I can construct quadratic models to solve problems.* Below that is the supporting learning target that Ducharme introduced to students the previous day: *I can find the zeros of a quadratic function by completing the square.* Students complete a reflection form about what was easy and challenging for them about the homework, and then they check their "complete the square" solutions using the quadratic formula. This leads into a lively classwide debate about the pros and cons of using "complete the square" versus the quadratic formula. "I like to have them take a stand like that," Ducharme says. "It increases their engagement. Suddenly they are speaking passionately about quadratic models!"

It isn't until about 35 minutes into the class that Ducharme points out the new daily learning target to the students: *I can identify and factor a difference of two squares.* She brings them back to the FOIL problems they had done in the first 10 minutes of class. As they explore the patterns in the solutions, awareness begins to dawn on the students. They see that their solutions to those problems have put them well on their way to the conceptual understanding they need to meet the new learning target.

Ducharme is strategic about when she introduces students to the daily learning target. She doesn't think it's a good use of time to introduce the learning target before her students have had a chance to do some grappling on their own. She says, "It will be meaningless to them unless they've had some experience with it." In this case, Ducharme knew that the students should be able to see the patterns based on the rules they have already learned about quadratics. "This is the fourth year I've taught these learning targets," Ducharme says, "and by now I've had enough experience to know how to build students to those 'aha' moments."

Choosing When to Introduce Learning Targets Depends on What Kind of Lesson You Are Teaching

By way of example, let's take a closer look at two related but different lesson structures. Workshop 1.0 – the ubiquitous Workshop Model – follows the traditional "I do/We do/You do" structure, beginning with a mini-lesson, followed by guided practice with teacher support, and then independent practice by students. Workshop 2.0, on the other hand, begins with students grappling individually and constructing meaning through peer discussion rather than with teacher modeling. A mini-lesson happens only after students have first had a chance to grapple.

Workshop 1.0 is often a better choice when students are learning a new skill that requires teacher modeling and when they may not be able to anchor new learning to past learning. In this case, you will most likely want to introduce the learning target right at the outset of the lesson so that students are grounded in the purpose of the lesson first. Table 1.7 shows the Workshop 1.0 lesson structure – the introduction of the learning target and opportunities to check in on the target with students are highlighted.

A Workshop 2.0 lesson is a good choice when you are prioritizing students grappling with a challenge first, and they have enough strategies to know how to begin. Once students have tried to make sense of a challenging text or math problem, and perhaps failed in that first attempt, they are more likely to be invested in learning the skill or knowledge required to meet the learning target. After students have grappled and the learning target is introduced, then teachers can conduct a mini-lesson to "mop up" misconceptions revealed during the grapple phase. This is the strategy used in the case study referenced previously. Tables 1.8 and 1.9 show the components of a Workshop 2.0 lesson for literacy and math, respectively, and highlight the logical places for learning targets to be introduced and checked in on.

Workshop 1.0 and 2.0 are just two possible lesson structures. No matter what structure you use, or what you call it, the important thing to keep in mind when it comes to introducing the learning target is when it is most *needed* by students. At what point in the lesson will revealing the learning target capture students' attention and interest? How can the target be used to motivate students to dig in and feel motivated to learn new things?

Table 1.7 Workshop 1.0 lesson structure

Component	Purpose
Introduction	• Build students' curiosity and need to know linked to the purpose of the lesson. • **Introduce and unpack the learning target.**
Mini-lesson ("I do")	• Provide direct instruction through explicit modeling of the task (not just what to do, but how to think through the process). • Focus on one trait, strategy, or aspect of quality at a time in direct support of the learning target. • Prepare students for success during application by providing a model of proficiency.
Guided practice ("We do")	• Gradually release responsibility. Create a "safe space" for students to practice the task with support; give students experience with success. • Assess student readiness to move into practice/application. • Address student misconceptions (group or individual).
Practice/application ("You do")	• **Reconnect to learning target and support students to set a goal for application time related to the learning target.** • Give students the opportunity to practice/apply the particular skill or concept, independent of the teacher. • Provide intentional differentiation.
Share	• Honor student work, ideas, and voice. • **Share progress toward the target; celebrate successes.**
Debrief	• Assess students' proficiency in relation to the learning target (self-assessment; teacher assessment). • Make connections between the specific learning target and the larger context. • Build lasting understanding by synthesizing as a group. • Identify next steps and set goals.

Table 1.8 Workshop 2.0 lesson structure for literacy

Component	Purpose
Engage	• Build students' curiosity and need to know linked to the purpose of the lesson.
Grapple	• Build students' self-reliance, confidence, and perseverance through grappling with complex text.
Discuss	• Build students' skills to justify their thinking, make coherent arguments based on text evidence, consider the ideas of others, and be metacognitive about their own approaches.
Focus	• **Introduce and unpack learning target.** • Provide explicit instruction if needed to "mop up" whatever students don't figure out on their own, focusing on a particular skill or concept. • Respond to gaps in understanding, misconceptions, or good ideas from students. • Gradually release responsibility. Create a "safe space" for students to practice the task with support; give students experience with success.
Apply	• Allow time for students to practice the particular skill or concept, providing intentional differentiation. • **Pause the whole class periodically during work time to provide a structured opportunity for students to monitor progress on the learning target and set a goal for the next segment of application time.**
Synthesize	• **Clarify the learning target(s), assess progress, and identify next steps/set goals.** • Address misconceptions, generalize conceptual understanding, and build lasting understanding through synthesis.

Table 1.9 Workshop 2.0 lesson structure for math

Component	Purpose
Engage and grapple	• Build students' curiosity and need to know linked to the purpose of the lesson. • Build students' self-reliant problem-solving skills. • Grapple with an interesting, complex problem or problem set related to the learning target(s).
Discuss	• Build students' skills to be metacognitive about their own approaches, justify their mathematical reasoning, and consider others' mathematical reasoning.
Focus	• **Discuss the learning target(s).** • Provide explicit instruction if needed to "mop up" whatever students don't figure out on their own, focusing on a particular skill or concept. • Respond to gaps in understanding, misconceptions, or good ideas from students. • Gradually release responsibility. Create a "safe space" for students to practice the task with support; give students experience with success.

Apply	• Time for students to practice the particular skill or concept in a collaborative learning culture.
	• Options:
	  • May return to original problem
	  • Analyze models of student work—strong and weak
	  • Rotate through stations
	  • Work on one or more additional problems, focusing on the learning target
	• **Pause the whole class periodically during work time to provide a structured opportunity for students to monitor progress on the learning target and set a goal for the next segment of application time.**

Synthesize	• **Clarify the learning target(s), assess progress, and identify next steps/set goals.** • Address misconceptions, generalize conceptual understanding, and build lasting understanding through synthesis.

TRY THIS: BE STRATEGIC ABOUT HOW YOU "UNPACK" LEARNING TARGETS WITH STUDENTS

Like a lot of things, posting and unpacking learning targets risks becoming a rote formality if you don't give care and attention to the process of engaging students with them. One of our most important messages here is to give yourself the time and flexibility to dig into the learning targets and discuss them thoroughly with your students. The point of unpacking a learning target with students is making sure they understand the target and that they know what success will look like. Here are three key tips to consider when unpacking learning targets:

1. Review domain-specific and academic vocabulary in the learning target.

2. Focus on the verb in the target (e.g., describe, sort, analyze) and ensure that students know what cognitive work they will be doing in the lesson.

3. Ensure that students understand what success will look like. How will they know they have mastered the learning target?

It is important to vary your approach. Unpacking learning targets in the same way every day will cause some students to tune out, limiting their ability to take ownership of the process. For example, if your learning target is: *I can compare and contrast birds and mammals,* why not start with some low-risk – even fun – comparing and contrasting: Compare and contrast the Patriots and the Steelers (or Beyoncé and Taylor Swift, or *1984* and *Animal Farm,* or whatever will capture your students' interest). After students have had some fun, and hopefully a little spirited debate about this topic, you will be able

It is critical to give the process of unpacking a learning target the time it needs. Students must be clear about where they're headed and what success will look like.

Photo credit: EL Education

to unpack what it means to compare and contrast (i.e., what success on the learning target will look like) with students who are engaged and ready to get started.

Unpacking learning targets often takes three to five minutes, but there is no hard and fast rule. Teachers often rush through this process so that they can get to the lesson; however, unpacking the learning target can be viewed as a valuable part of the lesson in and of itself. It can and should be viewed as valuable learning time.

Explore this topic further by viewing the video and considering the questions in Video Spotlight 1.1.

Video Spotlight 1.1: Unpacking a Learning Target to Clarify Terms and Concepts
https://vimeo.com/313842309

This video features a middle school math teacher from Polaris Charter Academy in Chicago. Because the learning target contains an important algebraic concept, the teacher spends time unpacking that concept with students before they begin the work.

Video Reflection Questions
1. The teacher in this video takes time to carefully unpack key vocabulary, like *linear* and *variable*. When you use learning targets in your class, how do you make sure that the key vocabulary in the targets is understood by your students?
2. How does it help students to unpack learning targets together in groups, versus on their own?

Challenge #4: I teach young children. Learning targets are really abstract for them. How can I help my students understand and own them?

TRY THIS: MAKE UNPACKING THE LEARNING TARGET A PUZZLE TO SOLVE

For primary students who can't yet read, unpacking learning targets in a more traditional way (e.g., by asking one student to read the target out loud and then inviting other students to explain the words in the target) doesn't always work. Our youngest students often need a more innovative and engaging hook to help them truly understand where they are headed with their learning.

Try translating your learning target into a Mad-Lib style puzzle with strategically placed blanks in place of key words. Then engage students in a dialogue to solve the puzzle. A puzzle like this not only gets students truly excited to engage in their learning, it is also a wonderful way to teach critical academic and domain-specific vocabulary. The following Close Up provides an example used in a kindergarten study of bird adaptations.

Close Up: Unpacking a Primary Grades Learning Target

Steven, a kindergarten teacher in Boston, wrote the following learning target for a lesson in which students would study pictures of bird beaks in order to draw conclusions about how different birds use their beaks for various purposes.

Learning Target: *I can closely view pictures to gather information about bird beaks.*

To introduce the target to his students, many of whom still weren't reading, Steven wrote the following on the board and read it out loud:

I can closely _____ _____ to gather _____ about _____ _____.

"Before we begin today, we have a puzzle to solve," Steven told his students. "We've got all these photographs out on our tables. What do you think we are going to do with these photographs?" Students shouted out words like "look at them," "read them," and "study them."

"That's right," said Steven, "we are going to view them with our eyes." Then he wrote *view* in the first blank and, so that even nonreaders would be able to remember the word in that blank, he drew some eyes over the word. Now the learning target looked like this:

I can closely view _____ to gather _____ about _____ _____.

Next he asked Frances, a student in the back row who was starting to wiggle distractedly, "What are we going to view?"

"The pictures," Frances answered. (She was paying attention all along.)

"What can we put above the word to help us remember that?" Steven asked. He drew a picture of a picture. Before long the learning target looked like this.

I can closely view pictures to gather _____ about _____ _____.

Now Steven's students were really getting intrigued about what words and pictures would go in those other blanks.

"Why would we *closely* view pictures," he asked. "What would we hope to find in them?"

"Things," one student answered. "Colors," said another. "Details," said another.

Steven took his cue and synthesized their ideas. "So if we saw things and colors and details, we could gather a lot of information, couldn't we?" And then he filled in the next blank and drew a thought bubble over it as a symbol for information.

I can closely view pictures to gather information about _____ _____.

Finally, he invited students to look at a few of the pictures and fill in the last two blanks. Students noticed right away that all of the pictures had bird beaks in them.

Although Steven's students were only five, they now had a clear and memorable understanding of what they would do and learn in the investigative lesson that day. Before long they were gathered around the photos at their tables, pencils and note-catchers in hand, closely viewing the pictures in search of important information for their ongoing study of birds.

TRY THIS: USE A STORY OR POEM TO FOCUS STUDENTS ON THE LEARNING TARGET

The EL Education K–5 Language Arts Curriculum includes a kindergarten module on Toys and Play that offers another example of introducing learning targets to our youngest learners. This example confronts the challenge of learning targets being too abstract for young children in a different way – with story. Before introducing the learning target in the first lesson, the teacher reads the story of "The Magic Bow," which ends with a brief poem that students hear repeatedly throughout the Toys and Play module. Before long, students can recite the poem themselves and use it as a kind of mantra to help them maintain focus, believe in themselves, and work hard to learn new things. Read the story and poem in Figure 1.5. Consider how you can use stories and poems to help your primary age students take aim at their learning.

Figure 1.5 The Magic Bow: Taking aim at learning targets

"The Magic Bow"

Once upon a time, there was a little old woman who owned a magical bow. This bow would allow anyone who used it to do something amazing that they had never been able to do before.

A person would take up the bow, fit it with an arrow, take aim at their heart's desire, and "voila!" they would be able to do what they had always dreamed of learning. Whether they dreamt of learning to climb a tree, or play a musical instrument, or remember all meanings of all of the words in all of the world, the bow would help them achieve their goals.

People came far and wide to ask the woman to borrow her bow. And she would gladly share it with anyone who asked kindly. But one day, a greedy person came and stole the magic bow. Everyone was devastated. Many people thought that this was a terrible thing. They thought that no one would ever achieve their heart's desires again. They thought that no one would ever learn to do anything amazing again.

Of course the old woman knew better. She told the people who came to her that is wasn't the bow at all that helped them learn something new, but the effort they put forth and belief in themselves that gave them this power. From then on she gave the people who sought her this poem to help them remember the true power of learning:

Think of the thing you desire to learn.
Believe in yourself and your efforts will earn,
The ability to learn something new.
Now take your aim at the target true.

Created by EL Education for Instructional purposes.
Lexlle: 870L

Challenge #5: I have a high percentage of English language learners in my class. I'm never sure how much the learning targets help them stay focused on their learning because of language barriers.

TRY THIS: USE CONSISTENT ROUTINES TO UNPACK LEARNING TARGETS

English language learners (ELLs) deserve the same rich, compelling, and challenging curriculum that other students receive. They have the same cognitive needs as any student, which makes it critical that you *not* change learning targets by making the vocabulary or concepts simpler. Instead, offer supports that give ELLs equitable access to understanding rich and rigorous learning targets. Unpacking learning targets is an opportunity for all students – including ELLs – to learn academic and domain-specific language in context.

What follows are several strategies to employ when unpacking and using learning targets throughout a lesson that will support ELLs to understand where they are headed with their learning:

- Focus on the meaning and purpose of a key phrase within the learning target. For example, using the learning target *I can explain how the author uses reasons and evidence to support a point,* ask students questions like:
  - Can you figure out why we say *to support a point*? (to show purpose for reasons and evidence)
  - Why do we use the word *to*? (to signal that we will provide a purpose or reasons)
  - What follows the word *to*? (a verb + a noun/an action + a thing)
  - What if we remove *to*? (we no longer are alerted that the sentence will have a purpose or reasons)

- To better integrate the affective aspects of learning a language with academic content, check for comprehension by asking ELLs to summarize and then personalize the learning targets:
  - Can you put the learning target in your own words?
  - How do you feel about the learning target? (to assess if they feel overwhelmed and to discuss strategies to make progress toward the target)

- If you introduce more than one learning target at the same time, ask ELLs to use sentence frames with temporal words to put the learning targets in their own words (e.g., First we will _____; Then we will_____; Last we will _____. These steps link to the assessment by _____).

- If the learning target is connected to previous learning targets that day or in previous lessons, ask ELLs to recall and describe one time that they practiced working on the previous few learning targets.

- Pause the lesson to ask ELLs to give specific examples of how they have worked toward each learning target in the lesson so far. Invite them to rephrase the learning target again now that they have had experience with it.

- Ask students if they can figure out why you are introducing this particular learning target today. Why is it important? How does it help them with the lesson or unit?

- Emphasize different forms and meanings of the vocabulary in the learning target, particularly the key verbs. For example, using the learning target: *I can link two different ideas in one sentence*, emphasize the different forms and meanings of the word *link*:
  - Let's stand up and link arms. What part of speech is *link* in the first learning target? What part of speech is *link* when we link arms? (verb)
  - What other part of speech can *link* be? What does it mean? (a relationship or connection between two things; also, a loop in a chain)
  - Look at the links we made with our arms when we linked arms. As we write today, think about this question: How are our linked arms like our linked ideas when we write?

- Learn and practice vocabulary within the context of the topic and text. For example, in a second grade unit on schools and community, students read the learning target: *I can write about my observations after closely viewing community pictures*. They discuss the meaning of *observations* in this sentence and then observe school communities through some mystery pictures. Afterward, students talk about what they observed before they write about it. ELLs can also compare shades of meaning (e.g., observe, see, notice, spot), use sentence frames to describe what they observe ("I see _____. One thing I observe is _____."), and contrast the observing and noticing process to the inquiring, evaluating, and wondering process.

- Use word walls or vocabulary logs to track and learn selected vocabulary.

 Challenge #6: I'm good at introducing the learning targets for every lesson, but I'm not so sure what I should do after that. How do I return to them throughout the course of a lesson?

TRY THIS: CATCH AND RELEASE

When you first begin using learning targets, it can feel a bit forced to keep referring to the target throughout your lesson. However, orienting students back to the target at major intersections in the flow of the lesson is a key to student ownership. It keeps the "why we are doing this" front and center for students. Over time your pointer finger will habitually track back to the learning targets on your board, and reminding students of the target will become part of the natural conversation in your lessons.

Here are some of the key intersections to attend to in your lesson plan, moments when students may need to be reminded of the target:

- Just before a mini-lesson

- When students are released to apply their learning

- When you are circulating and notice that several students are off track or off task

- When students ask questions about key vocabulary or concepts

- When you bring the whole group back to share, discuss, or debrief

One key to success with this practice is student involvement in tracking progress. You want to hear from them about how they think they are doing individually and as a class (e.g., "What do you think? Did we hit the target yet? Show me."). You want students to say things like "Yes, we've met the target. Here's the evidence." Rather than your assessing their progress, asking them to assess themselves and provide a rationale for their response will engage students more fully in meeting learning targets. There are many tools and protocols that can help you involve students in this process (see the next section Try This: Put Students in the Driver's Seat).

Catch and release doesn't always have to be a formal process that breaks the flow of the lesson (i.e., stopping the whole class and directing their attention to the learning target). You can naturally weave catch and release into the lesson through questions, reminders, or quick checks for understanding that you direct to individual students, small groups, or the whole class.

TRY THIS: PUT STUDENTS IN THE DRIVER'S SEAT

Often when we think of tracking student progress, we think of it as something that is done *to* students, rather than something done *with* students. Clearly you will need to track students' progress, but we urge you to also include them in the process. If we give students the tools to understand where they are headed with their learning, help them track progress along the way, and then debrief with them not only what they learned but how they learned it, we put them in the driver's seat. After all, students are the ones who are in control of their learning, not us. If they feel motivated to persevere when the going gets tough because they understand where they are headed and why, that will take them much further than our encouragement or admonishments.

There are many possible ways to engage students in the process (in Chapters 2 and 3 we explore this topic in more depth). Here are just a couple of examples:

- *Simple protocols.* In the previous section, Try This: Catch and Release, we list key points during a lesson when you might want to "catch" students to check in on learning targets. If you "catch" the whole class, you can have them check in with each other using simple protocols like Turn and Talk. Ask questions like, "Where are you in relation to our first learning target? Back up your answer with evidence."

- *Individual and whole-class tracking forms*: Learning target trackers are helpful for you and the class to get a picture of whole-class progress. You can also create the same form on a sheet of paper for students to reflect on individually before adding their dot to the whole-class tracker, or you can create one like Table 1.1 at the start of this chapter. Figure 1.6 shows another kind of form for tracking progress over time. Chapter 3 contains many more examples.

Figure 1.6 Sample form for tracking progress over time

⊚ I can identify the lower case letters.

Name: Boston

letters	Progress check in Date: 1/30/11	Progress check in Date:	Progress check in Date:	Progress check in Date:	Progress check in Date:	Progress check in Date:
a						
b						
c	▓▓▓▓					
d						
e						
f						
g						
h						
i						
j						
k	▓▓▓▓					
l						
m						
n						
o	▓▓▓▓					
p	▓▓▓▓					
q						
r						
s						
t						
u						
v						
w						
x	▓▓▓▓					
y						
z						

Preschool

TRY THIS: DEBRIEF, DEBRIEF, DEBRIEF

Debriefing learning with students, usually at the end of a lesson, is essential. This is students' opportunity to reflect on their learning targets individually and as a group. They can determine what they still may need to learn to meet a given learning target fully, and they can consider how they will apply their new learning or skills to future learning.

Asking debrief questions to the whole class and waiting for volunteers to answer is a strategy that should be used very sparingly. Instead, there are many different protocols that can be used to maximize student voice and participation in the process. It's important that every student is engaged in reflection. Just a few of the many protocols that are effective for debriefing learning include[3]:

---

[3] Fuller protocol descriptions, including step-by-step instructions, can be found in our 2015 book *Management in the Active Classroom*, which also includes many more examples.

- *Think-Pair-Share/Write-Pair-Share*: In response to a question or prompt, students think individually for a set amount of time. When cued, students turn to a partner and each shares his or her thinking, also for a limited amount of time. Pairs then share with the large group.

- *Back-to-Back and Face-to-Face*: Partners stand back-to-back and wait for the teacher to ask a question or give a prompt. After listening to the prompt and thinking, they wait for the teacher to signal "face-to-face" and each take turns speaking and listening. This can be repeated with the same or different partners as many times as is helpful.

Learning target trackers give teachers and students a visual indicator of whole-class progress toward meeting targets. On this tracker, different color dots represent progress at different points in the learning process. M.A.D.E stands for Mastery, Accomplished, Developing, Emerging.

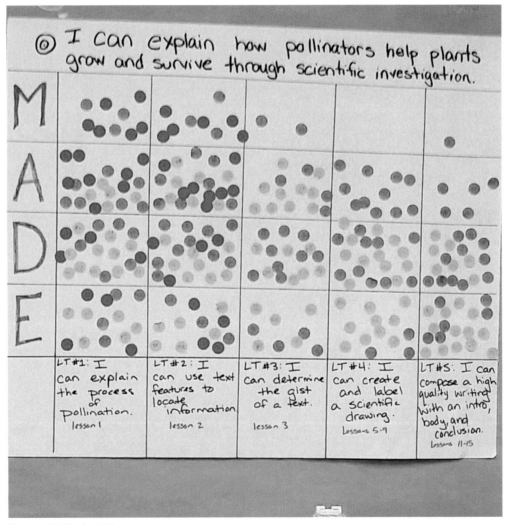

Photo credit: Wanda McClure

- *Human Bar Graph*: Teachers identify a range of levels of understanding or mastery (e.g., beginning, developing, accomplished) as labels for three to four adjacent lines. Students then form a human bar graph by standing in the line that best represents their current level of understanding. This provides a visual representation of whole class understanding.

- *Exit tickets*: Any relevant questions, prompts, or graphic displays of student thinking can be captured on an index card or small sheet of paper and viewed by the teacher or other student to determine a student's readiness for the next step or to assess learning from a lesson.

Note: Debriefs, protocols, and exit tickets are all discussed in greater detail in Chapter 2. For now you can explore this topic further by viewing the video and considering the questions in Video Spotlight 1.2.

Video Spotlight 1.2: Scaffolding Discussion Skills with a Socratic Circle
https://www.edutopia.org/video/scaffolding-discussion-skills-socratic-circle

This video features students at The Springfield Renaissance School in Springfield, Massachusetts, engaged in a deep conversation using a Socratic seminar as a scaffold for evidence-based discourse. Educator Linda Darling-Hammond offers commentary throughout the video and highlights the efficacy of the teacher's debrief strategy. This video was produced by Edutopia.

Video Reflection Questions
1. A few students participated in the Socratic seminar by tracking the conversation and then reporting out what they found. Why is this an effective debrief strategy, not only for those few students, but for the whole group?
2. In the video, Linda Darling-Hammond describes the students' exit ticket reflection as metacognitive. How does metacognition in a debrief help students transfer their learning from one setting to the next? If students don't have a chance to debrief, what learning opportunities are lost?

Challenge #7: I post my learning targets on the board or on chart paper, but as soon as students leave the room or move on to the next learning target, they forget what work relates to what learning target.

TRY THIS: WRITE THE LEARNING TARGET ON EVERYTHING

Well, not *everything*, but including the learning target on all handouts, homework assignments, anchor charts, and other related work keeps the target front and center for students. It also builds their understanding and ownership of where they're headed with their learning so that they can organize a body of evidence that demonstrates how they are progressing toward meeting it. See the following photos for two examples.

Learning target posted at the top of an assignment

Photo credit: EL Education

Learning targets displayed with student projects and related standard

Photo credit: Anne Vilen

Challenge #8: I know that learning targets for character are a good idea, but I don't take them as seriously as academic learning targets, and therefore, I don't take the time to really focus on them with my students.

TRY THIS: CONNECT CHARACTER LEARNING TARGETS AND ACADEMIC LEARNING TARGETS IN A MEANINGFUL WAY

If you are like most teachers, you feel a lot of pressure to cover all of the academic standards you are responsible for. Too often, it just feels like you can't take time to talk about character learning targets. We feel strongly that this is a mistake! In the end, your investment in helping students be respectful, courageous, collaborative learners will make everything go better in your classroom. We believe that sets of academic learning targets should always include at least one related character learning target that will support students to meet their academic learning targets. EL Education's definition of character includes Habits of Effective Learners (i.e., work habits, such as initiative, responsibility, perseverance, collaboration) and Habits of Ethical People, such as empathy, integrity, respect, compassion.

Character issues are often a big impediment to students' ability to meet academic learning targets. Students who struggle to work collaboratively, those who give up if they don't understand something right away, or those who don't see the value in revising their work get in the way of their own learning. Character learning targets that are aimed at what might be difficult in a lesson, and that are unpacked with students just like academic learning targets, will support students' academic and character growth. It's worth the time.

Used alongside your standards-based academic targets, character learning targets can really help students understand how they need to work in order to be successful learners. This is especially true when the character learning targets are specific and contextualized for the task or concept you are teaching.

Once you have crafted a character learning target, remember that it's just as important to unpack that target as it is the academic learning target. Students need to know exactly what it looks like and sounds like to demonstrate the character learning target. Here's an example of what the unpacking dialogue for the character learning target pictured might sound like:

TEACHER: Juan, can you read our first target?
JUAN: *I can give feedback to my peers respectfully.*
TEACHER: Talk to your tablemates. What do you think "respectfully" looks like and sounds like? What will we see and hear as you are doing your peer feedback protocol?

Possible Student Responses:

- You'll see us looking at each other.

- You'll see us not interrupting, but listening until the person is finished with their sentence.

- You'll hear us giving kind, specific, and helpful feedback.

- You'll see us giving each person a chance, so nobody gets left out.

The character learning target at the top of this list will help students meet their two academic learning targets.

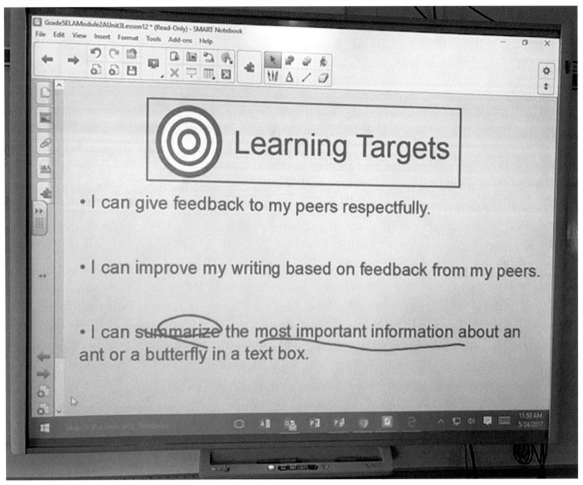

Photo credit: Anne Vilen

TEACHER: So, let's write some of those things up here next to "respectfully." These are the things I'll be looking for and listening for as I circulate during your peer conferences.

How can you integrate character learning targets into your daily lessons? The most helpful place to start is to look at the academic learning target(s) for an upcoming lesson and consider what character learning target would be most supportive to students' effort to meet the target(s). Do this for a week until you get the hang of it – and you have debriefed with students – and then try to be disciplined about including character learning targets with every set of academic learning targets you write for your lessons. Table 1.10 shows a few examples of what this might look like.

Table 1.10 Connecting academic and character learning targets

Academic Learning Targets	Relevant Character Learning Targets
I can write a scientifically accurate migratory species profile.	I can give kind, specific, and helpful feedback to my peers. I can incorporate feedback from my peers to improve my work.
I can describe how friction affects the motion of various objects.	I can collaborate effectively with my lab partner to generate accurate written data.
I can gather relevant evidence from exhibits during our fieldwork at the museum.	I can demonstrate respect and responsibility when representing our Crew off campus.
I can write my paragraph in cursive.	I can demonstrate a commitment to craftsmanship to make my writing legible and beautiful.
I can read out loud with my partner.	I can demonstrate academic courage.
I can convert decimals into percentages and percentages into decimals.	I can persevere by asking relevant questions when math is hard.
I can accurately record information from my animal research in my project notebook.	I can stay on task and focused through our entire independent research period.
I can learn the rules of a new game.	I can use words to explain rules I understand. I can use words to ask questions when I don't understand.
I can use evidence to evaluate arguments in a debate.	I can listen first to understand and then to be understood.

Check Yourself Checklist

Using Learning Targets throughout a Lesson Checklist

Review your lesson plan and check off all that apply:

❑ I have strategically chosen when to introduce each learning target based on what's best for the lesson.

❑ I have built in enough time to thoroughly "unpack" each learning target so that students will understand where they're headed and how to begin.

❑ I have identified opportunities throughout the lesson when I may need to reorient students to the learning target(s).

❑ I have made plans to post the learning target(s) and include them on handouts and other classroom materials.

❑ The lesson connects character learning targets and academic learning targets in a meaningful way so that students can see how their character helps them make progress academically.

❑ I have created a tool or tools that will help students monitor their progress, individually and as a class (e.g., target trackers).

❑ I have built in time to debrief progress toward the learning target(s) at the conclusion of the lesson or chunk of learning.

(This checklist is available in the online toolbox at http://www.wiley.com/go/lotolcompanion.)

Learning Target 3: I can create sets of learning targets that ensure my students are aiming for grade-level standards.

 Challenge #9: I'm struggling to translate standards into learning targets. I have so many standards to cover. Should there be a learning target for every standard? Is it a one-to-one relationship?

TRY THIS: DISSECT THE STANDARDS BEFORE WRITING LEARNING TARGETS

Now that we have looked closely at many of the lesson-level considerations necessary when writing and using learning targets, it's time to step back and explore how learning targets can be used to help students meet grade-level standards.

Standards are often complex and layered with meaning. Just as you unpack learning targets with your students, it's important to unpack standards for yourself so that you fully understand the expectations for what students should know and be able to do. This often works best when you have the opportunity to do this with your peers – your grade-level team or department – so that you can collectively discuss and debate the meaning of standards and what it would look like for students to meet them. It's not until you have done this that you can be sure that your learning targets will help students meet the standards.

Figure 1.7 shows the key steps for unpacking a sample standard. After going through this process with a sample standard of your own, you will likely never look at your standards the same way again! We want you – preferably in collaboration with teammates or colleagues – to dissect every word to really get at what the standard requires of students and how that impacts your curriculum and instruction. In the section that follows we will look closer at how standards can be bundled together in logical ways to guide the creation of learning targets.

TRY THIS: BUNDLE STANDARDS STRATEGICALLY

It's not necessary, or even wise, to create a learning target for every standard. After unpacking your standards (see Figure 1.7) you will discover that some will require multiple learning targets to address fully. And many standards can be bundled with others, particularly content standards (in science and social studies) and literacy standards, to make logical sequences of learning targets.

As with any design work, conceiving a long-term arc of purposeful student learning is messy, creative, multifaceted, and nonlinear. Figure 1.8 offers some key steps to consider when working to bundle standards to guide your curriculum.

Once you have done this work, you can create your long-term and supporting learning targets, based not just on each stand-alone standard but on bundles of standards that fit well together. As a reminder from *Leaders of Their Own Learning,* a long-term learning target may guide you and your students for an entire unit, case study, or long-term project. Supporting learning targets break the long-term target down into targets for lessons or arcs of lessons. Many teachers also use daily learning targets to further break down supporting targets.

Figure 1.7 Key steps for unpacking standards
SOURCE: The complete version of this document is available in the online toolbox at http://www.wiley.com/go/lotolcompanion.

Step 1
Locate your standards and choose a priority: one strand, one grade level, and one or two standards. (Use your school's curriculum map as a guide for your selection.)
Sample Standard: CCSS RI.2.2. Identify the main topic of a multi-paragraph text as well as the focus of specific paragraphs within the text.

Step 2
Get oriented to the standard(s) and annotate.

- Read standard once for gist. How might you nickname this standard? Why? How does it grow K–12?
- What words seem most important in this standard? Why?

Sample response for CCSS RI.2.2. Identify the main topic of a multi-paragraph text as well as the focus of specific paragraphs within the text.

- Read standard once for gist. How might you nickname this standard? Why? How does it grow K–12?
  - **Main idea standard**
  - As students progress through the grades, they must determine multiple main ideas and themes of texts, identify and explain how key details support those main ideas, and summarize the text.
- What words seem most important in this standard? Why?
  - **Identify, main topic, multi-paragraph, focus, specific paragraphs**
  - These are important words because they signal two different skills embedded in one standard. Students will also need to know what "main topic" and "focus" mean. They also inform the type of text that is needed in order for students to meet this standard.

Step 3
Reread standard more closely.

- What is the thinking this standard requires of students?
- What would mastery of this standard look and sound like?
- What scaffolding would students need to get there?

Sample response for Standard CCSS RI.2.2. Identify the main topic of a multi-paragraph text as well as the focus of specific paragraphs within the text.

- What is the thinking this standard requires of students?
  - Understand that individual paragraphs have specific foci and the paragraphs work together to support the main topic of a larger portion of text
  - Understand concepts of main topic and focus
  - Know strategies for finding focus of a single paragraph
  - Know strategies for connecting foci of single paragraphs to determine the main topic of the multi-paragraph text
- What would mastery of this standard look and sound like?
  - Student applies strategies to find focus of a single paragraph.
  - Student applies strategies for connecting foci of single paragraphs to determine the main topic of the multi-paragraph text
- What scaffolding would students need to get there?
  - Define main topic and focus.
  - Ensure that students understand text structure (e.g., paragraphs).
  - Practice finding main topic of one paragraph first.
  - Move to finding main topic of multi-paragraph text and finding specific foci of individual paragraphs.

Step 4
Focus on specific word choice in the standard: the verbs, nouns, adjectives, whether there are any "ands" or "ors."

- What are the implications for instruction? Assessment? Writing prompt?
- Look at the standard at the grade level above and below. Based on word choice, what seems key about the grade-specific demands of this standard? (e.g., In RI.7.1, students identify several pieces of evidence. In RI.8.1, students identify the strongest evidence. The grade 8 standard is more challenging, requiring students to be able to weigh evidence.)
- Revisit the nickname you created for your standard. Now that you have read the standard more closely, consider whether you might adjust your nickname.

(cont. online)

Figure 1.8 Key steps for bundling standards
SOURCE: This document is available in the online toolbox at http://www.wiley.com/go/lotolcompanion.

Step 1

Know your content standards deeply (see previous Try This section on unpacking standards). Think about not only what the standards are, but why they matter. What are the enduring understandings you want to stick with students?

Step 2

Prioritize your content standards. Of the myriad standards, which will you select as the heart of students' learning – the focus of units, case studies, or long-term projects? Why are those priorities?

Step 3

Know your literacy standards deeply (see previous Try This section on unpacking standards). Unpack the literacy standards (Common Core State Standards [CCSS] or your state literacy standards). Focus on specific words that signal the increased challenge from one grade level to the next.

Step 4

Prioritize your literacy standards. Note that certain standards (e.g., CCSS W.3 about narrative writing or CCSS R.6 about point of view) may actually "drive" the focus or inquiry of units, case studies, or long-term projects. By contrast, other standards will always be in play (e.g., CCSS RI.1 about citing evidence, CCSS R.4 about vocabulary learning strategies, or CCSS RI.10 about reading complex text).

Step 5

Strategically bundle content and literacy. The standards are like ingredients – as if someone has stocked your refrigerator for you. Teaching teams can then decide what meals to make. Bundle standards that are synergistic or complementary. Begin with content. Then consider how certain literacy standards or ingredients naturally go together (e.g., in chemistry, as students learn about the pros and cons of nuclear power, you might teach CCSS RST.8 about analyzing arguments alongside CCSS W.1 about crafting written arguments). Tip: When bundling literacy standards, consider physically cutting up your standards into strips that you can manipulate and literally bundle together (see photo):
- Physically cut up the standards and distribute them across the year. Focus first on the "main ingredients" that will drive student work, projects, etc. (e.g., focus on CCSS W.1–3 types of writing, or Speaking and Listening standards if students will be creating a presentation of some sort).
- Then layer in Reading standards; then remaining Speaking and Listening standards and Language standards.

Step 6

Consider the progression and spiraling of literacy standards. Some standards are so foundational to an effective classroom that they need launching early in the year (e.g., CCSS SL.1 about collaboration). Others are so technical they need to be spread across multiple units, case studies, or long-term projects (e.g., CCSS L.1 about the conventions of standard English). And some are challenging enough that they need more scaffolding and repetition (e.g., CCSS W.2 explanatory writing).

In the following Close Up from Jeanne Boland's eighth-grade class at The Odyssey School of Denver, you can see how what she calls an "uber" long-term learning target, a set of additional long-term targets, and supporting targets nest together to create a coherent learning path for students. You can also see how both content standards and literacy standards are featured. When studying this content, it was particularly germane for her students to focus on these literacy learning targets, which were applicable on almost any given day.

Physically manipulating your standards will help reveal the ways that they can be logically bundled together.

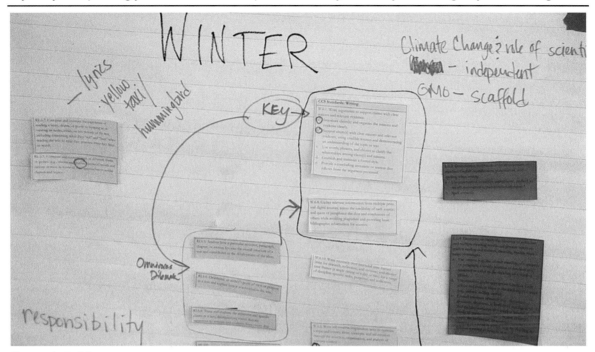

Photo credit: EL Education

Close Up: Nested Learning Targets

Uber Long-Term Learning Target

I can propose a peace plan for the Middle East that takes into account the needs of all parties.

Long-Term Learning Targets

1. I can describe what present-day life is like in Israel and the occupied territories.

   These sample supporting learning targets helped guide specific lessons related to Long-Term Learning Target 1.
   - I can identify which individuals, groups, and nations are involved in the conflict.
   - I can identify the current realities of the occupation (violence, separation wall, checkpoints, permits, conscription, etc.) for Israelis and Palestinians.
   - I can begin to compare/contrast Israeli and Palestinian views of each other and the conflict. I can describe why Israel and Palestine need a peace plan.

2. I can explain why the Middle East is defined as a distinct geographic region of the world.
3. I can compare and contrast the three major religions that arose in the Middle East.
4. I can analyze how religion has influenced the Israeli-Palestinian conflict.
5. I can explain both Israeli and Palestinian claims to live in and control the land.
6. I can name and describe significant events in the history of the Israeli-Palestinian conflict.
7. I can describe and empathize with a variety of perspectives on significant events in the history of the Israeli-Palestinian conflict.
8. I can describe nonviolent resistance and peace-building efforts by Palestinians, Israelis, and internationals.
9. I can create a series of annotated maps that tell the "story" of the Israeli-Palestinian conflict over time.
10. I can actively and respectfully participate in Socratic seminars about the Israeli-Palestinian conflict.
11. **I can identify point of view and bias within a text.**
12. **I can use the strategy of determining importance to set a purpose for reading a variety of texts.**
13. **I can annotate texts and take notes that help me answer historical questions and further my inquiry.**

Long-Term Learning Targets 11–13 in bold are literacy-focused; they were joined to different content standards and woven into instruction throughout the unit.

Challenge #10: I'm pretty good at writing learning targets, but I struggle to choose or craft assessments that clearly demonstrate that my students have met a target (and are therefore on their way to meeting required standards).

TRY THIS: START BY TRANSFORMING STANDARDS INTO STUDENT-FRIENDLY, *MEASURABLE* LEARNING TARGETS

Turning standards into learning targets involves much more than tacking on the words "I can" in front of a standard. Standards are often inscrutable for students – they do little to motivate or engage them. Learning targets must be a simple sentence, with one verb, that students understand and that motivate them to reach for the target.

For example, in one first-grade classroom, a state standard called for all students to "understand the monetary value of standard U.S. coinage." This is a reasonable and useful standard, but putting the words "I can" in front of that sentence would not make it understandable or motivating to any first grader, not to mention that the verb *understand* would be difficult to measure. The teacher in this classroom used the learning target: "I can make change for a quarter in many different ways." This was exciting for the students. They all got good at it and could demonstrate it to their friends and families. When they were done, they had met the intent of the state standard beautifully.[4]

The target also needs to use verbs that suggest how you can measure students' progress. Verbs like *understand* or *know* are especially problematic. Since you can't actually see inside your students' heads, it's hard to measure what they understand or know. That's why, when you write the learning target, you'll want to choose a verb that makes sense to students and that allows you and your students to measure progress. Verbs like *explain, write, sort, match, assemble* give you and your students a clear picture of what success will look like (refer back to Learning Target 1 of this chapter if you need a refresher on the importance of verbs).

TRY THIS: CREATE A STANDARDS-TARGETS-ASSESSMENT DOCUMENT

Another way to ensure that your assessments actually measure student progress toward learning targets is to create a Standards-Targets-Assessment document (STA). An STA is a tool to help you align standards, targets, and assessments. Some teachers also use STAs as de facto curriculum maps. Table 1.11 is an excerpted example from an STA for a fourth-grade study of North Carolina history.

The following questions will help you design your own STAs.

- What type of assessments best fit the learning targets? (Consider multiple choice, extended written response, performance assessment, or product.)

- How do the assessments enable students to demonstrate the specific knowledge, reasoning, and skills in the learning targets?

- Will a single assessment measure multiple learning targets? Or, do you need multiple assessments of different types?

- Do the assessments enable you to assess students individually? (Group projects are often not good summative assessments of knowledge and skills, but can be excellent assessments of character learning targets.)

---

[4] This example comes from our 2016 book *Learning That Lasts: Challenging, Engaging, and Empowering Students with Deeper Instruction.*

Table 1.11 Sample standards-targets-assessment document

Standard	Long-Term Target	Summative Assessment
Social Studies		
Understand how human, environmental, and technological factors affect the growth and development of North Carolina.	*I can describe what happened in the Trail of Tears experience.*	RAFT (role-audience-format-topic) assignment, supported by primary sources
ELA		
CCSS R3. Explain events, procedures, ideas, or concepts in a historical text.	*I can compare and contrast the perspectives of Cherokee leaders, white settlers, and the federal government.*	Research-based student-led mini-lesson (5 min.) on the impact of one natural resource
CCSS R6. Compare and contrast a firsthand and secondhand account of the same event or topic.	*I can find information in primary and secondary sources.*	Trail of Tears illustrated timeline from two perspectives
CCSS W3. Write narratives to develop real or imagined experiences or events using effective technique, descriptive details, and clear event sequences.	*I can explain how natural resources affected commerce and settlement on Cherokee lands.*	
CCSS W9. Draw evidence from literary or informational texts to support analysis, reflection, and research.	*I can explain some impacts of European colonization.*	

TRY THIS: ASSESS LEARNING FREQUENTLY

It is essential to create student-friendly learning targets with measurable verbs. These verbs suggest the kind of assessment that will be most appropriate. For example, a short answer format would not be appropriate when students are matching or assembling. Multiple choice will not work when students are explaining.

In addition to matching the type of assessment to the verb in the learning target, it is also important to assess progress frequently. Using quick *ungraded* assessments during or at the end of a lesson will let students know if they're on their way to meeting the learning target(s) without putting too much emphasis on testing. One or two math problems or a short written response to a question will give you the pulse check you need to adjust instruction if necessary, and will help prepare students for higher-stakes assessments that will be graded.

In the section Try This: Debrief, Debrief, Debrief, from Challenge #6, we describe protocols that can be used to help students reflect on their learning. These same protocols (or similar) can be used for quick assessments throughout a lesson:

- Think-Pair-Share/Write-Pair-Share

- Back-to-Back and Face-to-Face

- Human Bar Graph

- Exit Tickets

Chapter 2 offers many more tips for quick and frequent assessments.

In supporting schools and districts over the past 10 years to effectively implement learning targets, one thing is clear: school leadership is the key to success. If teachers see this strategy as a mandate from above – a practice they will comply with but don't really value – there is little hope for its success. School leadership must create a culture where teachers can learn, individually and in teams, how to make the practice of using learning targets a foundational part of their instruction. Teachers need freedom to experiment, to fail, to revise, and to discuss honestly what is working for them. They need to grapple with the practice until they see its power and make it their own. This can take months or even years to achieve. Many veteran teachers are still learning more every day about how to create and use learning targets effectively in their lessons.

What does that mean for your leadership? It means leading this change with the right spirit: We are going to take this on together as a school and learn as we go. It means modeling the use of learning targets in meetings and in teacher goals. It means celebrating teachers for having a growth mindset with learning targets and supporting teachers to meet regularly to share their learning about how to make targets work for them. It means patience with the faculty as they get better at this practice.

Holding teachers accountable in this work is important, but accountability should focus on a shared commitment to try things out, learn from them, and share learning with other teachers. If the accountability structure for leadership is reductionist – "Every teacher will have learning targets on her whiteboard every lesson or else. . ." – then teachers may be obedient but it will just be compliance. A more powerful accountability structure would include visiting classrooms through learning walks and sharing general data of what you learn with the staff. The best way to look for successful use of learning targets in a classroom is not the whiteboard, but the students. You can ask students: "What are you working on?" or "What are you trying to learn today?" If they tell you what their learning targets are you know that targets are a part of the culture of their classroom.

Video Spotlight 1.3 is a great example of skillful leadership focused on implementing student-engaged assessment practices throughout a school.

 Video Spotlight 1.3: Leading Professional Learning on Student-Engaged Assessment
https://vimeo.com/286915631

This video features four types of adult professional learning focused on student-engaged assessment at Amana Academy in Alpharetta, Georgia:

- Data-informed professional learning
- Coaching teachers
- Walkthroughs
- Learning walks

 Video Reflection Questions

1. Principal Cherise Campbell names several strategies that facilitate consistent use of student-engaged assessment practices at Amana Academy. What two or three strategies do you think would have the most leverage at your school and why?

2. Is there anything holding you back from trying new strategies that would allow for greater schoolwide consistency with student-engaged assessment practices? How might you get past these barriers.

What follows are a few tips to help school leaders facilitate consistent and effective practice across the school so that, ultimately, students can take greater ownership of their learning. Table 1.12 then summarizes the key action steps for teachers and students that will lead to success.

Top Tips

- Crafting and using learning targets well is challenging. Teachers need time to learn from you and each other, and to practice. Establishing a school culture where teachers can take risks, discuss mistakes, and keep learning is invaluable to this practice.

- Weave learning targets into the fabric of the school. Adults can benefit from the clarity they provide, just like students can. Craft learning targets for professional development, parents' nights, etc.

- Accountability and compliance are not the goal. Rather than simply looking for evidence of learning targets being written on the board in every classroom, take note of particularly strong learning targets you see. Create structures to lift up these good examples (e.g., via a staff newsletter, at the start of staff meetings) so that everyone can learn from them. Take note of teachers who are struggling with the practice and provide additional support.

- Build time into the school calendar for teachers to understand standards deeply and map their curriculum (or review existing curriculum maps). It is essential that grade-level teams and departments have the expectation and time to dig into standards together – to discuss and debate their meaning and to describe what it would look like if students met them.

Table 1.12 Learning targets: Steps to success

What Should Teachers Do?
Work collaboratively with grade-level and/or content area colleagues to deeply understand standards and what student work that meets standards will look like.
Craft high-quality learning targets that help students know exactly what they are aiming for with their learning.
Write learning targets on the materials that students will reference throughout the learning process (e.g., handouts, anchor charts).
Refer to learning targets throughout lessons and align activities to support students to meet them.
Craft learning targets that are aligned to standards and bundled strategically to support a compelling curriculum.
Craft learning targets that require students to engage in a variety of cognitive processes.
Integrate character learning targets and academic learning targets.
Align standards, learning targets, and assessments.
What Should Students Do?
Engage with the learning target – explain it in their own words with a partner or small group; discuss specific vocabulary; ask clarifying questions; and explore how they will demonstrate how they have met the target.
Articulate how each learning activity is helping them make progress toward learning targets.
Self-assess where they are in relation to a learning target.
See the connection between *how* they are learning (i.e., their character learning targets) and *what* they are learning (i.e., their academic learning targets).
Understand how they will be assessed from the beginning of a learning experience.

As you have read Chapter 1, maybe you have had an opportunity to try some of these strategies and techniques along the way. If not, come back to this post-assessment after you have had a chance to do so. Give yourself whatever time you need to address the learning targets and challenges in a meaningful way. Then take a moment to check your progress in Table 1.13, which is the exact same Learning Target Tracker that appeared at the beginning of this chapter.

Circle or place an X along the continuum from Beginning to Exceeding: **How would you rate your progress toward each learning target** *at this point in time?* Use the space provided to make notes regarding any remaining challenges you may be having or ideas for new and different strategies you want to try.

Table 1.13 Chapter 1 learning target tracker

Learning Target 1: *I can craft high-quality learning targets.* Beginning-----------------------------------Developing-----------------------------------Meeting-----------------------------------Exceeding Notes:
Learning Target 2: *I can use learning targets throughout a lesson to build students' understanding and ownership of their learning.* Beginning-----------------------------------Developing-----------------------------------Meeting-----------------------------------Exceeding Notes:
Learning Target 3: *I can create sets of learning targets that ensure my students are aiming for grade-level standards.* Beginning-----------------------------------Developing-----------------------------------Meeting-----------------------------------Exceeding Notes:

Checking for Understanding during Daily Lessons

Checking for Understanding during Daily Lessons

Using Data with Students

Learning Targets

STUDENT-ENGAGED ASSESSMENT

Student-engaged assessment is a system of interrelated practices that positions students as leaders of their own learning.

Models, Critique, and Descriptive Feedback

Standards-Based Grading

Student-Led Conferences

Passage Presentations with Portfolios

Celebrations of Learning

What Is Checking for Understanding?

Checking for understanding during daily lessons encompasses a wide range of techniques—formal and informal, oral and written, verbal and nonverbal—used by teachers and students to track what students understand and can do throughout a lesson. As a result of this ongoing assessment, teachers and students make adjustments to what they are doing to ensure that gaps in understanding are addressed and that students who have mastered concepts may comfortably move on to another learning task.

Checking-for-understanding techniques include the following:

- Writing and reflection
- Student discussion protocols
- Quick checks
- Strategic observation and listening
- Debriefs

The checking-for-understanding practices described in Chapter 2 of *Leaders of Their Own Learning* are seen by many teachers as the most important and, often, the most difficult practices to implement well in their classrooms. Learning targets can be precisely crafted, posted in the classroom, and unpacked with students every day, but if students can't articulate their progress toward meeting the target, they won't become leaders of their own learning. It's not about what you are teaching; it's about what students are learning. When the tasks we ask students to complete feel meaningful and purposeful to them and when we equip them with the tools they need to use learning targets and track their own progress, they become truly engaged in the learning process.

Harvard educator David Perkins reminds us that true understanding of concepts is not always easy to measure and is often not demonstrated by school assessments (D. Perkins, personal communication, 2017). True understanding may require that students apply learned concepts to new contexts or teach the concepts to others to demonstrate that they have fully grasped them. This chapter is not focused on assessing this deeper level of understanding. Here we focus on *quick checks* for basic understanding and question-asking strategies that can be built into daily lessons. This is a different lens than investigating deep understanding.

At the same time, however, we also want to emphasize that to be most effective, quick checks must go beyond what many of us are accustomed to. It's tempting—and common—to turn to our students and say "everyone got it?" and move on. Checking for understanding is most impactful when a well-chosen strategy is matched to a challenging and meaningful task, and, most importantly, when the information you glean from that check for understanding impacts your instruction. See what we mean in Video Spotlight 2.1.

> It's not just the recalcitrant rebel kid. It is also the quiet girl in the front row. For those children, the checking-for-understanding strategies give them a voice.
>
> —*Jessica Wood, teacher, The Springfield Renaissance School, Springfield, Massachusetts*

Video Spotlight 2.1: Redirecting a Lesson with Exemplars
https://vimeo.com/121494565

In this video, Anne Simpson, from Two Rivers Public Charter School in Washington, DC, supports her kindergartners' developing understanding of text-to-text connections. When her lesson doesn't go exactly as planned, she redirects the class by using one student's exemplar.

Video Reflection Questions
1. It's not unusual for a teacher to realize part way through a lesson that it's not working. How did Simpson figure that out, and how did she pivot her instruction?
2. How did using a model of a student who understood the concept help other students with their understanding?

In this chapter we build on the techniques offered in *Leaders of Their Own Learning* to help you meet four learning targets. Along the way, we explore solutions to the common challenges many teachers face when working toward each learning target.

Learning Targets for Chapter 2

- I can build a culture of trust, growth, and collaboration in my classroom so that students can honestly assess their progress.
- I can use checking-for-understanding techniques that help students assess their progress toward learning targets and allow me to monitor their progress.
- I can use questions effectively to check for understanding.
- I can plan effective debriefs.

Before we dive in, take a moment to assess yourself on each of the learning targets for this chapter. In Table 2.1, circle or place an X along the continuum from Beginning to Exceeding: **How would you rate your progress toward each learning target** *at this point in time?*

We'll give you a chance to assess yourself again at the end of the chapter.

Table 2.1 Chapter 2 learning target tracker

Learning Target 1: *I can build a culture of trust, growth, and collaboration in my classroom so that students can honestly assess their progress.* Beginning------------------------------------Developing------------------------------------Meeting------------------------------------Exceeding Notes:
Learning Target 2: *I can use checking-for-understanding techniques that help students assess their progress toward learning targets and allow me to monitor their progress.* Beginning------------------------------------Developing------------------------------------Meeting------------------------------------Exceeding Notes:
Learning Target 3: *I can use questions effectively to check for understanding.* Beginning------------------------------------Developing------------------------------------Meeting------------------------------------Exceeding Notes:
Learning Target 4: *I can plan effective debriefs.* Beginning------------------------------------Developing------------------------------------Meeting------------------------------------Exceeding Notes:

Learning Target 1: I can build a culture of trust, growth, and collaboration in my classroom so that students can honestly assess their progress.

Challenge #1: I haven't developed enough of a positive culture in my classroom and, as a result, my students are afraid to accurately assess their understanding in front of other students.

TRY THIS: REFRESH YOUR CLASSROOM NORMS

Have your classroom norms become just another poster on the wall? To you, the norms may be a no-brainer . . . of course we should "be respectful." But for some students, the practice may be more challenging than the concept. Asking students to assess their own understanding, especially in front of other students, requires a safe and respectful classroom culture. It's an essential starting place. Students will need to feel safe sharing their struggles in front of other students and must view making mistakes as a normal part of learning and growing. If students feel that they may be made fun of for assessing themselves honestly, they will quickly learn their own strategies to mask the struggles they may be having.

If you don't already have classroom norms in place, it will be important to develop them. Dig into this topic further by viewing the two videos featured in Video Spotlight 2.2.

Video Spotlight 2.2: (a) Creating Class Norms
https://vimeo.com/124448656

(b) Fostering Belonging with Classroom Norms
https://www.edutopia.org/video/fostering-belonging-classroom-norms

This first short video features teachers and students from multiple K–12 classrooms tapping into their hopes and dreams for their class in order to develop the norms they'll live by all year.

The second video, produced by Edutopia, was filmed at King Middle School in Portland, Maine. Teacher Bobby Shaddox grounds his students in their class norms every day by asking his students what social studies will look like, sound like, and feel like when they are supporting the norms.

Video Reflection Questions
1. After viewing these videos, why do you think norms are so important to students' ability to accurately and honestly check for understanding?
2. If you already have classroom norms in your classroom, what new ideas did the videos give you for how to *use* them differently during lessons?
3. If you don't already have classroom norms in place, what steps will you take to make them a part of your classroom? If you need help, what resources can you draw on?

Even if you already have norms in place, it may be time to give them renewed attention. But how can you refresh your norms in a way that helps them come alive in your classroom and that gives students a clear sense of how to take greater ownership of them? Sometimes it's as simple as engaging your class in a conversation about the norms. Depending on your comfort level facilitating such conversations, an open discussion of questions like "How do you think we're doing using respectful language?" can be quite fruitful.

Or, you may decide it will be more productive for you and your students to use a protocol that will get them talking to each other or engaging physically with their reflection on the norms. Table 2.2 lists a few protocols you can use to engage students in self-assessing their own progress toward upholding each norm. (Note: Protocols are explored more fully in the pages that follow.)

Table 2.2   Sample protocols for assessing progress on classroom norms

Protocol	Description and Use
Back-to-Back and Face-to-Face	Pairs of students start off standing back-to-back. When asked a question (usually by the teacher) they think briefly about their response and, when instructed, turn face-to-face. Each student then answers the question in turn, listening carefully when his or her partner is speaking. When discussing norms, possible questions/prompts might include: • "How are we doing as a class upholding our norm _____?" • "How do you personally feel you have done upholding our norm _____?" • "Give your partner two examples of how you upheld _____ norm this week/month/semester." • "Give you partner two examples you saw of one of your classmates upholding the norm _____ this week/month/semester."
Thumb-ometer	When asked a question, students respond with a thumbs up, sideways, or down to indicate agreement or disagreement (or something in between). This protocol generally does not involve conversation; it is best used to give students and teachers a quick pulse-check. Possible norms-based questions/prompts might include: • I sat with someone at lunch that I don't normally sit with. • I took time today to acknowledge the effort of one of my classmates. • I participated actively in my small group work today.
Fishbowl	A Fishbowl protocol can be used versatilely in many kinds of lessons. In the inner circle a lesson or discussion takes place, while in the outer circle students observe. These observers are process checkers and have some kind of question to keep in mind as the discussion or lesson proceeds (e.g., are boys and girls participating equally?). Fishbowls are a nice opportunity to blend academics and norms and help students see that they aren't separate entities in the classroom. The inner circle can be discussing academic content while the outer circle is checking in on the norms. The following list of possible questions/prompts shows how academics and norms can be blended using a Fishbowl: • What body language did you observe in students who were listening while others spoke? • Place a check beside the names of students who speak during the discussion. At the end of the discussion tally the check marks. Did everyone in the circle speak during the discussion? Did anyone speak more than once? If so, what was the highest number of checks? • What evidence did you see of students building off of other students' comments during the discussion? • What evidence did you see of students citing evidence from their text when making points during the discussion?

TRY THIS: USE GROWTH-ORIENTED STATEMENTS

Checking for understanding will inevitably lead to some students initially faltering. How you and your students respond to missteps has a singular influence on the climate of trust in the classroom. Students need to know that it's okay for them to make mistakes. They also need to know that, ultimately, they are accountable for learning from those mistakes and setting things right. Using growth-oriented language will support your students to see mistakes as an opportunity to learn. Here are some phrases you can try:[1]

• Mistakes grow your brain.

• It is really important to make mistakes.

---

[1] Retrieved from: http://motionmathgames.com/say-wrong-answer-while-encouraging-growth-mindsets

We spied this poster at The Franklin School of Innovation in Asheville, North Carolina. When students use self-talk that demonstrates and reinforces growth, they begin to view checking for understanding as a way to help them learn and grow, not just to comply with teacher directions.

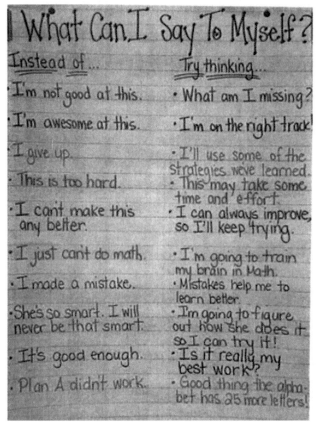

Photo credit: Anne Vilen

- The best way to improve is to learn from mistakes.
- It's great to challenge yourself.
- Easy is a waste of time.
- I love to learn from mistakes.
- Working hard grows your brain.
- You're pushing yourself, which is excellent, but you've made a mistake. Try again.
- You've made an interesting mistake. What can you learn from it?

TRY THIS: ASK A COLLEAGUE TO OBSERVE YOUR NORMS IN ACTION

It can be hard to assess progress without objective feedback. As you work to build a positive culture for checking for understanding in your classroom, consider inviting a fellow teacher or administrator to observe your class and look for two things:

1. Evidence of students upholding the classroom norms (see Figure 2.1 for a simple form an observer might use)

2. Evidence of growth-oriented language between you and your students and among students themselves

After the observation is complete, reflect on the observation data and ask yourself:

- What specific examples do I see of students upholding classroom norms?

- If some norms are obviously not being upheld, what can I do to refresh expectations and give students a chance to practice?

- What specific things did I say to foster students' growth mindset?

- In what ways did students encourage each other?

- How will I use learning targets and checking for understanding in an upcoming lesson to encourage all of my students to grow?

Figure 2.1 Sample form for observing students upholding classroom norms
SOURCE: This document is available in the online toolbox at http://www.wiley.com/go/lotolcompanion.

Norm	Evidence (include student names)

 Challenge #2: My students don't view learning as a collaborative effort. They don't want to share their work or talk with other students about what they know.

TRY THIS: USE PROTOCOLS TO HELP STUDENTS WORK TOGETHER PRODUCTIVELY AND COLLABORATIVELY

Protocols are an excellent way for students to practice talking with each other about any number of topics, including classroom norms (see Challenge #1) and academic content.

What Is a Protocol?

A protocol consists of agreed-upon, detailed guidelines for reading, recording, discussing, or reporting that ensure equal participation and accountability in learning. Importantly, protocols allow students to talk to each other, not just to you. As a result, students build independence and responsibility. Protocols also give you a chance to observe students discussing academic content. Since strategic observation is one important checking-for-understanding technique highlighted in *Leaders of Their Own Learning*, it's important that you have something worthwhile to observe! Protocols are a great tool for that purpose.

Protocols can range from very quick protocols like Back-to-Back and Face-to-Face (see Video Spotlight 2.3 and Figure 2.2) to longer lesson-length protocols like Science Talks.[2] The skeleton that holds up any protocol includes:

- Organized steps for the procedure
- Time frames for each step
- Norms for participants
- Specific roles for procedures

The first time a protocol is used, it must be explicitly taught and rehearsed. During successive uses, it will need to be reinforced multiple times. Providing table tents, graphic organizers, or an anchor chart with the bulleted steps of the protocol, and/or "role cards" that describe each person's role in the protocol, will help students stay on task and do the protocol with fidelity. We suggest starting small with three to five protocols you can have in your back pocket for a variety of situations.

Video Spotlight 2.3: Classroom Protocols in Action
Back-to-Back and Face-to-Face https://vimeo.com/164447189

This video is narrated by students, and can be shown to students to help them learn the Back-to-Back and Face-to-Face protocol. The Back-to-Back and Face-to-Face protocol is a great one to get started with if protocols are new to you and your students. Though this video features young students demonstrating the Back-to-Back and Face-to-Face protocol, it's a protocol that is appropriate for any age, including adults. Figure 2.2 is a full description of the Back-to-Back and Face-to-Face protocol.

Video Reflection Questions

1. How might you use this video to encourage students to talk to each other in your classroom? Look ahead to an upcoming lesson and work in the Back-to-Back and Face-to-Face protocol and/or the video.
2. If you teach older students and don't wish to show them this video, how will you help them understand the purpose of the protocol? How would you describe the purpose? Is there a different protocol that you would prefer to use that would serve the same purpose?

---

[2] Both the Back-to-Back and Face-to-Face video and the protocol in Figure 2.2 come from our 2015 book *Management in the Active Classroom*, where you can find many more protocols, including the Science Talk protocol referenced here, and 26 additional videos.

Figure 2.2 The Back-to-Back and Face-to-Face Protocol
SOURCE: This document is available in the online toolbox at http://www.wiley.com/go/lotolcompanion.

Purpose

This protocol provides a method for sharing information and gaining multiple perspectives on a topic through partner interaction. It can be used for reviewing and sharing academic material, as a personal "ice breaker," or as a means of engaging in critical thinking about a topic of debate.

Materials

- Questions to be asked between student partners, prepared in advance

Procedure

1. Have students find a partner and stand back-to-back with him or her, being respectful of space.

2. Give students a question or statement that they will share a response to with a partner.

3. Have students think about what they want to share and how they might best express themselves.

4. When you say, "Face-to-face," have students turn, face their partners, and decide who will share first if you have not indicated that a certain person should go first.

5. Have students listen carefully when their partner is speaking and be sure to make eye contact with him or her.

6. When given the signal, students should find a new partner, stand back-to-back, and wait for the new question, statement, etc.

7. This may be repeated for as many rounds as needed/appropriate.

Variations

- Partners may be assigned.

- Partners may also stay together for the length of the protocol.

- The class may stand in two concentric circles with one circle rotating to a new back-to-back and face-to-face partner for each new question or prompt.

- The protocol may be repeated several times in a row with the same partners to give students multiple opportunities to check their understanding and receive information from their partners.

Here are few great resources for finding protocols for almost any classroom purpose:

- Book: *Management in the Active Classroom* by Ron Berger, Dina Strasser and Libby Woodfin

- Video Collection: http://eleducation.org/resources/collections/protocols-in-action-videos

- Book: *The Power of Protocols: An Educator's Guide to Better Practice, Second Edition* by Joseph P. McDonald, Nancy Mohr, Alan Dichter, and Elizabeth C. McDonald

- Book: *Protocols in the Classroom: Tools to Help Students Read, Write, Think, and Collaborate* by David Allen, Tina Blythe, Alan Dichter, and Terra Lynch

- Website: National School Reform Faculty (www.nsrfharmony.org)

- Website: School Reform Initiative (www.schoolreforminitiative.org)

TRY THIS: USE CONVERSATION CUES TO SUPPORT ENGLISH LANGUAGE LEARNERS AND THEIR PEERS

Conversation Cues engage English language learners (ELLs) and their peers in thoughtful and extended academically oriented conversations. Conversation Cues are questions teachers can ask students to promote productive and equitable conversation, helping to gauge students' thinking and understanding. The questions encourage students to have productive discussions and generate new ideas. Conversation Cues are based on four goals[3] that encourage each student to:

- (Goal 1) Talk and be understood (e.g., "I'll give you time to think and sketch or discuss this with a partner" and "Can you say more about that?")

- (Goal 2) Listen carefully to one another and seek to understand (e.g., "Who can repeat what your classmate said?")

- (Goal 3) Deepen thinking (e.g., "Can you figure out why the author wrote that phrase?")

- (Goal 4) Think with others to expand the conversation (e.g., "Who can explain why your classmate came up with that response?")

By introducing Conversation Cues one goal at a time, you can slowly build the capacity of all students to engage in rich, collaborative discussions. For example, some students who are shy, introspective, or have less knowledge or language ability in some contexts may respond more readily to a Goal 1 Conversation Cue: "I'll give you time to think and write or sketch," while other students may be willing and able to respond to a Goal 4 cue: "How is what Lupe said the same as or different from what Young Bin said?"

Conversation Cues help all students begin to think deeply about the material, to explain their thinking, and to learn to listen to various points of view as they consider the material. You can encourage students to gradually begin using appropriate Conversation Cues themselves, along with other discussion conventions, to expand their independent interactions with their peers. Table 2.3 includes a complete set of Conversation Cues.

TRY THIS: MAKE THE PROCESS OF LEARNING PUBLIC

When students play in an orchestra or on a sports team, their individual and collective learning is public. They watch each other stumble, fall, and, eventually, work together to succeed. With the right team culture, they support and bring out the best in each other. Yet, when students are working on history or math, their learning is often hidden and private. Making the process of classroom learning public will foster a more collaborative learning environment, which will ultimately support students' ability to assess their progress and strive for improvement.

Some strategies you can try include:

- Having students explain their thinking to each other, including their learning *process* (see photo)

- The intentional use of multiple drafts of student work as models (see Chapter 4)

- Documentation panels that document the learning process (see photo and Chapter 6)

- Celebrations of learning that document the learning process (see Chapter 6)

---

[3] These goals are adapted from Sarah Michael's and Cathy O'Connor's Talk Science Primer, Cambridge, MA: TERC, 2012. http://inquiryproject .terc.edu/shared/pd/TalkScience_Primer.pdf. Based on Chapin, S., O'Connor, C., and Anderson, N. (2009). *Classroom Discussions: Using Math Talk to Help Students Learn, Grades K–6*, 2e. Sausalito, CA: Math Solutions Publications.

Table 2.3 Conversation cues

Conversation Cues	
Cue	**Expected Response**
Goal 1: Help all students talk and be understood	
Think and Process Language Internally	
"I'll give you time to think and write or sketch." "I'll give you a minute to think and write or sketch." "I'll give you time to discuss this with a partner."	
Elaborate upon or Expand	
"Can you say more about that?" "Can you give an example?"	"Sure. I think that _____." "Okay. One example is _____."
Clarify	
"So, do you mean _____?"	"You've got it." "No, sorry, that's not what I mean. I mean _____."
Goal 2: Help students listen carefully to one another and seek to understand	
Repeat or Paraphrase	
"Who can repeat what your classmate said?" "Who can tell us what your classmate said in your own words?"	"She said _____." "He was saying that _____."
Goal 3: Help students deepen their thinking	
Provide Reasoning or Evidence	
"Why do you think that?" "What, in the (sentence/text), makes you think so?"	"Because _____." "If you look at _____, it says _____, which means _____."
Challenge Thinking	
"What if _____ (that word were removed/the main character had done something different/we didn't write an introduction)? I'll give you time to think and discuss with a partner." "Can you figure out why _____(the author used this phrase/we used that strategy/there's an -ly added to that word)? I'll give you time to think and discuss with a partner."	"If we did that, then _____." "I think it's because _____."
Think about Thinking (Metacognition)	
"What strategies/habits helped you succeed? I'll give you time to think and discuss with a partner." "How does our discussion add to your understanding of _____ (previously discussed topic/text/language)? I'll give you time to think and discuss with a partner."	"_____ helped me a lot because _____." "I used to think that _____, and now I think that _____."
Goal 4: Help students think with others to expand the conversation	
Compare	
"How is what _____said the same as/different from what _____ said?"	"_____ said _____. That's different from what _____ said because _____."

(continued)

Table 2.3 Continued

Conversation Cues	
Cue	**Expected Response**
Agree, Disagree, and Explain Why	
"Do you agree or disagree with what your classmate said? Why?"	"I agree/disagree because _____." "I think what he said is _____ because _____."
Add on	
"Who can add on to what your classmate said?"	"I think that _____."
Explain	
"Who can explain why your classmate came up with that response?"	"I think what she's saying is _____."

Students explain their learning about crayfish to each other.

Photo Credit: Anne Vilen

Creating documentation panels that are beautiful and that stimulate thinking and reflection is a valuable process for students. Not only do the panels reflect that learning is a process, involving multiple drafts and growth, they demonstrate for students that learning is a collaborative effort.

Photo credit: EL Education

Check Yourself Checklist

Creating a Positive Classroom Culture for Checking for Understanding Checklist

Check off all that apply:

- ❏ My students and I have created classroom norms and students discuss and/or reference them regularly.

- ❏ My students and I use growth-oriented language when we make mistakes (e.g., I'll need to put more effort into this vs. I'm terrible at this)

- ❏ My lessons have plenty of time built in for students to talk with and learn from each other.

- ❏ We celebrate the learning process publicly in our classroom.

(This checklist can be found in the online toolbox at http://www.wiley.com/go/lotolcompanion.)

Learning Target 2: I can use checking-for-understanding techniques that help students assess their progress toward learning targets and allow me to monitor their progress.

 Challenge #3: I'm having a hard time finding checking-for-understanding techniques that give me the information I need (and I don't want to spend a lot of time teaching new techniques to my students).

TRY THIS: FOCUS ON JUST A FEW TECHNIQUES

Helping your students learn new protocols and checking-for-understanding techniques takes practice, particularly if students are used to answering questions or responding mostly to you, versus their peers. Introducing too many new techniques that require student discourse or collaboration all at once can be confusing or frustrating. This approach may also result in students spending so much energy learning the technique that they can't focus on its real purpose, which is for them to honestly and accurately reflect on their learning. The key to success is stability and consistency.

Try choosing a technique that you can reuse multiple times over the course of the next week or two. If the technique is a protocol with multiple steps, create an anchor chart of brief directions that students

Anchor charts with visual cues will support your students to remember the steps and purpose of protocols and checking-for-understanding techniques.

Photo credit: Anne Vilen

can refer to. Use the protocol at least four times before assessing what works and what doesn't. When you feel like the technique is serving its purpose well, introduce another until you have a handful of techniques that your students are able to use effectively and that serve all the purposes you need.

TRY THIS: SEEK OUT NEW TECHNIQUES

Classic "quick-check" techniques, like the Thumb-ometer, are perennial favorites because they are easy to use and can give you a quick look at whole-class understanding. But when a Thumb-ometer is over-used, students often respond with a reflexive thumbs up whether they have met the learning target or not. If you see 25 thumbs up, you may be seeing compliance, not true understanding.

If the Thumb-ometer is broken, it's time to introduce something new. When deciding what checking-for-understanding technique is best for a lesson, remember that it's all about how it will help you know whether students are meeting the learning target. When choosing a checking-for-understanding technique, you will save you and your students time and make the technique more purposeful by first asking yourself the following questions:

1. Do I need students to write it down in order to be able to check their understanding?

2. Do I need to hear or see *each* student demonstrate their understanding?

Students demonstrate the Thumb-ometer.

Photo credit: Sarah Wing

3. Do I want to check "whole-group" understanding or individual understanding?

4. Can students self-report their level of understanding accurately?

5. When is the right time to check for this understanding (before students have work time? at the end of the lesson?)?

6. Are there certain students who, due to learning or language challenges, may not feel safe reporting in public about how much they understand? Do I need to check in individually with them?

Then choose a technique that fits the purpose of the lesson you're teaching and your needs for assessment. Table 2.3 on pages 70 and 71 of *Leaders of Their Own Learning* lists a number of quick-check techniques including:

- Factual or brief-response checks
  - Go-Around
  - Whiteboards
  - Do Now
  - Clicker technology

- Monitoring confusion or readiness checks
  - Explain It Back
  - Table tags
  - Thumb-ometer or Fist-to-Five
  - Glass, Bugs, Mud

- Status checks
  - Sticky Bars
  - Learning Lineups
  - Human Bar Graph
  - Scatterplot Graph

- Checks to probe deeper understanding and reflection
  - Hot Seat
  - Admission and exit tickets
  - Presentation assessments

Table 2.4 on the adjacent page provides several more.

 Challenge #4: I'm never sure when to use which technique during the course of a lesson. I want to be judicious and efficient and not wear my students out checking for understanding too frequently.

TRY THIS: PLAN OUT WHEN YOU WILL CHECK FOR UNDERSTANDING

The best way to ensure that you are using a variety of checking-for-understanding techniques that are well-matched to the kind of assessment you need is to build them into your lesson plans. The ubiquitous Thumb-ometer or Fist-to-Five may be useful some of the time, but it won't meet all of your needs, and using it too much will inevitably diminish students' desire to be truly reflective. If the concept or skill you are teaching is complex, you'll probably want a more finely calibrated tool for measuring students' understanding.

Like anything you do in the classroom, it will be more difficult to choose the best checking-for-understanding technique on the fly. Things can be chaotic in the classroom, so you'll want to plan it out. Figure 2.3 shows a sample lesson plan with checking-for-understanding techniques built in. Following the lesson plan, Figure 2.4 shows the Strategic Observation Tracker

Table 2.4 Quick-check techniques

Technique	Description	Works Well When. . .
Flip Check	Students have a card to represent two possibilities (i.e., yes/no, north/south, China/India, multiply/divide). As you ask a series of questions, students "flip" to the response they believe is correct.	Students are memorizing simple facts to distinguish between two categories and you need a quick visual tool for seeing their answers.
Whole-Class Learning Target Tracker	This is a large "Tracking my Progress" sheet on which students will self-assess against the learning target(s), often using a sticker that they place anonymously on a rubric. This will give you and your students a "collective pulse."	You want data on progress that can be analyzed collectively. The class can set collective goals (e.g., for behavior or transition time) and see progress toward them.
Personal Learning Target Tracker	This is an individual "Tracking My Progress" sheet. Students mark their progress on a rubric, often at the beginning, middle, and end of a lesson that is aiming at a particular learning target or over a series of lessons aiming at a long-term target.	You want students to see their progress over time, particularly when learning targets are long-term or when they are revisited throughout a unit of study. Keeping the tracking sheets in their binders will help students see the progress they have made and where they need to keep working and learning.
Rapid Fire Brainstorm	Students stand up in a circle. You start with a ball or soft object and toss it to a student as you simultaneously ask a question. (Questions are usually quick facts like vocabulary, multiplication tables, or geography.) When a student catches the ball, she responds to the question and then tosses the ball to another student. Depending on the topic and the group, students can ask the questions as they toss the ball, or you can ask all of the questions.	Students are memorizing simple facts and trust each other enough to report answers quickly out loud. It would be important to establish a growth-mindset culture before using this quick check so that students feel comfortable "messing up." If possible, allow students to ask each other the questions–this engages their brains with the material in a different way.
Concept Map/ Interactive Word Wall	After learning content or vocabulary, give students a list of words or concepts and ask them to create a "story" or "map" that connects or links the concepts/ vocabulary together. For instance, if the topic is the Civil War, and ideas like, "north," "south," "draft riots," and "Lincoln" have been discussed, give a list of these words and concepts. This technique works best if each word/concept is on its own piece of paper (along with bridging words) and students can manipulate and place them in a way that tells the story. This can be done in partners, small groups, or by the whole class collectively (each person gets one word to add to the story and explain).	Students are learning to use academic or domain-specific vocabulary to discuss ideas. It would be important to structure the discussion so that all students participate and have clear boundaries for staying on topic and on task so that you can circulate and listen.
Bumper Sticker	Students synthesize their learning into one condensed idea/statement that is pithy and memorable (like a bumper sticker).	A complex idea can be boiled down to a single statement. This is especially useful if each student contributes one bumper sticker so that the most important aspects of the concept surface when sharing the bumper stickers.

for teachers to use during this lesson to track the strategies students use to represent functions in this math lesson.

In the video featured in Video Spotlight 2.4 you can get a glimpse of how one middle school teacher makes choices about which checking-for-understanding technique to use when. After viewing the video, dig deeper by considering the reflection questions.

Water Usage in Las Vegas Lesson Plan

Title	Water Usage in Las Vegas
Grade level	8/9
Discipline(s)	Math

Long-Term Learning Targets Addressed

CCSS.MATH.CONTENT.HSF.IF.B.4
For a function that models a relationship between two quantities, interpret key features of graphs and tables in terms of the quantities, and sketch graphs showing key features given a verbal description of the relationship. *Key features include: intercepts; intervals where the function is increasing, decreasing, positive, or negative; relative maximums and minimums; symmetries; end behavior; and periodicity.*

CCSS.MATH.CONTENT.8.F.B.4
Construct a function to model a linear relationship between two quantities. Determine the rate of change and initial value of the function from a description of a relationship or from two (x, y) values, including reading these from a table or from a graph. Interpret the rate of change and initial value of a linear function in terms of the situation it models, and in terms of its graph or a table of values.

Supporting Learning Targets Assessed	Ongoing Assessment
LT#1: I can explain what happens at the point of intersection of two functions. LT #2: I can analyze the connections between different ways of representing two functions. Character Target: I can engage positively with others to learn things and create work that is larger and deeper than I could create on my own.	Strategy Tracker Exit Ticket

Agenda Overview	Teaching Notes
Workshop 2.0	

Lesson Vocabulary	Materials
Function, graph, table, equation, axis, point of intersection, linear, slope, y-intercept	Student handout—one per student. Chart paper and marker per triad.

	Duration
	5 min

Instructional Plans

	Duration
	5 min

Grapple:

- **Students**: Independent. First attempt at solving problem.
- **Teacher**: (CFU: Strategic Observation and Listening. Use Strategy Tracker.)
  - ○ Read problem aloud and have students follow along.
  - ○ Use **anticipation guide** to identify next steps to help students make progress
  - ○ Record observations on **strategy tracker**.
  - ○ Focus on fostering growth mindset and reinforcing independent silent work— narrate the positive with perseverance. "A chance to try out your own thinki first. See what you know and what you don't know. A chance to build up you math brain."

> The teacher is cued to start using the Strategic Observation Tracker (see Figure 2.3), which captures important information about student thinking process and forms the basis for the synthesis/debrief.

Figure 2.3 Continued

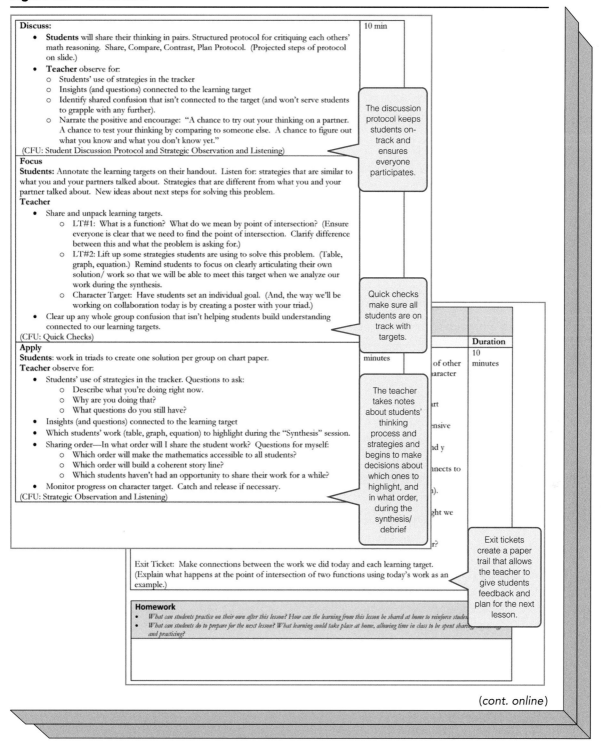

Discuss: 10 min
- **Students** will share their thinking in pairs. Structured protocol for critiquing each others'
  math reasoning. Share, Compare, Contrast, Plan Protocol. (Projected steps of protocol
  on slide.)
- **Teacher** observe for:
  - Students' use of strategies in the tracker
  - Insights (and questions) connected to the learning target
  - Identify shared confusion that isn't connected to the target (and won't serve students
    to grapple with any further).
  - Narrate the positive and encourage: "A chance to try out your thinking on a partner.
    A chance to test your thinking by comparing to someone else. A chance to figure out
    what you know and what you don't know yet."

(CFU: Student Discussion Protocol and Strategic Observation and Listening)

> The discussion protocol keeps students on-track and ensures everyone participates.

Focus
Students: Annotate the learning targets on their handout. Listen for: strategies that are similar to
what you and your partners talked about. Strategies that are different from what you and your
partner talked about. New ideas about next steps for solving this problem.
Teacher
- Share and unpack learning targets.
  - LT#1: What is a function? What do we mean by point of intersection? (Ensure
    everyone is clear that we need to find the point of intersection. Clarify difference
    between this and what the problem is asking for.)
  - LT#2: Lift up some strategies students are using to solve this problem. (Table,
    graph, equation.) Remind students to focus on clearly articulating their own
    solution/ work so that we will be able to meet this target when we analyze our
    work during the synthesis.
  - Character Target: Have students set an individual goal. (And, the way we'll be
    working on collaboration today is by creating a poster with your triad.)
- Clear up any whole group confusion that isn't helping students build understanding
  connected to our learning targets.

(CFU: Quick Checks)

> Quick checks make sure all students are on track with targets.

Apply
Students: work in triads to create one solution per group on chart paper.
Teacher observe for:
- Students' use of strategies in the tracker. Questions to ask:
  - Describe what you're doing right now.
  - Why are you doing that?
  - What questions do you still have?
- Insights (and questions) connected to the learning target
- Which students' work (table, graph, equation) to highlight during the "Synthesis" session.
- Sharing order—In what order will I share the student work? Questions for myself:
  - Which order will make the mathematics accessible to all students?
  - Which order will build a coherent story line?
  - Which students haven't had an opportunity to share their work for a while?
- Monitor progress on character target. Catch and release if necessary.

(CFU: Strategic Observation and Listening)

> The teacher takes notes about students' thinking process and strategies and begins to make decisions about which ones to highlight, and in what order, during the synthesis/ debrief

		Duration
minutes	of other character	10 minutes

Exit Ticket: Make connections between the work we did today and each learning target.
(Explain what happens at the point of intersection of two functions using today's work as an
example.)

> Exit tickets create a paper trail that allows the teacher to give students feedback and plan for the next lesson.

Homework
- *What can students practice on their own after this lesson? How can the learning from this lesson be shared at home to reinforce students*
- *What can students do to prepare for the next lesson? What learning could take place at home, allowing time in class to be spent sharing*
  and practicing?

(cont. online)

Figure 2.4 Strategic observation tracker to accompany the lesson plan in Figure 2.3
SOURCE: This document is available in the online toolbox at http://www.wiley.com/go/lotolcompanion.

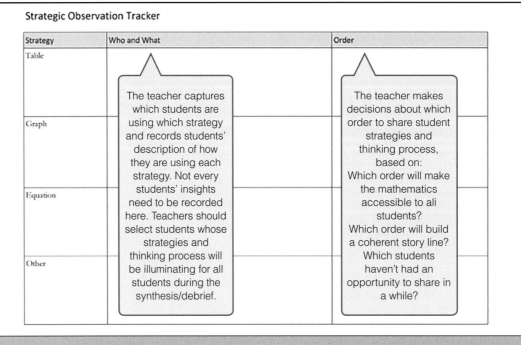

Strategic Observation Tracker

Strategy	Who and What	Order
Table		
Graph	The teacher captures which students are using which strategy and records students' description of how they are using each strategy. Not every students' insights need to be recorded here. Teachers should select students whose strategies and thinking process will be illuminating for all students during the synthesis/debrief.	The teacher makes decisions about which order to share student strategies and thinking process, based on: Which order will make the mathematics accessible to all students? Which order will build a coherent story line? Which students haven't had an opportunity to share in a while?
Equation		
Other		

Video Spotlight 2.4: Reading and Thinking Like Scientists, Day 1: Strategies for Making Meaning from Complex Scientific Text
https://vimeo.com/117019945

In this video, King Middle School science teacher Peter Hill guides his students through a challenging text and uses a variety of techniques to check for understanding. Working with the school's ELL teacher, Hill scaffolds his lesson to best support his students.

Video Reflection Questions
1. How would you describe the range of techniques that teacher Peter Hill uses to check for understanding in the video?
2. What role do the differentiated note-catchers play in individual students' ability to check their understanding as they read?
3. In the video, teacher Peter Hill reads a portion of the text, pauses for students to text-code, and then asks them to talk to a partner about their reflections on the reading so far. Is this an effective strategy for helping him and his students assess their progress understanding the challenging scientific concepts they are reading about? Why or why not?

Figure 2.5 gives you a chance to test yourself. Match the checking-for-understanding technique in the right column to the information you might be trying to gather in the left column.

What is the best checking-for-understanding technique to use?

Match the checking-for-understanding technique in the right column to the information you might be trying to gather in the left column.

My Need	Checking for Understanding Technique
I want students to have written evidence that I can collect to see if they have met the learning target.	Thumb-ometer
I want to see what my students were thinking as they read a text.	Exit Ticket
I have 60 seconds at the end of class and I just want to know if students are clear about their next steps before the next lesson	Human Bar Graph
I want to assess how well students can follow a protocol and collaborate with each other.	Strategic Observation
I want to get students moving and articulating their new learning.	Note-Catcher
I want students to see our collective strengths and growth edges so that we can set goals as a group.	Back-to-Back and Face-to-Face

Challenge #5: I struggle to efficiently track student progress while I'm observing them at work or engaged in discussions.

TRY THIS: USE TRACKING FORMS

Like most teachers, you are probably accomplished at multitasking. Nevertheless, recording what you hear and see while you are circulating during a student-run discussion protocol or during work time can be a real challenge. Taking extensive notes just isn't feasible, especially if you are checking the understanding of 25 or more students.

Tracking forms like those in Figures 2.6, 2.7, and 2.8 can help you move beyond anecdotal impressions of student progress. You can use these forms with whatever existing system you have in place to informally grade students (e.g., check marks, ratings 1–4).

Figure 2.6 Small group discussion tracker
SOURCE: This document is available in the online toolbox at http://www.wiley.com/go/lotolcompanion.

Date:
Discussion Topic:

Note: It may not be possible to track everything at once while students are working. Circle the column heading(s) that you want to focus on for this observation.

Name	Student is paying attention and listening to peers.	Discussion is on point (student seems to understand content).	Student asks questions.	Student responds to questions.	Student maintains a respectful tone and volume.

Figure 2.7 Problem-solving strategy tracker
SOURCE: This document is available in the online toolbox at http://www.wiley.com/go/lotolcompanion.

Date:
Problem:

Name	Student is confident enough to get started on problem.	Student is taking a reasonable approach to the solution.	Students' computations thus far seem accurate.

Figure 2.8 Contribution/collaboration matrix
SOURCE: This document is available in the online toolbox at http://www.wiley.com/go/lotolcompanion.

Directions: Place student names in the box that matches the level of their contribution and collaboration.

		Collaboration	
		Low	High
Contribution	High		
	Low		

These tracking forms may suit your purposes well. If not, create your own. As you design your own tracking forms, ask yourself the following questions:

- What behaviors or evidence will demonstrate meeting the learning target?

- Can I hear or observe that evidence?

- How much time will I need to listen or observe to know if each student is meeting the learning target?

- How many students can I observe/listen to during the course of a single lesson?

- Will I want to observe/listen for these criteria more than once? How often?

- Do I want to record notes while I observe/listen or will tallies, grades, or check marks suffice? What format will allow me to easily record my observations/listening?

- Do I want to record evidence from a group or from individual students?

- How will I use the information I collect?

- Will I share the evidence with students? With a colleague?

- How much am I looking for trends (how the group is doing in general) versus outliers (what kids are struggling and need help, or are way ahead and can help as models)?

Learning Target 3: I can use questions effectively to check for understanding.

Challenge #6: I ask lots of questions, but they don't elicit rich or engaging classroom discourse.

TRY THIS: INVITE INQUIRY BY PLAYING VERBAL VOLLEYBALL

In many classrooms, teachers do most of the asking and students do most of the answering. Often the same few students provide the answers. In a true inquiry-based classroom, by contrast, students – all students – are empowered to be engaged in the learning process and to be questioners themselves.

To invite this kind of inquiry in your classroom, be mindful of whether your students are playing ping-pong or volleyball. In ping-pong (Figure 2.9), you ask a question, a student answers, then you ask another question and another student answers. The dialogue is always between teacher and student.

In volleyball (Figure 2.10), students frequently ask questions of other students or respond to their peers' answers by adding on or asking a new question. Encouraging students to direct their questions

Figure 2.9 Ping-pong style questions

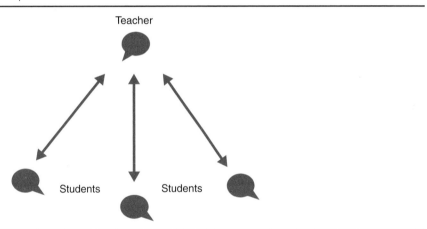

Figure 2.10 Volleyball style questions

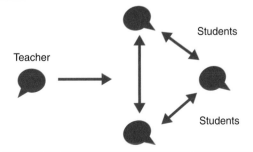

and answers to peers rather than to you can enhance the spirit of inquiry in your classroom. You'll also get a more accurate picture of what each student really understands because students are doing more of the talking and more students overall are involved in the discussion.

A great exercise to become aware of the question and discussion patterns in your classroom is to have another adult (e.g., colleague, coach, assistant) create a discussion diagram for you during an observation of your lesson. In secondary classrooms, a student could be enlisted to create this chart. The task is fairly simple: create a diagram of the classroom where all the students are sitting and draw lines for communication from one person to another. It can also be further coded using color or pattern, if you wish, to identify types of communication (e.g., question, response, statement) or type of question (e.g., memory question vs. higher order question). It is almost always surprising to see on paper patterns that we tend to miss in the flow of conversation.

Use the following strategies to improve discussion patterns in your classroom:

- Ask an open-ended question. Then say, "I'm looking for at least three hands." Wait for three raised hands and invite all three students to share their ideas before you speak again.

- Instead of asking questions that have clear answers, ask students, "What questions does this raise for you?" Record students' questions and turn them back to the class.

- When a student answers a question, rather than saying whether the answer is right or wrong, respond with "What do others think?" Elicit more responses, and more questions, before moving on.

- Change your physical proximity to your class so that you are not the center of attention. You might even sit down and be an equal participant in the class discussion.

- Encourage students to ask questions or direct answers to each other rather than to you. An anchor chart with question stems like those that follow will support your students to keep the discussion going:
  - "I'd like to build on what ___ said."
  - "I disagree with ____ because___."
  - "I found additional evidence to what ___ said before. . ."

- Praise strong, probing questions, even if students (or you) don't have answers. Making great questions visible in your classroom and returning to them frequently as students learn more shows that curiosity opens doors to learning.

TRY THIS: ASK NEUTRAL QUESTIONS AND KEEP YOUR RESPONSE NEUTRAL

When you observe another teacher's lesson, the correct response to many questions is clear to you just by the tone of the teacher's voice or the expression on her face. It's equally clear to students. When a teacher pauses in a math lesson to ask, "Now is this a *reasonable* answer to this problem?" with a skeptical and frustrated voice, all the students know to answer in chorus, "Nooooo." When she says, "Jamal, does that look right to you?" with a frown, he is bound to say, "No, I don't think so." Almost all of us as teachers do this without thinking, and it does much more harm than we realize.

When we telegraph the correct response by our voice or expression, we lose the power of the question to act as a check for understanding. Even worse, we allow all the students to turn off their brains. They don't actually have to consider whether the answer is reasonable or correct: you have just told them with your tone or face. Everything improves when we adopt a neutral tone. Let's say a math teacher says, with a placid face, "Jamal, tell us how you approached this problem." The students are not clear if she picked on him because he was on track or off track. When Jamal explains his solution, the students watch the teacher's face for a clue as to whether he is right or wrong. If she avoids this trap and keeps her face neutral – doesn't slightly smile in satisfaction or frown in frustration – the students are confused. Is he right or not? When she says, with balanced tone, "Interesting. Tell us why you took that approach?" the students will look even more closely at her face. Did she say "interesting" in a critical way or a pleased way? Is he right or wrong? If they can't tell, then they now have real work to do. They actually have to look closely at Jamal's solution and figure out whether they think it is correct.

By taking a neutral tone, this teacher was able to check for Jamal's understanding, and even more importantly, check for understanding for much of the class. When she asks the group, still with a neutral tone, "Who feels Jamal is correct here; or incorrect? Who can give their opinion on this?" She can look at faces, listen to responses, and get a sense of how many students understand the problem.

 Challenge #7: It's one thing to check for understanding on low-level questions, but I need new strategies for asking questions with a higher cognitive demand so that I can check for a deeper level of understanding.

TRY THIS: PREPLAN STRATEGIC QUESTIONS

How many questions did you ask your students today? The answer is probably more than 200, but when it comes to questions, quality matters more than quantity (Vogler, 2008). High-quality questions, planned in advance, are a strategic way to find out what *every* student knows.

Strong strategic questions are preplanned and designed to help students learn *even more*, not just to assess their learning. They raise more questions, opening the door to more knowledge. Even more important is the content of the question itself. Does it ask students to analyze or evaluate evidence? Have students learned enough about the topic, and enough disciplinary vocabulary, to be able to analyze and evaluate the issue?

Table 2.5 provides question stems for all the levels of Bloom's Revised Taxonomy. Using question stems from all levels of the taxonomy will help ensure that you are asking questions with a range of cognitive demand.

Table 2.5 Question stems for Bloom's Revised Taxonomy

	Verbs	Sample Questions
Remembering	name, match, select, choose, order, label, list, arrange, identity, locate, define, duplicate, memorize, recognize, relate, recall, repeat	What is. . .? How is. . .? Where is. . .? When did . . . happen? Can you list three. . .?
Understanding	tell, describe, explain, discuss, express, report, restate, review, translate, paraphrase	Which statement supports. . .? How would you summarize. . .? What is meant. . ..? What is the main idea of. . .? Can you explain to me. . .? How would you explain this to a younger student?

(continued)

Table 2.5 Continued

	Verbs	Sample Questions
Applying	use, draw, sort, write, solve, demonstrate, infer, dramatize, employ, interpret, operate, practice, schedule	How would you use. . .? How would you solve. . . using what you have learned? How would you organize. . . . to show. . .? What approach would you use to. . .? Can you show me how you. . .?
Analyzing	question, infer, test, experiment, compare, contrast, analyze, calculate, categorize, criticize, differentiate, discriminate, distinguish, examine	What inferences can you make. . .? What conclusions can you draw. . .? How would you categorize. . .? What is the relationship between. . .?
Evaluating	argue, assess, choose, compare, defend, estimate, judge, predict, rate, select, support, value, evaluate, appraise	How would you evaluate. . .? What criteria would you use to assess. . .? How could you determine. . .? What choice would you have made. . .? How would you prioritize. . .? How would you justify. . .?
Creating	create, do, perform, read, speak, operate, model, dramatize, measure, collect, compose, construct, design, develop, formulate, manage, organize, plan, assemble prepare, propose, arrange, write	What is an alternative. . .? Could you invent. . .? What could you design to. . .? *Assuming they have tried creating something (e.g., an essay, a robot):* Why did you choose this approach for this part? What ideas did you reject, or try out unsuccessfully? What is working best for you in this piece? What is still not as strong as you wish?

Figure 2.11 shows a set of questions a sixth-grade teacher made at the start of his class's study of states of matter (i.e., solids, gases, liquids). He preplanned questions that would help his students care about states of matter and understand why it's important to know about them.

TRY THIS: DEVELOP A SET OF GENERIC QUESTIONS

While planning your questions in advance is the key to pushing students to those higher levels of thinking, it's also important to go with the flow of the lesson, to anticipate and also to be responsive to what students really say in the dialogue of the classroom. This means listening deeply to students and demonstrating first and foremost that you really want to know what they think. Here are several powerful questions every teacher should be asking more students, more of the time:

- What do you think of _____'s response? Do you agree? Why?

- How did you get to that?

- How do you know?

Figure 2.11 Preplanned questions and teacher reflections from Genesee Community Charter School in Rochester, New York

SOURCE: The complete version of this document is available in the online toolbox at http://www .wiley.com/go/lotolcompanion.

Question	Teacher Reflection
What kinds of things are in the world? (Students make their own lists and I chart responses.)	I want an entirely open-ended, what's-he-talking about, everyone-could-answer, I-know-I'll-be-surprised-by-what-they-say kind of question. I want them to be scratching their heads and thinking where is this going? This is **analysis**, where they take a big concept (the physical world) and break it down into parts (whole to parts).
Now, what do all these things have in common? ***Can you find categories to combine several items from your list?***	Students must look for similarities, find categories, and make generalizations. It's still wide open. Some students will get it. Some will still be scratching their heads. This is **synthesis**, where they take a list of disparate items and look for generalizations and categories of things they have in common (part to whole). I am setting them up for the challenges scientists face in classifying things. That is one of the very big ideas behind the states of matter—that scientists classify things. They look for commonalities and for the classifying schematics that organize and categorize the world we perceive. This process helps students better appreciate the system Aristotle used to classify things.
Scientists look for the unifying theory, the one theory or organizing principle that explains how everything is organized and connected. One of the first attempts at this organization goes back to ancient Greece and a man called Aristotle. He looked around and decided everything in the world was made up of four elements. ***Raise your hand if you can tell me one of the elements.***	I introduce the "holy grail" of scientific investigation—the unifying theory. Then I go back to trace the origin of this theory that tries to explain the observations we make. Here is the first question that requires some **background knowledge** to answer. There is a right answer to this one, but I will only let each student say one, so it will draw out the drama and let more kids get involved. I write their answers on the board and eventually we come up with— earth, fire, air, and water.
Now what order would you put them in? Does it matter? (Students Write-Pair-Share so everyone is involved in answering the question, discussing it with someone else, and hearing from a range of students.)	There are all kinds of possible answers to this question, but what I am looking for is the thinking behind their organizing schemas. I also want to highlight one order I hope will come up—earth, water, air, and fire—which begins to reflect the order of the states of matter. I also ask them to write-pair-share to make sure that everyone gets involved. Then, I'll ask for people who haven't shared yet to tell me about their order, or their partner's. Again, this encourages more students to participate (even ones who didn't have a good answer themselves might tell me about their neighbor's idea). The big idea is to get them thinking about classification, properties, and order; then coming up with a theory and defending it with some **reasoning**.
Now, when Aristotle referred to earth, he did not mean just dirt or the planet. He meant anything solid, keeping its own shape. ***What examples do you see?*** (Then I explain what Aristotle meant by water, air, and fire and students generate more examples.)	Here I am anticipating their schema will connect to different things when they consider "earth," so I want to get us all on the same page. I also want to lay the groundwork for them to make the connection to states of matter.

(cont. online)

- Can you give me an example?

- Can you tell me more?

- Can you show us some evidence for that?

- How would you test that hypothesis?

- What questions do you still have?

Of course, in the clock-is-ticking moment of instruction, it's easy to fall back to lower-level questions with easy answers (often ones you blurt out yourself!). It's important to develop an awareness of the different types of questions and which ones work best in the classroom banter between students. Dig into this topic further by viewing the video and considering the questions in Video Spotlight 2.5.

When kids are thinking about their answer, that's when they're learning. When I'm giving them the answer and they're trying to remember it, that's not learning. That's just remembering.

—*Mona Iehl, third-grade teacher, Polaris Charter Academy, Chicago*

Video Spotlight 2.5: Teaching Students to Prove Their Mathematical Thinking through Questions, Charts, and Discourse
https://vimeo.com/123960860.

In this video, Mona Iehl's third-graders at Polaris Charter Academy in Chicago are guided to new understandings by Iehl's strategic use of questions.

Video Reflection Questions
1. How did teacher Mona Iehl's questioning strategy encourage grappling among her students? Why was this important to her as a teacher?
2. What impact did her focus on being "neutral" have on students?
3. Go back and review Figure 2.10: Volleyball Style Questioning. In this video, you see the students engaging in volleyball style discourse during the debrief portion of the lesson. What impact do you think this had on their learning?

TRY THIS: ARRANGE FOR A TARGETED OBSERVATION OF YOUR QUESTION-ASKING PATTERNS

Invite a colleague to observe a lesson using an observation note-catcher like the one shown in Figure 2.12 to record the types or patterns of questions you ask and who answers them. Then reflect together on the results. Are you giving all students opportunities to answer questions? Are you asking questions that push them to think more deeply? Did you miss any opportunities to ask higher-quality questions? Figures 2.13 and 2.14 show how space on the back of a note-catcher like this can be used to keep track of who the teacher called on and how many times, which is useful for analysis after the lesson.

Figure 2.12 Questioning observation note-catcher

SOURCE: This document can be found in the online toolbox at http://www.wiley.com/go/lotolcompanion.

Instructions for the observer: For every question you hear from the teacher, place a check in the appropriate column. Was it a remembering question or a higher-order question?

Reflections:

What did you notice as you observed?

Question	Remembering Question	Higher-Order Question	If possible, write down the question (especially if higher-order)
1			
2			
3			
4			
5			
6			
7			
8			
9			
10			
11			
12			
13			

If possible, on the back of this paper, draw a diagram that shows the layout of the classroom and the pattern of questions that were asked during the observation. Who did the teacher call on? How many times? Did questions from the teacher lead to students asking each other questions or did they only come from the teacher? See Figures 2.13 and 2.14 for example diagrams.

Figure 2.13 Fifth-grade question diagram

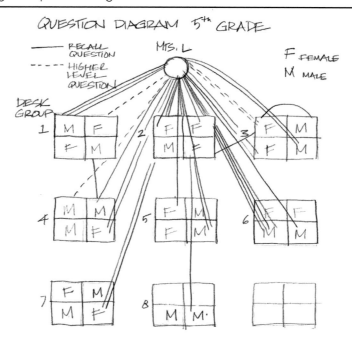

Figure 2.14 Eighth-grade question diagram

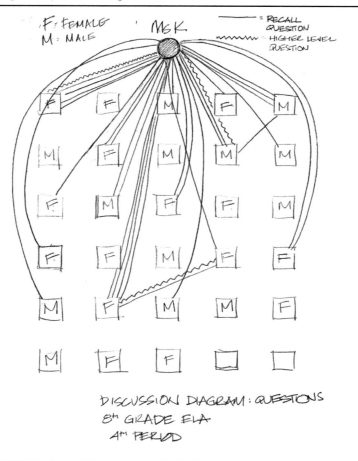

The Leaders of Their Own Learning Companion

Learning Target 4: I can plan effective debriefs.

Challenge #8: I always run out of time for the debrief at the end of my lessons. I struggle to prioritize it even though I know it's important.

TRY THIS: ESTABLISH A NEW ROUTINE

As any teacher can attest, lessons don't always go as planned, and time can be one of the most elusive elements of classroom instruction. There's never enough. Since it happens last in a lesson, the debrief is often the first thing to go when time is tight. However, a good debrief or synthesis helps students name their take-away from the lesson so that they can bring it back in the following lesson and learn more – this is called "transfer" and it's the key to learning how to learn. The debrief is an important 5 or 10 minutes!

If the debrief routinely falls off the map, it might be time to establish some new routines in your classroom:

> An effective debrief is the last chance during a daily lesson for a teacher to check for understanding, help students synthesize learning, and promote reflection so that students can monitor their own progress
> —*from Leaders of Their Own Learning, p. 74.*

- Invite a student to be the timekeeper and give the student permission to "stop the train" at least five minutes before the period ends so that you can debrief.

- Teach students to circle up or move to a designated part of the room quickly. When this becomes a routine, you will have more time for the debrief and you and your students will get into the habit.

- If you haven't had time to plan a debrief that is specific to the day's lesson, use debrief questions that are effective for any lesson: "What did you learn today?" "How did you learn it?"

- Develop a repertoire of protocols to use during a debrief, such as Concentric Circles, Think-Pair-Share, or Back-to-Back and Face-to-Face. Using protocols will help ensure that all students have an opportunity to reflect on their learning. Even when you're short on time, all voices can be heard.

TRY THIS: DEBRIEF DURING THE LESSON (YOU DON'T HAVE TO WAIT FOR THE END)

It is not always necessary to think of a debrief as a separate and distinct final five minutes of a lesson. In fact, sometimes synthesizing learning and getting a true sense of student progress toward a learning target can take much longer and is a valuable lesson (or chunk of a lesson) in and of itself. What follows is a sample script to give you a feel for what this might look like.

Sample Script

Third-grade learning target: *I can represent my mathematical thinking using both a model and a number sentence.*

TEACHER:	Let's circle up on the carpet to discuss your progress.
TEACHER:	Carlos, can you read our learning target for us again?
CARLOS:	Our learning target was "I can represent my mathematical thinking using both a model and a number sentence."
TEACHER:	Show me a thumbs up if you think you met the target today.
STUDENTS:	(All but three show a thumbs up)
TEACHER:	Karen, how do you know you met the target? Can you share your math journal with us and explain your mathematical thinking?
KAREN:	(showing her math journal) I made a picture of squares next to each other to show each inch in the placemat. That gave me 15 inches in a row and 10 rows. It took me a long time to make 150 squares! Then I did it the short way. I just wrote 15 × 10 and added the 0 to the 15 to get 150.
TEACHER:	Help me understand. Did you add the 0 to the 15?
KAREN:	No, I mean I multiplied 15 times 10. I moved the 1 over to the hundreds place, the 5 to the 10s place, and the 0 in the ones place.
TEACHER:	Turn and talk to a partner about Karen's model. Is this how you made your model? How is it the same and how is it different?
TEACHER:	(after a few minutes): William, I noticed that you didn't put your thumb up. Did talking with your partner help you feel better about representing your thinking using a model? Tell us about your model. How was it the same or different than Karen's?
WILLIAM:	Actually, it was the same! I didn't really understand before that the model could be a drawing. I thought it had to be using blocks or something like that.
TEACHER:	Kaila, you also had your thumb up. Which of Karen's strategies do you think is a more efficient way to get the area of the placemat?
KAILA:	Probably the number sentence. You get the same answer, but the squares take forever.
TEACHER:	We were working on perseverance today. What helped you meet our learning target about mathematical thinking?
ERIK:	I got started right away, so I'd have enough time to build my model. And it helped me to work with Carlos. He's a good explainer.
TEACHER:	So when you come to math tomorrow, we're going to use the number sentences again, but this time we'll have even bigger numbers to practice with! Be sure you do what Erik did. Choose a partner who helps your thinking rather than someone who distracts you.

 Challenge #9: When debriefing a lesson, I'll have students turn and talk or reflect with a peer, but I'm not capturing what they've learned.

TRY THIS: USE EXIT TICKETS STRATEGICALLY

Exit tickets are a great way for you to take something with you from the lesson that will help you assess individual students' understanding. With this evidence of student understanding in hand, you can more effectively plan subsequent lessons. It's important to be clear about the purpose of an exit ticket so that it gives you the information you need. You want to avoid exit tickets that are the same every day, that feel like a rote routine, or that are used as an accountability structure (e.g., "Your *completed* worksheet is your exit ticket from class").

Every exit ticket should be designed to give you truly useful information about where students are on skills or concepts, or how they are feeling about their learning. Varying the kinds of questions and tasks is key. Some options for exit tickets include:

- A single well-designed problem or question that reveals understanding of a skill or concept: One question, as opposed to a whole worksheet, gives you a quick look at both individual and whole class understanding. Exit tickets won't be useful if you can't review them quickly and efficiently in order to inform instruction right away.

- A small task that requires students to apply their learning to a new context (e.g., "Give an example of this historical conflict from today's world"; "Explain how football would be different on Mars.").

- An opportunity to reflect, especially if you feel like students may be struggling in some area: asking students to list two things they learned and one thing they felt confused about can be clarifying for them and for you.

- Asking for questions: What questions are you left with after today's lesson? What questions do you have about this area of study?

- A personal check in on how students are feeling in your classroom or around their self-image within this area of study: Do you feel like you belong, that your ideas are valued, and that you have the confidence to contribute? (This kind of personal reflection is a perfectly good use of exit tickets but is not something you would want to do every day.)

- A chance for students to give you feedback as a teacher (e.g., "What could I have done a better job explaining today? Have I been inclusive and fair to all students?"): these questions help students feel a sense of empowerment within the learning environment and can also be quite revealing about what students feel as well as what they understand and what they don't.

TRY THIS: USE TRACKING FORMS

We already covered this topic in Challenge #5, so we won't repeat ourselves. We just want to remind you to use forms like those in Figures 2.6–2.8 to keep track of what students are saying, how they are making sense of problems, how they are interacting with their peers, and myriad other purposes. You can create tracking and observation forms for any purpose. While students are debriefing in pairs or small groups, listen in and take notes so you have a record of their progress toward learning targets.

Check Yourself Checklist
The "Don't Forget the Debrief" Checklist
Check off all that apply:

❏ I have a small set of debrief protocols of all kinds—whole group share, pair share, individual reflection, oral, written—that I am comfortable facilitating.

❏ I plan which debrief protocol I will use, based on which feels most suited to each lesson.

❏ I devote at least five minutes at the end of every lesson or, depending on the lesson, during the flow of instruction, to debrief learning.

❏ If time runs short for the debrief I have planned, I have "back-up" debriefs—that take less time—that I can use so that students still have an opportunity to synthesize their learning.

❏ During debriefs, I ask students to provide evidence of their learning and to identify the next steps they will take to make progress toward their learning target(s).

❏ Whenever possible, I help students connect the dots between any daily learning targets and long-term learning targets or academic standards.

(This checklist can be found in the online toolbox at http://www.wiley.com/go/lotolcompanion.)

As a leader, it's important to have empathy and patience for teachers in recognizing how common it is to have poor habits in this area, and how difficult it is to break those habits. All teachers feel the need to keep the lesson moving forward, so it's normal for them to say, "Does that make sense?" or "Everyone get that?" and take a few nods in the front row as a signal to move on to the next step. Actually figuring out if students do understand something – especially the quiet ones or the ones who are masking their confusion – is not easy. Checking for understanding effectively while still keeping a lesson moving forward is an art that takes lots of practice.

If you expect teachers to adopt better strategies, you need to first model those strategies yourself in staff meetings and professional development. You need to give teachers time to try out strategies, discuss them with peers and refine them, and to build new habits over time. This should be seen as an area for staff inquiry and learning rather than as a new mandate.

This chapter is full of specific strategies, for example: hand signals such as the Thumb-ometer or Fist-to-Five check. A school leader can mandate that all teachers use those strategies, but a more effective and supportive approach might be to help teachers build the safe, honest classroom culture, with good teacher-student relationships, that makes it possible for teachers to implement and refine the strategies over time.

Leaders have an important role to play in supporting teachers' learning and setting schoolwide expectations. What follows are some of our top tips for leaders. Table 2.6 then summarizes the key action steps for teachers and students that will lead to success.

Top Tips

- Model checking-for-understanding techniques with teachers. As we pointed out in the Lessons for Leaders section of Chapter 1, using learning targets with teachers during professional development, staff meetings, and other gatherings will help focus their learning. Hand-in-hand with the learning targets should be checking-for-understanding techniques. Pause to have teachers turn and talk or write down a response. Debrief learning with them. The same things you want teachers doing with students will support their learning as well.

- Identify a handful of protocols that you and your staff feel offer the best opportunities to check for understanding that you want every teacher to master and use in their classrooms. Create and post anchor charts for these protocols in the room where staff meet, plan, or eat lunch.

- Create an accessible, digital bank of note-catchers, strategic observation recording tools, or reflection prompts that teachers share and add to.

- Create and post learning targets and target trackers for school improvement goals. Invite teachers to revisit these trackers at staff meetings so that they become part of the leadership conversation about long-term growth.

- Provide significant time and expectation in staff meetings and team meetings for teachers to discuss honestly what strategies and protocols they are using, and what is working well and what is not.

- Include checking-for-understanding techniques on your classroom observation tool. Invite teachers to reflect on their efficacy and make plans for improvement if necessary.

Table 2.6 Checking for understanding: Steps to success

What Should Teachers Do?
Create quality learning targets and assessments and ensure that students understand what is expected of them.
Build a classroom culture of trust and collaboration.
Preplan strategic questions to assess understanding throughout each lesson.
Build lesson plans that support students in meeting learning targets, emphasize student participation, and include ongoing checks for understanding throughout.
Check for whole-class understanding using a variety of techniques and make adjustments to instruction as necessary. Ensure that all students are included.
Check for individual understanding using a variety of techniques and use data to make decisions about next instructional steps to meet the needs of all students.
Over time, build a repertoire of checking-for-understanding techniques to engage students with varied learning styles in self-assessment. Increasingly emphasize ownership and capacity to self-assess.
What Should Students Do?
Make an effort to understand the learning targets and connect them with the purpose of each lesson and learning activity.
Communicate honestly about what they understand and what they don't.
Support thinking and ideas with evidence.
Monitor their own understanding throughout a lesson and advocate for support as needed; support peers with their understanding.
Self-assess progress in relation to a specific learning target.
Participate in class and turn in work (e.g., exit tickets, reflection journals, quizzes) that demonstrates progress in relation to one or more learning targets.
Become more proficient at self-assessing their level of understanding as the variety of strategies employed by the teacher expands to meet their learning needs.

Post-Assessment: Track Your Progress: Chapter 2

As you have **read** Chapter 2, maybe you have had an opportunity to try some of these strategies and techniques along the way. If not, come back to this post-assessment after you have had a chance to do so. Give yourself whatever time you need to address the learning targets and challenges in a meaningful way. Then take a moment to check your progress in Table 2.7, which is the exact same Learning Target Tracker that appeared at the beginning of this chapter.

Circle or place an X along the continuum from Beginning to Exceeding: **How would you rate your progress toward each learning target** *at this point in time?* Use the space provided to make notes regarding any remaining challenges you may be having or ideas for new and different strategies you want to try.

Table 2.7 Chapter 2 learning target tracker

Learning Target 1: *I can build a culture of trust, growth, and collaboration in my classroom so that students can honestly assess their progress.*
Beginning----------------------------------Developing----------------------------------Meeting----------------------------------Exceeding
Notes:
Learning Target 2: *I can use checking-for-understanding techniques that help students assess their progress toward learning targets and allow me to monitor their progress.*
Beginning----------------------------------Developing----------------------------------Meeting----------------------------------Exceeding
Notes:
Learning Target 3: *I can use questions effectively to check for understanding.*
Beginning----------------------------------Developing----------------------------------Meeting----------------------------------Exceeding
Notes:
Learning Target 4: *I can plan effective debriefs.*
Beginning----------------------------------Developing----------------------------------Meeting----------------------------------Exceeding
Notes:

Using Data with Students

Checking for Understanding during Daily Lessons

Using Data with Students

Learning Targets

Models, Critique, and Descriptive Feedback

STUDENT-ENGAGED ASSESSMENT

Student-engaged assessment is a system of interrelated practices that positions students as leaders of their own learning.

Standards-Based Grading

Student-Led Conferences

Passage Presentations with Portfolios

Celebrations of Learning

What Is Using Data with Students?

Using data with students encompasses classroom practices that build students' capacity to access, analyze, and use data effectively to reflect, set goals, and document growth. Using Data with Students includes the following activities:

- Students use their classwork as a source for data, analyzing strengths, weaknesses, and patterns to improve their work.
- Students regularly analyze evidence of their own progress. They track their progress on assessments and assignments, analyze their errors for patterns, and describe what they see in the data about their current level of performance.
- Students use data to set goals and reflect on their progress over time and incorporate data analysis into student-led conferences.

In the age of high-stakes testing, the word *data* can be off-putting. We and our students are continually bombarded by test scores, statistics taken out of context, and evidence that may not be reliable or credible. Students and their families, especially families of students who have often struggled academically, may dismiss data as "just numbers" that don't hold meaning or promise for them. This is all the more reason why teaching students to use and analyze data accurately and to good purpose, that is, to benefit students and give them control over their own learning, matters.

When students evaluate data about their own progress, when data is reviewed *with* them rather than something done *to* them, students develop the skills to lead their own learning. Through these practices, data becomes something that is useful to students, a tool that empowers them to reach goals they set for themselves. Nevertheless, for teachers, establishing the routines and creating the tools to use data effectively with students is a challenge. Using data with students means making time for looking at data, creating protocols for saving and analyzing data, and, most importantly, creating a culture in which students and families value data.

In this chapter we build on the techniques offered in Chapter 3 of *Leaders of Their Own Learning* to help you meet three learning targets. Along the way we give you an opportunity to explore the common challenges many teachers face when working toward each learning target.

> When students are equipped to analyze data for their own learning, whether from large-scale summative assessments or daily formative assessments, the power of data as an engine for growth is centered where it has the greatest potential to improve learning – with students
>
> —*Ron Berger*

Learning Targets for Chapter 3

1. I can create a data-informed culture in my classroom.
2. I can teach students to use data to evaluate their progress in relation to a learning target.
3. I can support students to set meaningful and effective goals.

Before we dive in, take a moment to assess yourself on each of the learning targets for this chapter. In Table 3.1, circle or place an X along the continuum from Beginning to Exceeding: **How would you rate your progress toward each learning target** *at this point in time?*

We'll give you a chance to assess yourself again at the end of the chapter.

Table 3.1 Chapter 3 learning target tracker

Learning Target 1: *I can create a data-informed culture in my classroom.* Beginning----------------------------------Developing--Meeting----------------------------------Exceeding Notes:
Learning Target 2: *I can teach students to use data to evaluate their progress in relation to a learning target.* Beginning----------------------------------Developing--Meeting----------------------------------Exceeding Notes:
Learning Target 3: *I can support students to set meaningful and effective goals.* Beginning----------------------------------Developing--Meeting----------------------------------Exceeding Notes:

Learning Target 1: I can create a data-informed culture in my classroom.

Challenge #1: My students and their families have a rigid idea of what data is. How do I help them see the bigger picture?

TRY THIS: BROADEN YOUR DEFINITION OF WHAT COUNTS AS DATA

In many schools, the calendar is punctuated with one test after another: interim tests, benchmark tests, and high-stakes end-of-year tests. Each of these tests generates data that can easily feel more like a threat than a helpful tool. While quantitative results from these kinds of tests *are* data, they may not be as helpful to students, or even to teachers, as the quantitative and qualitative data that come from the work students do every day. Think about all that your students do – homework, exit tickets, journals, classroom discussions. These are all data! The list that follows contains a few more examples of data students generate every day. Can you think of any more examples? Fill in your own ideas at the bottom of the list.

What Counts as Data. . . .
- Homework assignments
- Daily "Do Now" entrance tickets
- Lab notebook entries
- Reading running records
- Projects
- Gist statements from close reading lessons
- Observation notes
- Writing folders
- Students' notes and note-catchers
- Exit tickets
- Math test corrections
- Class discussion participation
- _____
- _____
- _____
- _____
- _____
- _____

Video Spotlight 3.1 features teachers using an index card protocol, which allows them to identify data focused on ensuring that students feel a sense of belonging in their classrooms. During team meetings, every student's name is spoken aloud so that each teacher can consider whether or not data related to that student's academics and behavior need to be discussed.

Video Spotlight 3.1: Knowing Every Child through Index Card Rosters
https://www.edutopia.org/video/knowing-every-child-through-index-card-rosters

This video features a team of teachers at King Middle School in Portland, Maine, using an index card protocol to regularly review students' behavior and learning to ensure that every student is seen, supported, and celebrated. This video was produced by Edutopia.

Video Reflection Questions
1. What are the sources of data that the teachers use to discuss students' academic and behavioral needs?
2. What is the role of norms in the team meeting?
3. How important are the index cards? What would be different if the team didn't use index cards but instead generated names based on the students who were already top of mind?

TRY THIS: POINT STUDENTS TOWARD DATA IN DAILY WORK

Now that you're thinking more broadly about what counts as data, make it a habit to help students understand data differently too. Making it a habit means that the culture of data is embodied in what students do, say, and value each day in your classroom. When you are in the habit of paying attention to results and growth, and when you frequently notice and wonder about patterns and trends, your students will also begin to pay more attention to the data in their daily work. What follows are examples of sentence stems you can use in your classroom conversations with students that will help them see data in every activity:

- Where do you see evidence of . . . ?

- Let's find the data in . . .

- Count the number of . . .

- Where do you see growth between X and Y?

- What does your work tell you about your progress toward our learning target?

- Can you sort your _____ into categories (weak, average, strong)?

- Can you write a reflection about the patterns you notice in your work?

TRY THIS: COMMUNICATE TO FAMILIES THE WHY AND HOW OF CLASSROOM DATA ROUTINES

Getting families to buy in to your daily data routine is a big part of building a positive data culture. Some families can rattle off the scores from their child's high-stakes tests but may not be tuned in to the kinds of daily data that you are collecting (which is ultimately a better barometer of progress). To secure family support, inform them about the rationale and specific protocols for your data routines. Figure 3.1 is a frequently asked questions (FAQ) document that can be used to help families understand how data is used in your school. This FAQ may not suit all of your needs – we encourage you to modify it or create your own.

Figure 3.1 Sample FAQs for families

SOURCE: This document is available in the online toolbox at http://www.wiley.com/go/lotolcompanion.

How does using data with students help them be leaders of their own learning?

What does it mean when we say students are *leaders of their own learning?* It means that students reflect on evidence from their daily classroom learning to set academic goals and make a plan for achieving them. We believe families play an important part in supporting students to lead their own learning. Here are answers to some of the questions we're frequently asked about how students use data in our classrooms.

Why do students analyze their own data?

In order to figure out how we can improve at something, we need to know how we're doing so far. Data that reflect the knowledge and skills a student is trying to acquire will help the student create an action plan for improvement. When students themselves analyze the data and create the action plan, they are much more motivated to improve.

What counts as data?

The most useful data for students (and teachers) comes from daily classroom activities. Students track homework quality and completion, daily "Do Now" entrance tickets, notebook entries, small-group discussions, math test corrections, participation rates, projects, and other assignments. Teachers and students work together to determine the most useful data to collect depending on the subject matter and how to record it.

What about standardized tests results?

Students may also reflect on state test results and/or interim test data from MAP testing or other assessments. However, we do not simply teach to the test. We believe that daily classroom data provides students with a more detailed picture of growth than the standardized test data she/he receives just a couple times a year.

When do students look at data?

In some classes students have a regular daily or weekly time set aside to analyze data and make plans for improvement. In other classes, looking at data happens midway through a project or at key points throughout a unit. Teachers often "debrief" data with an entire class at the end of a lesson. Students often reflect on their own data following an assessment and before preparing to take the next step toward a more advanced skill.

How do students use data?

Students analyze their data in order to determine which learning targets they've met and which they haven't yet achieved. Once they have identified these "data points," they create action plans with specific strategies for addressing the gaps. They set goals for what they want to achieve by the end of the unit, term, or year.

What can I do to support my student in leading their own learning?

Invite your child to share her/his data notebook! Discuss the data together and invite your child to explain the action plan she/he has created to reach specific goals. Ask questions! And, know that you'll see more data as evidence reflecting specific learning targets when you attend your child's student-led conference each term. Showing your interest in and understanding of your child's data is the best way to support your child in leading their own learning.

Challenge #2: My students don't get excited about academic data. They don't see it as useful or meaningful.

TRY THIS: LEVERAGE YOUR STUDENTS' INNER DATA GEEK

For many students, "data" can at first seem scary, confusing, or just plain boring. Getting students excited about "evidence" of their academic growth can be a real challenge. It helps to tap into the ways in which kids, even six- and seven-year-olds, already collect and use data to keep track of their favorite sports team or their treasured possessions. In fact, in real life many of them are natural "data geeks." Figure 3.2 provides a protocol for exploring the value of data with students in their own terms.

Figure 3.2 Lesson plan for exploring the value of data
SOURCE: This document is available in the online toolbox at http://www.wiley.com/go/lotolcompanion.

Engage
Invite students to brainstorm a list of all the kinds of "data" the local basketball team collects about players and games in the course of a season. For example, someone keeps track of points, free throws, three-pointers, assists, rebounds, blocks, and fouls. A player's stats include minutes played and shot percentage for all categories of shots. In addition to quantitative statistics, the coach likely also reviews video of games and of individual players' shooting or passing technique.

Discuss
Invite students to turn and talk about how players use that data to develop a winning strategy.
Share out some of their answers with the whole group.

Focus
Share the lesson learning target: *I can identify types of data that will help me know how I'm doing in school.*
Explain that getting better at school requires a growth mindset. When students believe they can get better at school by working really hard, practicing a lot, and paying attention to the right skills and knowledge – just like those basketball players – they sink more baskets. But as a classroom team, we all have to believe that and help each other to improve together. Keeping track of and paying attention to our data will help us do that.

Apply
Assign students to small groups and have them choose an activity that requires data collection.
Give them examples to choose among or to spark their thinking, such as:
- Multiplayer video games
- Building a following on social media
- Collecting (e.g., stuffed animals, comics, charm bracelets)
- Joining a fantasy sports league
- Supporting a political campaign
- Tracking popular music trends
- Selling Girl Scout cookies
- Competing (e.g., in cheer, dance, snowboarding, horseback riding)

Ask each group to identify at least three types of data that might be collected by those interested in this activity. Once they have made a list, groups should discuss:
- How would people in this activity use that data?
- How would they know if they are "getting better" at this activity?

Invite groups to share their conclusions with the whole group.

Synthesize
Ask students: Now that you have shown that people use data in all sorts of activities in order to improve their performance, let's make a list of the kinds of information we would collect if we wanted to get better at school.
Create an anchor chart of students' answers so that you can refer to it frequently as you and your students gather and analyze academic data to track your progress.

TRY THIS: IDENTIFY DATA THAT LIFTS STUDENTS UP RATHER THAN KNOCKS THEM DOWN

Working with data runs the risk of shining a light on weaknesses that many students have not paid attention to in the past. This can unintentionally demoralize many students. Instead, focusing on the data that reveals the small steps students are taking toward success will help you and your students shift from the fixed mindset that says "I've always been a failure, and I can't change that" to a growth mindset that says "I'm making progress by changing this one habit" or "I can see how this one skill helps me . . ."

Emphasize that repetition, practice, using feedback to improve technique, and dogged persistence are the ingredients for success over time. For example, we saw a third-grade girls basketball coach generate data for her players in a novel way. Initially she was collecting the usual basketball stats: points and assists. However, since these were beginning players and the games were very low scoring, these statistics were usually all zeros, and it was dispiriting for the players. To yield more helpful data, she assigned each parent in the stands a player who was not their child. Parents were asked to record more detailed data, such as ball touches, passes, picks, defensive stops, and moving to open spots. Now every player had statistics to analyze and improve: they could all be proud about advancing specific aspects of their game even if they didn't score points, and they all improved quickly (and, as a bonus, parents became boosters of students who were not their own children).

TRY THIS: INVESTIGATE THE PRACTICE OF LOOKING AT DATA BY ANALYZING HOW OTHER STUDENTS DO IT

To help students understand the value of a particular writing technique, you might analyze a piece of writing that uses that technique and the impact it has on the reader. Similarly, to help students understand the value of looking at data, try analyzing how other students have gathered data, and how they have used it to improve their work. The Close Up that follows takes us into Jessica Ayers's second-grade classroom at The Noah Wallace School in Farmington, Connecticut, where she has students analyze data collected by students the previous year.

Close Up: Learning to Analyze Data Using Other Students' Process as a Model at The Noah Wallace School in Farmington, Connecticut

Jessica Ayers introduces students to tracking their own reading data by first interpreting data other students have gathered, and then creating their own data trackers. She came up with this lesson after years of having students track their progress on the following *teacher*-created tracker:

Learning Target: *I can read longer and stronger.*	Monday	Wednesday	Friday
I went back to reread.			
I used "stop and jot."			
I looked up a tricky word.			
I stuck with my book.			

Although this simple tracker captured the data that was useful to Ayers, for students it was just another teacher tool, and they didn't use it very carefully. That's when Ayers refocused her lesson by unpacking the word *track* in her learning target: *I can **track** my goal to push myself to read longer and stronger each day.*

"If you're going to *track* your goal," she said to her students, "you need a way to collect information about your reading over time. A graph is a mathematical tool that gives you information over time. Do you think we could create graphs that can help us read better?"

Next, Ayers invited students to work with a partner to analyze graphs that other second-graders had created. Students studied graphs like those in Figures 3.3–3.5.

Then students discussed what they noticed in the graphs and how the students who created them could use the information to understand their reading progress. The class worked together to develop a list of criteria for a good reading tracker that included:

- It should show how you're doing on your goal.
- You need to be able to use it a bunch of times so you can see how you've grown.
- You can show how well you did something with happy, straight, sad faces.
- You can use bars, lines, or tallies to show how many times you did something.

Finally, students created their own trackers. They got feedback from a partner and the teacher based on their criteria list and revised their trackers before they put it in their data notebook. Ayers says, "This lesson is successful every year because it provides students with a choice about how they track their own learning. When the idea comes from the student rather than a teacher-generated tracking sheet, it is more authentic and engaging."

[Note: For more examples of students unpacking models to generate the criteria that guide them to create their own high-quality work, see Chapter 4.]

Figure 3.3 Student graph 1

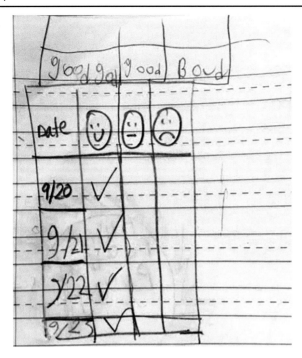

Figure 3.4 Student graph 2

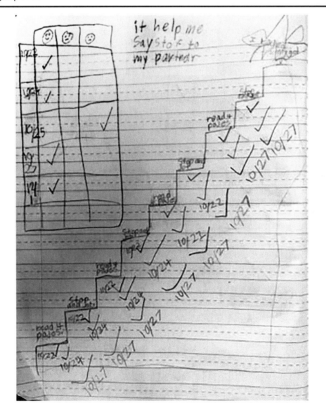

Figure 3.5 Student graph 3

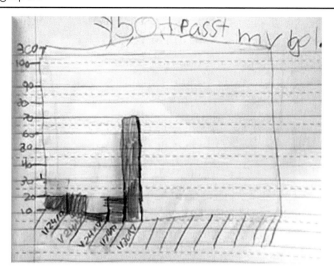

 Challenge #3: Looking at the data feels like another thing to do. How do I make time?

TRY THIS: BUILD LOOKING AT DATA INTO YOUR ROUTINE

Creating a data-informed culture means data is always at the center of your pedagogical decision making. It informs your choices about what to teach next, how to group students, and how fast or slow to pace your lessons. However, looking at data doesn't have to take a lot more time. For example, rather than just recording who turned in homework and who didn't (which you are probably already doing), sort the homework into three piles as you go through it. Make one pile for exceeds expectations, another for meets expectations, and a third for "not yet." Note which students are in which group. This simple triage can help you identify what each group of students needs to learn next. In the next lesson, establish differentiated groups based on this triage. Then provide differentiated scaffolding or differentiated lessons to help students reach their goals.

Looking at data with your students may also seem to be additional work and time that doesn't fit into your classroom schedule. Once you implement this practice though, you'll discover that analyzing and setting goals based on their own data makes students' time more purposeful and more intentional. They'll reach their learning targets more efficiently, and you'll spend less time cajoling, corralling, and reteaching students who are behind.

As a guiding principle, we encourage you to switch from asking, "What more can I do to analyze data?" to "What more can my students do to describe, reflect on, and sort their own data?" and "How can my students find patterns and create goals and action plans?" There is nothing more important than getting students involved in this process and becoming leaders of their own learning.

Many teachers can identify some time in the week that is difficult to fill with regular instruction – a short period on early release day or the brief time before a big transition. If you've got one of those in your schedule, it can be an ideal time to regularly look at data with students and to establish an expected routine that is always used for this purpose.

TRY THIS: GET STUDENTS DOING THE WORK . . . AND THE THINKING

Do you give students exit tickets to assess whether they are thinking critically and reflecting purpose-fully? Do you then get overwhelmed by the pile of exit tickets staring back at you at the end of the day? If so, you are not alone. It can be a challenge to make time to actually read them, much less analyze them carefully for clues to change instruction. To avoid spending your dinner hour and down time plowing through them all, enlist students in quality self-assessment.

The protocol in Figure 3.6 could be used to have students themselves sort anonymously authored exit tickets in order to articulate trends in the group's understanding. This would help you to adjust instruction in subsequent lessons. View the video in Video Spotlight 3.2 to see students engaged in tracking their data over time.

Figure 3.6   Collaborative exit ticket data sort protocol
SOURCE: This document is available in the online toolbox at http://www.wiley.com/go/lotolcompanion.

Norms
- We exercise a growth mindset.
- We set goals based on evidence.
- We honor others' growth mindset (by not revealing whose exit ticket is whose).
- We respect each other's feelings (by being kind, specific, and helpful).

Procedure
1. In your group circulate the exit tickets you've received.
2. Assess the answers in response to our three targets. (Talk to each other! You may need to deliberate on some of these to reach consensus about which answers meet the targets and which do not.)
3. For each ticket, record a tally mark on the Exit Ticket Data Sort Note-Catcher for each target. If the exit ticket does not met the target, record a tally in the "Not Yet" column. If it does meet the target, record a mark in the "Met the Target" column.
4. Compare the number of tally marks in column two for all three learning targets. Which learning target has the most "Not Yets"? Therefore, which target does your group feel we most need to work on before the next assessment?

Exit ticket data sort note-catcher

Type of Target	Target	Met the Target	Not Yet
Knowledge	I can identify key events that impacted World War I.		
Reasoning	I can use at least three pieces of evidence from our reading to show the impact of one event on the course of the war.		
Skill	I can construct a coherent one-paragraph argument using complete sentences.		

Based on our data, our high-priority learning target is:

Video Spotlight 3.2: Students Own Their Progress
https://vimeo.com/43990523

In this video, sixth-grade students at Genesee Community Charter School in Rochester, New York, track their strengths and challenges through analysis of their own homework and test data. Students articulate how they use this data to focus their studies and improve their skills.

Video Reflection Questions
1. What impact do the systems and structures for data collection and analysis in this classroom have on students' ability to self-assess their progress?
2. What role does data analysis play in the quality of these students' goals?
3. How would this process be different without the strong anchor of the learning targets?

Learning Target 2: I can teach students to use data to evaluate their progress in relation to a learning target.

Challenge #4: With so many students, it's impossible for me to keep track of each student's data on a daily basis. How can I enlist students in organizing, tracking, and storing their own data effectively?

TRY THIS: ESTABLISH ROUTINES FOR ACCESSING AND STORING STUDENT DATA

The first step to managing data effectively is strong organization. Students need the organizational skills to bring their binder to class, put their note-catcher in their cubby, file their portfolio alphabetically in the class crate, or save their work in the correct folder on the shared class drive. As with any routine, taking time at the beginning of the school year (or course) to teach, rehearse, and reinforce organizational routines related to student data will pay off in the long run. Dig into this topic further by viewing the accompanying video and considering the questions in Video Spotlight 3.2.

Video Spotlight 3.3: Paper Management
https://vimeo.com/124448650

This video illustrates a variety of paper management systems that help students keep track of their data.

Video Reflection Questions
1. What are the biggest organizational barriers to your students being independent with their papers and data?
2. What systems could you put in place in your classroom to improve your students' ability to be more independent and engage more meaningfully with their data?

Once you've set up your classroom so that students can access and store their data, remember that you need to teach them how to use this system. It's essential that you provide rehearsal, regular practice, and reinforcement that holds students accountable for getting their data and returning it to a place where you can also find it easily. For young students this may be a folder in a cubby or a binder on a shelf. For older students this may be a grade-level folder or drive on your school's computer network, with subfolders for each subject area. Data trackers can also be integrated into digital portfolios.

TRY THIS: PROVIDE A DATA TRACKER THAT IS EASY FOR STUDENTS TO USE

Once students understand where to find their data, you'll need to create, reproduce, or facilitate a lesson in which students create day-to-day trackers and note-catchers for the variety of data you want them to analyze. High-quality data trackers explicitly reference learning targets or long-term goals. They capture useful data over time so that students can track progress, not just performance at a single point in time. And they provide a visual way for students to analyze trends and patterns.

Figures 3.7–3.12 feature a collection of trackers for a variety of subjects and grade levels. As you review these trackers, consider how you can customize or adapt these tools to fit the needs of your students, your subject area, and your classroom systems.

Primary Grades Data Trackers

Figure 3.7 Independent reading tracker
SOURCE: This document is available in the online toolbox at http://www.wiley.com/go/lotolcompanion.

☺ ☺ ☹

Date	I chose a "just right" book.	I did a picture walk.	I used my strategies to read the text.	I can tell you all about my book!

Figure 3.8 Number sense tracker
SOURCE: This document is available in the online toolbox at http://www.wiley.com/go/lotolcompanion.

Daily Number Sense Quiz
Show the number _____ in the following ways:

Tally Marks	Tens and ones blocks
Equation	_____ tens and _____ ones

I showed the number correctly in _____ ways
Graph your progress on your tracker!
LT: I can show my number of the day in four different ways.

# of the day								
4 ways								
3 ways								
2 ways								
1 way								
Date								

Elementary Grades Data Trackers

Figure 3.9 Math quiz tracker from the Noah Wallace School in Farmington, Connecticut
SOURCE: This document is available in the online toolbox at http://www.wiley.com/go/lotolcompanion.

Name_____
Instruction: Place a check mark in the box that matches your quiz scores for each month: Exceeds, Meets, or Not Yet

I can show evidence of my math progress.
Place Value Quizzes

Exceeds 8–10 points						
Meets 4–7 points						
Not Yet 0–3 points						
	September	October	November	January	March	May

Subtraction Quizzes

Exceeds 8–10 points						
Meets 4–7 points						
Not Yet 0–3 points						
	September	October	November	January	March	May

Adapted from Jessica Ayers, Noah Wallace School, Farmington, CT.

Figure 3.10 Growth mindset target tracker
SOURCE: This document is available in the online toolbox at http://www.wiley.com/go/lotolcompanion.

Name:_____
I can demonstrate a growth mindset during independent work time.
During reflection time, fill in the box for each habit you have demonstrated during work time. Be prepared to share evidence for your assessment during debrief!

Date	I seek out challenging work.	I keep trying even when the work is hard.	I try again when I fail and use new strategies.	I use all my resources before I ask the teacher.	I encourage others to keep trying.	Evidence to share

Secondary Grades Data Trackers

Figure 3.11 Math test error self-analysis

SOURCE: This document is available in the online toolbox at http://www.wiley.com/go/lotolcompanion.

Math Test Error Self Analysis

Name:_____   Date:_____

Test Topic_____

Number of times you've taken this test (or a different version)_____

Number of problems on the test_____ Number Correct_____

Percent Correct_____

Error Analysis

  Type A: Careless Error (just a stupid mistake; you know the facts and operations

  Type B: Graphic Error (copied the problem wrong, read your writing wrong, lined up columns poorly, etc.)

  Type C: Confused by how to do the operation

  Type D: Wrong operation used

  Type E: Clueless (no idea how to start or what operation to use)

List each problem number you got wrong and assign an error code letter to each:

Total Errors of each type:

A:_____ B:_____ C:_____ D:_____E:_____

What patterns do you notice? What does this test show you?

How careful do you feel you were on this test? (circle one):

Super Careful   *Very Careful*   *Careful*   *Not Careful*   *Awful*

How pleased were you by your performance? (circle one):

Very   *Pretty Much*   *Somewhat*   *Not Much*   *Ugg!*

TRY THIS: BUILD DATA NOTEBOOKS WITH STUDENTS

A data notebook is an organized collection of data trackers, a one-stop shop for busy students that tabulates all of their data across subject areas and throughout the year. Data notebooks are often organized by subject area; each subject area section begins with a goal determined by the student after some initial analysis of pre-assessment data. The format of individual trackers within each section depends on the type of data your students are tracking over time. For example, you can design trackers for the number of correct words on a spelling test, reading levels, quiz scores, turning in complete homework, contributions to Socratic seminars, evidence of strong work habits, etc. A data notebook also includes strategically placed "pauses" for reflection and goal setting. Both the data and student's synthesis of it provide evidence to be shared at student-led conferences or other communications of student growth and achievement.

Figure 3.12 Written work error self-analysis
SOURCE: This document is available in the online toolbox at http://www.wiley.com/go/lotolcompanion.

Written Work Error Self Analysis

Data Collection of Mechanical and Grammatical Errors from the First Page of the Work

Name:_____   Date:_____

Number of Compositions Analyzed_____

Time Period (first and last dates of compositions)_____

Total Errors – Mean_____

Total Errors – Median_____

Total Errors in Each Category

Layout

Neatness _____
Margins _____
Heading _____
Spacing _____
Title _____

Punctuation

Periods _____
Capitals _____
Commas _____
Apostrophes _____
Quotations _____
Colons, Semi-Colons _____

Organization

Paragraphs _____
Opening _____
Clarity _____
Sentence Order _____

Spelling

Total Spelling _____
Proper Nouns _____
There, Their, They're _____
Too, to, two _____
Words with ie, ei _____
Plurals _____
Conjunctions _____
Careless (Easy Words) _____

Grammar

Full Sentences _____
Run-On Sentences _____
Tense _____
Subject-Verb Agreement _____
Subject-Object Pronouns _____
Extra Words (Like, etc.) _____

Ask yourself the following questions to inspire the design of a data notebook for your grade level and subject area:

Organization

- Will students "build" the data notebook themselves as we go or will I create a template for the notebook and provide it to students in advance? What "container" (e.g., three-ring binder, notebook, manila folder, digital portfolio) will make the notebook accessible and flexible for my students?

- What sections do students need in the notebook (e.g., by subject area? course units?)

- How will the sections be organized so that students can easily find their way through the notebook?

- What standards, skills, or knowledge do I want students to track?

- What work habits or mindsets do I want students to track?

Using data notebooks supports students to develop routines for reflecting on their progress toward learning targets.

Photo credit: EL Education

Tracking Progress

- How will I pre-assess the skills, knowledge, and work habits?

- What data provides the best picture of progress toward our long-term learning targets?

- What trackers provide the best picture of that data?

- What tracker formats or forms will be most user friendly for my students?

- How will the trackers be organized in the notebook?

Reflection

- When will my students pause to reflect on their data and set goals?

- What forms will students use to draw conclusions about their data?

- What forms will students use to set goals?

- How will I make changes to the notebook mid-course or mid-year as I make adjustments to my learning targets or the pace of my course?

- How will students use the notebook in conversations with parents or others?

- Do I want to have a place for family or teachers to respond to students' notebooks?

TRY THIS: TEACH STUDENTS TO TRACK THEIR DATA INDEPENDENTLY

Once students know where to find their data and how to use the trackers you have provided, give them time and support to track their data independently as a regular part of learning. The video featured in Video Spotlight 3.4 shows students at The Odyssey School of Denver using data trackers systematically to track their progress on a self-guided math unit.

Video Spotlight 3.4: Menu Math at Odyssey School of Denver
https://vimeo.com/108609925

This video features seventh-grade students at The Odyssey School of Denver using "menu math." Menu math is a unique approach to math instruction that allows students to master content, deepen their habits of inquiry, and know themselves as learners. Each menu takes students through a self-directed process of practice, instruction, and assessment as they work toward mastery of learning targets.

Video Reflection Questions
1. What evidence do you see of a "data-informed culture" in this classroom? Why is this important to the success of menu math?
2. Describe how these students' use of their own data empowers them to lead their own learning. Do you think something like this could work in your classroom? Why or why not?

Challenge #5: My students don't see illuminating trends that can motivate them to persist in their learning. How do I get them to analyze data more effectively?

TRY THIS: INTRODUCE STUDENTS TO THE WORLD (AND THE WORDS) OF STATISTICS

Sometimes the challenge for students is understanding whether or not their data is valid and how to interpret it. If you are working with upper elementary or secondary students, understanding a little from the field of statistics, including some of the terminology, may help your students to analyze their data. For example, students could learn about margin of error, outliers, and the line of regression by collectively reflecting on a scatter plot comparing their work habits to their academic grades. Figure 3.13 is a lesson plan that does just that, using a sample of scores from The Springfield Renaissance School in Springfield, Massachusetts.

TRY THIS: HAVE A DATA INQUIRY CONFERENCE

Imagine you skipped your mid-morning muffin all week, only to step on the scale and discover that you hadn't lost even a single pound. Looking at data with students can prompt the same kind of disappointment and discouragement. What do you do when you hear a student say, "Wait. . . I did all the right things, and I still didn't improve!" Having a data-inquiry conference with students who are confused or discouraged to explore what's really going on will help students put their best foot forward.

During your conference, engage the student as a fellow scientist working to get beneath the data and understand its complexity. What follows are three strategies for investigating what the data means and how to make it more useful for setting goals and identifying next steps:

1. **Make sure the data is reliable and valid.** For example, if the data comes from an interim test like MAP (Measures of Academic Performance), a retest in optimal conditions will help determine if the result reflects the student's knowledge and skills or something else. It's helpful to ask what the conditions were when the student generated the data. Did something happen at home that morning? Was the student sick or sleep deprived? Talking with the student and retesting can help answer some of those questions.

Figure 3.13 Sample statistics lesson
SOURCE: The complete version of this document is available in the online toolbox at http://www.wiley.com/go/lotolcompanion.

Use the following scatter plot graph to have a conversation with students about the relationship between Habits of Work* and academic learning targets. It is especially helpful if you project the graph so that you can annotate it as you discuss.

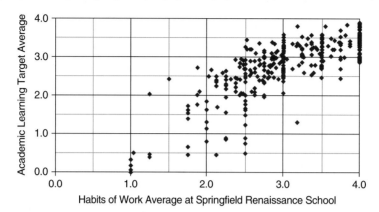

Use the **Numbered Heads Together protocol** as follows to facilitate collaborative analysis of the graph.

1. Explain to students that they will work as a table to analyze the graph and learn statistical vocabulary.
2. Give students a few minutes to study and talk about the graph at their tables.
3. Encourage students to identify (or record) notices and wonders about the graph.
4. Then ask students to number off by four at their tables.

Whole-Group Discussion with Small-Group Assist
Explain that for each round of questions, individual students will respond for their table group. Before they respond, they will have one more minute to confer with their table group before sharing the answer with the whole class. Encourage respondents to provide new information from the graph, not just to repeat what the last student said.
Invite the 1's at each table to respond to the following question:

1. What did you notice in this graph? What do these data say? (facts, not inferences).

   When students notice that students with high academic learning target averages generally also have high habits of work, draw and explain the **line of regression**.

   Invite the 2's at each table to confer and respond to the following question:

2. What do you infer is going on for the student who has a 3.25 in habits of work, but only a 1.25 academic average?

   Explain the term **outlier** and their implications for averaging and generalizing from data.

   Invite the 3's at each table to confer and respond to the next question:

3. What do you infer is going on for the student who has a 2.5 academic average and only a 1.5 habit of work average? Given what else we know, how do you think this student might perform if he/she also had a higher habit of work average?

   Invite the 4's at each table to confer and respond to the next question:

   What factors would make this graph **reliable** over time? What factors would make it less reliable?

Explain that **reliability is a combination of validity (meaningful data) and reproducibility**. Discuss what might create a **margin of error** in this graph (e.g., subjective scoring of habits).

Debrief
Invite students to discuss and share implications for their own data collection and documentation practices. How can they make sure their data is meaningful and reliable?

---

* Work habits such as responsibility and perseverance are referred to as Habits of Work at Renaissance and students receive grades for them. At other schools they may be called Habits of Scholarship, Habits of Work and Learning, Habits of Effective Learners, or something else.

(cont. online)

2. **Break the data down.** Work with the student to determine precisely which parts of the assessment resulted in a low overall score. Then ask:
   a. What can you do to improve in those areas?
   b. Are there discrete skills or understandings that would boost your score?
   c. What specific behaviors can you change to improve on your data next time?

3. **Investigate discrepant data.** In science, unexpected or discrepant results push investigators to ask deeper questions about the minute differences in experimental conditions or other factors that yield different results. Students can use their own discrepant data in the same way by asking these questions:
   a. What was "different" about my learning environment when I got this unexpected result?
   b. Would I benefit from taking the assessment again?
   c. Have I identified the right strategy for making progress toward the target?
   d. What or who can help me be consistent in working toward my goal?

Individual data inquiry conferences are an opportunity to focus students on manageable next steps so that they can feel positive about their progress.

Photo credit: Anne Vilen

When conferencing with students, be sure to stay positive and focus on small, manageable next steps. Remember to celebrate incremental successes *and* point out the data that shows students' actions have moved them toward their goals. This is what we call using data as a flashlight rather than a club, a tool for illuminating patterns and trends rather than a way of catching students at failure. This puts students in the driver's seat as interpreters of their own data, in charge of their own academic progress.

Check Yourself Checklist

Creating Effective Systems for Data Collection Checklist

Check off all that apply:

❑ Is there a place in the classroom for students to store their data? Can they do so independently?

❑ Do data trackers have learning targets written on them?

❑ Do data trackers capture useful data over time so that students can track progress, not just performance at a single point in time?

❑ Do data trackers provide a visual way for students to analyze trends and patterns?

❑ Do data trackers allow students to track their data as independently as possible?

(This checklist is available in the online toolbox at http://www.wiley.com/go/lotolcompanion.)

Learning Target 3: I can support students to set meaningful and effective goals.

 Challenge #6: My students learn "in the moment." How do I help them see the big picture and use today's learning to set goals for tomorrow?

TRY THIS: TEACH STUDENTS TO SET EFFECTIVE GOALS

A goal gives students a specific target to aim for and a benchmark to celebrate as they fly by it on their way to the next goal (and the next goal after that). Yet setting realistic and attainable goals does not come naturally to students who are used to dreaming of the big win or cheering for the underdog upset. One way to get students to set S.M.A.R.T. goals is to conduct a critique lesson that helps students understand the ingredients of goals that lead to success: Specific; Measurable; Attainable; Realistic; Timely

What Is a Critique Lesson?

Through critique lessons, students and teachers analyze model work together to define the qualities of good work in a specific genre or to think about the ways all students can improve their work through revision. This form of a critique is a lesson, with clear objectives, typically focused only on positive qualities in the work. It is designed to support the learning of all students, not primarily to improve a specific piece of work by one student.

(Note: Critique lessons are discussed in much greater detail in Chapter 4.)

In the following Close Up, second-grade teacher Jessica Ayers conducts a critique lesson with her students that helps them set S.M.A.R.T reading goals that align with the reading data trackers they created in the lesson described in the Close Up: Learning to Analyze Data Using Other Students' Process as a Model at The Noah Wallace School in Farmington, Connecticut, at the beginning of this chapter. It is important to note that although the Close Up that follows features second-graders, it could be conducted, with few changes, with students of any age.

Close Up: Setting S.M.A.R.T. Goals with Second-Graders at The Noah Wallace School in Farmington, Connecticut

Jessica Ayers recognizes that goal setting and data tracking are part of a regular cycle of looking at data. In her second-grade classroom, students gather data on their reading strategies, fluency, and work habits. Using their data, students set goals for the next cycle of learning based on the learning target: *I can set a goal to push myself to read longer and stronger each day.*

Ayers conducts a critique lesson[1] that begins with sharing several sample reading goals with students including:

- I will read better and better.
- I will increase my fluency to read 50 words per minute.
- I will use sticky notes when I read.
- I will record the gist of the story.
- I will use the read, reread, summarize strategy.
- I will read one book for the whole independent reading time.

---

[1] You can find the PowerPoint slides that accompany this Close Up in our online toolbox.

Students analyze one of these sample goals with a partner and respond to the following questions:

1. What part of reading is the goal for?
2. How will this student know if she is meeting the goal?
3. Why do you think she set this goal?

After students share their thinking, the class works together to cross out goals that are vague, hard to measure, or confusing. Then Ayers asks them to choose one of the S.M.A.R.T. goals remaining on the board or to write a reading goal for themselves that is specific, easy to measure, and that makes sense for them based on their own reading strengths and challenges.

Students then work with the same partner to analyze their personal goals for "smartness." Partners ask and discuss:

- What is your goal about?
- How will you know if you are meeting it?
- Is it just right—not too easy, not too hard?
- Will it help you reach our long-term targets?
- When will you complete your goal by?

Finally, partners give each other feedback on their goals using the following sentence stems:

- This goal is S.M.A.R.T. because. . .
- You can make this goal S.M.A.R.T.er by adding/taking out . . .

Once students have revised their goals, they save them in their data notebooks right alongside the tracker they created for themselves. Setting goals and collecting data to determine their own progress empowers students. "They love being able to prove they are reaching their goals!" says Ayers.

TRY THIS: APPROACH GOAL SETTING IN A VARIETY OF WAYS

Once students understand what good goals look like and have had some practice creating their own, you can further support them by building goal setting into various forms, tools, and routines in your classroom. What follows are a few examples, including a Video Spotlight:

- Sometimes students can identify S.M.A.R.T. goals but have more difficulty articulating specific action plans to reach those goals. Figure 3.14 invites students to literally map the journey toward their goal with words and illustrations that include developing new behaviors or work habits. The possibilities for timelines and illustrations are endless.

- For young students, just learning about S.M.A.R.T. goals, you may need to provide a goal-setting checklist like the one in Figure 3.15 that invites students to choose specific behaviors that will help them reach a goal.

- Figure 3.16 shows a data tracker for an eighth-grade unit on argument writing. Students begin by taking a pre-assessment and recording their scores for nine learning targets. Then they choose three or four key learning targets that they want to focus on throughout the year. Students graph their progress on these learning targets after each argument-writing assessment (fall, winter, spring) and write a specific goal and action step that will help them achieve that goal by the end of the year.

- Figure 3.17 is a similar math target tracking tool that incorporates goal setting.

- The 3-2-1 Exit Ticket featured in Figure 3.18 is a way to help students connect today's learning to the big picture and begin to set strategic goals for the future. This exit ticket asks students to reflect on *what I learned*, *how I learned it*, and *how I'll use it tomorrow*.

- Video Spotlight 3.5 features a first-grade teacher finishing her spelling assessment by conducting goal-setting conferences with her students.

Figure 3.14 My goal map

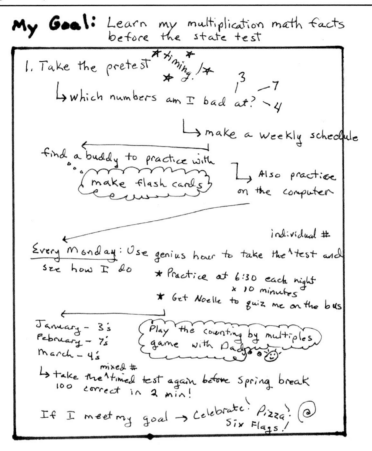

Figure 3.15 Goal setting worksheet for literacy
SOURCE: This document is available in the online toolbox at http://www.wiley.com/go/lotolcompanion.

I want to get better at:

Reading
- ❑ Choosing a book that is "just right" for me
- ❑ Choosing different types of books than I usually read
- ❑ Sounding out words and looking them up
- ❑ Using silent reading time to READ
- ❑ Rereading
- ❑ Writing the gist before I read more

Writing
- ❑ Revising my work
- ❑ Trying out new ideas
- ❑ Coming up with writing ideas
- ❑ Writing complete sentences
- ❑ Using capitals and ending punctuation

Figure 3.16 Goal setting tool for argument writing from Irving A. Robbins Middle School in Farmington, Connecticut

SOURCE: The complete version of this document is available in the online toolbox at http://www.wiley.com/go/lotolcompanion.

Argument Writing Skills	Learning Targets	Fall Score	Winter Score	Spring Score
Focus and Organization	**CLAIM:** I can write a claim that is maintained throughout the essay.			
	INTRODUCTION: I can inform the reader of the topic of the essay.			
	INTRODUCTION: I can preview the supporting arguments of the essay.			
	BODY PARAGRAPHS: I can organize the supporting paragraphs/counterclaim including topic and concluding sentences.			
	CONCLUSION: I can summarize the focus of the writing.			
	CONCLUSION: I can extend why the central idea matters.			
Support and Elaboration	**EVIDENCE:** I can use relevant and informative evidence that develops and illustrates the claim.			
	REASONING: I can use explanation and analysis of evidence to explain how the evidence supports and illustrates the claim.			
	COUNTERCLAIM: I can address the alternate or opposing claim.			
	COUNTERCLAIM: I can support the alternate or opposing claim with sufficient evidence.			
	COUNTERCLAIM: I can refute the opposing claim with analysis and reasoning.			

Graph your scores (Exceeds, Meets, Needs improvement, Below standard) for the Reasoning Learning Target on the chart below. Then choose **three other learning targets** that you will focus on and set goals for this year. Graph your scores for those targets using a different color for each line. After each assessment, you will add to this graph.

Exceeds			
Meets			
Needs			
Below			
	Fall	Spring	Winter

(cont. online)

Figure 3.17 Math goal-setting tracker from Irving A. Robbins Middle School in Farmington, Connecticut

SOURCE: This document is available in the online toolbox at http://www.wiley.com/go/lotolcompanion.

Name: _____   Date: _____

Solving Systems of Linear Equations by Graphing
Use the following scale to assess where you are right now on the learning targets.

3: I've got it!
2: I'm making progress, but need additional practice.
1: I'm not there yet.

Then choose from the menu of Improvement Plan Action Steps OR come up with an action step of your own to create an improvement plan that will help you meet the learning target and write it in the box below each learning target.

I can solve a system of linear equations by graphing.	1	2	3
I can accurately identify and label the solution to a system of equations as: an ordered pair (x,y), no solution, or infinitely many solutions.	1	2	3
I can solve a system of linear equations when given a problem-solving application.	1	2	3

Improvement Plan ACTION STEPS

1. Use your RESOURCE JOURNAL.
2. Check odd answers in the back of the book.
3. Watch a video about the concept you are struggling to understand.
4. Email the teacher your questions before class.
5. Have the problem in front of you during class.
6. Use your class notes when you are doing your homework.
7. Do the homework with good quality.
8. When correcting homework, use pen to make notes about your errors. Record the correct answers and try to find where you went wrong.
9. Get started on a problem even if it seems too challenging.
10. Make multiple attempts instead of skipping problems.
11. Re-do homework problems you didn't understand originally.
12. Come for extra help.
13. Use your textbook.
14. Work with a study partner from the course.
15. Teach the concept to someone else.
16. Homework/classwork reflection on sticky note.
17. Share a mistake with the class.
18. Ask someone with more math experience.
19. Use the learning target to describe what you don't understand.
20. Google the learning target that you find challenging.
21. Ask questions during class.
22. Be honest with yourself about your level of understanding.
23. Make an appointment with your teacher.

Created by the Math Department of Irving A. Robbins Middle School

Figure 3.18   3-2-1 exit ticket

List three new things you learned about _____ today.
   1.
   2.
   3.

List two skills you used to learn those things (e.g., close reading, group discussion).
   1.
   2.

What is one strategy you can use tomorrow to build on your learning?
   1.

Video Spotlight 3.5: K–2 Skills Block: End of Cycle Assessments
https://vimeo.com/159828967

This video shows first-graders participating in the end-of-cycle reading and spelling assessment with their teacher in the K–2 Reading Foundations Skills Block, part of EL Education's K–5 Language Arts Curriculum. It specifically shows the spelling portion. The teacher administers the assessment with a small group, evaluates their responses, and confers with each student to set an individual goal.

Video Reflection Questions
1. What's the data in this video? How is it used to set goals?
2. What strategies does the teacher use to make the data accessible for these young students to analyze?

Using data with students is key to a student-engaged assessment system. Leaders are in a position to connect the dots from classroom assessment to schoolwide assessment in a meaningful and coherent way. But in today's educational world, student-achievement data has become so charged and high stakes that many teachers live in fear of it rather than embracing it and using it well. School leaders have an important role to play in leading a safe professional culture where data is seen as an opportunity for inquiry and learning, rather than an ominous final judgment.

The most important maxim for leaders is "First, do no harm." Don't make teachers and students afraid of data by using it to admonish and judge. Model curiosity, transparency, and a desire to learn from data. Whenever possible, give raw data to teachers and let them find trends, make hypotheses, and suggest ideas. It's a common practice in schools these days for school leaders, or math/ELA coaches, to go through all the raw data from student assessments (yearly state assessments or district term assessments), analyze those data for trends, find areas of weakness, and then report to teachers *what they did poorly and need to improve.* It's no wonder teachers live in fear of data. While this practice is a well-meaning attempt to save teachers time, it does not yield the rich understanding that teachers will get if they grapple with raw data themselves. If teachers dig into the actual data, they will likely discover positive, confusing, and discouraging trends. But if *they are the ones discovering those trends,* they will feel trusted and empowered to work together, with leaders, to come up with areas for focused improvement. What follows are key moves for leaders to support the successful practice of using data with students throughout a school. Table 3.2 summarizes the key action steps for teachers and students that will lead to success.

Top Tips

- Model a data-informed culture by regularly looking at evidence with teachers and other leaders. Evidence can include traditional student performance data (interim or end-of-year test results) or qualitative day-to-day data like exit tickets, observational notes, or lesson plans.

- Support all staff to identify trends, set goals, and suggest strategies based on data. Provide protocols that teaching teams and other leadership teams can use to analyze data collaboratively and effectively.

- Build teachers' capacity for analyzing data by reviewing the evidence for progress on school goals together. Then adjust strategies and goals in response to the evidence.

- Develop grading and reporting systems that recognize growth as well as achievement. Communicate a focus on growth to staff and to families. When students' academic skills and knowledge are growing quickly, and when their work habits are becoming more consistent, they will also, eventually, see gains in achievement.

Table 3.2 Using data with students: Steps to success

What Should Teachers Do?
Identify a variety of types of data to collect from daily work as well as assessments.
Establish a data culture that encourages students and families to value and learn from data, and that supports all students to grow toward goals.
Create routines for looking at data with students and creating action plans for meeting goals.
Design and teach students to use tools for tracking their progress toward learning targets.
Conference with students to support them in analyzing data and tracking their progress independently and effectively.
What Should Students Do?
Embrace a culture of feedback, in which data is useful information that helps them grow and reach goals.
Use progress trackers to measure growth toward learning targets and standards.
Analyze their own data and reflect meaningfully on progress and goals.
Discuss their progress with other students, families, and teachers, using data as evidence to support claims about learning.
Set S.M.A.R.T. goals for learning and achievement that build on progress and sustain growth.

As you have read Chapter 3, maybe you have had an opportunity to try some of these strategies and techniques along the way. If not, come back to this post-assessment after you have had a chance to do so. Give yourself whatever time you need to address the learning targets and challenges in a meaningful way. Then take a moment to check your progress in Table 3.3, which is the exact same Learning Target Tracker that appeared at the beginning of this chapter.

Circle or place an X along the continuum from Beginning to Exceeding: **How would you rate your progress toward each learning target *at this point in time?*** Use the space provided to make notes regarding any remaining challenges you may be having or ideas for new and different strategies you want to try.

Table 3.3 Chapter 3 learning target tracker

Learning Target 1: *I can create a data-informed culture in my classroom.*
Beginning----------------------------------Developing------------------------------------Meeting----------------------------------Exceeding
Notes:
Learning Target 2: *I can teach students to use data to evaluate their progress in relation to a learning target.*
Beginning----------------------------------Developing------------------------------------Meeting----------------------------------Exceeding
Notes:
Learning Target 3: *I can support students to set meaningful and effective goals.*
Beginning----------------------------------Developing------------------------------------Meeting----------------------------------Exceeding
Notes:

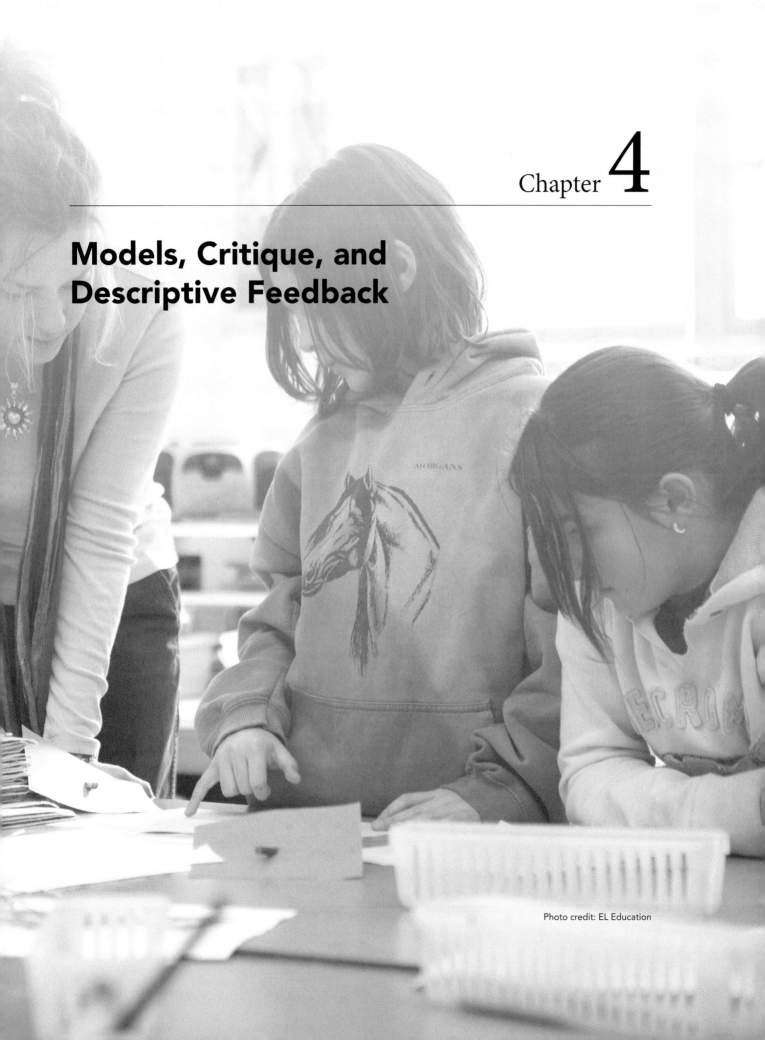

Chapter 4

Models, Critique, and Descriptive Feedback

Photo credit: EL Education

STUDENT-ENGAGED ASSESSMENT

Student-engaged assessment is a system of interrelated practices that positions students as leaders of their own learning.

Checking for Understanding during Daily Lessons

Using Data with Students

Models, Critique, and Descriptive Feedback

Learning Targets

Standards-Based Grading

Student-Led Conferences

Passage Presentations with Portfolios

Celebrations of Learning

**Models,
Critique, and
Descriptive
Feedback**

What Are Models, Critique, and Descriptive Feedback?

Models are exemplars of work used to build a vision of quality within a genre. Models do not have to be perfect but must be strong in important dimensions. They can be drawn from current or prior student work, student work from other schools, work from the professional world, or can be teacher created. They are often used in critique lessons.

In **critique lessons**, students and teachers analyze model work together to define the qualities of good work in a specific genre or to think about the ways all students can improve their work through revision. This form of a critique is a lesson, with clear objectives, typically focused only on positive qualities in the model work. It is designed to support the learning of all students, not primarily to improve a specific piece of work by one student.

Descriptive feedback is typically individual feedback. It may take place in the form of a teacher-student conference, written comments from the teacher, or during a peer-to-peer feedback session. Descriptive feedback is most effective when it focuses on one dimension, or a few dimensions, of the work, rather than trying to address all the issues in the work at one time.

Supporting students to create high-quality work is a great challenge for all of us. As teachers, we feel compelled to cover a great deal of content and to give many small assignments. As a consequence, the quality of student work that is turned in is often weak – even in very good classrooms. Nothing is exemplary. While it's true that not every assignment needs to be polished into a final draft, if students *never have the opportunity* to create work of truly high quality, they will not develop high standards for their scholarship and craftsmanship, and they will not understand their true capacity.

There is no easy solution, but there is a clear pathway. Students need:

- A clear vision of what quality looks like, built through analyzing models together

- Time that allows them to get off the treadmill of turning in endless small assignments in order to save some time for priority assignments that carry the expectation of excellence and of improvement through multiple drafts and revisions

- Effective critique from peers, teachers, and perhaps outside experts during the revision process

Teachers often worry that if they use models of quality work, students will copy from those models. At EL Education, we believe that "copying" is one of the most important ways we all learn, and should be encouraged and guided. William Zinsser, one of the world's leaders in writing instruction and author of the bestseller *On Writing Well*, opens an essay on the craft of writing with these words: "Writing is learned by imitation; we all need models (2012, p. 45)."

Of course, students should not plagiarize. But if we want them to learn to write strong essays or swing a tennis racket correctly, they will need to study models and copy technique. In this chapter we build on Chapter 4 of *Leaders of Their Own Learning* and we provide new tools and examples, guided by four learning targets.

> Looking at models showed me the flaws in different people's paragraphs, which reminded me not to make those same mistakes. The good models showed what good reasoning and citations look like. That helped me understand where I am with argument writing and what I need to improve on.
>
> —*Eighth-grade student, Irving A. Robbins Middle School, Farmington, Connecticut*

Learning Targets for Chapter 4

1. I can distinguish between assignments that should be revised and polished into quality final drafts and those that can be just practice and reflection.
2. I can choose engaging and effective models to help students understand what "good" looks like in that genre of work.
3. I can conduct an effective critique lesson that motivates students and gives them concrete takeaways they can use in their work.
4. I can structure descriptive feedback so that it helps students see their strengths and how to improve their work.

Pre-Assessment: Track Your Progress: Chapter 4

Before we dive in, take a moment to assess yourself on each of the learning targets for this chapter. In Table 4.1, circle or place an X along the continuum from Beginning to Exceeding: **How would you rate your progress toward each learning target** *at this point in time?*

We'll give you a chance to assess yourself again at the end of the chapter.

Table 4.1 Chapter 4 learning target tracker

Learning Target 1: *I can distinguish between assignments that should be revised and polished into quality final drafts and those that can be just practice and reflection.* Beginning--------------------Developing----------------------Meeting---------------------Exceeding Notes:
Learning Target 2: *I can choose engaging and effective models to help students understand what "good" looks like in that genre of work.* Beginning--------------------Developing----------------------Meeting---------------------Exceeding Notes:
Learning Target 3: *I can conduct an effective critique lesson that motivates students and gives them concrete takeaways they can use in their work.* Beginning--------------------Developing----------------------Meeting---------------------Exceeding Notes:
Learning Target 4: *I can structure descriptive feedback so that it helps students see their strengths and how to improve.* Beginning--------------------Developing----------------------Meeting---------------------Exceeding Notes:

Learning Target 1: I can distinguish between assignments that should be revised and polished into quality final drafts and those that can be just practice and reflection.

 Challenge #1: There's so much to do in my curriculum. I don't have time for my students to critique and revise their work.

TRY THIS: CATEGORIZE WORK EFFECTIVELY – NOT ALL WORK NEEDS TO BE REVISED

Professional writers, artists, engineers, historians, and scientists don't turn every piece of work into a beautiful, polished, museum-quality artifact. Sometimes they simply explore their ideas or the materials of their medium in a messy fashion. Other times they produce something that is neat and organized for internal critique, but not polished for an external audience. And still other times, they revise and improve through many, many drafts to create a work of art of technical or aesthetic importance.

For some teachers, the expectation for almost all student work is in the second category: "if it's neat, it's complete." Even with this low expectation, the work they receive from many students is not actually neat, nor is it thoughtful or well organized. We suggest that if students have opportunities to occasionally create beautiful, sophisticated work that surprises students and families with its quality, their standards rise for *all* of their work. In order to carve out time to support students to create high-quality work that will raise their personal standards, teachers need to categorize assignments more effectively, just as professionals do. Sort the work you typically assign into these categories:

1. Work that can be exploratory and messy, where the ideas may be high quality and the skills are important to practice but the physical work does not need to look polished or perhaps even be completed – this is *practice* work

2. Work that should be neat and organized, and will be turned in but need not be revised and improved through multiple drafts

3. Work that should be "museum quality" – polished through multiple drafts with support – for an audience beyond the classroom

This means that some of the assignments you have previously expected students to finish and turn in for a grade may actually belong in category 1. Many skills can and should be practiced through exercises that students never revise for a finished product. There is no set of rules for this distinction, but in general we suggest that category 3 work, where critique and revision are important, is:

- Shared with a broader audience – displayed, published, presented; or

- Important for the student to "get right" in order to understand the genre or concept (e.g., a student needs to create an effective persuasive essay or geometric proof to understand the form and affirm that she can do this)

There are also practice activities that are simply part of the learning process and do not require the creation of a successful final draft – category 1 work. For example, if elementary students are preparing to interview senior citizens at a local senior center and create a book for them with short biographies and painted portraits, the final draft work for this book should absolutely be critiqued and revised to "museum quality." The incremental skills needed to succeed at this project require a lot of practice. The practice may be assessed as a work habits grade (in some schools this may be called Habits of Scholarship, Habits of Work, or Habits of Effective Learning) or, in some cases, as an academic grade (for a skill learning target like "*I can paraphrase and quote interview responses accurately.*"). But the work students do while practicing these skills does not need to be revised or polished for an audience. For the book of biographies and portraits, for example, students might need low-stakes practice with all of the following skills:

- Interviewing peers or family members
- Note-taking or transcribing recordings
- Writing introductory and closing paragraphs
- Writing descriptive language
- Sketching faces
- Controlling the paint brush
- Blending painted colors

TRY THIS: SUPPORT STUDENTS TO MAKE EDUCATED CHOICES ABOUT WHAT TO REVISE AND POLISH

Sometimes students, like studio artists or writers, are working on multiple things at once. Learning to choose which piece is most worthy of revision and completion is part of honing artistic judgment. Figure 4.1 is a revision checklist designed to help students make choices about what to revise and polish.

Figure 4.1 Student checklist for worthy revision
SOURCE: This document is available in the online toolbox at http://www.wiley.com/go/lotolcompanion.

I choose to revise this piece of work because. . .

❏ It challenges me.
❏ It gives me a chance to use new skills.
❏ It lets me be creative and original.
❏ I want to revise it for detail and craftsmanship.
❏ I will share it with an audience other than my teacher.
❏ It is really complex work, worth spending more time on to get it right.

❏ It is modeled on a real work format or standards from the professional world.
❏ It really matters to me, and I want to feel proud of the finished product.
❏ It contributes to the world in a meaningful way.

Challenge #2: It's hard to predict how long it will take for students to refine their work. How do I create a plan that supports students to do quality work?

TRY THIS: SCAFFOLD THE STEPS TO COMPLETE THE WORK WITH PRECISION AND CARE

To determine how much time your students need to do quality work, schedule the scaffolding for the piece of work into your unit timeline. In general, the process almost always takes longer than you imagine or plan for. It is rare to *overestimate* how long it will take students to create quality work.

Table 4.2 Planning to support critique and revision

Questions to Ask during Planning	Ideas
What mini-lessons or specific skills do I need to teach? Do students need time to practice these skills incrementally or can they apply them directly to the task I've assigned?	
What graphic organizers will help my students organize the information they'll need for their work?	
How much in-class or out-of-class time do students need for research, information gathering, planning, and drafting their work?	
Will students need time to revisit texts or research after drafting?	
When will I share models with students to help them construct a shared understanding of quality?	
When will students receive feedback from me or others?	
How much time do students need to revise thoughtfully? Will they need to revise multiple times?	
How will students get appropriate feedback to help them with final edits, refinements, or presentation skills?	
Which students will need more structure and support through additional graphic organizers, opportunities for feedback, support from specialists, and so on?	

Begin by identifying the steps students will need to take to create the work and how many drafts students will likely need to do their best work. The number of steps and the amount of time depend heavily on the grade level of your students and complexity of your product, so there is much to consider. In our 2014 book, *Transformational Literacy: Making the Common Core Shift with Work That Matters*, we note that "the writing process is circuitous and recursive, punctuated with fits and starts, wrong turns, dead ends, and course corrections" (p. 139). The same could be said of the creative process for any worthy product. Table 4.2 is adapted from a writing-specific list in *Transformational Literacy*. It may help guide your thinking as you plan the scaffolding for the work.

Now, map out these steps on an actual calendar, which may also include other lessons or daily learning targets. How can you use your time wisely to ensure that students have enough time to do high-quality work?

TRY THIS: TEST DRIVE THE TASK SO THAT YOU CAN ANTICIPATE CHALLENGES

If you've never assigned the task before, you should absolutely try it yourself first. After you do the assignment, pause to reflect on the questions in Figure 4.2. Keep this figure handy so that you can return to it each time you create a new task for students. It's important not to present them with tasks that haven't been tested against the kinds of questions you see in Figure 4.2.

Project-based learning guru Jeff Robin created a short, animated video about the importance of "doing the project yourself first" as you plan for instruction. You can see that video on his website: http://www.jeffrobin.com/planning-and-letting-go.html. Once you've test-driven the task, you may even want to share your product with your students as one model of a finished product.

TRY THIS: CO-MANAGE THE TIMELINE WITH STUDENTS TO BUILD OWNERSHIP OF SUCCESS

Communicating the timeline for critique and revision to students so that they can use a public calendar to plan their own work and stay on track throughout the project is key. You can communicate your timeline to students on the whiteboard, on a classroom chart, by digital calendar, on the assignment, or in

Figure 4.2 Questions to ask yourself when test driving a task
SOURCE: This document is available in the online toolbox at http://www.wiley.com/go/lotolcompanion.

1. Now that you've done the task, did it match well your goals for what you want students to know, and to know how to do?
2. Did the balance of what you spent your time doing in order to complete the task align well with the priorities of what students need to learn?
3. What was sensible and clear in carrying out the task you assigned and what was not?
4. What unexpected challenges arose for you that prompted you to pause, learn something new, or return to a previous step?
5. Which parts of the work were surprisingly hard or time consuming?
6. What tricks or shortcuts did you discover along the way that could also benefit your students?
7. What would you change about the assignment now that you've tried it yourself?

A teacher shares with a class her own models of project pages and explains the challenges and strategies she used in creating them.

Photo credit: Ron Berger

some other way. The important thing is that students themselves know and own what phases of a project are due when and how to manage their time between these benchmarks so that they can stay on track with critique and revision. This means that the timeline/calendar of work must be public: it can't just live in your plan book. It works best when the class as a whole reflects together on their progress relative to the timeline. In many cases, students can help to build and revise the timeline. Video Spotlight 4.1 highlights teachers using an interactive flow chart on a whiteboard to engage students in tracking their progress through the writing process.

Video Spotlight 4.1: Using a Flow Chart to Keep Student on Track
https://vimeo.com/313436214

In this video, two sixth-grade teachers from King Middle School in Portland, Maine, help keep their students on track as they write paragraphs about individual heroes. This video is excerpted from the first of a two-part video entitled *Scaffolding Research-Based Writing with Sixth Graders*. If you are interested in the full Part 1 video, you can view it at: vimeo.com/127193559. Part 2 is featured in Video Spotlight 4.7.

Video Reflection Questions
1. How did the strategy of moving their sticky notes through the flow chart outlined on the whiteboard support both the teachers and the students to stay on track and on target?
2. How did the graphic organizers help students stay on track and on target?
3. What evidence did you see of students being leaders of their own learning?

Check Yourself Checklist

Planning for Quality Work Checklist

Review the list of assignments you have planned for an upcoming unit and check off all that apply:

❏ There is a healthy balance of category 1 (simply practice), category 2 (neat, thoughtful, organized, but perhaps just one draft), and category 3 assignments ("museum quality" refined and polished through drafts). (Note: These categories are discussed in Challenge #1.)

❏ I have identified and planned for all of the incremental skills students will need to *practice* in order to be successful with category 3 assignments.

❏ I have scheduled enough time for practice, revision, and polish.

❏ (If you are a secondary teacher) I have conferred with my colleagues so that all of our category 3 assignments are not piling up on students at the same time.

❏ I have built in systems and structures that allow students to be independent and take ownership of their success.

(This checklist is available in the online toolbox at http://www.wiley.com/go/lotolcompanion.)

Learning Target 2: I can choose engaging and effective models to help students understand what "good" looks like in that genre of work.

 Challenge #3: I'm not sure what good work looks like.

TRY THIS: LEARN THE ATTRIBUTES OF HIGH-QUALITY WORK

In order to help students produce high-quality work, it will be important to first ground yourself in a clear definition of high quality. Figure 4.3 features EL Education's Attributes of High-Quality Student Work.

As you review the Attributes of High-Quality Student Work, consider the following questions:

1. What is an example of a "complex" piece of work created by one of your students or one of your colleague's students? Defend your answer.

Figure 4.3 Attributes of high-quality student work
SOURCE: This document is available in the online toolbox at http://www.wiley.com/go/lotolcompanion.

The descriptions below are intended to provide educators with common vision and terminology as they engage in using student work to improve teaching and learning, be it shorter task work or products that are the result of long-term projects. These attributes are not intended to constrain a conversation about quality, and not all descriptors must be present for a piece of work to be high quality. They are intended to provoke deeper conversation and act as a starting point for formulating a shared understanding of quality.

Complexity

Complex work is rigorous: it aligns with or exceeds the expectations defined by grade-level standards and includes higher-order thinking by challenging students to apply, analyze, evaluate, and create during daily instruction and throughout longer projects.

Complex work often connects to the big concepts that undergird disciplines or unite disciplines.

Complex work prioritizes transfer of understanding to new contexts.

Complex work prioritizes consideration of multiple perspectives.

Complex work may incorporate students' application of higher order literacy skills through the use of complex text and evidence-based writing and speaking.

Craftsmanship

Well-crafted work is done with care and precision. Craftsmanship requires attention to accuracy, detail, and beauty.

In every discipline and domain, well-crafted work should be beautiful work in conception and execution. In short tasks or early drafts of work, craftsmanship may be present primarily in thoughtful ideas, but not in polished presentation; for long-term projects, craftsmanship requires perseverance to refine work in conception, conventions, and presentation, typically through multiple drafts or rehearsals with critique from others.

Authenticity

Authentic work demonstrates the original, creative thinking of students – authentic personal voice and ideas – rather than simply showing that students can follow directions or fill in the blanks.

Authentic work often uses formats and standards from the professional world, rather than artificial school formats (e.g., students create a book review for a local newspaper instead of a book report for the teacher).

Authentic work often connects academic standards with real-world issues, controversies, and local people and places.

Authenticity gives purpose to work; the work matters to students and ideally contributes to a larger community as well. When possible, it is created for and shared with an audience beyond the classroom.

2. Which aspect of complexity is most difficult for your students to achieve? What are your students' greatest barriers to producing high-quality work in this aspect of complexity? How can you help them overcome that barrier?

3. How do you bring in multiple perspectives to your assignments?

4. In your discipline or unit of study, what concepts need to be rendered with accuracy and detail?

5. What does "beautiful in conception and execution" mean to you?

6. What formats and standards from the professional world can students at your grade level follow?

7. What authentic audience would make the work purposeful for your students?

TRY THIS: DISCUSS STUDENT WORK WITH COLLEAGUES AND ANALYZE "WHAT'S GOOD"

For many of us, it's one thing to read and comprehend the Attributes of High-Quality Work as a stand-alone document and a whole different thing to articulate what's good in an actual piece of student work. It's important to note that we are not using models to encourage students to copy actual text from other students, but rather to notice and name the strategies and features that create quality within that format. Those strategies are not just *fine* to copy, but also *smart* to copy. Seeing many models and having the opportunity to talk with colleagues about "what's good" in the model will help you develop the language for discussing them with students. It will also help clarify what you and your colleagues value in student work. See teachers in action doing just this in Video Spotlight 4.2.

Video Spotlight 4.2: What Does Good Work Look Like?
https://vimeo.com/313883577

In this video, teachers in a Harvard University workshop led by Ron Berger called "What Does Good Work Look Like?" look together at actual student projects (all of which are available on the website Models of Excellence: The Center for High-Quality Student Work)[1] and discuss where they see quality in the work.

Video Reflection Questions
1. How do these brief presentations of student work inspire these teachers to get excited about students' capacity to create beautiful work?
2. Was your own education like the train trip through Europe without stops that Ron Berger describes? What kinds of projects will help you change the itinerary for your own students?

Now that you have learned more about the Attributes of High-Quality Student Work and seen a video of teachers analyzing student work, we invite you to do the same. Figure 4.4 is a Quality Work protocol designed to walk you and a group of colleagues through a thoughtful process of analyzing student work. (Note: See the next section Try This: Use a Model to Inspire Your Students for more information about finding models of student work.)

This protocol is deep – it is designed to take 2.5 hours. When you have the time for it, we are sure you will find it worthwhile, as there are few ways we know of that are better than this protocol to engage teachers

---

[1] https://modelsofexcellence.eleducation.org

Figure 4.4 The Quality Work protocol

SOURCE: The complete version of this document is available in the online toolbox at http://www.wiley.com/go/lotolcompanion.

Overview

EL Education is distinguished in the educational landscape by an explicit focus on high-quality student work as an essential part of student achievement. One reason that others avoid this topic is that it is messy. Quality cannot be easily defined and quantified. EL believes, however, that when schools regularly engage in the difficult process of working together to define, recognize, and analyze quality work (and even quantify when possible), the results are positive and powerful. When a student is done with schooling, she is judged for the rest of her life not primarily by her ability to perform on tests, but by the quality of person she is and the quality of work she does. Developing an ethic of quality in students is vital.

EL Education has worked closely with Harvard's Steve Seidel, who is an international expert in the field of quality in general and quality student work in particular. After over a decade of work as a part of Harvard's Qualities of Quality Project, Steve shares with us two key points:

1. Quality is best viewed not as an end-state, but as a discussion. A stellar symphony orchestra or sports team can only keep quality high by constantly analyzing and critiquing—discussing quality during rehearsals and practices and after performances. If the analysis and discussion stops, quality will deteriorate. EL Education schools engage in this discussion about quality through a variety of routines and structures by looking at student work together, planning curriculum that addresses issues of quality, engaging in regular critique with students, etc.

2. It is not possible to create an effective single rubric for "high-quality work." Rubrics are useful when they name concrete, specific features that students and teachers can recognize in work. A useful rubric for a first grade Haiku will look very different from a rubric for a high school physics lab report. Across grade levels, disciplines and formats (e.g., geometry proof; book review), specifics differ and matter. We can, however, generalize attributes of quality students can aspire toward in any piece of work, which can be used to calibrate a general sense of quality and recognize patterns and trends in student work, and for that reason we use EL Education's *Attributes of High-Quality Work* as an anchor document in this protocol.

Purposes

- Engage in discussion to develop a shared vision of quality work characterized by complexity, craftsmanship and authenticity.
- Identify patterns related to quality across student work to inform goal setting and action steps Like an instructional learning walk, this protocol provides participants with the opportunity to view many examples quickly and search for patterns of strength and areas for growth based on common criteria.
- Create a "body of evidence" that a school can use to reflect on how student work has changed and improved over time. This body of evidence is also what schools reference when applying to become a credentialed EL Education school.

(cont. online)

deeply in understanding what good work looks like. Many schools in the EL Education network engage staff members in this protocol at least twice each year. If the time involved is prohibitive for your school, read through the protocol and decide how you can trim its length while still maintaining its core elements.

 Challenge #4: I don't know where to find good models for my students. Where do I look? What do I look for?

TRY THIS: USE A MODEL TO INSPIRE YOUR STUDENTS

You can talk about what a good comparative essay, book review, or lab report looks like, but if students have never actually seen one, it's just a bunch of words to them. They need a picture in their mind of what a good example looks like. But finding strong models can be a challenge if you don't know where to look. Sometimes teachers have models from former students or from teacher colleagues, but that is not always the case. EL Education and Harvard Graduate School of Education have selected and curated hundreds of models of excellent Pre-K–12 student work on the website Models of Excellence: The Center for High-Quality Student Work. All the work is free and can be downloaded in full or in part. Having a strong model like those available on this site means that much of the work is done for you – you don't have to go searching for a strong model, and students will be able to picture what a good example looks like.

You can lead your class in teasing out the aspects of quality that you and your students recognize in the work, but even apart from this, the model alone can provide vision and direction for students. For example, at Meadow Brook High School in Chesterfield County, Virginia, high school freshmen were involved in a project on personal identity. They wrote short autobiographical essays and created pointillist self-portraits and then used those pieces for exhibitions and discussions to learn about each other. Because drawing a self-portrait is challenging for many students, the process was scaffolded by using digital photographs and teaching students how to transform those photos into pointillist portraits using fine-point markers. Most importantly, they used models to set a standard for quality, and models can make all the difference. Notice the power of the self-portrait in Figure 4.5 (available on the Models of Excellence website), and imagine how it would help to inspire students to strive for quality work.

Models also serve to inspire students. In the video featured in Video Spotlight 4.3, Ron Berger tells the story of how he captured the attention of skeptical students simply by showing (not telling) them models of home blueprints designed by students. Instead of explaining the math skills students would need to create this product or talking about the knowledge architects must have to do this work, he simply allowed students to explore and marvel at the creativity and innovation in the model.

Figure 4.5 Pointillist self-portrait by ninth-grader

Video Spotlight 4.3: Inspiring Passion-Driven Education with Yo-Yo Ma and Ron Berger
https://vimeo.com/313883577

This video, featuring Ron Berger's presentation at Yo-Yo-Ma's Passion-Driven Learning Conference at Harvard Graduate School of Education, interlaced with footage of Yo-Yo Ma performing at the conference, explains how models alone can motivate students.

Video Reflection Questions
1. How did the models inspire the eighth-grade students to be "passion driven"?
2. What types of project models would inspire your students to tackle skill building they may have thus far been resistant to or that may be challenging for them?

TRY THIS: SEARCH FOR MODELS WITH SPECIFIC STRENGTHS

Often, as teachers, we give similar assignments year after year, but don't think to collect models of the best work we encounter to use as models with current students or in subsequent years. Written work can be photocopied; posters, artwork, and three-dimensional work can be scanned, color-copied, or photographed; and performances can be captured on video. If you develop a habit of building archives – digital or physical – of student work models, you will be ready in a range of situations to give students a clear picture of what quality looks like and sounds like.

The work does not need to be perfect. It only needs to be strong in one aspect. An essay with a great opening line or concluding paragraph, for example, can be a powerful example you can use to focus on that feature. A clever approach to a mathematical problem might not be written neatly and clearly, but the solution may be illuminating.

Consider for example the common assignment of a history paper. Most of us completed a research paper in this style during our time as a student, perhaps at a number of different grade levels. It's a worthy assignment, but the resulting papers are not always compelling in style, insight, or scholarship. Most students have never seen a compelling history paper written by a student and can't even imagine one, so they have no idea what to aim for. The history paper featured in Figure 4.6,[2] written by an eighth-grade student, can be a powerful tool to change that pattern. When we have used parts of this paper as a model with teachers or high school students in a critique lesson, they are so intrigued that they demand to read more, are excited to finish the paper, and want to share it with others.

What Makes This Paper a Strong Model?

There are many things that make the paper, "Revolutionary Rum," exemplary. The author presents an original historical thesis – a new idea – for the primary cause of what is arguably the most important event in American history: the Revolutionary War. Despite the fact that almost every student and teacher already has a firm opinion about this, hardened by textbooks and lectures, many readers of the paper are so impressed by her argument that they immediately question their thinking and feel she just may be right. The argument is not just fresh: it is remarkably well framed and evidenced. The quality of the research and writing sets a high bar for high school students, or even college students. And her idea is provocative: *rum* was the cause of the American Revolution!

---

[2] You can read more about Revolutionary Rum, and download the full 23-page paper, on the Models of Excellence website (https://modelsofexcellence.eleducation.org/writings/revolutionary-rum-economic-exploration-ignited-american-revolution). You can also find the full paper in our online toolbox.

Figure 4.6 Revolutionary Rum
SOURCE: The complete version of this document is available in the online toolbox at http://www.wiley.com/go/lotolcompanion.

Revolutionary Rum

During Paul Revere's renowned ride from Boston to Lexington warning John Hancock and Samuel Adams of the British approach, he stopped to drink a rum toddy in a Medford, Massachusetts tavern. Many would assume his drink of choice would be "Liberty Tea", a substitute for real tea made from tisanes and consumed in protest of British tyranny.[1] The dumping of British East India Company tea during the Boston Tea Party is recognized as the first purposeful revolutionary act by the English colonies. Because of this deed, tea is seen as the revolutionary drink, but it was rum that incited the American Revolution. Rum, an alcoholic beverage made from molasses and cultivated from sugarcane in tropical regions, initiated New England's exploration of a self-reliant economy. When Britain began to tax the rum trade, the colonies' most lucrative asset, colonial resentment grew, fostering contempt towards Parliament. The colonists encountered a mother country excessively regulating them, while Parliament encountered disobedient colonies. Attempting to gain control of her settlements, Parliament taxed colonial foreign trade, initiating an exchange of regulation for rebellion between the motherland and the colonies. Therefore, British regulation of the rum trade was *the* spark that ignited the rebellion which founded our nation.

Rum's influence on the founding of America arose from Europe's desire to colonize the New World. Colonialism is the practice of domination by one country subjugating another region for monetary or influential gain.[2] During this period, European countries saw colonialism as the avenue to power. As high speed ships became readily available, Europeans found that moving

---

[1] Liberty Tea was made from tisanes and was used as a tea substitute in the boycott against the Tea Act. Tisanes are spices, herbs, or other plant material besides tea leaves.
Perry, Dr. Leonard. "Liberty Tea." Liberty Tea. University of Vermont, n.d. Web. 12 Apr. 2016.
<http://pss.uvm.edu/ppp/articles/liberty.html>.
[2] Stanford University. Stanford University, 09 May 2006. Web. 13 Feb. 2016
<http://plato.stanford.edu/entries/colonialism/>.
Russia, the Netherlands, Spain, England, and France were all trying to use colonialism to build their empires.
Lesson of Our Land. Indian Land Tenure Foundation, 2016. Web. 20 Feb. 2016.
<http://www.lessonsofourland.org/lessons/european-colonization-around-world>.

(*cont. online*)

But what makes this paper a particularly useful model is that it also demonstrates specific strategies and structures that students can borrow right away to make their own papers stronger, such as:

- The bibliography is eye-opening
  - Every entry is annotated in terms of its personal contribution to the author's knowledge and its contribution to the book. Just reading this 10-page bibliography gives you a clear sense of the author as a thinker and historian. The connection between what the author read, what she learned, and how she used that knowledge (or chose not to use it) in the paper is transparently explained. The bibliography is actually fascinating to read: how often is that the case?
  - The balance of primary sources and secondary sources, and the amount and types of sources used, gives the reader a vision of how strong historical research is actually done. She includes a remarkable number of books, articles, foundational government documents, and web resources from a wide range of sources, used for information, quotes, graphics, and general background knowledge. A deep degree of scholarship is evident just from the scope of the bibliography.

- The writing is fresh and engaging – like an engrossing historical novel – without sacrificing professional scholarship. Just consider page one:
  - It opens with a great hook – the first sentence reads: "During Paul Revere's renowned ride from Boston to Lexington warning John Hancock and Samuel Adams of the British approach, he stopped to drink a rum toddy in a Medford, Massachusetts tavern." Wait, what? The famous midnight ride of Paul Revere? He stopped to drink rum? Could that be true? It would make sense if this were a novel, but in a history paper. . .
  - Her thesis is bold and clear: "Because of this deed (the Boston Tea Party), tea is seen as the revolutionary drink, but it was rum that incited the American Revolution."
  - The text has a lyric, literary quality: "The colonists encountered a mother country excessively regulating them, while Parliament encountered disobedient colonies." This is historically true, and at the same time the language evokes a familiar family analogy, resonant in the lives of many adolescent readers.
  - The citation footnotes on page one are thoughtfully used and professionally written.

TRY THIS: CHOOSE A WEAK MODEL THAT ILLUMINATES COMMON MISTAKES OR MISCONCEPTIONS

Is it ever a good idea to show students a poor model of student work? The answer to this frequently asked question is yes, but only under careful conditions. If this strategy is used carelessly, it can damage the classroom culture of ethical, respectful character. It can send the wrong message about how we should treat each other and speak about each other's work. Following are some guidelines for using weak student work as a model:

- The work must be anonymous – from another school or a distant year, without an identified author. Students should not be able to trace who created it, and the author of the work should not be able to recognize that his or her work is being used.

Figure 4.7 A weak model of student work: Survey data conclusion statement
SOURCE: This document is available in the online toolbox at http://www.wiley.com/go/lotolcompanion.

"In the ____ School Community, the eighth grade students sent out surveys based on voting and people's opinion about voting. One of the questions stated in the survey was 'Is it important to vote?' A whole group, 93%, which is 96 people, said it was important to vote. Twenty-nine men said it was important to vote and that was 85%. There were 67 females that stated it was important to vote and that rounded off to be 97%. The results have been stated according to the question and the data.

The conclusions that can be drawn from this data is that only 29% of men said it was important to vote and 97% of women said it was important to vote. As you can see that 12% more women believes that voting is important than men. Women probably think voting is more important than men do because many men are probably not into voting. Especially young men, they probably think drug selling is more important. Therefore the conclusion is that more women think that voting is important than men."

- A teacher-created model with intentionally embedded errors, presented as your own work or as an example of what a student might do, is a good approach.

- The work must be critiqued with kindness and respect. Even if it has glaring and perhaps even comical errors, if teachers and students make fun of the work (even if it is teacher work) it sends the message that it is okay to ridicule the work of others.

It is important to understand also that most weak student work is not instructive – it just shows lack of effort, and students see enough of that kind of work every day. To be helpful for student learning, the flawed work must demonstrate common misconceptions or mistakes that students may be able to recognize and discuss and hence avoid making those same mistakes themselves.

For example, a common activity that is used in schools at almost every grade level is to ask students to create a survey connected to their studies, administer that survey to others, and then to chart and draw conclusions from the resulting data. A common challenge for students is to understand what conclusions they can actually draw from the data they collect. Consider the excerpt, adapted from an eighth-grade social studies project, shown in Figure 4.7. This conclusion statement was accompanied by a bar chart.

The example in Figure 4.7 is full of errors and misconceptions that could be helpful to analyze and discuss with students to help clarify what would be expected in a report of this type. Some of the errors are simply careless (e.g., using the number 29 as a percent in paragraph two, instead of 29 men/85% as it is in paragraph one). Some errors are in grammatical conventions in the writing. Some errors are stylistic consistency (e.g., writing out numbers versus using digits; listing the "n" [the sample size] first or the percentage first). Paying attention to all of these details matters in a quality report.

But the most important concept to discuss here is what we can actually conclude from a sample of 29 men and 67 women who answered this question. What more information might we want that this report does not make clear (e.g., Who are these men and women; how were they chosen; under what conditions did they fill out this survey)? Many students reading this example are able to recognize that the author went far beyond the data in his or her speculative inference, but it is not so easy for most students to explain how to properly word a conclusion for this data in a clear and valid way.

TRY THIS: USE MODELS THAT DEMONSTRATE MULTIPLE PERSPECTIVES AND APPROACHES, ESPECIALLY IN MATHEMATICS

Using models of student work or professional work that represent a range of perspectives is a powerful way to open the eyes of students to thinking more critically and creatively about their work. One particular use of models of multiple perspectives is to engage students in analyzing different approaches to mathematical problems.

One of the challenges in teaching and learning mathematics is that many problems have a single correct solution, and racing to that solution is often seen as the point of student work – as opposed to understanding the concepts embedded in the problem. When that is the case, the fastest students or groups win the race. Others are often left behind, and almost everyone suffers in terms of developing deep conceptual understanding.

One way to address this issue is to provide students, individually, in groups, or as whole class, with multiple approaches to solving the same problem – without a clarification of what is correct in process and solution. This approach makes the task too complex to be a race. Students must struggle to understand what other students are thinking, understand the concepts well enough to judge what is correct and what is helpful, and then articulate that thinking in words, diagrams, and symbols.

The Mathematics Assessment Project[3] hosts a free online resource of mathematical problems for secondary students that includes a set of actual student solutions for the problems – correct and incorrect – with different approaches and levels of understanding. The "Formative Assessment Lessons" provided on the site include a protocol for analyzing these solutions in student groups. For example, one eighth-grade problem asks students to estimate the amount of matchsticks that can be created from a single pine tree, given the dimensions for each. The lesson includes three different student solutions to using mathematical models, diagrams, and equations to reach a reasonable solution, each with its unique insights and confusions.[4]

These examples and others like them, including your own students' work, can be used as *models* of problem solving to teach mathematical concepts. Review Video Spotlight 4.4 to see how one teacher lifts up the models her own students create to analyze important fourth-grade mathematical concepts.

Video Spotlight 4.4: Using a Problem-Based Task with Fourth-Graders to Create Deep Engagement in Math
https://vimeo.com/117861347

In this video, a fourth-grade teacher at Two Rivers Public Charter School in Washington, DC, guides her students to explain their own thinking through models of a variety of solutions.

Video Reflection Questions
1. How does the teacher support students to ask questions about their peers' model math solutions?
2. How does the debrief help students clarify their understanding of what makes a good math solution?

---

[3] http://map.mathshell.org
[4] You can access this problem at http://map.mathshell.org/download.php?fileid=1691

If you are teaching math, test-drive your next lesson by anticipating multiple possible student approaches to solving a problem and possible resulting solutions – correct and incorrect. Then, *after* the lesson, gather and sort students' work into the various strategies to assess next steps for different groups. This process will also provide models of student work you can use with other classes or in future years.

Check Yourself Checklist

Choosing a Model Checklist

When deciding on the right model to use with your students, check off as many of the following as possible:

❏   It sets a high but realistic bar that my students can aim for.

❏   It invites wonder and analysis; it will inspire students to create.

❏   It is intriguing and compelling: students will appreciate looking at it closely.

❏   It demonstrates types of thinking I want my students to do.

❏   It models unusual commitment to detail, accuracy, and craftsmanship.

❏   It demonstrates specific techniques I would like my students to use.

❏   It shows a unique approach to questions we are trying to answer.

❏   It demonstrates standards or expectations of a specific real-world format.

(This checklist is available in the online toolbox at http://www.wiley.com/go/lotolcompanion.)

Learning Target 3: I can conduct a critique lesson that motivates students and gives them concrete takeaways they can use in their work

Challenge #5: I am not sure where to begin with a critique lesson.

TRY THIS: BEGIN WITH A FEW KEY CHOICES

Once you have chosen a strong model, you are ready to plan the details of a critique lesson. As is often the case, the devil is in the details, and different types of critique lessons are appropriate in different situations. Usually you or a collaborating teacher will be leading the critique lesson. However, sometimes you may want to invite an outside expert from the school or the professional world to conduct the lesson. If you bring in an outside expert, you, or ideally your students, will need to teach the expert your classroom norms and protocols for critique. Once you have decided on who will lead the critique lesson, consider these three different types of critique lessons:

1. A **catch and release** critique: While students are working, you circulate and look for strong *student models of specific features of the work*. Periodically you pause to "catch" the class for a brief, clarifying critique of work that is currently being created, and then release students back to the work.

2. A **gallery critique**: Lots of work is posted on the wall or on tables, or short excerpts of many written pieces are viewed together. The models for a gallery critique could be from current students, from models created by anonymous students in a previous year, or from the professional world.

3. An **in-depth critique** of a single piece (or a few pieces) chosen ahead of time: This is typically student-created, but could also be from the professional world.

Video Spotlight 4.5 features a video that illustrates a series of critique lessons – a gallery critique led by a teacher, a peer critique, and a critique lesson led by an expert – as second-grade students create detailed scientific illustrations of snakes.

Video Spotlight 4.5: Inspiring Excellence Part 4: Using Models and Critiques to Create Works of Quality
https://vimeo.com/85779855

This video features second-graders at Conservatory Lab Charter School in Boston critiquing a model of scientific drawings. It shows how even young children can engage in critique sessions to learn very specific strategies for creating strong illustrations.

Video Reflection Questions
1. How does the teacher break down the illustration process into specific aspects of quality?
2. How does she leverage whole-class critique, peer critique, and expert critique to bolster students' understanding of quality?
3. What strategies does she use to support students to be leaders of their own learning?

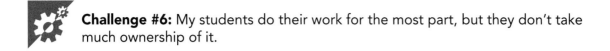

Challenge #6: My students do their work for the most part, but they don't take much ownership of it.

TRY THIS: DESIGN A CRITIQUE LESSON THAT INVITES OWNERSHIP, INQUIRY, AND UNDERSTANDING

Of all the feedback we've received from teachers since the publication of *Leaders of Their Own Learning*, among the most frequent is that it's hard to facilitate effective critique lessons that motivate all students to do high-quality work. Our most viewed video, with millions of views, is *Austin's Butterfly*, which illustrates Ron Berger's critique lesson with elementary school students discussing a first-grader's progress on his scientific illustration of a butterfly: https://eleducation.org/resources/austins-butterfly.

A good critique lesson is empowering for students: it amplifies students' voices and unique perspectives and honors their membership in a community of creative experts. You don't want to spoon-feed your own critique to your students. You want to get them involved. A lesson that engages every student in looking deeply at the model and sharing their insights will ratchet up students' ownership of the lesson and their commitment to using their learning to improve their own work.

The respectful and strategic teacher-student dialogue of a good critique lesson is perhaps the hardest thing to master. For example, when students critique a model, it's fine to slightly reword student comments to make them more clear and useful. When a student offers a grain of something important, build on it yourself (e.g., "Jalen, what I hear you saying is that the opening grabs you – has a good hook – is that right? That is an important observation! I'll write that on our anchor chart."). If students notice that Anton has used an especially efficient strategy in a math problem, label that "Anton's approach." Forever afterward, the suggestion to "try Anton's approach" will make Anton beam with pride, and it will be a shorthand way for other students to easily remember the strategy. Also, if students have missed something important in the work that you wish they would address, bring it up yourself as a question and prompt them to name it (e.g., "Did any of you notice what Madison did here in this part. . .?"). Table 4.3 shows sample sentence stems for various purposes during a critique. The table is in no way

Table 4.3 Sentence stems for encouraging engaging critique lessons

Purpose	Sample Sentence Stems
To restate a student's comment using more precise language or vocabulary	• Destiny, what I hear you saying is that. . . • Chris, am I correct in saying that you are suggesting. . . • Karina, there is a scientific word for exactly what you are describing. It is. . . • Terrific, Aidan! In English grammar we call that a. . .
To engage a particular student or make a student feel proud	• Sergio, what do you think about what she did in this section. . . • Wow, I was so impressed with the improvement by. . . • We saw this same good idea from Jalen last week. . . • We could call this "Kristina's Strategy." • Brianne, your eye is so sharp! Can you say more about. . .
To ensure a point is made that students haven't yet made themselves	• Your comments made me think of. . .. • Great! Another feature we could name is. . . • I love these observations! I want to add. . . • There is one more thing we all need to consider. . .

complete; we encourage you to add to it with your own favorite phrasing that will work best for you and your students.

The best way to build understanding and ownership with students is to ask them questions that invite them to examine the model like real investigators. A lesson that ignites curiosity and students' "need to know" engages students because they understand that in order to do their own work, they need to understand how the model represents quality, and in what dimensions. Model-dependent questions – questions that push students to identify the exact words or numbers or features of the model that show an answer to the question – are key. It's also important that all students feel accountable to probing the model and answering the questions. By summarizing the strategies that students notice on an anchor chart along the way, you also create a helpful resource for students to refer back to as they do their own work. Video Spotlight 4.6 features two videos that illuminate the power of critique lessons.

Video Spotlight 4.6: (a) A Group Critique Lesson
https://vimeo.com/44053703

(b) Ron Berger: Teachers as Learners
https://www.youtube.com/watch?v=ulG65R6hH6Y&app=desktop

In the first video, Ron Berger leads an in-depth critique lesson with third-grade students from Presumpscot Elementary School in Portland, Maine. With guidance from Berger, students use a piece of student writing as a model from which to identify criteria for a quality story.

In the second video, filmed at High Tech High in San Diego, Berger is interviewed about the power of models and critique and the importance of a safe classroom culture for critique. This video was produced by High Tech High.

Video Reflection Questions

1. What phrases and questions did you hear Ron Berger use in the first lesson that caused students to become enthusiastically engaged in dissecting this piece of writing.
2. How would you describe the role that the model played in the critique lesson in the first video? How might the critique lesson have been different if students had been reading a published story (i.e., not written by another student)?
3. Did the interview with Ron Berger in the second video make you think differently about the use of models in school? Describe any insights you may have had.

TRY THIS: USE A CRITERIA LIST INSTEAD OF A RUBRIC

Sometimes a critique lesson is an excellent launch pad for creating a rubric with students. Connecting the rubric criteria explicitly to the points elicited during the critique lesson will significantly increase student understanding of and engagement with the rubric. However, much of the work in creating a rubric is spent in the time-consuming details of creating the gradations of partial success (i.e., what distinguishes the category "exceeding expectations" from "meets," "approaching," and "not yet"). Often there is no need to involve students in that work, and it is not the best use of their time. Indeed, if what you need is a list of features that represent good work in that genre in order to guide students to create high-quality work, a rubric may not be needed at all. Creating a criteria list is simpler, clearer, and more feasible. A criteria list is basically the highest column on a rubric – the "exceeding expectations" category.

When analyzing models of student work, creating a list of the strong qualities gleaned from the examples is what builds that criteria list. It can be posted on a chart or turned into a print or digital document that students can use as they work. It is not usually as simple as a checklist – though checklists are also useful – because the criteria may be nuanced and require judgment or discussion (e.g., while a checklist may say "bibliography includes at least five sources," a criteria list for a quality bibliography may have descriptors such as "balances primary and secondary sources," "gives evidence for the credibility of online sources," "uses sources that the professionals in the field use").

There is also a hybrid version of the criteria list/rubric, as in Figure 4.8, a Public Service Announcement (PSA) criteria list, which also functions as a rubric. Students found their original rubric, which spelled out all levels of success, to be unwieldy, with too many criteria and too many gradations of quality. As a result, their teacher instead decided to illuminate the same criteria for quality through precisely worded learning targets that are closely connected to their required writing standards. Teachers shared this tool with students early in the project as they unpacked the learning targets. Students then used it as a reflection tool and to guide their peer critique during successive drafts when writing their arguments.

Figure 4.8 Social activism PSA criteria list with learning targets from Irving A. Robbins Middle School in Farmington, Connecticut
SOURCE: This document is available in the online toolbox at http://www.wiley.com/go/lotolcompanion.

Standards and Corresponding Criteria		Evidence	E	M	N	B
STANDARD *Research and Inquiry* **Score:**	**LEARNING TARGETS** **I can** conduct a short research project to answer questions (including self-generated questions).	**Generating Questions**				
	I can draw on multiple sources to focus my inquiry.	**Research Notes** **Works Cited**				
STANDARD *Speaking and Listening* **Score:**	**I can** integrate multimedia and visual displays into a presentation to clarify information and add interest.	**PSA**				
	I can present a memorable concept which emphasizes key points in a focused, coherent manner with relevant evidence, valid reasoning, and well-chosen details.	**PSA**				
STANDARD *Speaking and Listening* **Score:**	**I can** deliver the presentation with appropriate eye contact, adequate volume, and clear pronunciation.	**Presentation**				
	I can present the problem clearly by emphasizing the key points and well-chosen details with valid reasoning.	**Presentation**				
Feedback:						

Exceeds 95 + **Meets** 90. . .85. . .80 **Near** 75. . .70 **Below** 65. . .60 **Lacking** 50
Created by Bonnie Frascadore, English language arts teacher, Irving A. Robbins Middle School

Learning Target 4: I can structure descriptive feedback so that it helps students see their strengths and how to improve their work.

 Challenge # 7: Giving students feedback takes too much time.

TRY THIS: MASTER THE ART OF THE CONFERENCE

Especially if you have multiple classes of students every day, providing written feedback on dozens of papers can easily consume an entire weekend. In-class conferences are a strong alternative, but making time to conference with every student requires careful scheduling and practice at divvying up time effectively and equitably. To make that equation more complicated, when students are in different phases of the writing process, they may also need different kinds and amounts of feedback. One way to navigate this challenge is to conference with students on a "need to know" basis – optimizing when your feedback will have the greatest impact on the next draft. Consider giving feedback on students' written plans rather than on their first drafts. Consider conferencing on second drafts after students have received feedback from a peer on the big ideas in their first drafts. Once you've determined *when* is the right time to conference with students, these questions will help you determine *how* to proceed.

- How many students can I effectively conference with in the time that I have?

- How can I structure the task and work time so that all students are engaged?

- How can I prioritize the order of conferences so that students receive feedback when they need it most?

- How can I focus my conferences so that students leave with a sense of direction and purpose?

Furthermore, because students often need very specific and very different kinds of feedback, this is an excellent time to invite a support teacher, knowledgeable parent, expert, or other adult to provide additional conference support. In Video Spotlight 4.7, return to King Middle School in Portland, Maine, for the second part of Scaffolding Research-Based Writing with Sixth-Graders to see how two teachers work in parallel to ensure that all 80 of their students get the feedback they need to produce a strong piece of writing.

 Video Spotlight 4.7: Scaffolding Research-Based Writing with Sixth-Graders, Part 2: Staying on Track and on Target
https://vimeo.com/127193596

In the second part of Scaffolding Research-Based Writing with Sixth-Graders, two teachers structure their writing lessons so that students who need one-on-one conferences with them get the time they need. Students also provide each other with peer feedback based on rubrics they have cocreated and of which they feel ownership and deep understanding.

 Video Reflection Questions
1. How do these teachers keep the conferences with their 80 students focused and short?
2. What benefit does the status flag have for both the teachers and the students?
3. What makes the peer conferences so successful?

After conferencing with several students, a Catch and Release Critique Lesson (which we introduced in Learning Target 3, Challenge #5) might be a good next step. This kind of brief, in-the-moment critique lesson would allow you to address a common issue that has arisen as you have conferred with students. It is a great way to give helpful feedback to the whole class before you proceed with individual conferences.

 Challenge #8: I give verbal and written feedback to students all the time, and they don't seem to learn from it. They continue to have the same weaknesses in their work.

TRY THIS: USE YOUR FEEDBACK TO IMPROVE *FUTURE* WORK (NOT THE CURRENT WORK)

Think back to when you were a student yourself. Your teacher gave you assignments, and you probably just wanted to get them completed and accepted as good work, or at least passable work. She marked up your paper, made some comments, and you changed what she asked for so that she was satisfied. If you had weaknesses in certain conventions or grammatical structures, in framing your thesis or writing a strong conclusion, for example, fixing this particular paper and getting it accepted was still your real focus. The critique did not launch you on a personal mission to address your areas of weakness as a writer.

But that is exactly what we really need critique to do for students. As teachers, we act as if this assignment, and getting it right, is what matters. But in truth, the assignment doesn't matter at all unless it teaches something new. Just getting a paper or a math problem set corrected and acceptable is fairly meaningless. Instead, we need to use our critique time with students to help them discover and consider what they are struggling with and share ideas together of how they might improve. We want students to recognize and own the area they need to learn about and practice, to commit to improving their skills, and to create a plan with you about how they will improve and demonstrate their new learning.

For example, let's say you have a student whose written papers are painfully stilted. He follows the outline format and organizer you have given out but does so literally, with no voice or persuasive language. His essays read like this: "In this essay I will explain why ___. My first point is ___. The evidence I found for that is ___. My second point is ___. The evidence I found for that is ___. My conclusion is that ___." You have encouraged him in written comments on his papers, or verbally in conferences, to elaborate, to use detail, to vary his sentence structure and paragraph structure, but you get this same kind of essay each time. And this student is not the only one with this problem, just a more extreme example of what many students do, causing you to make similar comments on many student papers.

So, you change your tactics. You decide that getting these particular papers fixed is not the purpose of your comments on papers, or, if you have time, your conferences with students. Instead, you lead a critique lesson with the class, using an inspiring essay by an anonymous student that has the strengths that you wish their essays did. You analyze the strengths carefully, name them, and discuss with students how to borrow strategies from this paper. Then you ask each student to fill out an index card or a form in which they each commit to the strategies they will use in their next paper. Fixing their current papers is no longer important; creating a much-improved *next* paper is the goal.

When you receive your next set of essays, your written comments are based on the commitments that students have made: where did they succeed; what more could they do? If you have the time to conference one-to-one with targeted students or all students, you pull out their cards of improvement commitments and go through them carefully while looking at their essays. The conversations you have with students are no longer about meeting *your* expectations but about reaching goals that *they* set.

TRY THIS: BRING IN EXPERTS TO PROMOTE PROFESSIONAL THINKING AND VOCABULARY

Students have been getting feedback from their teachers ever since they started school. After a while, the teacher's voice in their heads may sound dull and uninspiring. By contrast, when experts from the community or professionals who make their living from the skills and themes that students are trying to learn come into your classroom, magic happens. Experts can teach your students how professionals think about your topic. They can demonstrate and coach students in the skills and vocabulary of the discipline. And students take expert feedback very seriously, especially if implementing it with care and determination will enable them to create something that looks and has the impact of professional work. The case study that follows illustrates the power of community experts.

Case Study

Enlisting Community Experts to Improve and Deepen Student Work at the Interdistrict School for Arts and Communication (ISAAC) in New London, Connecticut

When a group of 94 diverse sixth-grade students took on a challenging project to interview local refugees and immigrants and create a professional-quality book to honor their courage and their stories, they analyzed models of interviews, photographs, and books from the professional world. They looked at models created by other students, and they critiqued their own work continually in the process. They worked with an immigration lawyer to build expertise in the legal issues of immigration and refugee status. They worked with a professional photographer who taught the students photographic technique and the language of light and composition. And they worked with an expert from Yale medical school—a specialist who taught doctors how to interview patients about health histories, including patients who may be shy or not fluent in English—to build students' skills as interviewers and teach them the vocabulary of *listening*.

After they had learned from the professionals, ISAAC students invited feedback from the experts on their own work in progress. Then they went back to their own drafts and revised again and again. "We made mistakes, and we kept persevering," said one student. "We were responsible for sharing their story with the world, and we knew we had to be professional."

The result of this magnificent collaboration between community experts and powerfully engaged students was an award-winning interactive art exhibit that was exhibited in libraries, universities, art galleries, and the Connecticut Statehouse. The student work also culminated in a published book honoring the immigrants' stories with text and photographs—with the proceeds from book sales going to help the immigrants' lives. At this time, multiple immigrants have had the legal expenses for their green cards covered by book profits.

You can learn more about this impressive project, and how they used models, critique, and descriptive feedback, in an exhibit on the Models of Excellence website: https://modelsofexcellence.eleducation.org/tours/community-faces-4.

Students from ISAAC worked with an adjunct faculty member from Yale Medical School to learn interview skills.

Photo Credit: Mike Kuczenski

 Challenge #9: Peer conferencing feels like a waste of time. How do I help my students give and get high-quality feedback?

TRY THIS: TEACH STUDENTS WHAT KIND, SPECIFIC, AND HELPFUL FEEDBACK LOOKS LIKE AND SOUNDS LIKE

Learning to give and receive high-quality feedback is a skill that students can only develop in a culture that values respect, deep listening, and gratitude. When students perceive feedback as "coaching" rather than instructing or criticism, and when they are empowered to coach others, they gain confidence and competence. To foster a culture of coaching in your classroom, begin by teaching students how coaching sounds different from criticizing. "Kind, specific, and helpful" is a useful mantra to repeat often with your students, but students may not automatically know what these adjectives look like and sound like in action. At your next critique session, unpack these words with the following explanations:

1. **Be Kind:** Always treat others with dignity and respect. This means we never use words that are hurtful, including sarcasm.

2. **Be Specific:** Focus on particular strengths and weaknesses, rather than making general comments like "It's good" or "I like it." Provide insight into why it is good or what, specifically, you like about it.

3. **Be Helpful:** The goal is to positively contribute to the individual or the group, not to simply be heard. Echoing the thoughts of others or cleverly pointing out details that are irrelevant wastes time.

Table 4.4 Kind, specific, and helpful sentence stems

Criteria	What does this mean?	What does it look like?	What does it sound like?
Be kind	Always treat others with dignity and respect	Listening carefully	• "I like the way you have. . .because it meets these criteria." • "I can see you worked hard to. . ." • "I wonder. . ." • "This really helps me understand. . ."
Be specific	Focus on particular strengths and weaknesses	Identifying the parts that you think were done well using the criteria Identifying the parts that you think could be improved using the criteria	• "This part meets these criteria by. . ." • "I notice. . ." • "Remember when we learned about. . .? You could apply that here." • "Have you thought about adding/revising. . .in order to. . .?" • "I can't see evidence of this criterion in your work. Where do you think you could revise to show evidence of this criterion?"
Be helpful	Positively contribute to the individual or the group	Helping a peer identify where he or she can improve	• "Perhaps you could revise this. . . in order to improve. . ." • "If this were my work, I would. . ." • "As a first step, I suggest. . ." • "What would happen if. . ."

Use Table 4.4 as a starting point to co-create with your students an anchor chart for what kind, specific, and helpful feedback looks like and sounds like in your classroom. Depending on your students' age, language proficiency, and overall needs, your classroom anchor chart may look much different than what you see in Table 4.4 (e.g., you may include symbols or images in the "looks like" column; you may add a column to also include sentence stems in the home language of your students). There are no rules. The only criteria is that students have a helpful tool that will support them to give each other feedback that truly is kind, specific, and helpful and that helps them each improve their work.

TRY THIS: PROVIDE A CLEAR FOCUS OR A PROTOCOL FOR PEER CRITIQUE

For student coaching to be effective, students have to be (young) experts in the feature of the work that is the focus of coaching, and they need a clear structure for offering their critique in a way that is memorable and retraceable. For example, when art teacher Mary Ann Athens asked her students to create close-up oil pastel paintings of dragon eyes, she didn't simply say "give your partner some critique on his or her draft." If she had, many students would not have known how to be helpful. Instead, she led short lessons focused on drawing the iris of the eye, using Smaug from the *Lord of the Rings* film as a model. She showed them a model she herself had created, pointing out how the shape (round, pointy, pebble shaped, diamond shaped) and colors of the scales make the eyes engaging, mysterious, or scary. Then, when she asked students to pair up and give each other advice about how to improve the eyes in

Middle school students at Evergreen Community Charter School in Asheville, North Carolina, drew dragon eyes after studying the model on the left, drawn by art teacher Mary Ann Athens. On the right is a dragon eye drawn by a seventh-grade student, Aimee.

Photo credit: Mary Ann Athens

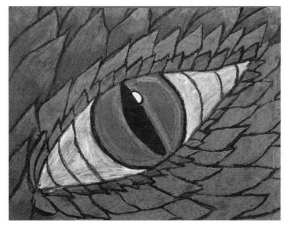

Photo credit: Mary Ann Athens

their drawings, they had many concrete and useful suggestions. They had, in a sense, become experts on dragon eyes.

A protocol that provides clear procedures, a focus for the critique, time frames, and accountability ensures all students are engaged and working collaboratively and productively to improve their own and each other's work. Video Spotlight 4.8 illustrates two protocols for leading peer feedback sessions that invite total participation and meaningful critique. Figure 4.9 is written version of a protocol featured in one of the videos, and Figure 4.10 is an additional protocol for peer feedback that can be used with pairs or small groups.

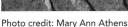

Video Spotlight 4.8: (a) Praise, Question, Suggestion
https://vimeo.com/84899365

(b) Using a Speed Dating Protocol to Think Critically about Writing
https://vimeo.com/124633818

The first video features the Praise, Question, Suggestion protocol. Eighth-grade students give each other kind, specific, and helpful feedback by offering praise, asking specific clarifying questions, and making suggestions that will help their partner make progress toward learning targets. The full Praise, Question, Suggestion protocol can be found in Figure 4.9.

The second video features a "speed dating protocol" to facilitate students offering each other specific feedback on a high-stakes writing assignment.

Video Reflection Questions
1. What structures are in place that support students to be kind, specific, and helpful in both of these videos?
2. What structures hold students accountable for giving productive feedback and for revision?

Purpose

This protocol can be used to offer critique and feedback in preparation for revision of work. It should be used after a draft of what will become a finished product is completed. This process will help students see what is working and then ask questions and offer suggestions, leading to revision and improvement. It is important for students to understand that the focus should be on offering feedback that is beneficial to the author. Explicit modeling is necessary for this protocol to be used successfully.

Materials

- Product descriptors and rubrics
- Revision checklist or questions
- Anchor chart for protocol norms

Procedure

1. Provide product descriptors and rubrics as clear guidelines of the expectations and criteria for the piece of work that will be critiqued. If the work is written, providing copies for the critique group is helpful.

2. As a whole group, create or refer to a list of revision questions based on the criteria for the piece of work.

3. Model the procedure with the whole group before allowing small independent feedback groups.

4. Have students work in groups of two to five.

5. The first student presents or reads the draft of her piece. She may ask peers to focus on a particular revision question or two that she is struggling with from the list.

6. Peers first focus on what is praiseworthy or working well. Praise needs to be specific. Simply saying, "This is good" doesn't help the author. Comments such as, "I notice that you used descriptive picture captions" or "You have a catchy title that makes me want to read your piece" are much more useful.

7. Next, ask questions and offer helpful suggestions: "This part is unclear. I wonder if it would be better to change the order of the steps?" or "I can't tell the setting. Maybe you could add some details that would show the reader where it is taking place?" or "I wonder if adding a graph to highlight your data would be effective."

8. Feedback should relate to the revision questions identified by the group or presenter.

9. After each member of the group has offered feedback, the presenter discusses which suggestions she wants to implement and thanks the group.

10. Others then present their work in turn and cycle through the feedback process.

Variations

- Give time guidelines for each part of the protocol so students don't get "stuck" on a particular type of feedback.
- Feedback can be written on sticky notes and given to the author.

TRY THIS: USE A NOTE-CATCHER TO HELP STUDENTS FOCUS ON ONE FEATURE AT A TIME

A clear and well-communicated protocol helps students know what to do during their peer conference, but few of us can remember what our critical friends say unless we write it down in some fashion. Providing students with a note-catcher for this purpose will hold them accountable for capturing the feedback they are given and provide a record both the teacher and the student can track back to when

Figure 4.10 Peer feedback protocol for pairs
SOURCE: This document is available in the online toolbox at http://www.wiley.com/go/lotolcompanion.

1. **Get Set:** Sit side by side so that both author and respondent can see the work being read.
2. **Get Organized:** Decide whose paper you will focus on first. Put it in front of you so you both can see it.
3. **Get Started:** First author explains his/her work and exactly what type of feedback would be helpful (in other words, what questions does s/he have or what is s/he confused about that s/he would appreciate help with). Then the author reads his/her work out loud, while the partner listens carefully and follows along. Reading aloud may cause the reader to notice flaws in his or her work. If necessary, s/he can pause to make notes. The other partner may also make notes on a separate piece of paper or mark dots on the draft as a reminder of a spot to go back to.
4. **Keep Going:** When the author has finished reading, the partner begins by saying something positive about the work ("warm" feedback), then moves on to constructive sharing of issues or suggestions ("cool" feedback). The author's job during this time is to listen and take notes on his/her own copy of the draft.
5. **Finish Up:** When the partner has provided feedback, the author may ask clarifying questions (without being defensive or rejecting feedback). Then the author indicates what his/her next steps will be.
6. **Repeat:** Repeat steps 3-5 for the other partner.
7. **Be Responsible for Your Learning:** Each member of the group should end the conference by collecting the copy of his/her work, the notes, and written action steps.

Variation for Small Groups:
This protocol can also be completed in small groups. In this case each group member should be provided with a copy of every piece of work and group members should decide on the order in which they will be shared. Steps 3-5 can then be completed in turn for each group member. During Step 4, each group member provides warm and cool feedback in turn while the author takes notes.

Peer critique can be especially productive and effective when students have learned the language of critique and use a clear protocol.

Photo credit: EL Education

Figure 4.11 Poster mock-up feedback note-catcher

SOURCE: This document is available in the online toolbox at http://www.wiley.com/go/lotolcompanion.

Author: _____ Critical Friend: _____

Learning Target: I can improve the craftsmanship of my poster

During your peer conference, LISTEN and record the feedback you get from your critical friend.

Element	Praise	Questions	Suggestions
Composition • Prioritization of information • Using artistic elements well (e.g., color, contrast) • Well-planned use of space			
Clarity of Message • You learn what's intended • Messages are clear and bold; not busy and cluttered			
Text Elements • Labels and captions • Titles • Text blocks			
Eye Appeal • Visual power (i.e., does it grab you?)			
Neatness and Care			
My action plan for my next draft:			

comparing successive drafts. Importantly, the feedback note-catcher, labeled with the learning target, is also an opportunity to identify the specific feature of the work that you want students to focus on in the conference so that they do not spend their time "editing" the first draft of an essay or discussing style and tone, for example, when the learning target addresses the validity of an argumentative claim. Figures 4.11 and 4.12 feature two sample note-catchers, which can be adapted for different grade levels or purposes.

TRY THIS: SUPPORT STUDENTS TO REFLECT ON AND EVALUATE FEEDBACK

Authors, artists, and creative professionals value the feedback they receive but they don't usually respond and revise wholesale. Instead, they synthesize and evaluate the feedback so that they can integrate it into their vision for the project at hand. Ultimately, the author is responsible for how the project turns out. To encourage student accountability and thoughtful use of feedback, explicitly teach a process for synthesizing and evaluating feedback. Figure 4.13 leads students through a written reflection process, but the same sequence could be used in a one-on-one conference or small group lesson.

Figure 4.12 How rock-solid is my argument note-catcher
SOURCE: This document is available in the online toolbox at http://www.wiley.com/go/lotolcompanion.

Learning Target: I can build a solid argument made of claim, evidence, and backing.
Author: _____ **Critical Friend:** _____
Exchange papers and do the following:

- Highlight in blue the writer's claim.
- Highlight in yellow the 3 BEST statements of evidence for that claim (e.g., the reasons).
- Circle facts, statistics, and examples that support the evidence (e.g., the backing).
- Underline the counterclaim.

Pause to discuss: review both papers and make sure that you agree on what is highlighted and circled before you proceed.
The critical friend answers these questions:

1. **As the author develops the claim, does the logic hold up? Why or why not?**

2. **What facts, statistics, or examples should the author add to strengthen the evidence?**

3. **What facts, statistics, or examples derail or distract from the claim?**

4. **Has the author sufficiently addressed the counterclaim?**

5. **Is this a solid argument? Why or why not?**

Figure 4.13 3-2-1 revision action plan
SOURCE: This document is available in the online toolbox at http://www.wiley.com/go/lotolcompanion.

Three suggestions my critique partners made that will help me improve my work:
1.
2.
3.

Two questions my critique partners raised that have got me thinking:
1.
2.

One piece of praise my critique partners gave me that I'm really proud of:
1.

TRY THIS: GIVE FEEDBACK ON STUDENTS' FEEDBACK

It takes time, years even, for students to polish the art of giving high-quality feedback and responding constructively to the feedback they receive. Learning this skill has value in its own right, so even if your students don't master it this year, giving them practice at peer critique is still worthwhile. You may not see students' work measurably improve as a result of a peer conference, but they are still learning the real-world skills of listening, perspective taking, evaluating, synthesizing, and revising.

To help students get better at giving kind, specific, and helpful feedback, try anonymously collecting (in writing or by recording comments as you listen to students conference with each other) their comments on a specific assignment. Do a gallery walk of the comments (without students' names on them, of course) and ask students to label them "kind," "specific," or "helpful." Then debrief with the class:

- What makes a comment helpful?

- Which comments felt kind?

- What do the comments labeled "specific" have in common?

- How could the comments that were *not* kind, specific, or helpful be rephrased to follow the norm?

TRY THIS: GIVE CREDIT FOR ENGAGING DEEPLY IN THE REVISION PROCESS

You know it's important to use feedback to inform and guide revisions in pursuit of high-quality work. But your students may see peer and even teacher conferences as just going through the motions. They *hear* the feedback, but they don't really *listen* to it. Instead of getting frustrated when students turn in the same dull writing or lackluster poster with each "revision," empower students by underscoring the connection between feedback and revision in the rubrics they use. Figure 4.14 is an example of one row of a rubric that gives students a chance to self-reflect on the *process* of revision as well as the product. Consider making it standard practice to add this row or something similar to your rubrics.

Figure 4.14   Rubric row for reflecting on revision of work
SOURCE: This document is available in the online toolbox at http://www.wiley.com/go/lotolcompanion.

I can apply feedback to improve my work.	3 or more peers gave me feedback. All feedback is recorded and attached to my drafts. My final paper shows evidence that I reflected on and responded to feedback from peers and teacher.	2 peers gave me feedback. All feedback is recorded and attached to me drafts. My final paper shows evidence that I made some changes in response to feedback.	I participated in feedback conferences, but I didn't save my feedback so you can't tell if I made changes in response to feedback.	I didn't receive any feedback.

Reflect on Your Process: Review your feedback note-catchers and your drafts. How did you use your peer feedback to improve your work (be specific)?

_____

_____

_____

_____

Check Yourself Checklist

Peer Critique Checklist

Before the peer critique. . .

- ❏ Teach students the purpose and language of feedback.
- ❏ Return frequently to learning targets and ensure that students understand them.
- ❏ Model giving effective feedback.

During the peer critique. . .

- ❏ Provide a step-by-step, specific protocol/procedure.
- ❏ Model the protocol.
- ❏ Group students intentionally (by interest, readiness, writing trait, social skills, etc.).
- ❏ Focus the critique on one or two traits that have been taught or designated as learning targets.
- ❏ Provide a recording sheet or other means to hold authors and critics accountable.

After the peer critique. . .

- ❏ Follow through and hold students accountable for next steps (e.g., refer back to conference outcomes in feedback on the next draft).

(This checklist is available in the online toolbox at http://www.wiley.com/go/lotolcompanion.)

One of the most important things leaders can do is model a growth mindset and commitment to quality work that communicates to everyone at the school: "This is a school where we give and receive kind, specific, and helpful feedback. This is a school where we revise and polish our work and our teaching to realize our vision of excellence and beauty."

Within a few minutes of walking through any school building, a school's priorities are clear, and the hallways speak loudly: if the only things displayed are athletic trophies, that sends a message. If the hallways are also filled with powerful, beautiful, and sophisticated student work, exhibited with professional care, everyone walking through those hallways – students, families, staff and visitors – gets the message that in this school there is a culture of quality. That can't happen without visionary leadership that charges and supports teachers to care about quality student work – not simply good test scores – and invests in the time for staff to lead its creation and curation.

Leaders can support individual teachers and the school as a whole at this focus by providing training, tools, and time for teachers to build their capacity. The quality of student work, improved by models, critique, and descriptive feedback, needs to be a regular focus of staff meetings, team meetings, and department meetings. Teachers need to adopt the habit of bringing student work to discussions with colleagues, using protocols to analyze how they can boost understanding and craftsmanship. All of this starts with leaders who make it clear that this is a priority for staff time. Following are a few tips for leading a culture of growth throughout your school community. Table 4.5 then summarizes the key action steps for teachers and students that will lead to success.

Top Tips

- Establish a culture of constructive critique for teachers by using the protocols and strategies in this chapter to critique lesson plans, curriculum maps, projects, or schoolwide event plans. Model a growth mindset by frequently critiquing yourself as a leader, and maintain a safe, supportive climate for all staff to give and receive feedback.

- Create a schoolwide bank of models in a variety of genres. Help teachers and students see how the bar of excellence rises as students develop their knowledge and skills and move up through the grades. Use the website Models of Excellence: The Center for High-Quality Student Work[5] as a launchpad for exploring new product ideas and for deepening the implementation of projects already under way.

- Use the Attributes of High-Quality Work (see Figure 4.3) as a benchmark for student work throughout the school. Foster this common language when discussing teacher work as well as student work.

- Invite teachers to model great critique lessons or share feedback protocols and note-catchers with their colleagues.

- Analyze student work, including drafts and feedback, regularly and collaboratively. Come to this work with a spirit of inquiry. Can you discover what this student did to understand the criteria for excellence and then to bring those criteria to life through creative effort?

Table 4.5 Models, critique, and descriptive feedback: Steps to success

What Should Teachers Do?
Find high-quality models and examine them for specific features and techniques that can be used in critique lessons.
Lead engaging critique lessons that invite student inquiry, ownership, and understanding.
Use professional language to develop a shared understanding of "what's good" and support students to realize those features.
Use protocols to conduct effective critique and feedback lessons.
Use recording forms to track progress through revisions and to help students reflect on and evaluate the feedback they receive.
What Should Students Do?
Analyze models together to get a vision of what high quality looks like in the genre they are creating.
Use that analysis to create a criteria list for what they are aiming for in their own work.
Revise in response to feedback from adults and peers.
Use kind, specific, and helpful language to give feedback to peers.
Reflect on and evaluate the feedback they receive; demonstrate ownership and intention in making revisions and throughout the creative process.

---

[5] https://modelsofexcellence.eleducation.org

As you have read Chapter 4, maybe you have had an opportunity to try some of these strategies and techniques along the way. If not, come back to this post-assessment after you have had a chance to do so. Give yourself whatever time you need to address the learning targets and challenges in a meaningful way. Then take a moment to check your progress in Table 4.6, which is the exact same Learning Target Tracker that appeared at the beginning of this chapter.

Circle or place an X along the continuum from Beginning to Exceeding: **How would you rate your progress toward each learning target** *at this point in time?* Use the space provided to make notes regarding any remaining challenges you may be having or ideas for new and different strategies you want to try.

Table 4.6   Chapter 4 learning target tracker

Learning Target 1: *I can distinguish between assignments that should be revised and polished into quality final drafts and those that can be just practice and reflection.* Beginning--------------------Developing----------------------Meeting--------------------Exceeding Notes:
Learning Target 2: *I can choose engaging and effective models to help students understand what "good" looks like in that genre of work.* Beginning--------------------Developing----------------------Meeting--------------------Exceeding Notes:
Learning Target 3: *I can conduct an effective critique lesson that motivates students and gives them concrete takeaways they can use in their work.* Beginning--------------------Developing----------------------Meeting--------------------Exceeding Notes:
Learning Target 4: *I can structure descriptive feedback so that it helps students see their strengths and how to improve.* Beginning--------------------Developing----------------------Meeting--------------------Exceeding Notes:

Chapter 5

Student-Led Conferences

Photo credit: EL Education

Checking for Understanding during Daily Lessons

Using Data with Students

Learning Targets

Models, Critique, and Descriptive Feedback

STUDENT-ENGAGED ASSESSMENT

Student-engaged assessment is a system of interrelated practices that positions students as leaders of their own learning.

Standards-Based Grading

Student-Led Conferences

Passage Presentations with Portfolios

Celebrations of Learning

What Is a Student-Led Conference?

Student-Led Conferences

A student-led conference is a meeting with a student and his or her family and teachers during which the student shares his or her portfolio of work and discusses progress with family members. The student facilitates the meeting from start to finish. Student-led conferences can be implemented at all grade levels, K–12.

Student-led conferences are an essential part of a student-engaged assessment system because they give students an opportunity to explain their own progress as learners. Many of our most successful EL Education network schools point to student-led conferences as *the most powerful practice* that has transformed their school culture, improved family collaboration, and boosted students' ownership of their work.

Student-led conferences make the age-old practice of parent-teacher conferences more engaging and informative for parents. However, the structures and systems that create successful conferences can be challenging, and many educators believe that students – especially young students – are not capable of leading their own conferences. This chapter is designed to help you establish and polish student-led conference practices so that *all* students can succeed at presenting their own work, resulting in engaged and informed families, and everyone playing a role in the school's learning community.

In this chapter, we build on Chapter 5 of *Leaders of Their Own Learning*. We begin by analyzing schoolwide structures such as calendars, schedules, and space allocations. We then dive deep into the nitty-gritty of how teachers and students prepare for conferences so that when the big event arrives, everyone is confident and successful. Along the way, we'll address four learning targets that will help you overcome the common challenges many teachers face when implementing student-led conferences.

> Student-led conferences show students taking ownership of their work, reflecting upon the "big ideas," and demonstrating skills of self-presentation. They are good PR for your school. Families love them. We have nearly 100% participation. Schedule them whenever you need to – Saturdays, seven in the morning, eight at night – to get parents in there!
>
> —*Lynn Bass, Founding Principal, Tapestry Charter High School, Buffalo, New York*

Learning Targets for Chapter 5

1. I can collaborate with my colleagues to build a schoolwide system for effective student-led conferences.
2. I can structure portfolios and conference agendas so that families get the information they need and want.
3. I can ensure that students are prepared to lead a conference with a high-quality presentation.
4. I can prepare families to engage meaningfully in their student's conference.

Before we dive in, take a moment to assess yourself on each of the learning targets for this chapter. In Table 5.1, circle or place an X along the continuum from Beginning to Exceeding: **How would you rate your progress toward each learning target** *at this point in time?*

We'll give you a chance to assess yourself again at the end of the chapter.

Table 5.1 Chapter 5 learning target tracker

Learning Target 1: *I can collaborate with my colleagues to build a schoolwide system for effective student-led conferences.* Beginning----------------------------------Developing--Meeting------------------------------------Exceeding Notes:
Learning Target 2: *I can structure portfolios and conference agendas so that families get the information they need and want.* Beginning----------------------------------Developing--Meeting------------------------------------Exceeding Notes:
Learning Target 3: *I can ensure that students are prepared to lead a conference with a high-quality presentation.* Beginning----------------------------------Developing--Meeting------------------------------------Exceeding Notes:
Learning Target 4: *I can prepare families to engage meaningfully in their student's conference.* Beginning----------------------------------Developing--Meeting------------------------------------Exceeding Notes:

Learning Target 1: I can collaborate with my colleagues to build a schoolwide system for effective student-led conferences.

Challenge #1: Just scheduling all those conferences is a challenge!

TRY THIS: START BY STUDYING WHAT WORKS AT OTHER SCHOOLS

Often schools and teachers are on board with the value of student-led conferences and very much *want* to do them, but are overwhelmed by the logistics. Preparation and scheduling can be intimidating for any school and, especially in large secondary schools, it can lead to paralysis. Rest assured, it can be done (and it will be worth it)!

Student-led conferences work best when the entire school commits to this new structure, and the time devoted on the school calendar to traditional parent-teacher conferences is reassigned to student-led conferences. By working together, teachers and school leaders can create systems that support students to be effective and reflective reporters on their own learning. The Close Up that follows describes how teachers and leaders embraced the challenges of scheduling student-led conferences at a comprehensive public high school with more than 2,100 students.

Close Up: Organizing Student-Led Conferences at a Large High School

River Bluff High School in Lexington, South Carolina, opened in 2013 with a student body of nearly 2,000 students, and has grown since then. Despite the logistical challenges, and the fact that most high schools don't even hold parent conferences, teachers and leaders were determined this structure was possible for their school. Students would lead their own conferences and conferences would be meaningful—not just a quick sharing of report cards. They held their first student-led conferences in January of their second year of operation. "It was a cultural game changer," says Director for Student Life, Avis Cunningham. "It shifted the conversation from grades to good work. After fall courses, students were ready to talk about growth and goal setting for the second semester. We noticed an increase in work ethic as a result."

It wasn't easy figuring out where to hold 150 conferences simultaneously or how to prepare students to facilitate the conferences effectively. Leaders established a team to tackle the logistics and develop structures that would support teachers and students. The essential structure, according to Kelly Smoak, a social studies teacher on the team, is Crew (or advisories). At River Bluff, Crews of 10–15 students meet daily for 35–55 minutes. Crew leaders support students to prepare and rehearse, and the schedule and location of student-led conferences is all based on student Crews.

The student-led conference team created a guide for Crew leaders and students that established some consistencies all students would follow. They also provided regular training for Crew leaders in Faculty Crew sessions, in which they modeled lessons, so that all Crew leaders would introduce the basics of student-led conferences to their crews in the same way. Crew time created space for students to organize their digital portfolios, create an agenda for sharing evidence of learning, and practice leading a conference. Throughout the fall, Crew leaders circled up weekly in Faculty Crew after school to compare notes, share what was working, and to address challenges collaboratively. The student-led conference team also communicated regularly with parents, setting the purpose of student-led conferences and the expectation that every family participate.

In order to accommodate all families and students, the school held conferences for each grade level on four different evenings. The team set up and labeled Crew spaces in the school's large cafeteria. Students were trained to greet their family at the door and bring them quietly to the correct space for their conference. Crew leaders helped facilitate time keeping and transitions between conferences. Following the conferences, each Crew debriefed the experience. Their feedback informed improvements in the schedule and logistics for the following year.

"The size of the school makes this practice a real challenge," says Cunningham, "But what we've learned is that all those challenges can be overcome if you really want students to lead their own learning."

Student-led conferences have been around for a long time, and schools have found their own creative ways to make them work based on the needs of their communities. When we published *Leaders of Their Own Learning* in 2014 we offered many tools to help schools implement student-led conferences, and we will offer many more for you in this chapter. We encourage you to take those tools and make them your own because none will be perfect for your setting and your community. Figure 5.1 is an excellent example.

Figure 5.1 Student-led conference logistics checklist from Washington Heights Expeditionary Learning School in New York City and The Franklin School of Innovation in Asheville, North Carolina
SOURCE: This document is available in the online toolbox at http://www.wiley.com/go/lotolcompanion.

Pre-conference/Scheduling Logistics
- ❏ I have scheduled a conference for each student in my Crew.
- ❏ Each family knows when to arrive and where the conference will be held.
- ❏ I know the first and last names of any adults that will be attending the conference.
- ❏ I have created other arrangements for parents who cannot attend the regular conference times.

Pre-conference/Student Logistics
- ❏ I have helped students organize assignments and prepare for conferences.
- ❏ I have helped students learn appropriate speaking skills.
- ❏ I have set aside Crew time for students to practice student-led conferences with peers.
- ❏ I know my Crew! I know what classes they are excelling in and in which they struggle. I know if they are having trouble with behavior in a specific class or homework in another. I definitely know if a student is failing a class and I've spoken with the subject teacher to find out why. I know if the child's family is going through a difficult time. I know with whom each student lives and if there has been a change in the home environment. I know the names of my students' parents and I think I may recall the names of a sibling or two. I know if a student is habitually tardy or late. Nothing is a surprise to me.

Materials for Conferences
- ❏ I have a copy of the conference schedule posted outside my classroom.
- ❏ I have set up chairs in the hallway for families that arrive early.
- ❏ I have a group of desks arranged to promote small-group discussion. Multiple chairs are available.
- ❏ I have a copy of the conference schedule in front of me.
- ❏ I have a timer or watch and multiple pens.
- ❏ I have copies of parental concern sheets that I can provide and enough surveys for each conference. I have a folder in which to keep documents.
- ❏ I have a sheet on which to record parental concerns that cannot be addressed during the conference.

During the Conference
- ❏ I stick to the schedule. I make sure that each conference ends before the next begins.
- ❏ I let the student talk. I help the student if the parent is talking too much, and I try to redirect the conversation if the parent begins to get upset.
- ❏ I make sure all of the paper distribution and signing happens without taking away from the student's presentation.
- ❏ I welcome each family, preferably using names, and thank them for coming. I remind families that the student will do most of the talking and that it is best to save questions for the end.
- ❏ If a parent wants to meet with a teacher I can provide them with a parental concerns sheet and tell the subject teacher the next day.
- ❏ I thank each family for coming and reaffirm my availability for current or future concerns and give them a survey to fill out at home.

Post-conference
- ❏ Inform core teachers of parent concerns
- ❏ Collect parent surveys
- ❏ Send student-led conference thank-yous (created by the student) to be sent home no later than May 13th.

This student-led conference logistics checklist was published in Chapter 5 of *Leaders of Their Own Learning*. We borrowed it from Washington Heights Expeditionary Learning School (WHEELS) in New York City. The Franklin School of Innovation in Asheville, North Carolina, then borrowed it and made it their own. They left the first three sections largely the same, but then added two new sections at the end to better meet their needs. We urge you to borrow this list and make it your own to suit your school's logistical needs.

TRY THIS: RUN MULTIPLE STUDENT-LED CONFERENCES SIMULTANEOUSLY

The essential difference between student-led conferences and traditional parent-teacher conferences is that *students lead them*. This means that teachers don't necessarily have to be at the table for each conference; in fact multiple, conferences can be taking place at one time in the same room. Consequently, while 20 individual 20-minute parent-teacher conferences may take an entire day, the same number of student-led conferences can be held in half a day, with ample time for transitions (see Table 5.2 for an example).

Table 5.2 Sample schedule for simultaneous student-led conferences

	Number of students/class	Length of conferences	Number of conferences at one time	Total time with 5 min transitions
Primary	20	20 min + transition	2	4–5 hours
Elementary	24	20 min + transition	4	3 hours
Secondary	15 (in Crew/Advisory groups)	30 min	4	3 hours

In middle and high schools where students move between subjects throughout the day and have a team of teachers, each teacher can be responsible for overseeing a small group of student-led conferences. For example, if you have a Crew or advisory structure, this is the best way to ensure that every student conducts a student-led conference and that teachers have a manageable number of conferences to plan for – typically no more than 15. When all Crew leaders or advisory teachers take on the role of organizing student-led conferences for their small group, they also are compelled to be the point person for the students in their group. As point person, they are an advocate who is familiar with the group members' academic and social/emotional progress across subject areas (including classes the Crew or advisory leader does not him/herself actually teach).

Video Spotlight 5.1 highlights the inaugural year of student-led conferences at Conway Elementary in Escondido, California, where all students, including 40 kindergartners, conduct their student-led conferences simultaneously.

Video Spotlight 5.1: Station-Based Student-Led Conferences in Kindergarten
https://vimeo.com/291520157

In this video, kindergarten teachers prepare students to rotate through three stations where they lead their own conferences. The video also features interviews with families experiencing student-led conferences for the first time.

Video Reflection Questions
1. What are some of the things teachers have done to prepare students and make the logistics of rotation manageable and effective?
2. How have teachers and leaders made the conferences accessible to families who are not native speakers of English?
3. What lessons can you take away from this video to help your school implement student-led conferences more effectively?

TRY THIS: STAGGER STUDENT-LED CONFERENCES BY GRADE LEVEL

Scheduling conferences by grade level and running them on different days, weeks, or even at different times of year allows for greater flexibility and can put less logistical strain on the school as a whole. This strategy is also often better for teachers, as it allows conferences for each grade level to be scheduled optimally, relative to other grade level commitments (e.g., assignment due dates, off-campus trips, teacher meetings).

We know of one K–8 school that holds student-led conferences for sixth-graders during the third week of school, so that each student can share their goals (rather than their accomplishments) with parents and discuss how they've adjusted to the new routines and expectations of middle school. The same school holds a kindergarten open house for parents during that third week so that parents can get a group progress report from teachers and learn about what's going well and what the class as a whole is working on. During the one-hour open house, kindergarten students are with an assistant teacher, while parents are with the lead teacher. Then the kindergarten teachers schedule student-led conferences for their young students during the third *month* of school, which gives them time to teach students the presentation skills and protocol they'll need to succeed in leading their own conference. Not surprisingly, the idea for this creative approach to the logistics of student-led conferences came from teachers.

Staggered scheduling also has a number of other benefits, including the following:

- Not all families are on campus at the same time, which eases the parking burden.

- In secondary schools, groups from different grade levels can use the same space for conferences on different nights.

- Special education teachers and other specialists can rotate between grade levels and be available for questions or support.

- Teachers can design the specific structures of the conference time to meet the needs of their students.

- Families with children in multiple grade levels can focus on one conference at a time, rather than trying to double up on the same day.

TRY THIS: ENSURE ALL STAFF ARE "ON DECK" FOR STUDENT-LED CONFERENCES

Many hands make light work. The logistics of student-led conferences will be much more manageable if all staff play a role in making them a success. Whether your school holds conferences for all grades at the same time or staggers them across different evenings or days, it makes sense to identify roles for all staff, even those who are not directly involved in the conferences. Table 5.3 shows some of the important

Table 5.3 Logistical task list for student-led conferences

Task	Who can do this?
Directing visitors in the parking lot	
Welcoming visitors in the hallways or other public spaces; giving directions	
Distributing conference evaluations	
Supporting teachers and Crew leaders as needed	
Providing refreshments	

roles and tasks that will help make conferences a success. We suggest you use a table like this with the left-hand column modified to meet your particular logistical needs: fill in the right-hand column with the names or roles of people in your school who could help fill this need.

 Challenge # 2: Our families can't come to conferences during the school day and many don't speak English.

TRY THIS: DEVELOP STRUCTURES TO ACCOMMODATE WORKING PARENTS

In order for student-led conferences to truly become an impactful and important feature of your school – an opportunity for *every* student to lead the conversation about their learning – 100% family participation must be the goal. This means that systems and structures must be in place to ensure that the conferences are accessible to all. Before you schedule your student-led conferences, conduct a parent survey that can help you tailor conferences to family needs. Table 5.4, which highlights some of the main barriers and bridges to family involvement in student-led conferences, can help you pinpoint some of the things to ask about in your survey.

Table 5.4 Barriers and bridges to family engagement in student-led conferences

Barrier	Bridge
Parents work during school hours.	Hold many or most student-led conferences in the evening hours; offer some before-school time slots.
Parents would need child care for younger children in order to attend their student's conference.	Identify slots when child care can be available and provide it on-site, perhaps using your after-school program, teacher assistants, parent volunteers, or trained older students at the school.
Because of their own school experience, parents feel anxious about coming into the school or meeting the teacher.	Hold some student-led conferences at a local library or community center that is more accessible to parents.
Parents speak a language other than English.	Identify interpreters, parent volunteers, older, bilingual students, or others who can support families during their student's conference. Provide written materials in the parent's home language.
Parents have physical or mental disabilities that make participating fully in a conference difficult.	Identify special education teachers or others who can support families during their student's conference. Encourage caregivers or other family members to also attend the conference.
Parents have transportation challenges that make getting to a conference difficult.	Coordinate car pools or volunteers to provide rides to conferences. Raise funds to hire a ride-sharing service for transportation.
Parents are not familiar with or don't have access to online communication (e.g., email, a scheduling app).	Revise or create communications to families that don't require digital access or understanding.
Parents work in hourly jobs where they don't get paid if they aren't at work.	Many states have laws that require employers to compensate employees for time off to attend school events. (You can see a state-by-state list here: https://primepay.com/blog/state-state-guide-family-school-partnership-acts.)
Parents, due to challenging personal circumstances, cannot attend the conference.	If a parent can't attend a conference, invite another family member, relative, or caring adult (e.g., neighbor) who can attend the student's conference.

TRY THIS: PROVIDE INTERPRETERS AND TRANSLATIONS OF STUDENT-LED CONFERENCE DOCUMENTS AND SIGNAGE

For family members who are not fluent in English, student-led conferences can be especially daunting. Planning supports for these families will be especially important, particularly if the practice of coming into the school for conferences in the first place is one with which they are not familiar or comfortable.

All conference-related documents should be provided in the language that families speak. This task will be easier for some languages than others, depending on the availability of staff or community members who can translate. If a family speaks a language for which there is no available onsite translator, consider using an online service to translate key documents, including:

- The student handbook or other documents explaining what student-led conferences are and why they matter

- The initial invitation to the conference

- The schedule for the conference

- Directions or signage related to the conference in the hallways and classrooms

- Guidance explaining parents' role in the conference

- Suggested questions that parents might ask during the conference

- The conference evaluation, if there is one

In addition to providing translated documents, schools with significant populations of families who do not speak English fluently may need to tweak the schedule so that all families who need an interpreter have one available. Professional interpreting may not be feasible or affordable for a school for every conference. Consider freeing up bilingual staff members, recruiting bilingual volunteers from families and the broader community, or using older students from the school or from a sister school to act as interpreters.

Learning Target 2: I can structure portfolios and conference agendas so that families get the information they need and want.

 Challenge #3: Students want to share their best and favorite work, but families want and need to know the full story of how their children are doing, even if they are struggling.

TRY THIS: BALANCE BREADTH AND DEPTH IN STUDENT PORTFOLIOS

The agendas for student-led conferences and the portfolios of work that students share with their families during conferences are tightly linked. Depending on your process, the agenda you create for student-led conferences will drive the structure and contents of student portfolios; or, if student portfolios are already well established with an organizing principle that lends itself well to students' presenting their work to their families, the portfolio may drive the agenda for the conferences. There is not necessarily any one right way to approach the process – what matters is that the agenda and the portfolios speak to each other in logical and consistent ways so that the conferences flow.

In Chapter 5 of *Leaders of Their Own Learning*, we describe some of the key decisions teachers need to make regarding portfolios and conference agendas, including:

- Will all subjects be discussed?

- What will be the balance between students providing a general overview of their performance in all subjects versus discussing specific examples of their work in depth?

- What kinds of evidence will students present?

- How will character growth and work habits be addressed?

- To what degree will extracurricular activities be shared and discussed?

The answers to these questions enable students to compile a portfolio that provides snapshots into the school year and to present their growth and learning to their families at student-led conferences two or three times throughout the year. (For passage presentations, addressed in Chapter 7, portfolios take on a multiyear dimension.) In order for families to get the information they want (i.e., information they may be accustomed to getting from teacher-led conferences they have attended in the past, where the student wasn't present), it's essential for teachers to design the contents of the portfolio so that students' challenges and growth are reflected as well as their successes. *Balance* is the key.

You may need to deliberate extensively with your grade-level team to identify parameters for the portfolio contents that balance breadth and depth. A portfolio with breadth demonstrates that students are on track and meeting learning targets across the curriculum. A portfolio with depth means that students are able to demonstrate who they really are – how they learn best, what they are passionate about, what skills they have truly mastered – through compelling work that they feel proud of.

Figure 5.2 High school portfolio requirements for student-led conferences from Metropolitan Expeditionary Learning School in New York City

SOURCE: This document is available in the online toolbox at http://www.wiley.com/go/lotolcompanion.

Learning Targets for Student-Led Conferences
- I can speak clearly and articulately about my work.
- I can reflect on my growth as a learner.
- I can identify and describe my own strengths and weaknesses.

Choose five pieces of work from different subjects (from the current academic year).

1. Piece #1: An example of work you are proud of. The piece shows what you learned and what makes you feel successful. Choose work from a core class.
2. Piece #2: An example of work that you struggled with – it was a challenge. The piece shows what you learned and how you can improve on this kind of assignment next time. Choose work form a core class.
3. Piece #3: Make your own choice (core or elective; 1st or 2nd semester).
4. Piece #4: Make your own choice (core or elective; 1st or 2nd semester).
5. Piece #5: Make your own choice (core or elective; 1st or 2nd semester).

Name one habit of scholarship where you have improved, such as coming prepared for class or getting work in on time. Explain how you have improved and what that has meant to you.

Look carefully at the letter you wrote for the Current Grade and Goal Reflection Task. Read from your letter and be sure to name one goal you have for yourself and what you're doing/changing to make that goal come to life. Name specific subjects, works, etc. if needed. Summarize here what from your letter you want to discuss during this time.

Review the student-led conference portfolio requirements featured in Figure 5.2. As you review this example, consider circling the items that show the breadth of a student's learning – individual artifacts from a variety of subject areas or courses. Put a box around those items that show depth – the process behind a product or a deeper look into who the student really is as a learner. Then put on your parent hat. Is anything missing that you would want to hear about in a 20–30 minute conference? How might you adapt these requirements for the student-led conferences in your own classroom?

TRY THIS: BALANCE ACHIEVEMENT AND GROWTH IN STUDENT PORTFOLIOS

Another consideration when you and your students are identifying what will go into the portfolio is to select some artifacts that represent the student's current level of achievement and other artifacts that demonstrate growth over time. Especially for students who, for whatever reason, are not meeting grade-level learning targets, an artifact that shows the student is growing and making progress toward the target is important. Pre- and post-assessments of writing, reading, or math can be excellent indicators of growth. Revisions based on documented feedback can also show growth. The following photos show a sixth-grade student's revision of a graph displaying data collected in a science class at Genesee Community Charter School in Rochester, New York. This "before and after" view demonstrates that this student's skill at precisely representing the relationship between quantities and time increased through critique and revision.

A bar graph showing temperature over time

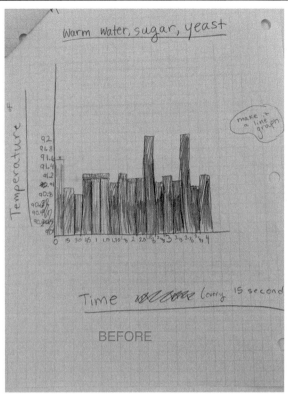

Photo credit: Chris Dolgos

After critique, the student revised the format of the graph to a line graph to more powerfully represent the impact of temperature over time.

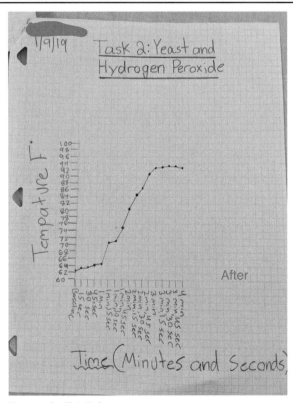

Photo credit: Chris Dolgos

TRY THIS: BALANCE QUANTITATIVE AND QUALITATIVE DATA IN STUDENT PORTFOLIOS

Student portfolios should provide both qualitative and quantitative data – both are important for families to see. Quantitative data, however, must be chosen and presented with care. Parents often seek comparative information: how their child is doing relative to others in the class, or to grade-level standards. It is important to carefully prepare students, particularly older students, to be able to address this in their presentations because focusing on student rankings within the class, school, or state can be reductive and harmful for student confidence and learning. Students with low rankings lose confidence and heart in school; students with high rankings become afraid to take risks in learning because they need to protect their place. Student-led conferences should not center on class rank or yearly test scores – conferences are much more effective when they use data to illuminate strengths, weaknesses, growth, and next steps.

We suggest a particular approach when students present quantitative data:

- *Not This.* "Here are my grades and here is where I rank in the class. My state test shows here that I am two years behind in my reading and one year behind in math."

- *But This.* "Our learning targets match grade-level state standards, so you can tell where I am compared to where I am expected to be by how I am doing on my targets. Here are the learning targets I am meeting or exceeding; here are targets I am pretty close to meeting; and here are targets that are still really challenging for me. I am proud of my growth in these targets – I will show you evidence here. Here is evidence of targets that are challenging for me, and some specific things I need to work on."

The evidence that students provide can be quantitative (e.g., quiz and test scores, number grades on assignments, rubric scores, lexile levels of books) and qualitative (e.g., examples of papers written for class, reflections on performance). For each subject area in Table 5.5, we have indicated one quantitative and one qualitative artifact that could be included to represent a student's achievement and/or growth. Considering the grade level of your students and the work your students have done this year, what else could you add to the list?

Table 5.5 Examples of quantitative and qualitative artifacts

	Quantitative	Qualitative
Reading	Lexile score	Read aloud of just-right book
Math	Unit test score	Math journal with written reflections on meeting learning targets
Social Studies	Homework completion rate	Project
Science	Science Fair place ranking	Science notebook

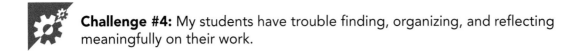

Challenge #4: My students have trouble finding, organizing, and reflecting meaningfully on their work.

TRY THIS: CREATE COMMON SYSTEMS FOR STUDENTS TO SAVE AND KEEP TRACK OF THEIR WORK

One of the biggest challenges of creating strong portfolios in any classroom setting is to determine what students will save and reflect on, when students will compile and tune their portfolios, and who will support them to do so regularly enough that portfolios mature over time into presentation-worthy documents. You may remember being in school yourself and having a desk or locker that was not well organized or perhaps even quite a mess. Before you blame yourself fully, recall how little time you were given to regularly clean and organize your spaces. It's the same with portfolios – they will only be up-to-date and organized if we provide students with ample time to do so.

In many elementary schools, students create and maintain their portfolios during Crew or morning meeting. In secondary schools, students are likely to do much of their portfolio maintenance during Crew or advisory but may do some tasks related to specific subject areas (e.g., reflect on a specific assignment) in regular academic classes. In addition, students with academic support or "pull-out" classes may get additional time in those classes for work on portfolios. The list of questions that follows, about how students will store, organize, and access their work, originally appeared in *Leaders of Their Own Learning* (p. 268):

- Where are portfolios kept in a classroom or school?

- Are portfolios kept across years or sent home each year?

- What kind of binders, folders, bins, or boxes are used?

- Will students use physical portfolios, digital portfolios, or both?

- If portfolios are digital, how will students be supported to manage files effectively? Who will have access to those files?

- How much do students get access to their portfolios? How often do they engage in portfolio tune-ups?

- How is oversized, 3D work, and multimedia work stored?

It's helpful if all students in a grade level follow the same system so that teachers can collaborate on the many forms, templates, and letters that support this system. Once you and your team have determined where you want students to store their portfolios-in-progress, you should also discuss how to get students involved and accountable for keeping track of their own work. Figure 5.3 is a tracking sheet organized by learning target, but you could just as easily design a tracking sheet organized by subject area or work habit. Make your own tracking sheet that captures the contents of the portfolio your students will create. Ensure that it is a tool your students can use effectively – individually or collectively – so that they are leading their own learning.

Figure 5.3 Accountability tracking sheet by learning target

Name:_____	Subject Area/Grade level _____	
Long-term LT# 1	**Assignments/evidence**	**Date reflection checked by teacher**
Long-term LT # 2	**Assignments/evidence**	**Date reflection checked by teacher**
Long-term LT # 3	**Assignments/evidence**	**Date reflection checked by teacher**
Long-term LT #4	**Assignments/evidence**	**Date reflection checked by teacher**

TRY THIS: INCLUDE AN INCOMPLETE WORK PAGE WHEREVER WORK IS MISSING

If a student chronically loses his or her work, or never turned it in in the first place, and that work is a required component in the portfolio, the portfolio should still include a placeholder for that work. The student's job during the conference, then, is to explain why the item – and the learning it represents – is missing. An incomplete work page marked "Missing Assignment," with a student's explanation of what's missing and why, creates an opportunity for a student and her family to discuss what needs to be done to address the missing work. Including this page in the portfolio is much more impactful for students and their families than simply not including the work.

TRY THIS: CREATE COMMON PROTOCOLS THAT STUDENTS USE TO REFLECT ON THEIR WORK AND DATA *AS THEY LEARN*, NOT JUST BEFORE THE CONFERENCE

One of the common mistakes teachers make the first year they try student-led conferences is to have students do all of their portfolio preparation in the few weeks just before the conference. In this scenario, many students will be unable to find their work, and those students who have saved assignments from months earlier are unlikely to remember it well enough to articulate what was challenging, what they learned, and how it connects to long-term learning targets. For this reason, common protocols that support students to reflect on their work *as they complete it* are essential for high-quality conferences. It is best for students to reflect on their work, in writing just after the work is completed (or after it is assessed). Figure 5.4 is a sample reflection form that can be used for this purpose.

A great way to engage primary-age students in this reflection process is to create preprinted sticky notes or stickers that they can match to items in their portfolio. Then, as they move through their portfolio during

Figure 5.4 Writing reflection form for student-led conferences from Two Rivers Public Charter School in Washington, DC

SOURCE: This document is available in the online toolbox at http://www.wiley.com/go/lotolcompanion.

Writing Process
This piece of work was chosen to show you the steps I use in the writing process. I would like you to notice:

_____
_____
_____

Pride
I selected this piece of work because I am really proud of:

_____

I would like you to notice:

_____
_____
_____
_____

Improvement
I chose this work to show how much I have improved at:_____
_____
I used to _____
Now I, _____

Perseverance
I included this piece of work because it is something I really tried hard to do well. I want you to see that: _____
_____
I am trying hard to: _____
I would like you to notice: _____

their student-led conference, the stickers will cue students to talk about that aspect of their work. The process of affixing stickers to the portfolio will require modeling and support so that students are thoughtful and reflective about where they place them. Here's a starter collection of possible categories for the stickers:

- This is my best work because. . .
- This was the hardest thing I ever did!
- If I had to do this again, I would improve. . .

- This shows my learning about. . .
- I got better at. . .
- Here's the evidence of my thinking. . .

Check Yourself Checklist

Student-Led Conference Agenda/Portfolio Contents Checklist

The items included on the agenda in students' portfolios. . .

❑ Represent important learning targets in at least four academic subject areas

❑ Give students some choices about what to include

❑ Require students to present and discuss their challenges, as well as their accomplishments

❑ Address work habits and character

❑ Invite students to pause, reflect, and interact with their family members

❑ Require students to use data—grades, test scores, exit tickets, reflections—as evidence of their learning

(This checklist is available in the online toolbox at http://www.wiley.com/go/lotolcompanion.)

Learning Target 3: I can ensure that students are prepared to lead a conference with a high-quality presentation.

 Challenge #5: My students have good portfolios, but their presentations are weak.

TRY THIS: PLAN BACKWARD TO ALLOW TIME FOR REHEARSAL

Maybe you've already given student-led conferences a try and even overcome some of the scheduling challenges. However, even when the logistics of conference day go smoothly, students' presentations can be less than stellar if they haven't prepared and practiced how to present their learning to an authentic audience. Just as students need time to reflect on a piece of work immediately after creating it, they also need time to prepare for how they will deliver their student-led conference. The first step in this process is calendaring time for this preparation to take place. If a calendar isn't put in place ahead of time, it will be hard to carve out the time on the fly. Figure 5.5 is an example of a calendar created by a team of teachers at The Franklin School of Innovation in Asheville, North Carolina, that keeps all teachers on track to prepare students for upcoming conferences.

After reviewing the calendar in Figure 5.5, list out the key tasks you think will be necessary to prepare your students for their student-led conferences. Then pull out a calendar and work backwards from the date of your conferences to ensure that everything on the list makes it into your plans. In the pages that follow, we'll explore the specifics of many of the kinds of tasks you are sure to put on your list.

TRY THIS: USE A MODEL TO LEARN WHAT A CONFERENCE SHOULD LOOK LIKE AND SOUND LIKE

As is true for any polished performance, the secret to a successful conference is rehearsal. Your timeline identifies opportunities for students to practice and receive feedback on their conference presentation. Before you can teach students what a high-quality conference looks and sounds like, you need to understand these criteria deeply. Many schools film and archive their own models over time. Until you have models from your own school, you can use the videos in Video Spotlight 5.2 to learn what a conference looks like and sounds like. These videos feature student-led conferences at the elementary, middle, and high school levels. (Note: Later in this chapter, in Figure 5.9, we offer a lesson plan to help you analyze videos like these with students as part of their preparation.)

 Video Spotlight 5.2: (a) Kindergarten Student-Led Conference
https://vimeo.com/49170218

(b) Middle School Student-Led Conference
https://vimeo.com/41363907

 (c) High School Student-Led Conference
https://vimeo.com/43992567

These three videos feature student-led conferences at the elementary, middle, and high school levels from Delaware Ridge Elementary School in Kansas City and Washington Heights Expeditionary Learning School in New York City.

Video Reflection Questions

1. Would you agree that the students are describing what they are learning versus what they are doing in school? Why or why not?
2. How do the conferences develop students' sense of ownership and responsibility for their work?
3. How would you describe the impact of the student-led conferences on the parents in attendance?

Figure 5.5 Sample student-led conference preparation calendar from The Franklin School of Innovation in Asheville, North Carolina

SOURCE: This document is available in the online toolbox at http://www.wiley.com/go/lotolcompanion.

	~ April 2016 ~					
Sun	**Mon**	**Tue**	**Wed**	**Thu**	**Fri**	**Sat**
3	4	5	6	7	8 *Generic scheduling letter & email (provided by SLC team) sent home to families* **SLC Robo Call*	9
10 *Make sure your Crew has binders to organize materials!	11 **Great day to review SLC materials**	12 **Great day to have a Crew lesson on how to reflect**	13	14	15	16
11th-15th: This week in Crew make sure you collect **_Binders_** to organize SLC materials. Review SLC materials with your Crew, **crew leaders must make a copy for each member of their crew.** Students organize materials in SLC binder						
17	18	19	20	21	22	23
18th-22nd: Students should collect work samples for SLC's. Classroom teachers should provide class time for work collection and LT gathering. Crew leaders need to review work samples (use the Crew Leader checklist) to ensure variety and authenticity. Once samples have been collected students should work to complete work/HOS reflection sheets. **Crew leaders need to be aware of families scheduling conferences and begin creating a schedule.**						
24	25	26	27	28 *Follow up on **unscheduled** SLC's, reach out to families that need to schedule*	29 ***TWD*** ***No School*** **SLC Robo Call*	30.
25th-28th: Students should have collected all work samples by this point. Students will work this week on final reflections and filling in their maps.						
1	2	3	4 *Send an email confirmation of SLC schedule to your Crew families*	5	6 ***STUDENT LED CONFERENCES***	
2nd-5th: Practice! Practice! Practice! Your Crew should practice with their peers **_multiple_** times. If a member of your Crew has practiced **_multiple_** times and has reflected thoroughly on work samples and HOS, that student can collect additional work samples to share **after** their SLC in the hallway.						

* *Students will write thank-you notes to their families the week of May 4th to be taken home no later than Fri. May 8th.*

TRY THIS: CREATE A SCRIPT THAT PROVIDES STUDENTS WITH SUPPORT TO MEET CONFERENCE GOALS BUT ALSO MAKES SPACE FOR THEIR AUTHENTIC VOICE

One of the trickiest challenges of preparing for student-led conferences is creating a script that provides a "just right" level of support for students and allows them to reflect on their learning with an authentic voice. This script is not truly a script: it is typically an outline, with sentence starters to help students begin each section. Most students need a structure that helps them tell the story of their learning. The story of learning, like any good story, has a beginning (an introduction), a middle (my learning claims and evidence), and an end (thank you and time for questions). But even the youngest students also need to have some choice in how they tell their story and room to infuse the conference with an authentic voice. Students with special needs, at any grade level, may need some extra support to organize and prepare their conference. (Note: Table 7.6 in Chapter 7 offers strategies suggested by learning specialists for preparing students for their passage presentations. You may find many of those same strategies useful here as well.)

Figures 5.6 and 5.7 show scripted sample agendas for elementary and middle school students, while Figure 5.8 shows a more open-ended agenda from which high school students can write their own script. Of note, Figure 5.6 is a script distilled from a PowerPoint template used by second graders at The Noah Wallace School in Farmington, Connecticut. The template, which students complete before their student-led conference, allows even these young children to share and reflect on their learning with professionalism and poise. You can see the full PowerPoint template in our online toolbox.

Figure 5.6 Primary student-led conference script from The Noah Wallace School in Farmington, Connecticut
SOURCE: This document is available in the online toolbox at http://www.wiley.com/go/lotolcompanion.

Introduction: Welcome to my conference. Today you will learn about my progress and goals in work habits, reading, writing, and math.
Here is a copy of my work habits charts from term 1 and 2.
I notice _____
My goal for the next term is _____
In the next slides, I am going to show you what I am most proud of in reading.
Here is a graph of my reading growth.
I notice _____
My goal for the next term is _____
This slide is about my reading fluency. Let me read a just-right book to you!
This slide is about my reading stamina work. I chose to work on _____.
This is where my reading really glows: _____
This is where I am still growing: _____
I can talk about the most important parts of an informational text.
I am most proud of this because _____
I would like to improve on _____
Do you have any comments or questions about my reading progress?

Created by second-grade students and teacher Jessica Ayers

Figure 5.7 Middle school student-led conference script from Two Rivers Public Charter School in Washington, DC

SOURCE: This document is available in the online toolbox at http://www.wiley.com/go/lotolcompanion.

Opening
- Introductions: Welcome your family to the conference, introduce all adults, and thank them for attending.
  - "Mom, this is my crew advisor_____. Mr./Ms. _____, this is my family member _____."
  - "I want to thank you for taking the time to come to my conference."
- Purpose: Explain why you are leading this conference and how the conference will work.
  - "This is an opportunity for me to share who I am as a learner."
  - "I'll begin by sharing some of the work in my portfolio. Then, we'll have some time to talk about the ways I've grown as a learner and establish goals for the next few months. Finally, we'll look at my report card."

Sharing the Portfolio
- Introduction to the portfolio: Explain the purpose of your portfolio.
  - "This portfolio contains some of my best work from the past few months. I'm going to show you a piece from one of my classes and explain how I completed this work and what this work shows about me as a learner."
- Work samples: Present your subject-area work.
  - "This piece is from my _____ class. The task was to _____."
  - "The key skills and knowledge in this piece include _____. Some of the important learning targets that this work addresses include _____."
  - "In my first draft you will notice that I succeeded in _____ but had challenges with _____ _____. I got feedback about _____."
  - "My final draft shows improvement in _____."
  - "In reflecting on this piece, I am proud of_____but need to continue working on_____."
  - This piece demonstrates the Two Rivers' expectation of I work hard/I care for my community/I am a team player/I am responsible and independent because _____."

My Data
- This section varies-depending upon the data featured.

Goal Setting/Closing of Portfolio
- Goal Setting: Reflect on how you hope to improve your work in the future.
  - "I am proud of my work in _____ and need to work on _____."
  - "Some ideas I have to continue developing as a learner include _____"
  - In the next few months I hope to _____."
  - "Do you have any questions about what I've presented or ideas about how I can produce my best work?"

Report Card/Logistics
- The Crew advisor comes to the table to distribute the report card.
- Discussion of report card: Are there any surprises? Are there any areas of improvement? What might be some specific goals for next report card?
- Logistics: This is an opportunity for the Crew advisor to address any outstanding logistics
- Thank you: "Thank you for supporting me by participating in my student-led conference."

The following questions will help you find opportunities for students to express their choice and voice in their student-led conferences. Use them to review and revise your agenda or script:

- Is there an opportunity for students to freely choose at least one item in their portfolio?

- Do reflection forms invite students to think about and articulate what they like about their choice item and why they chose it?

- Can students create their own cover or illustrations for the portfolio?

Figure 5.8 High school student-led conference agenda from Gilbert High School in Gilbert, South Carolina

SOURCE: This document is available in the online toolbox at http://www.wiley.com/go/lotolcompanion.

The purpose of the sophomore student-led conference at Gilbert High School is to reflect on your 10th-grade-year experiences in relationship to the questions that guide Sophomore Crew: **"Where am I now? How am I doing?"**

1. Consider these questions in relationship to both academics and character goals.
2. Provide evidence of your progress, strengths, and challenges in a presentation to family members and your crew leader.

Agenda

1. Share your "This I Believe" essay. Reflect on how your beliefs inform where you are and how you're doing.
2. Share two pieces of high-quality work that show how you are doing academically. For each piece selected, be sure to include:
   a. A copy of the final product (this can be a photograph or video if the piece is not done on paper)
   b. The process of creating this product
   c. A written reflection on the significance of this piece (why you chose to include it in the portfolio)
3. Share your learning target trackers from core classes as evidence of growth and mastery in each area of study.
4. Share your Brag Sheet – a record of academic, athletic, extracurricular, or civic positions, as well as any personal celebrations you would like to document.
5. Share your Crew Reflection – focusing on how Crew has impacted your academics and character
6. End with your Video-Diary message to a current ninth grader. What have you learned in 10th grade that will help a new student at Gilbert succeed and avoid any mistakes you've made?

- Are their opportunities for students to individualize the script, for example, to paraphrase or rewrite sentence stems that introduce the various parts of the agenda?

- Are there opportunities for students to "tell the story" of their learning in their own words, for example, to explain why something was especially challenging or rewarding or to describe the evidence of their learning?

- Does the presentation include opportunities for sharing accomplishments beyond core academics, such as arts, athletics, and out-of-school learning?

TRY THIS: ANALYZE A MODEL AND MAKE TIME FOR STUDENTS TO PRACTICE, REFLECT, AND REVISE IN RESPONSE TO FEEDBACK

As we noted in Chapter 4, in order to produce high-quality work, students need time to practice, reflect, and revise. The same is true if we expect students to present high-quality student-led conferences. Two Rivers Public Charter School in Washington, DC, provides a series of six lesson plans designed to introduce students to student-led conferences. You can find this collection and many more tools to support preparation for student-led conferences, including reflection questions, scripts, and questions for rehearsal, on their website, www.learnwithtworivers.org. The critique lesson plan in Figure 5.9, similarly, gives your students an opportunity to analyze a model closely, generate criteria for quality, and then practice through role play. The criteria for a high-quality student-led conference, which is best created *with* students through a process like that detailed in the lesson plan in Figure 5.9, can be left as is, or it can be turned into a rubric, which describes developing, accomplished, and exemplary levels.

Students will feel more confident and prepared for their student-led conferences if given a chance to rehearse.

Photo credit: EL Education

TRY THIS: ENLIST PARENTS TO SERVE AS PRACTICE PARTNERS

Parents are an untapped resource for rehearsing student-led conferences. There are often parents who have some flexibility during school time and who would be happy to come in for a few hours and rehearse with students (not their own child). Parents often enjoy helping in this way, students appreciate the attention and critique, and new relationships are created that help the school community. Even a parent who is not familiar with all of the educational goals can give helpful feedback about posture, eye-contact, speed and tone of voice, clarity of explanations, and other general presentation habits. Parents can be stationed in a corner of the room, in the hallway, or in a library/common space, and students can rotate through rehearsals. Make sure that parents have a copy of the portfolio table of contents/agenda and a rubric if you have one, and that they understand your classroom norms for providing kind, specific, and helpful feedback. (Note: You might consider referencing Figure 7.8 in Chapter 7, which offers guidance and sentence stems for offering kind, specific, and helpful feedback on passage presentations. It would also be useful as a tool to support students rehearsing for their student-led conferences.)

Figure 5.9 Lesson plan: Student-led conference preparation critique
SOURCE: This document is available in the online toolbox at http://www.wiley.com/go/lotolcompanion.

Day 1

Engage
- Ask students to turn and talk with a partner. Together come up with five things that keep their attention if they are listening to a speaker (e.g., a clear, loud voice).
- Share out a few.

Grapple
- Watch a model student-led conference video (for a collection of student-led conference videos see Video Spotlight 5.2 or go to https://eleducation.org/resources/collections/student-led-conferences).
- Discuss at your table what makes this student's conference good.

Apply
- Give each table three pink sticky notes (looks like) and three blue sticky notes (sounds like).
- Watch the model again. Write one specific "looks like" on each pink sticky note. Write one specific "sounds like" on each blue sticky note.
- Join two table groups together. Ask students in this larger group to organize their collective sticky notes into "looks like" and "sounds like" and then cluster together any sticky notes that are similar.

Synthesize
- Invite each super-table group to share one or two "looks like," then one or two "sounds" like criteria.
- Synthesize these into general presentation criteria and create an anchor chart to guide students' rehearsals.

Day 2

Engage
- Remind students of the presentation criteria anchor chart; unpack any criteria that students are unclear about.

Grapple
- Fishbowl a student-led conference rehearsal. The teacher could play student and present a conference, or invite a student who has done one before to demonstrate.
- Ask five students outside of the fishbowl to provide feedback based on the criteria list. (Remind students of feedback norms: be kind, specific, and helpful). Consider providing sentence stems to get students started.

Apply
- Pair students up and have them rehearse their student-led conference with a partner. Remind student to be kind, specific, and helpful when giving feedback and to use the criteria list/anchor chart to give feedback.

Synthesize
- Exit ticket: Ask students to write a goal related to the "looks like" or "sounds like" criteria that they want to work on most before their next formal rehearsal.

The Following Week
- Develop a formal presentation rubric or criteria list based on the anchor chart.
- In the next week or two, give students an opportunity to rehearse again with a buddy, a teacher, or someone in another class.
- Ask the partner to give feedback based on the presentation rubric.
- Return the exit tickets and ask students to journal on whether they met their goal.

Challenge #6: Students are too focused on what they did and not on what they learned.

TRY THIS: TEACH STUDENTS TO FOCUS ON THE LEARNING, NOT THE DOING

One of the most important things you can teach students about leading their conferences is how to deeply connect the evidence in their portfolio to their learning targets. In other words, students should be explaining how the work in their portfolio demonstrates *learning,* not just *doing,* and explaining where they are meeting targets, and where they have not yet met targets. Your ongoing dialogue with students about their data and their progress toward learning targets (see Chapter 3) is essential training for students to lead this same conversation with their families. Revisit Video Spotlight 5.2, featuring three videos from student-led conferences at the elementary, middle, and high school levels, to see how students themselves can reference learning targets and lead a nuanced conversation with their parents about the evidence that demonstrates their progress (or lack of progress) toward those targets.

TRY THIS: TEACH STUDENTS TO EMPHASIZE WHAT THEY ARE GRAPPLING WITH AND GROWING TOWARD

Parents sometimes feel frustrated if they leave a student-led conference with a good sense of what the student knows and can do currently but no idea what the student doesn't know yet and what she's working on improving for the future. One of the remarkable things about Rafael's student-led conference in Video Spotlight 5.2 is how deeply he reflects on the challenges of his upper-level Spanish course and what he's *not* yet able to do. He also identifies some specific actions – doing his homework, taking the risk to speak up in class even if it means being wrong – that will help him overcome those challenges. Deep reflection and articulating future goals should be a part of every conference. Table 5.6 provides some sentence starters that will help students reflect on learning targets they have mastered and those they are still making progress toward. When students use these sentence starters, you'll want to be sure that they also connect the comments to the specific evidence in the work they are reflecting on.

Table 5.6 Sentence starters for reflecting on mastery of and progress toward learning targets

Reflecting on Mastery	Reflecting on Progress
My work demonstrates my mastery of this learning target because. . .	Because I have not yet reached mastery on this learning target, I will. . .
<ul><li>It is accurate. . .</li><li>It is detailed. . .</li><li>It shows that I analyzed. . .</li><li>It shows that I evaluated. . .</li><li>It shows that I applied my learning. . .</li><li>It shows multiple perspectives on this topic, such as. . .</li><li>It uses evidence from reading and research, such as. . .</li></ul>	<ul><li>Research more thoroughly</li><li>Double-check my work</li><li>Reread and annotate</li><li>Discuss with my group</li><li>Follow through to revise</li><li>Consider other perspectives</li><li>Use evidence from the text</li></ul>

(continued)

Table 5.6 Continued

Reflecting on Mastery	Reflecting on Progress
My work demonstrates high-quality because. . .	To increase the quality of my work, I can. . .
<ul><li>It is accurate and functional</li><li>It is detailed</li><li>It is effectively organized</li><li>It shows my thinking</li><li>My grammar, punctuation, and spelling are correct</li><li>It is beautiful</li><li>It looks like a professional's work</li><li>It shows care and effort</li><li>I revised carefully to improve</li><li>It shows my original ideas and thinking</li><li>It demonstrates innovation</li><li>I really cared how it turned out</li><li>It has an audience beyond the teacher</li><li>It uses a real work format (e.g., a newspaper article)</li><li>It takes academic risks</li></ul>	<ul><li>Revise for precision</li><li>Take time to plan</li><li>Use all of my time</li><li>Focus on organization and ideas, not just grammar and punctuation</li><li>Ask for specific feedback and revise accordingly</li><li>Listen to the experts</li><li>Take a risk to be more original</li><li>Review the models more carefully</li><li>Use the rubric to guide my revisions</li></ul>
My work demonstrates my work habits because. . .	I can develop my work habits by. . .
<ul><li>I used outside resources to improve my work and thinking</li><li>I revised my work in response to feedback</li><li>I kept trying even when the work was hard</li><li>I followed directions and turned every part of the work in on time</li><li>I kept track of my materials throughout the project</li><li>I did my part to help my group succeed</li><li>I valued my group's contributions</li><li>My group took advantage of our different strengths to make our work better</li><li>I took the lead on this part. . .</li></ul>	<ul><li>Looking back on my notes and the assignment before I ask for help</li><li>Using a calendar to stay on track instead of doing everything at the last minute</li><li>Trying again when something is hard</li><li>Rereading the directions; comparing notes with other students</li><li>Organizing my materials</li><li>Trusting my group to support me</li><li>Contributing to and collaborating with my group</li><li>Being a leader when I have a good idea</li><li>Using all of my time</li><li>Paying attention to the deadlines</li></ul>

Learning Target 4: I can prepare families to engage meaningfully in their student's conference.

 Challenge #7: This is new for families. How do I help them let go of old assumptions about conferences?

TRY THIS: EDUCATE FAMILIES ABOUT WHAT TO EXPECT

When you are just establishing the practice of student-led conferences, or transitioning from traditional parent-teacher conferences to student-led conferences, there's a lot to communicate to families. It's understandable that it will take some time for family members to understand how the two formats are different and what they should expect at their child's conference. Be patient: the first year will be a transition for most families. In some schools, student-led conferences are a big success with parents in the first year; in other schools, the adjustment takes a few years. In our experience, almost no school or parent community wants to return to traditional conferences once they have made the switch.

Especially for families of elementary school students, it's important to communicate that students may be bringing fewer pieces of finished work home. Instead, students will be keeping these items in portfolios and sharing them during their student-led conference. Communications that help families make the transition come in many forms. The school website or student and family handbook is a good place to begin. King Philip Middle School, in West Hartford, Connecticut, for example, provides families with a number of articles that explain and share the rationale for student-led conferences. They also share videos of a student-led conferences, so that parents can see ahead of time what to expect.

Student or family handbooks are another important place to preview the practice of student-led conferences. The Springfield Renaissance School in Springfield, Massachusetts, includes this brief description in their handbook: "Three times a year all students prepare for and conduct a Student-Led Family Conference. Students present to a family member and their Crew leader a reflection of their current academic progress that includes concrete evidence from multiple classes showing strengths and weaknesses, evidence of their work habits, evidence of their contributions to the school community, and specific and measurable goals for the rest of the semester or school year. Through this process, students are able to develop important reflection and speaking skills."

At The Odyssey School of Denver, school communications clearly define the purpose of student-led conferences: "The purpose of student-led conferences is to engage/support students, parents and teachers in communicating progress toward academic learning and habits of a learner development. Students are the key communicator in the process as they learn to speak about their own strengths, struggles, goals and learning processes. This supports them in the process of becoming lifelong learners."

TRY THIS: CREATE TRADITIONS THAT WELCOME FAMILIES INTO THE LEARNING CONVERSATION

Beyond handbooks and websites, which some families may not always consult, information about student-led conferences should be communicated to every family through a letter or invitation. Better still, write a letter to all families with basic information, and then have students personalize an invitation

Figure 5.10 Letter to families from Two Rivers Public Charter School in Washington, DC

SOURCE: This document is available in the online toolbox at http://www.wiley.com/go/lotolcompanion.

Dear Middle School Families,

Your middle school student's conference is scheduled for this week. By now, your student's crew leader has contacted you or left a message, and we are aiming for 100% attendance.

What's the parent role during portfolio conferences? The adult's role is to ask probing questions that help students reflect upon the piece that they are presenting. We are trying to help students see improvements, next steps, or work habits that supported or impeded success.

I have never been part of a student-led conference. What are some good questions to ask during the portfolio portion?

- What was the process for creating this piece?
- What skills and knowledge does this piece demonstrate?
- How did you improve your work over time?
- How did your work change from the first draft to the final draft?
- How did you use feedback to improve the piece?
- What are you most proud of about this piece?
- If you were to do it over again, what would you do differently?
- What did the process teach you about your strengths and weaknesses in this class?
- What did you learn about yourself as a learner by creating this portfolio?

What are common parent concerns about portfolios? *First drafts are messy. Spelling is not perfect. Pieces of work get lost. Not all student work meets grade-level standards. Students sometimes struggle to explain their work.* Portfolios are meant to show the whole journey towards success, and the bumps along the way help us all support our student's success in the next semester. Please support growth by asking questions that make students think about their work. Criticism will lead a student to be less likely to share about herself.

What if I have specific questions for one of my child's teachers? You will meet with your student's crew leader. Should you have concerns that need to be addressed by a specific teacher, your crew leader will take notes and facilitate the connection. We can't wait to see you.

for their own family. Figure 5.10 offers an example of a letter to families that demystifies the process by addressing some of the common concerns families have, and offers a helpful list of questions they can ask during the conference so that they arrive feeling prepared.

Other welcoming traditions can also make a real difference in how families perceive conferences. Post some greeters in the parking lot. Have well-trained students in the hallways directing families around the school. Create welcoming and informative signage, and ensure that signs appear in multiple languages to accommodate families as necessary. Create table tents that include questions parents might ask during conferences to keep them positive and focused. Provide refreshments, like cider and cookies. These little details will go a long way to helping families let go of preconceived notions of parent-teacher conferences so that you can build a positive new tradition in your classroom and school.

 Challenge #8: Families don't understand their role in the conference. They take over instead of letting the student lead the dialogue.

TRY THIS: TEACH STUDENTS FACILITATION SKILLS

Leading a conference is a big step for many students, especially those who are used to or inclined to just sit back and listen to the grown-ups. When awkward silences ensue, family members might step in to "rescue" the child by taking over the conference. Moreover, if a parent is confused, frustrated, or impatient, he or she may try to "drive" the conference with pushy questions or a voice-over explanation that coopts the student's agenda.

There are a number of things you can do to prepare students to lead the narrative and help family members understand their role in the learning conversation. Start by explaining the student's and the family's role in advance. The following description of roles and responsibilities could be distributed at the conference and/or it could accompany the letter or invitation that goes to families ahead of time.

A student shares work with her parents during her student-led conference at Evergreen Community Charter School in Asheville, North Carolina.

Photo Credit: Anne Vilen

Role of the Student

- The student invites her family to the conference and communicates the importance of 100% participation.

- The student welcomes his family to the conference and ensures that everyone understands the agenda and their role.

- The student leads the conference. She initiates each part of the conference and lets participants know when it is appropriate to ask questions or offer feedback.

- The student makes sure families understand the relationship between learning targets and the evidence in the portfolio. He supports each claim about his learning with evidence.

- The student concludes the conference by inviting questions. She asks family members to give feedback on the conference survey. The student writes a formal thank-you note to his family after the conference.

Role of the Teacher

- The teacher guides students through the conference preparation process, but during the conference, he may not even sit at the table (especially if several conferences are occurring simultaneously).

- The teacher is available during the conference to support students who are struggling and, especially with younger students, to answer questions parents may have after the conference.

- The teacher ensures that all students complete their portfolios and lead a conference. If a family is unavailable, the teacher may enlist a colleague or administrator to stand in for the family.

- The teacher debriefs student-led conferences with students, so that everyone can learn from mistakes and improve on the next conference.

Role of the Family

- Family members arrive on time and wait to be invited to the conference table.

- Family members allow students to lead the conference and save questions until they are invited.

- Family members share any lingering concerns with the Crew leader or advisor, or the teacher who is monitoring the conference.

- Family members may be invited to give feedback and to help their student set goals based on the evidence in the portfolio. When identifying strategies to reach the goals, family members should consider ways to improve home routines that can help their student reach academic and character goals.

TRY THIS: CUE FAMILIES WITH OPPORTUNITIES TO PARTICIPATE APPROPRIATELY

Especially with younger students, you can gently remind parents of their role just before and even during the conference by explaining that students will do most of the talking and that there will be time to ask questions at the end. If you are not sitting at the table with the student, revise the script/agenda so that students start their conference by previewing the conference agenda. This allows families to know what's coming next and when they will have a chance to ask questions or comment on students' work. Many teachers also provide table tents with questions like those that follow, which support families to engage students appropriately during the conference.

Questions to Ask Your Child. . .

- What were the learning targets for this assignment?

- What skills did you have to use to complete it?

- What was the process for creating this piece?

- What did you read/research/investigate before you worked on it?

- What did you learn from doing this project?

- How did your work change from the first draft to the final draft?

- How did you use feedback to improve the piece?

- What are you most proud of about this piece?

- What would you do next time to improve this piece?

- What did the process teach you about your strengths and weaknesses in this class?

- What did you learn about yourself as a learner by creating this portfolio?

- What goals have you set for the remainder of the year?

- Why did you choose this goal? How do you plan to reach it?

TRY THIS: INVITE FAMILIES TO SET GOALS WITH THEIR STUDENT DURING THE CONFERENCE

It's important to emphasize that parents do have a role in the conference beyond just listening. In addition to asking productive questions, families can actually be part of helping their child to set or monitor progress toward goals during the conference. At some schools, the first student-led conference of the year is focused primarily on goal setting, based on baseline data from the beginning of the school year and the new challenges and priorities of the year ahead. At other schools, goal setting happens as one element of each student-led conference after the student's presentation of work. In Video Spotlight 5.3, an eighth-grade student leads his own "student-led meeting," attended by his teachers and his parents, in which he reflects on his challenges and growth and sets goals for leading his own learning. It portrays a different structure for a student-led conference than EL Education network schools typically use – one that brings in a large group of adults to the conversation – and is a provocative example. This conference demonstrates how students' academic growth is also connected to social and emotional development. When students reflect and report on their own learning, they are also better able to set impactful goals for the future.

Video Spotlight 5.3: Developing Agency with Student-Led Conferences
https://www.edutopia.org/video/developing-agency-student-led-conferences

This video, filmed at University Park Campus School, in Worcester, Massachusetts, features education experts, and an eighth-grade student, his teachers, and his parents all reflecting on the power of student-led meetings. This video was produced by Edutopia.

Video Reflection Questions
1. What does Alec say that demonstrates agency and responsibility – a willingness to change his work habits going forward?
2. How can you tweak the structure of student-led meetings or conferences in your own school to instill this kind of collaboration between students, teachers, and their families as students set goals for the future?

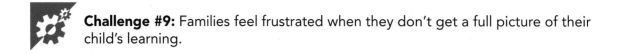

Challenge #9: Families feel frustrated when they don't get a full picture of their child's learning.

TRY THIS: PROVIDE DIFFERENTIATED CONFERENCE FORMATS WHEN NECESSARY

For some families, deep concerns about a student who is struggling in school make a student-led conference feel inappropriate. Families understandably want the school to intervene quickly and effectively. They want clear, direct, and goal-oriented communication, and they may feel this needs to come straight from the teacher, not from the student. They may also want some conversation where the student is not present. We suggest that a standard student-led conference remains an important structure to keep for these students, just like every student, and, additionally, another structure or strategy may need to be added. For example, the student can leave the room to allow for some adult-only discussion for a part of the conference, or a separate conference can be scheduled for adults at a different time.

At The Odyssey School of Denver, teachers and leaders have devised a solution to this problem by providing differentiated conference formats. Conferences for students who are struggling in a class where they are supported by a learning specialist or for a student who is struggling considerably are structured differently, with more adults at the table. Study Table 5.7, then review your roster of students and identify those for whom you may need to provide a separate and more fully supported conference.

Table 5.7 Differentiated conference formats at The Odyssey School of Denver

Type 1: Typical	Type 2: Push-in	Type 3: Intervention
This conference type is good for: • Most students • Students who are in good standing academically • Families that you have been in close communication with	**This conference type is good for:** • Students who may be performing well in most classes, but struggling in one that includes a specialist • Students who are not passing a class, but for whom major intervention isn't needed; instead, targeted interventions (e.g., behavior management) may be needed	**This conference type is good for:** • Students who are not doing well across the board • Students for whom it is necessary for ALL teachers and specialists to meet together to provide support
Time needed: • One 30-minute conference slot	**Time needed:** • One 30-minute conference slot	**Time needed:** • Two 30-minute conference slots OR backed up to a break (at least 45 minutes)
Who attends: • Crew leader, student, family	**Who attends:** • Crew leader, one specialist (could be for only a portion of the conference), student, family	**Who attends:** • Crew leader, as many teachers and specialists as possible, student, family

TRY THIS: INVITE FEEDBACK FROM FAMILIES

Just as students can use descriptive feedback to improve the quality of their work, it is important for teachers and leaders to use feedback to improve the structure of and support for conferences. Evaluation forms, like the ones in Figures 5.11 and 5.12, can help you gather useful suggestions to guide the improvement of student-led conferences in the future.

Figure 5.11 Student-led conference parent survey adapted from The Franklin School of Innovation in Asheville, North Carolina

SOURCE: This document is available in the online toolbox at http://www.wiley.com/go/lotolcompanion.

What grade is your child in?

Student-led conferences gave me deeper insight into the following aspects of my child's learning (check all that apply):
- ❑ What my child is learning
- ❑ My child's study habits such as finishing assignments/handing in work on time
- ❑ My child's growth as a learner
- ❑ My child's habits of scholarship

What was the most helpful mode of communication regarding student-led conferences?

- ❑ Hard copy letter from the principal
- ❑ Emails from my child's crew leader
- ❑ Robo call reminders

What was the most challenging part of participating in student-led conferences?

- ❑ Scheduling
- ❑ Not being familiar with the conference format
- ❑ Logistics (timing and transportation)
- ❑ Letting my child lead the conversation
- ❑ Other _____

What was the most rewarding part of student-led conferences for you?

What could we do better in preparing for and conducting student-led conferences next time?

Figure 5.12 Student-led conference parent survey from Oakhurst Elementary School in Decatur, Georgia

SOURCE: This document is available in the online toolbox at http://www.wiley.com/go/lotolcompanion.

Please rate on a scale of 5 to 1 with "5" being a statement you strongly agree with and "1" being a statement you disagree with.

1. My child was able to explain her/his growth as a learner.						
Strongly Agree	**5**	**4**	**3**	**2**	**1**	**Strongly Disagree**

2. I have a clearer picture of what my child learned this semester.						
Strongly Agree	**5**	**4**	**3**	**2**	**1**	**Strongly Disagree**

3. I believe student-led conferences helped my child strengthen his/her habits of scholarship.						
Strongly Agree	**5**	**4**	**3**	**2**	**1**	**Strongly Disagree**

4. What did you enjoy most about your participation in the **Student-Led Conference?**

_____

_____

Oakhurst Families: THANK YOU for participating in your child's conference today. Now, we have an assignment for you! Please write your child a positive, personal note about the conference. We hope this experience was as rewarding to you and your child as the process was to us! Thanks again for choosing to take an active role in your child's education. This letter will become part of your child's portfolio.

TRY THIS: DEBRIEF WITH STUDENTS AND COLLEAGUES

You've gleaned lots of strategies for improving your conferences from this chapter. You can come up with many more, and many that are tuned to the particular challenges of your school, by putting heads together with your own students and colleagues. Plan to debrief conferences with your students within a day or two after they are held. If possible, also debrief with colleagues. Following are some debrief questions that can drive a productive dialogue. Add a few of your own based on your experience with conferences:

- Describe the highlights of your conferences.

- What challenges or concerns came up that you didn't anticipate?

- Was your family(s) satisfied with your portfolio and supporting documentation? Were there documents that you would add to the portfolio?

- Did the logistics of your conference(s) go smoothly?

- Was I/were the teachers accessible during your conference(s)?

- _____

- _____

Gilbert High School in Gilbert, South Carolina, debriefed their first student-led conferences by simply sharing "notices" and "wonders" about the evening. You can see their notes from the debrief in Figure 5.13. Their list may inspire new questions and insights at your own school.

Figure 5.13 Student-led conferences faculty debrief notes from Gilbert High School in Gilbert, South Carolina

Notice	Wonders
• Over 95% of the SLCs were student led. • Parents seemed to be engaged in the conversations. • The student leaders escorting parents were very well received and they did a beautiful job. • The greeters at the front were well informed. • This was incredibly organized–(kudos to Libby and team). • There were LTs for the SLC and an agenda for all students. • Parents had prompts/questions they could use to engage in the conversations. • The space was very appropriate. • There was documentation of the process. • Signage was helpful and appropriate. • Survey for parents. • Celebration for students after conferences—field day and lunch. • The leaders welcomed parents and the sign-in process was very well organized and received. • The Brag sheets and examples of high-quality work were strong. • There were plenty of pieces of evidence/artifacts in the SLC. • Students seemed well practiced and parents seemed engaged in the SLCs. • The check in process was very well organized. • Crew leaders greeting the parents was a strong practice. • Students saw value in the SLCs. • Parents commented that the depth of the conversation with their child about their learning was greater than usual.	• Do we need to frame the SLC for parents as a group? • Should there be some type of admin welcome? • Does the use of electronics detract from the SLC? • When will we debrief with crew leaders about actual conferences? • Is there more and/or something else crew leaders should do during the conferences? • Did the other principals get an opportunity to be engaged in this process? • Do we need a walkie talkie to communicate with office staff? • If a parent does not show, could we have the student contact them via telephone first–then send them back to class and/or a teacher/admin instead of waiting? • What are students doing when they are not presenting? • Are students able to have some "regular" schedule on an SLC day? • By having substitutes "standing by" does it create an easy "out" of getting a parent/guardian to listen to SLCs? • I wonder if the iPads limit the presentation and/or conversation with the parents? • Do we need to support parents with small children better and how if so? • How many parents speak about bringing children home after SLC? Is it because of the team-building and/or being on a Friday? • Parent Guides to SLC in Spanish?

Lessons for Leaders: Chapter 5

Making the shift to student-led conferences is a major instructional, organizational, and cultural shift for a school. It's not easy! Families, students, and even teachers may feel overwhelmed and upset during the transition. School leadership is crucial in making this a positive and successful shift. Leaders must be confident and expansive in regularly communicating – in speaking and writing – the pedagogical reasons for the shift, the great potential to improve learning, and the expectation that every single student, family, and teacher will participate. Most importantly, leaders must be champions for the ways in which student-led conferences can positively impact school culture and student achievement. Video Spotlight 5.4 features a principal in New York City reflecting on the systems and structures that support successful and impactful student-led conferences at his school.

 Video Spotlight 5.4: Schoolwide Structures for Student-Led Conferences
https://vimeo.com/58187029

Principal Brett Kimmel of Washington Heights Expeditionary Learning School (WHEELS) in New York City describes the integrated approach used at his school to ensure that all students and families participate in meaningful student-led conferences.

 Video Reflection Questions
1. Within two months of opening as a brand-new school, WHEELS conducted their first student-led conferences. Based on what Principal Brett Kimmel says about student-led conferences, why do you think they decided to prioritize this structure?
2. Principal Kimmel talks about setting expectations for student-led conferences, including 100% attendance. Could you set this expectation in your school? What barriers do you face and how can you overcome them? (Note: Refer back to Table 5.4 for barriers and bridges to family engagement.)

School leaders can offer great support to teachers by ensuring that structures and systems are in place for success: procedures, guidelines, schedules, protocols, communication systems, and lots of faculty time for planning and preparation. It is important that teachers can meet with each other to draft, revise, and refine conference schedules, reflection tools, portfolio maintenance protocols, and conference agendas. School leaders also need to troubleshoot the transition during the first year: personally meeting with parents, students, and teachers who may have challenges with the structure.

Following are our top tips for leaders working to create a strong culture and a well-coordinated system of documents and procedures for student-led conferences. Table 5.8 summarizes the key action steps for teachers and students that will lead to successful student-led conferences.

Top Tips

- Review the many resources and tools in this chapter. Which ones fill a gap in your own system? Which ones can you adapt and revise to strengthen the tools you already have?

- Drive the scheduling of student-led conferences at the macro level. Where do they fit in your year-long calendar? How can you support teachers and families to ensure that every student leads a conference and every family is able to attend?

- Recognize and build on the expertise of your own faculty by selecting a team of teachers to spearhead needed professional learning on student-led conferences for the rest of the faculty. The same team can revise schoolwide documents and coordinate communication about student-led conference expectations and schedules to the rest of the staff.

- Build teachers' capacity to prepare for student-led conferences by carving out extra time for teachers who are new to the process to learn and prepare.

- Stay on top of early communications to families about student-led conferences. Make conferences accessible and welcoming for all families, including those who must overcome scheduling or language barriers in order to attend.

- Seek feedback from students, teachers, and families. Facilitate ways to debrief and respond to this feedback.

- Hone the message. In communications with families, teachers, students, and your district, be sure to present student-led conferences as part of an overall approach to supporting students to lead their own learning.

Table 5.8 Student-led conference: Steps to success

What Should Teachers Do?
Collaborate with other teachers and with school leaders to create a coherent system for student-led conferences, including scheduling and logistics that meet the needs of all grades.
Develop structures to increase access for families so that all families can engage in conferences effectively.
Design portfolios and agendas that balance breadth, depth, achievement, and growth so that students present a comprehensive picture of who they are.
Support and hold students accountable for working on their portfolios and preparing to reflect on their work "along the way" rather than just before the conference.
Provide students with models and tools to help them rehearse and get feedback on their student-led conference presentation.
Welcome and engage families as full partners in the conference experience.
Debrief conferences with each other and with students.
What Should Students Do?
Reflect on their work along the way. Gather evidence of their progress toward learning targets.
Follow systems and protocols for compiling a high-quality portfolio throughout the year.
Practice the conference presentation; listen to feedback and revise.
Lead the conference conversation. Describe and reflect on their learning with insight and confidence. Invite questions. Set goals.
Debrief conferences by reflecting on what worked, and what could be done better.

Post-Assessment: Track Your Progress: Chapter 5

As you have read Chapter 5, maybe you have had an opportunity to try some of these strategies and techniques along the way. If not, come back to this post-assessment after you have had a chance to do so. Give yourself whatever time you need to address the learning targets and challenges in a meaningful way. Then take a moment to check your progress in Table 5.9, which is the exact same Learning Target Tracker that appeared at the beginning of this chapter.

Circle or place an X along the continuum from Beginning to Exceeding: **How would you rate your progress toward each learning target** *at this point in time?* Use the space provided to make notes regarding any remaining challenges you may be having or ideas for new and different strategies you want to try.

Table 5.9   Chapter 5 learning target tracker

Learning Target 1: *I can help build a schoolwide system for effective student-led conferences.* Beginning---------------------------------Developing----------------------------------Meeting------------------------------------Exceeding Notes:
Learning Target 2: *I can structure portfolios and conference agendas so that families get the information they need and want.* Beginning---------------------------------Developing----------------------------------Meeting------------------------------------Exceeding Notes:
Learning Target 3: *I can ensure that students are prepared to lead a conference with a high-quality presentation.* Beginning---------------------------------Developing----------------------------------Meeting------------------------------------Exceeding Notes:
Learning Target 4: *I can prepare families to engage meaningfully in their student's conference.* Beginning---------------------------------Developing----------------------------------Meeting------------------------------------Exceeding Notes:

Celebrations of Learning

Checking for Understanding during Daily Lessons

Using Data with Students

Learning Targets

Models, Critique, and Descriptive Feedback

STUDENT-ENGAGED ASSESSMENT

Student-engaged assessment is a system of interrelated practices that positions students as leaders of their own learning.

Standards-Based Grading

Student-Led Conferences

Passage Presentations with Portfolios

Celebrations of Learning

What Are Celebrations of Learning?

A celebration of learning (which many schools may refer to as an *exhibition* of learning) is a culminating classroom, grade-level or schoolwide event in which students present high-quality work to the school community, families, and members of the greater community. Although we use the term celebration, and there is always joy in the event, it is not like the cast party after a play—it is the play itself. It is a public exhibition of student learning in academics and the arts that features student work and student reflection on learning. Expedition nights, culminating events, authors' nights, and many other names all fall under the umbrella term celebrations of learning. Celebrations of learning can include presentations, original performances, and demonstrations for an authentic audience.

Like student-led conferences, celebrations of learning entrust students themselves to tell the story of their learning, growth, and character. In celebrations, however, the emphasis is on telling the story through student work that may not fit easily into a portfolio, and telling it collectively to a community audience, not just to the student's own family. Celebrations also often focus on one particular topic, project, learning expedition, or unit of study, rather than an overview of all academic areas. And most importantly, celebrations are a collective event that builds community pride within a classroom or school and across the wider community, and—like a musical, dramatic, or team athletic performance—builds bonds among students.

Celebrations are truly celebratory, and they are also dynamic visual and auditory demonstrations of what students know and can do. Students share their best work—often writing, artwork, projects, and performances they have created, rehearsed, and polished over time. They also share the process of creating that work and the challenges and learning along the way. They are reflective presentations in which students connect what they have done and learned to learning targets, grade-level standards, and the journey they've traveled together to reach them. This means that in addition to student work, celebrations will likely feature photos of fieldwork and learning in action, student reflections and quotes, and posters with learning targets on display. It also means that students, not teachers, are the hosts of the event. They introduce and MC the program, greet visitors, respond to questions, and represent their classroom and school community as confident and competent narrators of the learning story.

> This is our first celebration of learning. . . where students present to an authentic audience "here is what I learned," not just here's my poem or here's my hero's journey paper. It's "here's the journey I went through. Here's what my journey looked like and felt like, and here's how I'm forever changed because I did that."
>
> —*Shari Griffin, teacher, Fox Creek Elementary, Littleton, Colorado*

In this chapter we build on the practices we explored in Chapter 6 of *Leaders of Their Own Learning* to help you meet three learning targets. Along the way we give you an opportunity to explore solutions to the common challenges many teachers face when implementing celebrations of learning in their schools.

Learning Targets for Chapter 6

1. I can choreograph the details of a celebration of learning.
2. I can support students to produce original, high-quality work for an authentic audience.
3. I can display student work with power and purpose.
4. I can prepare students to tell the story of their learning in a way that informs, enlightens, and moves the audience.
5. I can structure celebrations of learning so that families and community members can participate meaningfully.

Pre-Assessment: Track Your Progress: Chapter 6

Before we dive in, take a moment to assess yourself on each of the learning targets for this chapter. In Table 6.1, circle or place an X along the continuum from Beginning to Exceeding: **How would you rate your progress toward each learning target** *at this point in time?*

We'll give you a chance to assess yourself again at the end of the chapter.

Table 6.1 Chapter 6 learning target tracker

Learning Target 1: *I can choreograph the details of a celebration of learning.*
Beginning----------------------------------Developing----------------------------------Meeting----------------------------------Exceeding
Notes:

Learning Target 2: *I can support students to produce original, high-quality work for an authentic audience.*
Beginning----------------------------------Developing----------------------------------Meeting----------------------------------Exceeding
Notes:

Learning Target 3: *I can display student work with power and purpose.*
Beginning----------------------------------Developing----------------------------------Meeting----------------------------------Exceeding
Notes:

Learning Target 4: *I can prepare students to tell the story of their learning in a way that informs, enlightens, and moves the audience.*
Beginning----------------------------------Developing----------------------------------Meeting----------------------------------Exceeding
Notes:

Learning Target 5: *I can structure celebrations of learning so that families and community members can participate meaningfully.*
Beginning----------------------------------Developing----------------------------------Meeting----------------------------------Exceeding
Notes:

Learning Target 1: I can choreograph the details of a celebration of learning.

Challenge #1: There are so many details! How do I get it all done while I'm teaching?

TRY THIS: PLAN EARLY AND COLLABORATIVELY

Every school holds events – curriculum open houses, school plays, art shows, math nights, graduation ceremonies, to name just a few. A celebration of learning combines many elements of these sorts of events, with which you are likely already familiar. However, it is not just a time for showing families what students have been doing in school – it's an opportunity for students themselves to showcase the quality and relevance of their work and to celebrate the culture of the school with the entire community. Before you begin your planning process, it's important to get a picture of what a celebration of learning might look like. Watch the video in Video Spotlight 6.1 and consider the reflection questions that follow.

Video Spotlight 6.1: Fox Creek Elementary Celebration of Learning
https://vimeo.com/313905677

In this video, leaders, teachers, students, and families reflect on their first ever schoolwide celebration of learning at Fox Creek Elementary School in Littleton, Colorado. This video was produced by Fox Creek Elementary School.

Video Reflection Questions
1. How does the opening of the celebration of learning with a schoolwide presentation and greeters at the door set the stage for families and visitors?
2. What most surprises parents about their students' abilities as presenters?
3. How could a celebration of learning impact the culture of *your* school?

The structures and systems that drive the events that already exist at your school can also be used as a starter set to make a celebration of learning successful. Whether you are planning a celebration of learning for a single classroom or for an the entire school, asking the right questions, like those that follow, will help you assess what needs to be done, by whom, and when.

1. Which classrooms will be presenting?

2. Who will be invited (e.g., families, community members)?

3. What kind of experience do you want your community guests to have?

4. How will you advertise and promote the event?

5. What do you need to communicate to families ahead of time?

6. What's the timing of the celebration and the order of events?

7. What student work will you showcase?

8. Where will the work be displayed/presented?

9. How will the story of the work – the learning involved – be highlighted in addition to the work itself?

10. What questions do you hope families will ask? What do you want them to look for?

11. Will there be a program for the event featuring student work? Who will create it?

12. What equipment do you need for presentations (e.g., sound equipment, tables, podiums, lighting, props)?

13. What other logistics and hosting details do you need to plan (e.g., refreshments, welcome and directional signs, name tags)? Who will organize that work?

14. How will you know if you've been successful?

Especially if you are planning a schoolwide celebration of learning, it's important to share the load by involving teachers from multiple grade levels and school leaders in the planning. Parents can often be a terrific help as well, organizing logistics such as refreshments, social media, and promotion. Remember too that there is no one right format for a celebration of learning. Some schools plan an evening celebration that involves all grade levels; this means that every grade level and every classroom must be prepared to present their students' work at the same time. Other schools do celebrations by grade level, which allows for a bit more autonomy in the timing and involves less logistical coordination of space and staffing. In some schools, individual classrooms or subject areas organize celebrations of learning to showcase a particular project, product, or topic of study. All of these formats can be successful if the details are in place.

Figure 6.1 provides an example of how the Instructional Leadership Team at Kuumba Academy, in Wilmington, Delaware, began their collaborative planning for a schoolwide celebration of learning. Consider creating a similar action plan for your next celebration of learning.

TRY THIS: LEVERAGE THE POWER OF STUDENTS IN THE PLANNING AND PREPARATION

Remember that the purpose of a celebration of learning is for students to be fully engaged in sharing and demonstrating their learning. Students should be beaming with pride, actively interacting with the audience, and showcasing high-quality products that are professionally presented. Enlisting students' help in planning the celebration will make it both more authentic and more powerful. Kid-inspired celebrations bring down the house!

The list that follows identifies some support roles (in addition to the key role of presenting their work) that leverage the help of students:

❑ Create and address invitations.

❑ Create the program for the evening.

❑ Prepare documentation panels (or help a teacher do so).

❑ Clean up and organize classrooms, the school, and the school grounds in advance of the event.

❑ Act as greeters, tour guides, or runners; or work the setup, refreshments, and cleanup teams.

❑ Write an excitement-building article about the celebration of learning for the school newsletter, newspaper, website, and/or social media accounts.

❑ Make signs needed for the event.

(Note: In Learning Target 4 of this chapter we delve into the roles that students play *during* the celebration of learning itself.)

Figure 6.1 Celebration of learning planner from Kuumba Academy Charter School in Wilmington, Delaware
SOURCE: This document is available in the online toolbox at http://www.wiley.com/go/lotolcompanion.

When will celebrations of learning occur for each grade level?	
• May 22 for grades K–1 • May 26 for grades 2–4 • May 27 for grades 5–7	To Do: ❑ All draft documentation panels up by 5/19 ❑ Staff gallery walk on 5/20 with feedback ❑ Final doc panels ready on 5/22 for all parents

What is each grade level exhibiting?	
• Kindergarten: posters • 1st: animal book (Atrium) • 2nd: PSA (Public Service Announcement) (Library) • 3rd: PSA • 4th: brochures • 5th: graphic novels • 6th: magazine and posters • 7th:	To Do: ❑ Reserve atrium and library

What can be done to ensure high levels of attendance from families and community members?
To Do: ❑ See if we can offer breakfast for families when they attend ❑ Students create written invitations ❑ Teachers identify a community member to invite and make the outreach ❑ Teachers invite experts to attend ❑ Invite board members ❑ Postcard contest at three levels—top five get sent out for postcards ❑ Save the date to go out from admin by April 24th ❑ Thank you photograph

In what ways will families and community members be encouraged to be *active* participants in the celebration of learning?	
• Glows and Grows note-catcher for parents • 3-2-1 exit ticket • Digital portfolio on Facebook with hashtag • Involve PTA and student government	To Do: ❑ ILT checks in with grade-level teachers ❑ ILT reports to admin ❑ Price digital storytelling

How will teachers ensure that students demonstrate mastery of state and Common Core standards at the celebration of learning?	
• Ensure rubrics are aligned with standards. • Doc panels reference learning targets. • Students should be able to connect their work to standards.	

What will be on the documentation panels	
• Rubrics, rough-drafts, graphic organizer, reflections, learning targets, habits of scholarship, summary of case study, guiding questions, pictures/experts, representation from each student	

What steps need to be taken to prepare students for celebrations of learning?	
• Provide rehearsal time • Reflect and revise • Publish high-quality work • Prepare the presentation equipment and space • Display for impact	To Do: ❑ Ask EL Education school designer for feedback

TRY THIS: LEVERAGE THE POWER OF THE COMMUNITY IN PLANNING AND PREPARATION

Family and community members play an important role in any celebration of learning. First of all, they are the chief audience. They are also, often, eager to help support the logistics. By all means, be the stage manager of your event, but enlist the help of others for setup, cleanup, food, decoration, and promotion. The following list will help you identify tasks for family and community members:

- ❏ Announce or promote the event to groups in the community (e.g., school board or district office).

- ❏ Provide dinner or snacks for teachers and students before the event.

- ❏ Provide snacks and beverages during the event.

- ❏ Set up and staff fund-raising booths during the event.

- ❏ Help with parking and traffic flow.

- ❏ Help prepare documentation panels or displays of student work.

- ❏ Train and rehearse with student hosts/docents.

- ❏ Set up and take down chairs, performance equipment, or technology before and after the event.

- ❏ Host community members or VIPs in the audience; ensure they receive a special welcome and introduce them to student presenters, teachers, and school leaders.

- ❏ Promote the event on social media.

 Challenge #2: We are disappointed with the level of family and community attendance.

TRY THIS: START THE EVENT WITH A SCHOOLWIDE ASSEMBLY OR PERFORMANCE

Starting your celebration of learning with a well-promoted performance or presentation is a great way to gather the crowd, build excitement, and introduce the evening's agenda. Evergreen Community Charter School in Asheville, North Carolina, begins its celebration of learning with a student art gallery that is set up in the gymnasium. Winnona Park Elementary School in Decatur, Georgia, begins each celebration of learning with a student-led musical performance, followed by a short introduction in which the school principal previews what family members should look for in hallways and classrooms. Even if you are hosting a grade-level or individual classroom celebration, starting it with a slide-show, performance, or student presentation creates an opportunity for students to frame the celebration, connect student work to learning targets and guiding questions, and generally give audience members a few directions before the tour of individual work begins.

Second Graders present their learning about snakes at a celebration of learning at Conservatory Lab Charter School in Boston.

Photo Credit: EL Education

TRY THIS: BUILD A TRADITION THAT THE COMMUNITY CAN'T RESIST

Over time, a school's celebration of learning may become the event of the school year, something everyone in the school community – students, families, neighbors, community stakeholders, and teachers – looks forward to. A celebration of learning binds the school community together because it reminds everyone not just what students are learning, but *why* and *how* they are learning, and the difference it makes for the future. One way to turn a showcase of student work into the event of the season is to blend in other school functions – fund-raising, a pot-luck dinner, a service project, or a sports competition. Pretty soon people will be saying, "After the game, we'll go to your classroom to see your work, and then you can show us what's happening in other grades," or "Let's be sure to arrive early, so we get some of the tamales the third grade is selling." Figure 6.2 is a middle school celebration of learning program. Note the 20-questions trivia game to generate some friendly competition among teams of families and students.

We have also seen many schools in communities with prominent cultural backgrounds where the celebration of learning is simultaneously an affirmation of those cultures. If the celebration features food, music, clothing, or dance that connects to common family backgrounds and traditions (e.g., if the parent community is largely Mexican-American or Dominican-American, and the celebration features familiar foods), families feel honored and comfortable. The celebration may be joined with an outdoor picnic, games for children and adults, or an outdoor concert.

Figure 6.2 Middle school celebration of learning program from Wood Hill Middle School, Andover, Massachusetts

7 East (8:30 -10:00)   Rooms 124, 130, 133, 134, 136
    Katie Bent, Chris Brodeur, Chip Gregory
    Betty Singleton, Donna Sunderland, Thyra Sherman

Welcome to Team 7 East!
Please help us celebrate our completed and continuing work from 8:30-10:00 AM this morning.
Here's what you'll find as you travel through our wing:
    Ms. Sunderland's room:
    Trail Blazing Video and Walk-a-thon Video
    Ms. Bent's room:
    Social Studies projects on display
    Caesar Trial Pictures on display
    Mr. Gregory's room:
    Live poetry readings
    Mr. Brodeur's room:
    Pictures of field guide/website work in action
    Microscope PupilCAM's in use
    Plant specimens on display

    Hallway:
    Guatemala Picture Display
    Math Walking Rate Charts
    Walk-a-thon Picture Display
    Student Essays on Lockers

8 East (8:00 – 10:30)   Rooms 224, 230, 233, 234, 236
    Jane Anthony, Brian Carey, Scott Govoni,
    Laura Desjardins, Kim Leiberman

Team 8 East will showcase the work of an investigation focusing on Social Injustices through a look at period music, art and literature from the 1930's as part of the students reading of To Kill a Mockingbird.

Also, the 8 East team will be featuring various works of the students:
- Ms. Anthony showcasing student Weather Books and Human Body Books
- Ms. Desjardins showcasing Writing Folders
- Mr. Carey showcasing War of 1812 Newspapers, U.S. Foreign Policy Timelines, Civil War Letters to the Editor and Memorial Day Investigation.

Finally, after the student presentation of their Social Injustice Expedition students and parents will participate in a game of 20 Questions where each subject area teacher will create 20 questions as a review of the past year. Each homeroom along with their parents will form teams in a friendly competition in their attempt to answer the most questions correctly.

8 West (8:30 -10:30) Rooms 203, 204, 207
    Christine Hill, David Lawrence, Karen Parker

Learning Target 2: I can support students to produce original, high-quality work for an authentic audience.

Challenge #3: My students' work is too similar; if you've seen one example, you've seen them all.

TRY THIS: GIVE STUDENTS' CHOICE AND VOICE WITHIN A COMMON THEME OR TOPIC

It's not uncommon for families to arrive at a celebration of learning only to see 25 of the same teacher-created book templates posted on the wall. The lines have been filled in by students, but it's hard to distinguish one from another or to understand what choices students made as authors or what thinking they did to produce the work. Especially with young students, you may feel compelled to give students a template to begin from. There is value in students "copying" a model in order to learn new skills and work toward professional quality. At the same time, the work students produce should have an element of their unique personality, voice, thinking, and creativity.

Kindergarten students created a unique "person" to hold the book at the center that contains their early writing and learning about nutrition.

Photo Credit: Anne Vilen

If the student work is by its nature very similar for each student, it can still be personalized by displaying an accompanying author's or artist's statement, or, similarly, a scientist's, historian's, or mathematician's reflection on the work. Accompanying displayed work with a reflective statement by the author of that work does more than simply distinguish it for families; it puts the focus on *what was learned* in the creation of the work, not simply the work itself.

Another way to coach students toward variety and excellence is to use a common format for the work but to allow each student to choose a different subject. That way, the same background learning and lessons in content and skills applies to every student, but each has a distinct subject for his or her final product (e.g., every student learns how to write a strong book review, but they each review a different book). For example, second-grade teacher Jenna Gampel, from Conservatory Lab Charter School in Boston chose snakes as the topic of her students' science study and assigned each student a different snake to profile. Students researched, illustrated, and wrote a nonfiction story about their individual snake. The format was the same; the skills preparation was the same; but the students each created a unique written page and scientific illustration. They worked with a professional herpetologist, illustrator, and other experts along the way to their professional-quality audio e-book. They even got feedback from the experts to help them with pacing and presentation skills they would need in the recording studio. Watch the video in Video Spotlight 6.2, the first in a six-part series, for an overview of this remarkable work.

 Video Spotlight 6.2: Inspiring Excellence Part 1: Overview
https://vimeo.com/85779604

The Inspiring Excellence video series celebrates a powerful confluence of exciting original research that includes fieldwork and experts, artistic skill and critique, and sharp literacy practices. This video overview begins with second-graders at Conservatory Lab Charter School in Boston celebrating months of hard work and presenting the premier of their e-book *Slithering Snake Stories*. (Note: If you are interested in viewing the full six-part series about this project, you can do so at: https://eleducation.org/resources/collections/inspiring-excellence-videos.)

 Video Reflection Questions
1. How do students' individual passions and sense of purpose reveal themselves in these illustrations and stories?
2. How does the teacher's choice of different products each year, all on the topic of snakes, enable her to build on her teaching resources and lesson plans and also keep her celebration of learning fresh and exciting for herself and for her students?

 Challenge #4: Students and community members are excited about the celebration, but the quality of student work is not as strong as it could be.

TRY THIS: BE A STRONG GUARDIAN OF QUALITY

Even when work displayed at a celebration of learning is clearly original, it can disappoint an audience if it is poorly constructed or overly simple. In Chapter 4, we discussed a number of strategies for coaching students to produce work that shows complexity, craftsmanship, and authenticity. The most common problem in reaching quality is time. Almost all teachers underestimate how long it will take for students to create high-quality work, or feel too worried about coverage of academic content to be able to dedicate substantial time for preparation. Those pressures are real, but we encourage you to be bold and commit to carving out truly significant time for work creation, refinement, and rehearsal. It may feel scary at the time, but the payoff in boosting students' standards for pride in their work will pay off.

In the end, the work displayed at a celebration of learning should be work that students are proud to share with their families and with the community. It should also be work that evokes families' and community members' curiosity, wonder, and admiration. Truly high-quality work shows that students are capable of much more than their families, or even they, imagined. It is work that teaches the audience about both what and how students learn in your classroom or your school. It is the tangible evidence of a hands-on, minds-on approach to learning – work that yearns for a public audience.

In Video Spotlight 6.3, revisit Jenna Gampel's second-grade students as they prepare the writing and speaking about snakes that was later shared at their celebration of learning. Gampel dedicated a tremendous amount of time with students focused on the quality of this project – an audio e-book – and the resulting work was stunning.

(Note: For much more on supporting students to produce high-quality work, revisit Chapter 4.)

Video Spotlight 6.3: Inspiring Excellence Part 6: Writing and Speaking with Power
https://vimeo.com/85789701

This video features second-graders at Conservatory Lab Charter School in Boston crafting narrative nonfiction stories based on their research about snakes. They then practice reading their work aloud in preparation for the final production of their audio e-book in a recording studio.

Video Reflection Questions
1. How do the color-coded organizers Gampel provides help students connect their learning to their learning targets and stay on track to create high-quality work?
2. What are the specific techniques students learn for presenting their work aloud in the recording studio? Do you agree that this is time well spent? Why or why not?
3. How might you revise your plans for a future project to give it the "time and care" students need to create high-quality work?

Check Yourself Checklist

Preparing High-Quality Work for Public Display Checklist

Use this checklist to determine if student work is ready for public display:

❏ It demonstrates complex, rigorous thinking.

❏ If applicable, it articulates and analyzes multiple perspectives.

❏ It shows remarkable accuracy and detail.

❏ It demonstrates specific techniques that students have practiced and polished.

❏ It shows a unique approach to the question we are trying to answer.

❏ It uses professional vocabulary and format.

❏ It invites wonder and analysis.

❏ It reveals an original and engaging perspective on a local problem or solution.

❏ It is beautiful in conception and execution.

Source: This checklist is available in the online toolbox at http://www.wiley.com/go/lotolcompanion.

Learning Target 3: I can display student work with power and purpose.

Challenge #5: Students' individual work is high quality, but our display doesn't do it justice.

TRY THIS: TREAT THE WALLS OF YOUR SCHOOL LIKE A MUSEUM

We believe that the walls of a school can function as a museum of learning for students, staff, and guests, especially during a celebration of learning. This tradition has a rich heritage in the Reggio Emilia Preschool Program in Reggio Emilia, Italy, which attracts visitors from across the world. Creating excellent museum panels begins with providing the materials and teaching students to mount their work with mats, frames, or in the context of a larger story. Create a norm for how to display folders, drafts, and three-dimensional work on desks or tables. Take time to help students create labels and signage that make the work appealing and informative for the audience. Recruit an adult in the building or the community – a teacher, leader, or parent – who has passion and skill in building beautiful displays of work. Give that person time and support to work with students and on her own to build professional-looking exhibits. Think of your classroom or hallway walls as a museum of learning. Begin with these questions:

- What story does this work tell about teaching and learning at our school?

- How can we best share that story with our community?

View the video in Video Spotlight 6.4, which takes you on a walking tour of the hallways of a school that takes the curation of student work very seriously.

Video Spotlight 6.4: School as a Living Museum
https://www.teachingchannel.org/video/make-student-work-public-hth

This video follows Jeff Robin, art teacher at High Tech High in San Diego, California, as he describes the approach and impact of curating student work for public display throughout the school. Students display their authentic and original work using the principles of symmetry, repetition, and surprise to inspire visitors to the school with their learning and creativity. This video was produced by The Teaching Channel.

Video Reflection Questions
1. How does this "learning museum" inspire students to do high-quality work every day?
2. What does this video suggest about the role of the teacher and the role of the student in preparing work for a public audience?

TRY THIS: TELL THE STORY OF STUDENT LEARNING WITH A
DOCUMENTATION PANEL

EL Education schools promote the practice of using documentation panels to tell the story of student learning. The concept of documentation panels draws from the heritage of at least three sources:

- Explanatory panels in museums that give visitors background to understand and interpret exhibits

- The work of the Reggio Emilia Preschool Program in Reggio Emilia, Italy, which pioneered a unique level of commitment to documenting student thinking and work, and exhibiting it with artistic care

- The work of Harvard Project Zero, particularly the research project Making Learning Visible, which investigates ways in which individuals and groups construct, recognize, document, and share ideas and concepts

A documentation panel, though usually displayed on a wall of a school, differs from a typical school bulletin board in its purpose and content. Instead of simply exhibiting a set of final draft student work, documentation panels present what students studied and what they learned, making evident the process and context of the work. When looking at a bulletin board, one doesn't often have a sense of the unit in which the work was embedded; the rationale for the particular project; the process by which the work was created; the core concepts, content, and skills addressed during the project; what ideas the students were considering; and how students felt about their learning. A documentation panel attempts to make these elements visible.

A documentation panel features final draft student work, but it also presents much more, including earlier drafts of the work to give evidence of process, images to show the learning in action, and explanatory text that features both the teacher's voice and, prominently, students' reflections and comments about the work and the learning.

Table 6.2 provides guidance for building a documentation panel that tells the learning story. The adjacent photos provide several examples of documentation panels to give you a vision of telling your learning story with power and punch. Some of these examples of documentation panels were created solely or mostly by adults. Others were created with the help of students. In either case, notice how all of them intentionally place student voices, student work, and images of students learning at the heart of the story.

The best way to communicate the relationship between students' growth and achievement is to display their learning targets along with drafts and revisions so that their work tells the story of their learning process.

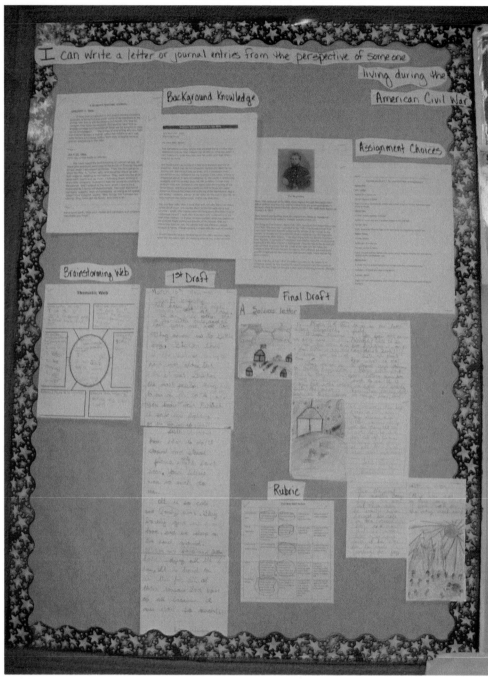

Photo Credit: Anne Vilen

Table 6.2 Building a documentation panel

Why document learning?
❏ It educates the community about school culture and philosophy.   ❏ It stimulates and deepens thinking and reflection about learning.   ❏ It creates a beautiful visual environment that shows learning.   ❏ It demonstrates what and how students are learning.   ❏ It makes the students involved proud, and inspires other students.
What elements will best tell the story of students' learning?
❏ Learning targets and guiding questions   ❏ A summary of the theme or story of the unit   ❏ Multiple drafts of student work   ❏ Rubrics   ❏ Written reflections and quotes about the process or product   ❏ Photos of student learning in action   ❏ Photos of fieldwork or interactions with experts   ❏ Evidence of sources used (e.g., experts, books for research)
Is the panel artistically and beautifully presented with student voice shining through?
❏ The design is visually appealing and crafted with care.   ❏ The design features the order in which students learned (a visual narrative).   ❏ The design showcases student work as the centerpiece of learning.   ❏ Labels, captions, and headings support and enhance images, narrative, and student work to tell a compelling story of learning and teaching.

Documentation panel from Genesee Community Charter School in Rochester, New York

Photo Credit: Ron Berger

Documentation panel from The St. Michael School of Clayton in St. Louis

Photo Credit: Ron Berger

Documentation panel from Rocky Mountain School of Expeditionary Learning in Denver

Photo Credit: Ron Berger

Documentation panel from Genesee Community Charter School in Rochester, New York

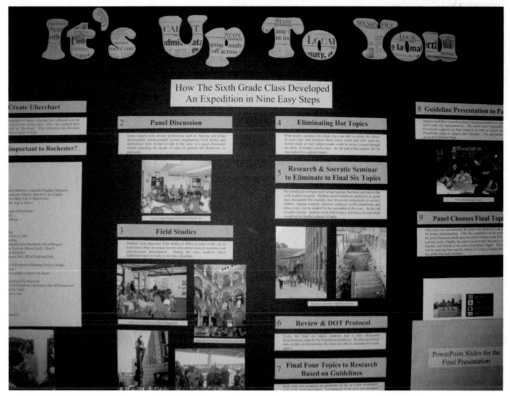

Photo Credit: Ron Berger

Documentation panel from The College School in St. Louis

Photo Credit: Ron Berger

Documentation Panel from The World of Inquiry School #58 in Rochester, New York

Photo Credit: Anne Vilen

Documentation panel from The St. Michael School of Clayton in St. Louis

Photo Credit: Ron Berger

Documentation panel from The Odyssey School of Denver

Photo Credit: Ron Berger

TRY THIS: COLLABORATE WITH COLLEAGUES TO CREATE SCHOOLWIDE CONSISTENCIES FOR DOCUMENTATION PANELS

To ensure that all teachers have a deep and common understanding of what a high-quality display looks like, many school faculties identify some common standards or consistencies for celebration of learning displays (see Figure 6.3).

If you are preparing for an upcoming celebration of learning, pause to take an observant walk through the classrooms and hallways in your school. Use a note-catcher like that in Figure 6.4 to record some "notices and wonders" about the work that is displayed with an eye toward making final revisions to documentation panels before the big event.

Figure 6.3 Celebration of learning display consistencies from Harborside Academy in Kenosha, Wisconsin

	Elements	Items to Collect/Provide/Create
Purpose	• Illustrates the steps of the project clearly and creatively. • Steps are a coherent sequence of linked experiences and products.	• Photos of work in progress • Photos of fieldwork or active learning • Drafts and revisions • Formative and summative assessments
Title	• Headline sums up the case study/learning expedition and also entertains	• Engaging headline for the case study/learning expedition
Objectives and Questions	• Learning Targets for knowledge, skills, and reasoning that support each product • Guiding Questions that drove the learning	• Clearly articulated learning target and guiding questions
Artifacts	• Student work representing critical moments in the learning process (revising, drafting, final product)	• Final student work • Student planning sheets • Drafts • Student critique and responses or reflections from critique sessions • Students' questions • Students' quotes • Learning anchor charts
Craftsmanship	• Sense of balance and creativity • Color and surprise • Age appropriateness • Clarity and accuracy • Words and pictures work together	• Photos • Narrative of the learning process • Markers, colored paper, borders, ruler, etc.

Figure 6.4 Documentation panel and student work note-catcher
SOURCE: This document is available in the online toolbox at http://www.wiley.com/go/lotolcompanion.

Features of the Celebration of Learning Display	Notices	Wonderings
I can identify the content areas being studied. (Content targets are posted.)		
I see evidence of literacy strategies practiced by students. (Literacy skills targets are posted.)		
I see evidence of arts and/or technology skills practiced by students. (Other skills targets are posted.)		
I see evidence of character/work habits practiced by students. (Character/habits targets are posted.)		
I see evidence of revision and craftsmanship. (e.g., rubrics, multiple drafts of work, craftsmanship targets are posted). "Works in progress" are labeled as such. Final draft products have been checked for accuracy and craftsmanship.		
I see high-quality student work rather than identical worksheets. Student work is supported with text that explains what students learned and how.		
I see evidence of student participation in fieldwork, experts, and/or service learning.		
I see evidence of student thinking, independence, and engagement. Documentation panels and student work on display show me that this is a place for hands-on, minds-on learning.		
Documentation panels explain student learning through an artistic arrangement of student work, explanatory text, learning targets, photos, quotes from students, draft and final work, and reflections.		

Learning Target 4: I can prepare students to tell the story of their learning in a way that informs, enlightens, and moves the audience.

 Challenge #6: Students talk about what the work is, rather than what they learned from doing it.

TRY THIS: PROVIDE STUDENTS WITH TOOLS THAT HELP THEM REFLECT ON THE LEARNING BEHIND THE WORK

One important and nuanced distinction between the typical student-work display that is common in many schools and a high-quality celebration of learning is the role that students themselves play in telling the story of their learning. A celebration of learning is only a student-engaged assessment structure to the extent that students are engaged in explaining to families and community members how the work displayed reflects their learning and growth over time. As you proceed throughout a unit, and especially leading up to a celebration of learning, be sure to frequently refer back to the long-term learning targets your students are aiming for, so that they can see how they are applying their learning through the work they are creating, revising, and polishing for the celebration. Invite students to revisit their learning target trackers or data notebook, so that they can see how they have grown throughout the unit. Then prompt students to reflect on the connections between their learning targets and the work they have created. Table 6.3 provides an example of using a variety of learning targets and the types of reflection questions you might ask.

Student reflections on fieldwork are posted alongside photos and student work.

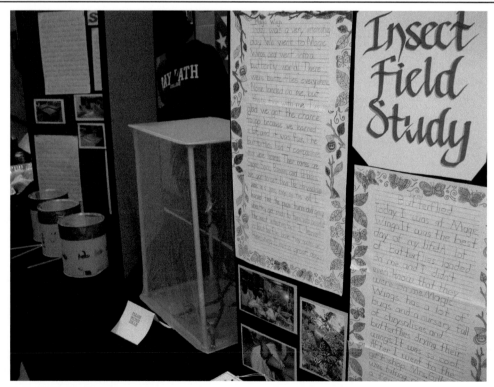

Photo Credit: Ron Berger

Table 6.3 Reflection questions and learning targets

Learning Target	Reflection Questions
I can create a graph that compares migratory pattern information from the past to more recent information.	What do you know now that you didn't know when you started this work? How does that knowledge show up in your product to inform your audience?
I can draw a scientific illustration that is beautiful and scientifically accurate.	What can you do now that you couldn't do when you started this work? How do those skills show up in your product?
I can write a migratory species profile that concisely and comprehensively summarizes key indicators about my species.	What type of thinking can you do now that has improved since you started this product (e.g., organize, analyze, categorize, prioritize)? How does your thinking show up in your product?

Figure 6.5 Student script for presenting work at a celebration of learning
SOURCE: This document is available in the online toolbox at http://www.wiley.com/go/lotolcompanion.

Introducing yourself:
Good evening. I am _____.

Introducing the work:
This is my _____.
I have chosen my work on _____ to highlight this evening.

Introducing the learning targets:
Our long-term learning targets for this project were _____.
To do this project, I had to learn how to _____.
I did a lot of research! (Describe *how* you did your research): _____
I am especially proud of my work on the learning target: _____
When you look at my drafts, you can see that I improved on: _____
If I were doing this again, I would: _____

Inviting the audience to engage
Are there any questions?
What would you like to know more about?

Thank you...
Thank you for supporting our work at _____.
I appreciate you taking time to honor our work.

Once students can answer questions like those in Table 6.3, support them to write a script for presenting their work that includes naming the learning targets and pointing out how they are reflected in the work itself. Depending on the format of your celebration of learning, individual students may be presenting their own work (gallery style) or a few student representatives may be introducing the project as a whole to your audience. Figure 6.5 is a tool that can guide individual students in preparing a script for presenting their work. This "fill in the blank" template is an especially good starting place for young students and students who have never presented before (or are anxious about doing so). As students get more familiar with presenting their work and explaining their learning, encourage them to add variety and personality to the presentation.

Figure 6.6 Sample group presentation script from The Franklin School of Innovation in Asheville, North Carolina

Student 1

Good morning parents, faculty, community members, and students. On behalf of the class of 2020, I would like to WELCOME you to our ninth-grade celebration of learning.

Our city is undergoing rapid change as it grows into one of the most popular tourist destinations in the United States. With this change come both benefits and challenges for our community. Three significant impacts are:

- Low wages pervasive in the service industry
- High housing costs and low availability as more people move to town
- Environmental impacts caused by increased traffic and industrial growth

To learn about and respond to these impacts, we created four significant products that you'll see tonight. Be sure to ask questions as you review your own student's work and look at the work other students have done too.

Student 2

In science class, we created a systems map for one aspect of air quality and a scientific research paper on healthy air quality. When you look at our maps and our writing, we invite you to notice how much we learned about the correlation between air quality and quality of life (in particular, health trends). Don't forget to look at our drafts! We revised and revised as we learned about using and organizing our evidence to support our research thesis.

Student 3

In math class, we created graphs for data gathered in science class and identified a correlation between social data and a pollutant data over time. Notice how our graphs communicate information and provide evidence to support our research claims.

Student 4

In social studies class, we wrote a solution-based, persuasive letter that we sent to city council. Do you think our evidence, and our claims, are convincing? Do you think the city council will adapt any of these solutions?

Student 5

In ELA class, we used the problems and solutions from social studies and science classes to craft a spoken word poem. We learned so much about using powerful word choice, facts, and form to craft our poems. And we practiced and practiced to meet our learning targets about volume, expression, and articulation. As you tour through each of these products, please be sure stop and listen in the coffee house downstairs, where we'll be performing these powerful poems.

When a group of representative students is opening the celebration for an entire class, a script that provides an overview of the topic and key learning will capture the audience's attention and prepare them to engage more deeply when they circulate to see individual work. Figure 6.6 is an example of a group script from a ninth-grade celebration of learning at The Franklin School of Innovation in Asheville, North Carolina. A group script like this example serves as a reference point for students to speak about their own individual work after the group introduction.

For young students who may not yet be ready to write lengthy reflections, you may need different tools and strategies for helping them talk less about what they *did* and more about what they *learned*. After you post the work for your celebration of learning, invite students to reflect on their learning in a whole-class debrief. Record students' brief comments on sticky notes and post the sticky notes right there by the work to demonstrate students' authentic thinking in response to a learning target. Students can reference these when talking about their work to families during the celebration of learning.

TRY THIS: SUPPORT STUDENTS TO SHARE THE STORY OF THEIR GROWTH, NOT JUST THE FINAL PRODUCT

One of the features that makes each student's product unique, even when at first glance it looks similar to another student's work, is that each student has experienced the process of creating the work differently. The challenge, the joy, the feedback received along the way, and how the student responds to that feedback is part of the learning story. When students present their learning to an authentic audience,

Figure 6.7 Gallery walk protocol for noticing changes in drafts
SOURCE: This document is available in the online toolbox at http://www.wiley.com/go/lotolcompanion.

Each student will need an early draft and a final draft of the same work.

Procedure
- Display the early draft and final draft side-by-side on the wall or on desks/tables.
- Give each student five sticky notes.
- Instruct students to visit five other students' work and closely observe how the final draft is different from the early draft. At each piece of work, students should write one "I notice" sticky note. Students should comment specifically and helpfully on what's different from the first draft to the final draft. Students should read the other sticky notes before writing theirs to ensure that they notice something *different* than what has already been noticed by another student (i.e., no repeats). (*Take time to model what specific and helpful comments sound like.* For example, "I notice that the final draft has more bright colors" *or* "I notice that you added a lot of detail and interesting words to your story.")
- Remind students that only five comments should be left on each piece of work so that students distribute themselves evenly across the class and every set of work gets five comments.

Once each student has five sticky notes, ask students to return to their own work and read the sticky notes that have been left by their peers.

The information on these sticky notes can then be used to help students prepare written and/or oral reflections on their growth.

talking about *how* they created the work and what they changed or improved along the way can have a powerful impact on the audience.

To help students prepare to talk about their growth, conduct a hosted gallery walk of drafts and final products using a protocol like that in Figure 6.7 that focuses students on noticing and describing the changes between early and late drafts of work.

Finally, once students have engaged in a process like that described in the protocol in Figure 6.7, they should practice talking about their growth, as evidenced in their drafts. This is a chance for students to hone the language explaining why they made the changes they did and how those changes have improved the overall quality of the work. As students practice, encourage them to discuss the challenges and rewards they encountered along the way as they revised.

 Challenge #7: Students don't have enough to do during the celebration.

TRY THIS: GIVE EVERY STUDENT A MEANINGFUL ROLE TO PLAY

There's nothing that can push a celebration of learning off the rails so much as students running around the exhibit space goofing around or disrupting presentations and displays because they aren't sure what their role is. If families or teachers find themselves having to discipline or chaperone students, the event can quickly become disappointing to everyone attending, and especially to students themselves. Instead, every student should have a meaningful part to play and a clear, rehearsed understanding of what to do throughout the celebration.

Beyond logistical roles, such as greeting families as they come in, or acting as ushers to help guests find their seats before performances, the more important roles to consider are those for how students will actually present their work. Table 6.4 lists several student roles matched to the format of their work and the things you may need to consider for that format and role.

Table 6.4 Examples of student roles and formats for presentation

Format	Student Role	Things to Consider
Scientific poster presentation	scientist, presenter	• Do I have enough space for all displays? • Will students present individually or in teams? • What visuals will students need to support their presentation?
Demonstration	engineer, crafts-man, physical scientist, athlete, mathematician	• How will students demonstrate their learning so demonstrations are unique? • Where will students perform their demonstrations? • Will demonstrations be interactive, so that the audience can participate?
Simulation or living museum role play	historian, character actor	• Where will students acquire costumes or props? • How will the audience interact with the actors? • How can signs or written displays supplement the story?
Panel presentation	expert panelist	• How long will the presentations be so that every student can participate? • How will the audience interact with questions or comments?
Intellectual debate	politician, advocate	• Will students debate each other or members of the audience? • How will students prepare so that multiple perspectives are represented? • How can all students participate?
Art gallery or history museum	artist, docent	• What space will we use to show our products in a beautiful setting? • Will students share their work as individual artists or take groups of audience members on "tours"?
Drama, musical performance, dance performance, or poetry reading	actor, singers, musician, dancers, poets	• Are there enough parts for all students to participate? • Can the performance kick off or conclude the evening? • Will we videotape the performance or run it live?
Honorary ceremony or documentary of service	leaders, citizens, public servants	• How can we involve every student in the presentation? • How can we create a setting that honors those we are serving? • What products can we display to show what we learned as well as our acts of service?

In Video Spotlight 6.5, see kindergarten students take on the role first of performer and then of scientist to share their learning about birds with their families and a community expert. With preparation and clarity of roles, as well as a presentation format that meaningfully includes all students, even five- and six-year-olds can demonstrate and explain what they know and can do with precision and poise.

Video Spotlight 6.5: Kindergarteners as Experts
https://vimeo.com/69120172

This video shows a dynamic and impactful celebration of learning at ANSER Charter School in Boise, Idaho, where kindergarten students conducted a year-long investigation of birds, including reading, writing, fieldwork, and learning from experts.

Video Reflection Questions
1. How do the presentation boards allow students to express their individual personalities and lend consistency and structure to their presentations?
2. Are you surprised at the poise these young students demonstrate? What strategies can you borrow from this classroom for preparing your own students to present with poise?

As part of a celebration of learning featuring eighth-grade students' deep study of community engagement, a student represents a local political action organization and responds to questions from a local radio show host.

Photo Credit: Anne Vilen

TRY THIS: USE A RUBRIC TO GUIDE STUDENTS AS THEY REHEARSE FOR CELEBRATIONS OF LEARNING

Rehearsal is a key ingredient for successful celebrations of learning. Rubrics or criteria lists that define high-quality presentations can be helpful guides for students as they practice and receive feedback. As you saw in Video Spotlight 6.5, when students have multiple opportunities to rehearse, first with an audience of their peers and then with a less familiar audience (e.g., older classmates, other teachers), they polish their presentation skills. Feedback that references a familiar rubric will help even the youngest students focus on a few key skills for delivering their message with competence and confidence. Figure 6.8 is an example of a music performance presentation rubric used to give feedback to kindergarten students working on a musical number.

Figure 6.8 Snake song performance rubric from Conservatory Lab Charter School in Boston
SOURCE: This document is available in the online toolbox at http://www.wiley.com/go/lotolcompanion.

Name _____   Date_____

Learning Target: *I can give a quality song performance that shows how much I care about our class snake and makes the audience want to find out more about her.*

Criteria	Bulls Eye	Almost There	Getting Started
Posture	Stands straight and tall for entire performance.	Stands straight and tall for most of performance.	Slouches back. Hunches shoulders.
Voice	Level 3 presentation voice. Can hear voice in all parts of room.	Level 2 or 3 presentation voice can sometimes be heard in all parts of room.	Can't hear voice at back of room.
Expression	Face shows interest and enthusiasm for entire performance.	Face shows interest and enthusiasm for part of the performance.	Face looks bored and uninterested.
Eye contact	Eyes on the audience for entire performance.	Eyes on audience for some of performance.	Eyes wander or look downward. Eyes not on audience.
Movement	Moves like a snake. Always in sync with music.	Moves like a snake. Sometimes in sync with music.	Movements are not clear and out of sync with music.

Name _____   Date _____

On the back of this page, reflect on your performance by answering the following questions:

(continued)

Figure 6.8 Continued

Performance Reflection

1. Write about something that went well or made you feel proud.

_____

_____

_____

2. Write about something that you want to keep working on for future performances.

_____

_____

_____

_____

_____

Learning Target 5: I can structure celebrations of learning so that families and community members can participate meaningfully.

Challenge #8: Family members and guests show up to look, but don't know what else to do.

TRY THIS: WELCOME AND INFORM

Celebrations of learning have the power not only to motivate and empower students, but also to inspire and engage communities in support of children and learning. Families and community members are not just a passive audience; they are key players in the celebration. Their questions, their praise, their engagement, and their service to the school community should be honored, encouraged, and supported as part of every celebration of learning.

Think about a party you've attended where you really only know the person who invited you. Maybe the party is in a new and unfamiliar place. And maybe it involves games or cultural traditions that you haven't experienced before. This is the same situation for families who are new to celebrations of learning, and who are perhaps also new to the school community. If you want your guests to feel welcome and comfortable, share the format of the event ahead of time and greet them with a smile. A clear structure that explicitly communicates what families and visitors should do and how they should interact with students allows them to let go of any initial awkwardness and fully engage in the experience.

Creating a program will help guests get acquainted with the order of events. If your school is holding a schoolwide celebration, you may also need to share information about logistics like parking, what to expect at each grade level, and the flow of visitors from classroom to classroom. In addition, be sure to have adult or student greeters on hand to help direct families to the right place and to answer any questions they have about the event. The website Models of Excellence: The Center for High-Quality Student Work has a set of celebration of learning programs that you can use as models and inspiration for your own event (https://modelsofexcellence.eleducation.org/projects/expedition-programs).

TRY THIS: ASK STUDENTS TO PRE-IDENTIFY EXHIBITS FOR THEIR FAMILIES TO VISIT

Teachers at Mary O. Pottenger Elementary School in Springfield, Massachusetts, noticed that many family members left their celebration of learning after they'd seen their own child's work. They decided to tackle this challenge in an especially innovative way. The entire school had a dress rehearsal version of the evening celebration during the school day. All classrooms, in shifts, toured other classrooms in the building to learn about other students' work and ask questions. During this preview, students took notes about which student work they would most like their own families to see. Then students shared these personalized recommendations with their families on a special form that parents received from their child when they arrived that evening. Parents also received a program that described what was being exhibited and performed in each classroom, along with a school map. Visiting the work of other students gave students and their parents an opportunity to compare notes and get excited about learning throughout the school.

As you prepare for your celebration of learning, invite your own students to visit the work of other students and take notes about what they would like their families to see on celebration night. Ask students to use a form like that in Table 6.5 to prepare for their families.

Table 6.5 Student recommendations for celebration of learning itinerary

My Top Five	Student/Grade Level	What You'll See	What I Want You to Notice
1			
2			
3			
4			
5			

TRY THIS: PROVIDE FAMILY MEMBERS AND GUESTS WITH FEATURES TO LOOK FOR OR ASK QUESTIONS ABOUT

Another way to ensure that guests feel a sense of purpose at the celebration of learning is to give them something specific to look for or ask about. Since a celebration is a time for *students* to share the story of their learning and accomplishments, encourage families and guests to ask questions and comment on the specific features that demonstrate learning. Use Table 6.6 to develop a set of specific questions that guests could ask about the work in your celebration of learning.

Table 6.6 Look-fors and questions for parents at celebrations of learning

Look-Fors	Questions for Students
Learning targets and guiding questions	What did you learn from doing this work? Did you answer your guiding questions? How will this learning help you prepare for what you will be studying next?
Photos and stories that show how we learned about this topic	What did you learn along the way that helped you create this work? Which experience was the most fun for you? Or the most challenging?
Evidence of craftsmanship	How did you revise your work to make it better and better with each draft? How did you learn the skills you needed to do this work?
Work habits and character	What role did character play in your success? Which work habits were most important for you to help you be successful with your learning?
Evidence of collaboration	What role did you play in your group? How did you contribute to the group's goals and efforts? What did you learn from your group?
Contributing to a better world	How does this work serve the needs of the larger community? How does it feel to be a part of that effort?

TRY THIS: DESIGN THE CELEBRATION FOR AUDIENCE INTERACTION

Another strategy that can be especially engaging for families and other guests is to intentionally design opportunities for students to demonstrate their learning and for families to get involved. For example, eighth-graders at Evergreen Community Charter School in Asheville, North Carolina, participated in a math project where they were given a certain amount of virtual money to invest. At their celebration, they shared the results of their decision making about money and the rationale for their decisions. Then they played the Investment Game online with their parents, walking their own families through the decision points in a virtual environment to discover if they got a new outcome.

There are dozens of things students could do with their guests in the context of a celebration of learning. The celebration of learning program featured in Figure 6.2 that highlights a 20 questions trivia game for families and students is a good example. Here are a few more with space for you to fill in your own ideas:

❏ Create art together.

❏ Try out simple machines created by students.

❏ Play math or board games created by students.

❏ Students can interview guests and record the data as part of a study connected to a particular class or for feedback on the celebration of learning itself.

❏ _____

❏ _____

❏ _____

 Challenge #9: I'm not sure how to include the community members and experts who don't have children at the school.

TRY THIS: TREAT COMMUNITY MEMBERS AS VIPS

One goal for any celebration of learning should be to bolster the relationship between the school and the community. To build that relationship, be sure to invite board members, neighbors, members of partner organizations, or visitors from other schools or educational organizations. If you have had experts assist your class with learning, fieldwork, or service, they should also be invited. Honor these special guests for the important role they play in the life of your school. Start by assigning especially capable students to host community members. Prepare the student hosts to provide an informative and engaging tour. Here are a few tips for student guides:

• Introduce yourself.

• Wear a name tag and provide one for your guest.

• Ask your guest how he/she is connected to the school.

• Provide the guest with an overview of the celebration of learning agenda and space.

- Ask, "What are you most interested in learning about our school?"

- Share the highlights of your celebration (and why your guests won't want to miss them).

- Introduce the guest to teachers and student presenters as you go.

- Invite the guest to ask questions and do your best to answer them.

If your celebration of learning includes any kind of contest (e.g., a science fair) or an opportunity for visitors to provide feedback or ask questions, community members can also serve as official judges or simply be asked to provide specific feedback based on their special expertise about the topic or the format. In some cases, you might even consider inviting the community expert to debrief the celebration with your class the following day.

Video Spotlight 6.6 features two celebrations of learning in which experts who students worked with throughout their projects were honored at the celebrations. In the first video, seventh-grade students in Maine presented their work to an auditorium full of community members they had previously interviewed for an oral history project on civil rights activism in their local community. In the second video, sixth-grade students in Rhode Island proudly shared the professional-quality photographs and profiles they had created of immigrants in their community with the immigrants themselves.

Video Spotlight 6.6: (a) Students Share Work That Matters with an Authentic Audience
https://vimeo.com/48803088

(b) Community Faces: Humanizing the Immigrant Label
https://vimeo.com/276987940

In the first video, students at King Middle School in Portland, Maine, share their learning about civil rights activists in their own community with the experts whose lives they have profiled in an illustrated oral history collection called *Small Acts of Courage*.

The second video features an inspiring project from the Interdistrict School for Arts and Communication (ISAAC) in New London, Connecticut. Students profiled immigrants in their community to break stereotypes about immigration and humanize the immigrant label. The immigrants whom they interviewed and photographed then attended the celebration of learning, which was much like an art gallery opening.

Video Reflection Questions
1. What steps did teachers and students take to honor community members who were part of each project?
2. What structures were in place to provide opportunities for all visitors to interact with students? What impact did this have?
3. What is the impact of an authentic audience like this on a celebration of learning? What inspiration does it give you when thinking of your own celebrations?

As a school leader, you have so much on your plate that it may be tempting to put support for celebrations of learning on the side burner and assume that other staff will plan and prepare things without your help. This would be a big mistake. First, celebrations are key events to build support for your school among parents, community leaders, and district leaders. A quality event – led by your high standards – can win over many stakeholders. Second, when teachers see school leaders carving out time for their planning and preparation, and see leaders pitching in to support with logistics and details, it boosts their trust and support for your leadership, and it will help them prepare for the event with greater confidence and success.

We all know that the value of a school doesn't just live in test scores. A celebration of learning is an opportunity to lift up the breadth of good teaching and learning taking place in the school. Following are a few tips for supporting teachers to implement high-quality celebrations of learning. Table 6.7 summarizes the key action steps for teachers and students that will lead to a successful celebration of learning.

Top Tips

- Invite input from teachers and parent leaders when planning dates, times, and structures. Be sure to consider faith holidays, the schedules of working parents, and the home languages of families when calendaring and communicating event plans.

- Consider whom in the community you want to reach out to with invitations and encouragement to attend. Use the event to build alliances with local businesses and with other community organizations (e.g., after-school programs, clubs, faith-based organizations).

- Lead the faculty in discussion and planning about what will make this a truly high-quality and memorable event for students, families, and other guests. Details matter. Brainstorm together strategies to lift the quality of student work, the displays and performances, and the logistics of the event. How can you surprise the community with quality?

- Coordinate the moving parts, including schedules, venue setup and cleanup, space assignments, parking, the event program, etc. If leaders can take care of managerial decisions, teachers can focus deeply on preparing and rehearsing with students.

- Provide materials for displays and performances to make things look attractive and professional. For example, many school leaders order standard, reusable presentation boards (e.g., large black foam core panels) for every classroom, so that displays look professional. Check with staff about what display and art supplies they need to make things look beautiful. If your budget is limited, consider finding a community partner or getting financial support from your parent-teacher organization. Save the teachers a great deal of frustration and help them be successful by sweating the small stuff.

- If there are audiovisual needs, such as microphones, computers, projectors, and screens, ensure that everything is available, set up, and tested for use.

- Problem-solve strategically. Remember that you are building a tradition, but some things will always need to be tweaked to accommodate changing school conditions, faculty, or anomalous considerations. We know of one school where the celebration of learning got so popular, that they decided to run it on two consecutive nights, with alternating grade levels participating each night. This created more space for parking and more room to move in the hallways, and it retained the opportunity for families to visit a full range of grade levels.

- Evaluate the success of each celebration. Invite families and community members who attend to fill out a brief survey on their way out the door.

- Debrief the celebration of learning with students and teachers. What went well? What can be improved for the next celebration? Design and use a rubric to describe what your next celebration will look like and sound like.

Table 6.7 Celebrations of learning: Steps to success

What Should Teachers Do?
Plan and communicate logistics in advance.
Display students' work to highlight its best features and embody student learning, voice, and individuality.
Support students to tell the story of the learning journey.
Be intentional about identifying and communicating ways in which families and communities can engage in and contribute to the celebration.
What Should Students Do?
Discuss the work and learning in a way that informs, enlightens, and moves the audience.
Reflect on the knowledge, skills, character, and growth conveyed by their work.
Contribute to documentation panels or other ways of telling the story of their learning.
Rehearse and present their learning to an authentic audience.
Engage families and visitors as honored guests.

Post-Assessment: Track Your Progress: Chapter 6

As you have read Chapter 6, maybe you have had an opportunity to try some of these strategies and techniques along the way. If not, come back to this post-assessment after you have had a chance to do so. Give yourself whatever time you need to address the learning targets and challenges in a meaningful way. Then take a moment to check your progress in Table 6.8, which is the exact same Learning Target Tracker that appeared at the beginning of this chapter.

Circle or place an X along the continuum from Beginning to Exceeding: **How would you rate your progress toward each learning target** *at this point in time?* Use the space provided to make notes regarding any remaining challenges you may be having or ideas for new and different strategies you want to try.

Table 6.8   Chapter 6 learning target tracker

Learning Target 1: *I can choreograph the details of a celebration of learning.*

Beginning----------------------------------Developing----------------------------------Meeting----------------------------------Exceeding

Notes:

Learning Target 2: *I can support students to produce original, high-quality work for an authentic audience.*

Beginning----------------------------------Developing----------------------------------Meeting----------------------------------Exceeding

Notes:

Learning Target 3: *I can display student work with power and purpose.*

Beginning----------------------------------Developing----------------------------------Meeting----------------------------------Exceeding

Notes:

Learning Target 4: *I can prepare students to tell the story of their learning in a way that informs, enlightens, and moves the audience.*

Beginning----------------------------------Developing----------------------------------Meeting----------------------------------Exceeding

Notes:

Learning Target 5: *I can structure celebrations of learning so that families and community members can participate meaningfully.*

Beginning----------------------------------Developing----------------------------------Meeting----------------------------------Exceeding

Notes:

Chapter 7

Passage Presentations with Portfolios

My Portfolio

Name:

Checking for Understanding during Daily Lessons

Using Data with Students

Learning Targets

STUDENT-ENGAGED ASSESSMENT

Student-engaged assessment is a system of interrelated practices that positions students as leaders of their own learning.

Models, Critique, and Descriptive Feedback

Standards-Based Grading

Student-Led Conferences

Passage Presentations with Portfolios

Celebrations of Learning

What Are Passage Presentations with Portfolios?

A portfolio is a selected body of student work – with reflections – that provides evidence of a student's progress toward standards, learning targets, and character growth. Passage presentations (often called presentations of learning, or portfolio presentations) are benchmark presentations at the end of pivotal transition years (e.g., fifth, eighth, twelfth). During passage presentations, students use their portfolios as evidence to reflect on their learning and growth and to demonstrate their readiness to move on to the next level of their education.

Throughout history, across many cultures, rites of passage ceremonies are common markers of growing up and committing to new roles or communities. In the United States, families and friends gather to witness and celebrate the growth of young people at events like quinceañeras, confirmations, bar mitzvahs, and weddings.

In American schools, students cross the stage to receive their graduation diploma cheered on by their families and friends, but traditional graduation ceremonies are rarely structured to focus on each individual student's growth, accomplishments, and unique journey. In contrast, passage presentations allow the community to appreciate and reflect on each student's important transition to the next grade level or into college or working life. Passage presentations create an opportunity for students to demonstrate – in their own voices and using meaningful evidence – their readiness to move on to a new school, grade level, or challenge, and to reflect on what they have learned and how they have grown. Unlike many graduation ceremonies, students themselves lead the passage presentations and tell the unique story of their own growth and preparation for the next step in their educational journey.

In this chapter, we build on Chapter 7 of *Leaders of Their Own Learning* to explore the challenges of creating passage presentations that are meaningful to students and the community, and portfolios that reflect personal growth, character, and academic readiness. We provide tools and examples to help individual teachers and school teams design high-quality passage presentations and the systems that support them. Four learning targets will guide you through the chapter.

> This is pretty much a way for me to leave my legacy behind. This is who I was and the struggles I went through, where I am at, and what I am planning for the future.
>
> —*Gerardo Herrera, graduate, Washington Heights Expeditionary Learning School, New York City*

Learning Targets for Chapter 7

1. I can communicate the purpose and audience for passage presentations, and how they are different from student-led conferences.
2. I can support students to create multi-year portfolios with reflections.
3. I can ensure that students are prepared to lead passage presentations with professionalism.
4. I can prepare families and community members for the important roles they play in passage presentations.

Before we dive in, take a moment to assess yourself on each of the learning targets for this chapter. In Table 7.1, circle or place an X along the continuum from Beginning to Exceeding: **How would you rate your progress toward each learning target** *at this point in time?*

We'll give you a chance to assess yourself again at the end of the chapter.

Table 7.1 Chapter 7 learning target tracker

Learning Target 1: *I can communicate the purpose and audience for passage presentations, and how they are different from student-led conferences.* Beginning---------------------------------Developing---------------------------------Meeting---------------------------------Exceeding Notes:
Learning Target 2: *I can support students to create multi-year portfolios with reflections.* Beginning---------------------------------Developing---------------------------------Meeting---------------------------------Exceeding Notes:
Learning Target 3: *I can ensure that students are prepared to lead passage presentations with professionalism.* Beginning---------------------------------Developing---------------------------------Meeting---------------------------------Exceeding Notes:
Learning Target 4: *I can prepare families and community members for the important roles they play in passage presentations.* Beginning---------------------------------Developing---------------------------------Meeting---------------------------------Exceeding Notes:

Learning Target 1: I can communicate the purpose and audience for passage presentations.

Challenge #1: I am not clear on the purpose and value of passage presentations.

TRY THIS: START BY WATCHING MODELS OF PASSAGE PRESENTATIONS

As we discussed in Chapter 4, showing students models is the best way to help them visualize an outcome. Video models of passage presentations can help you and your students understand what's important about passage presentations and how they are different from student-led conferences. You may already have video models from your own school; if not, you can use models from other schools.

Ron Berger used passage presentations for over 20 years with the graduating sixth-graders in his rural public elementary school, before they left town to attend the regional middle school. The tradition became a community event: grandparents, aunts and uncles, friends and neighbors eagerly attended the presentations each year. This structure is so valued by the community that it continues today, 15 years after Berger left the school to work full-time for EL Education. The tradition has been sustained through many teacher changes and nine different school principals!

Berger had students videotape every student presentation so there would be plenty of models to show to future classes when they entered sixth grade. Strong video models were used every year, and the video archive also allowed for choosing specific models to show to particular classes. For example, when a sixth-grade girl said, "There is no way my older brother did that presentation well," Berger was able to pull out her brother's old video; she and her classmates were amazed by his professional manner and strong presentation. (The student could also not believe that her brother looked that young in sixth grade and was ever that polite.) When a student complained that he had speech challenges so he should not be asked to present to an audience, the class watched a video of a powerful and beautiful presentation by a former sixth-grade girl with cerebral palsy, whose speech was challenging to understand for anyone who did not know her well. She was proud, confident, and successful – she carefully voiced short verbal introductions during her presentation, and also wrote a script so that her friend and presentation partner could voice the majority of the presentation for the audience, describing her work and her growth.

You can see a montage of Berger's students from the 1980s and 1990s leading passage presentations in Video Spotlight 7.1. The technology is old, so the film is grainy and the sound is not perfect, but the student work and student voice are clear as models.

Video Spotlight 7.1: Portfolio Presentations from Ron Berger's Classroom
https://vimeo.com/313907607

This video follows several sixth-grade students at Shutesbury Elementary School in Shutesbury, Massachusetts, as they reflect on their growth and accomplishments with academic challenges and personal passions. This video was produced by Ron Berger and recut by EL Education.

Video Reflection Questions
1. Why is it important for students to reflect on their challenges and growth edges?
2. How do students personalize their presentations with stories that are unique to them?
3. Which response to a question from the panel is particularly memorable? Why?

It's also important to note that while different schools structure their passage presentations somewhat differently, there are common elements that define the purpose and audience. Video Spotlight 7.2 features passage presentations from four different secondary schools that highlight the following characteristics:

- Students articulate their readiness for the next stage in their education.
- Community members are included as panelists who provide questions and feedback to students.
- Students uphold a high standard for presentation style and the contents of the portfolio.
- Students have the opportunity to personalize and individualize their presentations.

Notice too how these schools define the "stakes" of passage portfolios differently. In some cases, "passing" the passage presentation is a requirement for graduation or grade promotion. In others, the passage presentation is a required, public presentation, but is not evaluated.

Video Spotlight 7.2: Passage Presentations in Secondary Schools
https://vimeo.com/68481107

This video shows passage presentations with portfolios at four different schools. It illustrates the key features of passage presentations, as well as the unique style and structures that each school brings to this tradition.

Video Reflection Questions
1. How do these students use evidence to support claims about their learning and growth?
2. How do panelists' questions, encouragement, and feedback set students up for meaningful reflection and goal setting?
3. When you think about preparing your own students to do passage presentations, what are your hopes and anxieties about implementing this practice?

We often think of passage presentations as a structure that is introduced in middle or even high school, but some schools hold them much earlier. In many districts or schools, there is a structural shift between first and second grade, or between second and third grade – students move to another part of a building or to another school entirely. In other districts, a shift to another building happens after fourth or fifth grade. In any of these cases, a passage presentation can be a helpful tradition in celebrating the big step that students are taking. We have seen successful passage presentations at all of these grade levels.

Supporting younger students to conduct a passage presentation with style and poise may require a more scripted format, but with support and practice, young students are quite capable of reflecting on their learning and growth within this format. In the video featured in Video Spotlight 7.3, a third-grader shares his "greater moments" from the year, and what he learned along the way to becoming a fourth grader.

Video Spotlight 7.3: Third-Grade Passage Presentation at Tahoe Expedition Academy
https://vimeo.com/312847213

This video features one bubbly third-grader from Tahoe Expedition Academy in Truckee, California, sharing the challenges and strengths of his third-grade year. This video has been cut down to feature just one student. If you would like to see more passage presentations from his third-grade classmates, you can access the full video here: https://vimeo.com/218112635. This video was produced by Tahoe Expedition Academy and recut by EL Education.

Video Reflection Questions
1. What would you infer about Finn's preparation? What enabled him to present with zest and confidence despite his fear of public speaking?
2. If you teach younger students, how would you help them select and gather evidence about their "greater moments"?

Challenge #2: I haven't yet figured out how to turn passage presentations into a tradition that really matters to students and families, rather than just another event.

TRY THIS: EMPHASIZE THE TRADITION AS A RITE OF PASSAGE AND A MILESTONE FOR STUDENTS

One important distinction between student-led conferences and passage presentations is that student-led conferences happen every year, and often multiple times a year. Passage presentations, by contrast, come along only during critical transition years; they are truly markers of a "passage" from one phase of schooling to another. As such, they offer you an opportunity to imbue them with special meaning for students. The Close Up that follows is an example of how one school in New York City ensured that passage presentations would be significant and meaningful events for students and their families.

Close Up: Passage Presentations as a Rite of Passage at Metropolitan Expeditionary Learning School in New York City

At Metropolitan Expeditionary Learning School (MELS) in New York City, teachers begin the eighth-grade year—on the first day of school—by introducing passage presentations as an important tradition and then, in the first month of school, students learn about different rites of passage all over the world. They participate in team-building activities in which they design their own rites of passage. As the school year unfolds, students prepare to conduct their own passage presentation by focusing deeply on what they are learning about themselves by doing academic projects that they share during student-led conferences in November and March. They also present their classwork more frequently than in other years and hone their presentation skills explicitly in preparation for passage presentations in May. They write a personal narrative about a moment that changed them and compile their passage presentation portfolios knowing that their presentation before a panel of faculty, older students, and community members is the only way they'll be allowed to participate in the celebratory Passages Spirit Week and a Passages Dance and, finally, the Passages Night moving up ceremony that happens in June.

By introducing passage presentations early in the year, framing student-led conferences as background work for the ceremony of passage presentations, and magnificently celebrating student passage presenters, MELS faculty turn this school tradition into an engaging and motivating force for students. On Passages Night, students who have passed their passage participate in a moving pin ceremony where they self-assess their readiness to receive a MELS pin and receive it from a trusted mentor and faculty member in their Crew (advisory). Family member witnesses then speak to the student, publicly gifting their child with praise and words of wisdom to start him or her on their high school journey. At the end of the ceremony, the students come to the stage again and collectively read a choreographed poem about their experience at MELS.

"The ceremony," says assistant principal Hillary Mills, "is one of the most moving things that happens at MELS. Younger students are looking on and noticing what it means to be celebrated for being ready to go to high school. They even look forward to Spirit Week when they'll be able to shed their uniforms and dress up for the dance, just like they will in high school. It's a big deal, and they take it very seriously."

TRY THIS: HELP STUDENTS REFLECT ON THEIR UNIQUE AND PERSONAL VISION FOR THE FUTURE

To create a tradition that matters to students, make it less formulaic in format and more personal in content. Unlike student-led conferences, students don't need to follow the same script or set of requirements. At Codman Academy, in Boston, The Springfield Renaissance School, in Springfield, Massachusetts, and in many other EL Education network high schools across the United States, the senior passage presentation culminates a year of self-reflection, visioning, and celebration that includes 100 percent of seniors applying to college. Exploring their post-secondary options, writing their college application essays, and receiving the support and accolades of their peers and families immerses students in a year-long reflection on their time in high school and how overcoming challenges has prepared them for college. Many of these schools use the format of a "senior talk" for the passage presentation. Senior talks are profoundly personal for students and their families. For schools looking for a tradition that will "matter," and that will also help students reflect on their growth and focus on their futures, look no further.

Video Spotlight 7.4 features videos from two schools that use "senior talks" (sometimes called "final word" presentations) as the format for senior passage presentations. The first video features Codman Academy, which was the first EL Education network school to offer this powerful platform to seniors. Several Codman students, their families, and their teachers are featured in this short video. The second video features one student from The Springfield Renaissance School. Edward Brown reads aloud his entire senior talk on what it means to grow up, find your voice, and become a leader as a young African American man in America.

Video Spotlight 7.4: (a) Elevating Student Voice through Senior Talks
https://www.edutopia.org/video/elevating-student-voice-through-senior-talks

(b) Edward's Senior Talk
https://vimeo.com/81527464

The first video features seniors at Codman Academy in Boston presenting evidence of their growth and readiness for their futures to their families and school community. This video was produced by Edutopia.

In the second video, senior Edward Brown rehearses for his Senior Talk. After graduating from The Springfield Renaissance School in Springfield, Massachusetts, Edward went on to attend and graduate from Brown University. This video was produced by The Teaching Channel for EL Education.

Video Reflection Questions
1. In what ways do these students' senior talks demonstrate insight into the promises and pitfalls that await them in the future?
2. What does Edward reveal about how his passions and personal path are rooted in his experience in high school?
3. How would you describe the impact of senior talks on the students and their school communities? What opportunities are lost when schools don't give students a platform for this level of serious reflection?

In other schools, students conduct a senior capstone project involving extensive research or prepare a more traditional portfolio of evidence for the senior passage presentation that supports claims about preparation for their future. As you prepare to help your own students reflect on their strengths, challenges, and goals, consider using a reflection tool like the one in Figure 7.1 to help seniors envision their own futures in college and beyond.

TRY THIS: CLEARLY COMMUNICATE WHAT'S AT STAKE IN PASSAGE PRESENTATIONS

In many schools passage presentations are a required *and evaluated* part of moving up to the next grade level. Whether or not passage presentations are a formal gateway to the next grade level at your school, it's important to communicate to students and parents how much passage presentations "count" toward grade promotion and/or what happens if students don't "pass" their passage.

Figure 7.1 Triple-A visioning tool for seniors
SOURCE: This document is available in the online toolbox at http://www.wiley.com/go/lotolcompanion.

1. List your ASSETS. Be sure to include skills, knowledge, and mindsets (e.g., perseverance, reliability).

2. Imagine yourself five years from now. What ASPIRATIONS do you have? These can include personal goals (e.g., renting an apartment, buying a car, having children) as well as professional or work goals.

3. How will you APPLY your assets to reach your aspirations? In the next five years, what can you do to build on your strengths and move toward your aspirations?

In schools that require high-quality passage presentations, students who don't pass often have time in the last weeks of the school year to revise and redo their presentations. They may miss end-of-year trips or activities to stay back and prepare. In some cases, when students have not completed the work that needs to be in their portfolio, or have not passed their courses, they are required to attend summer school and complete their work during the summer before re-doing their passage presentation.

At Evergreen Community Charter School in Asheville, North Carolina, teachers evaluate the passage portfolio before students begin to prepare their presentations. A high-quality and complete portfolio is the first cut demonstrating readiness for the passage presentation and, ultimately, graduation. Once a student's portfolio has met expectations, students then focus on their presentation. The presentation itself is evaluated by a panel of community members, and a passing score on the presentation is required for graduation. Table 7.2 summarizes a variety of passage presentation highlights and requirements from five different EL Education network schools.

Table 7.2 Variations on passage presentations

Capital City Public Charter School, Washington, DC, grades K–12	
Grade levels for passages	4th, 8th, 10th, 12th
Content highlights	• 4th: Standard one-year portfolio • 8th: Multi-year portfolio • 10th: Multi-year portfolio and letter to twelfth-grade self • 12th: Senior capstone project (10-page research paper based on individual field work and inquiry)
How long is the presentation?	30–50 minutes
Who is on the panel?	The panel varies by grade level; senior expedition passage presentations include community members, senior mentors, board members, and teachers.
Who is in the audience?	Parents are invited; teachers and friends often attend.
How is it evaluated?	In fourth, eighth, and tenth grade, presentations are evaluated by teachers using a rubric. In twelfth grade, both the research paper and presentation are evaluated on a rubric. Students must pass both in order to graduate.

Metropolitan Expeditionary Learning School, New York City, grades 6–12	
Grade levels for passages	8th, 12th
Content highlights	• 8th: Multi-year portfolio demonstrating high school readiness • 12th: Final word presentation on student's growth and accomplishment
How long is the presentation?	15–30 minutes
Who is on the panel?	Teachers, community members, and seniors sit on 8th-grade passage presentation panels. Final word presentations have an audience, but no evaluative panel.
Who is in the audience?	Parents are invited, but aren't required to attend passage presentations. Students choose who they want to invite to Final Word presentations, including parents, peers, and teachers.
How is it evaluated?	Eighth-graders must pass in order to walk at graduation. They have time to "do over" if they don't pass the first time. Final Word presentations are graded by the English teacher, but are not a requirement for graduation.

Health and Science School, Beaverton, Oregon, grades 6–12	
Grade levels for passages	8th, 12th
Content highlights	• 8th: Reflection on student work and growth • 12th: Reflection on a significant experience related to school pathways (work internship, biomedical science, engineering); post-secondary goals based on research done in eleventh grade
How long is the presentation?	30–45 minutes
Who is on the panel?	Teachers and community members serve on the panel.
Who is in the audience?	The student's Crew teacher and parents provide an audience.
How is it evaluated?	Students must pass to graduate. Students have opportunities to redo their presentation if they don't pass.

Table 7.2   Continued

Evergreen Community Charter School, Asheville, North Carolina, grades K–8	
Grade levels for passages	8th
Content highlights	• Resume used to apply for campus service job • Letter of recommendation from community member • Reflection on extracurricular activity of choice • Reflection on high school or life goals
How long is the presentation?	20 minutes
Who is on the panel?	Board members, community experts, and parents from other grade levels serve on the panel.
Who is in the audience?	Parents are invited.
How is it evaluated?	Students must pass portfolio and presentation in order to walk at graduation. Those who don't walk are required to redo presentation in the summer before promotion to ninth grade.

The Odyssey School of Denver, Denver, Colorado, grades K–8	
Grade levels for passages	3rd, 5th, 8th
Content highlights	• Reflection on Habits of a Learner supported with portfolio evidence • Third-graders report on two habits, while eighth-graders report on four
How long is the presentation?	15–30 minutes
Who is on the panel?	Teachers, parent volunteers, and community members serve on the panel.
Who is in the audience?	Parents are not invited. Students are accountable to an authentic audience of community members
How is it evaluated?	Panelists evaluate the presentation based on a rubric, then write a letter to the student. Eighth-graders who pass both academics and Habits of Learning receive "distinction" on their diploma.

Fox Creek Elementary, Littleton, Colorado, grades K–6	
Grade levels for passages	6th
Content highlights	• Significant introduction of the student from a former teacher • Highlights of student work • Reflection on a significant failure • Reflection on "why I'm ready to go to seventh grade"
How long is the presentation?	20 minutes for presentation; 10 minutes for feedback
Who is on the panel?	No formal panel
Who is in the audience?	Each sixth-grader is "hosted" by a former teacher for his/her passage presentation, and the school schedule is reorganized for two days so that sixth-graders can present to an audience of younger students (K–5), as well as their family and teachers.
What about kids who don't pass?	Presentations are not formally evaluated, but the host teacher facilitates feedback and questions from students in the audience.

Figure 7.2 Letter to families from Metropolitan Expeditionary Learning School in New York City
SOURCE: This document is available in the online toolbox at http://www.wiley.com/go/lotolcompanion.

Dear Families,

As we enter your child's second month as an eighth-grader, we are writing to invite you to Student-Led Conferences and to explain an important end-of-year ritual that your child will take part in called the Passages Panel Presentation.

Panel Presentations and SLCs are important events here at MELS that reflect our core beliefs about teaching and learning. Here, learning is personal – a process of self-discovery through which we come to better understand ourselves and our place in the world at the same time as we develop new knowledge and skills. Learning is also about growth – we encourage students to compete with their own personal best as they strive to produce high-quality work and improve their habits. Finally, we believe that learning is reflective – when students consider their successes and failures, they can identify their own areas and strategies for future growth.

Passages Panel Presentations

The transition from middle to high school is an important milestone in a person's life, marking the transition from childhood to young adulthood. We believe this is a time not just for celebration but also for introspection. We want our eighth-graders to enter high school with an understanding of themselves as people and as learners, so that they are ready for the challenges that await them.

In June, your child will deliver a ten-minute presentation to a panel of adults from across the MELS community. In this presentation, they will speak about themselves, highlighting the ways that they have grown and changed since sixth grade. They will also discuss a project from this school year that they found especially interesting. The presentation is followed by a few minutes of questions from the panelists who will then provide the presenter with some feedback and let them know if their reflection and presentation were satisfactory. Any students needing to present a second time are given extensive support from Crew Advisors and panelists. Parents are encouraged to join us as audience members. More information will follow as that date gets closer.

Student-Led Conferences

Because we believe that students should be well-supported when asked to do difficult things, we have designed Student-Led Conferences in the eighth grade so that they will prepare your child for their Panel Presentation. For that reason, things might look a little bit different than they have in the past. Rather than providing an overview of performance in multiple classes, students will instead focus on just one project, with an emphasis on explaining the learning that is reflected in that work. As a result, parents wanting to look at Progress Reports and JumpRope comments are encouraged to review their child's SLC Portfolio before or after the conference. SLCs will take place in the evening on Thursday, November 9 and in the afternoon on the 10th.

TRY THIS: COMMUNICATE WITH FAMILIES EARLY IN THE YEAR

If passage presentations are a new idea for students, they will also be new for their families, even those who may already be accustomed to participating in student-led conferences. It is critical to communicate to families why passage presentations matter at your school and how they are different from student-led conferences. It's also important to include *all* families in this communication, especially those who, because of a language or cultural barrier, may not understand how important the passage presentation is. Figure 7.2 shows how leaders at the Metropolitan Expeditionary Learning School in New York City explain the difference. The letter also explains the importance of the passage presentation tradition as a reflection of the school's core beliefs about teaching and learning.

Learning Target 2: I can support students to create multi-year portfolios with reflections.

 Challenge #3: I have student work everywhere! I need clear systems for saving, storing, and managing students' portfolios over multiple years.

TRY THIS: COLLABORATE WITH COLLEAGUES TO CREATE SYSTEMS FOR CHOOSING, ARCHIVING, AND TRANSFERRING STUDENT WORK INTO PASSAGE PORTFOLIOS

In Chapter 5, we discussed a variety of systems for gathering, storing, and maintaining student portfolios within classrooms. When thinking about passage portfolios, the logistics become more complicated because now we are talking about multi-year portfolios and systems and consistencies that must be negotiated *across* classrooms and grade levels. In *Leaders of Their Own Learning*, we described key decision points that teachers will need to address in order to create a system for building passage presentation portfolios across multiple years:

- Where will students save work that may be included in the passage presentation portfolio?

- Are portfolios kept at the school across years or sent home each year?

- Will we use a digital portfolio system or physical portfolios (binders, bins, boxes) or both?

- If the multi-year portfolios are physical, such as binders, where are they stored (e.g., in classrooms, the library, a portfolio storage area)?

- If portfolios are digital, who will have access to those files?

- Who is responsible for supporting students to organize and maintain the passage presentation portfolio (subject area teachers? advisory/Crew teachers?)?

- How will physical work be transferred when students move up to a new grade level?

- How will we support students who are new to the school or for other reasons don't have work from previous years?

- How will we support teachers who are new to the school and new to our portfolio system?

- How will we support students to maintain and keep track of the work that may be included in their portfolios?

Because passage portfolios must be maintained over multiple years, it's critical that these questions be tackled collaboratively across the school so that students have consistent systems for accessing and adding to their portfolios.

Students will periodically need time to conduct "portfolio maintenance."

Photo Credit: EL Education

TRY THIS: LEVERAGE TECHNOLOGY TO CREATE DIGITAL PORTFOLIOS

Many schools today circumvent the challenges of maintaining, storing, and moving physical work folders or portfolios-in-progress by establishing a digital portfolio system. There are many software programs, including shared Google folders, that teachers and students can use to build a stable digital system accessible to everyone involved in creating portfolios. For schools with one-to-one laptop or tablet programs, where all students have ready access to technology, this may be a viable and powerful option. At River Bluff High School in Lexington, South Carolina, for example, where all freshmen receive tablets to use throughout their high school years, the first few months of freshman advisory, or Crew, include explicit lessons on how to set up and manage a digital portfolio and students are introduced to the tradition of passage presentations (which take place at the end of tenth and twelfth grade). In preparation for those events, students learn how to take and upload photos of their work, how to organize their work into folders, and how to save reflections and other data that will accompany that work as they move through their courses and up through the grades.

Challenge #4: I'm not sure what students should include in the passage portfolio.

TRY THIS: IDENTIFY PASSAGE PORTFOLIO CONTENT THAT IS PERSONAL AND POWERFUL, AND THAT ILLUMINATES THE PROMISE OF THE FUTURE

Portfolios for passage presentations, like those for student-led conferences, should provide a compilation of compelling evidence of a student's academic achievements and growth. The specific contents of passage portfolios, however, are often broader in scope (encompassing multiple years), deeper in their explication of specific student work, and may be more personal and creative than those used in student-led conferences. Because they are meant to show growth since the previous passage presentation, they provide evidence of academic challenges and successes across multiple years and subject areas. In addition, the portfolios may delve deeply into projects, disciplines, or experiences of particular interest to students so that they can truly reflect on and share the transformative experiences that have prepared them for their next challenge. Passage portfolios may include out-of-school learning and accomplishments in athletics, arts, citizenship, service, job-based learning, and faith. Finally, they may include things like career inventories, personal statements, maps of the future, or other items that illuminate students' promise and vision for the next leg of their academic journeys. Table 7.3 illustrates portfolio components to consider as you work with colleagues to create a list of artifacts or sections for passage portfolios.

Once you and your team have determined the parameters of what must be included in the passage portfolio, be sure to communicate those requirements clearly to students and families. Our online toolbox contains examples of these passage presentation portfolio guides designed for students and

Table 7.3 Examples of passage portfolio components

Artifacts That Show Personality	Artifacts That Speak with Power about Student Accomplishment	Artifacts That Show the Promise for the Future
• Introductory personal statement • Reflections on independent projects, extracurriculars, work, athletics, the arts, or personal passions • Student work from elective courses • Creative cover or illustrations throughout the portfolio • Work chosen by the student	• Resume • Transcript • Trend data from interim or standardized assessments • Major student-work projects, organized by subject area, grade level, or required standard • Student work, especially final drafts of long-term projects or work created for an authentic audience • Reflections on character or leadership • Service learning logs • Awards and recognitions • Recommendations or testimonials by others (e.g., coach, work supervisor, pastor)	• Letter to future self • Reflection on work habits • Reflection on challenges overcome or areas of growth • Career inventories • Personal metaphors or maps that depict "where I'm headed"

families. Explore the one(s) that match the needs of your school (all four documents are available in the online toolbox at http://www.wiley.com/go/lotolcompanion):

- *Capital City Public Charter School, tenth Grade*: This guide describes the requirements and expectations for a tenth-grade passage presentation and portfolio that includes a letter to the student's twelfth-grade self.

- *Capital City Public Charter School, twelfth Grade*: This curriculum map for the Senior Expedition culminates in a final passage presentation and outlines learning targets and expectations seniors must meet in order to graduate.

- *Evergreen Community Charter School, 8th Grade*: This guide for 8th-grade students outlines four components of a portfolio that communicates a holistic view of the student (self, academics, community, future) and the requirements for a 20-minute passage presentation.

- *The Odyssey School of Denver*: This guide for third-, fifth-, and eighth-grade students and their families provides an overview of passage presentations that focus on the link between work habits and academic achievement.

TRY THIS: ENOURAGE (OR REQUIRE) STUDENTS TO INCLUDE NONACADEMIC CHALLENGES OR OUT-OF-SCHOOL LEARNING AS A PART OF THEIR PASSAGE

One way that many schools distinguish passage presentations and portfolios from those created for student-led conferences is that passages focus as much on personal challenges and learning as on academic ones. As the word *passage* implies, students experience and reflect on stepping out of their comfort zone during their passage presentation year.

Several years ago, The Springfield Renaissance School in Springfield, Massachusetts deepened tenth-grade passages by adding a requirement that students take on a physical challenge for their sophomore year that they had never tried before (e.g., a new sport, a martial art, a new dance style, a trade). Another EL Education network school had a similar requirement for trying a new winter sport (e.g., nordic skiing, hockey, curling, winter camping). The journey of learning that skill, of trying something brand new, is the centerpiece of students' passage portfolios and presentations. And, since each student chooses their "something new" individually, according to their own passions, proclivities, and personalities, the skill and the story she tells is unique.

Students often have rich lives outside of school that are places of deep learning and growth for them. Asking students to show evidence of this learning through artifacts, video, or demonstrations can make the passage presentation unique, personal, and compelling. Over the years we have seen students perform live on the cello, violin, flute, and drums; juggle balls and clubs; show videotapes of horseback riding competitions, dance performances, basketball and soccer highlights; and feature live demonstrations of skills including dog obedience training and quickly disassembling and reassembling a chainsaw!

 Challenge #5: My students can't find or don't have academic work from multiple years.

TRY THIS: THINK OUTSIDE THE BOX

Supporting students who have transferred to your school from other schools or homeschool environments where they didn't archive their work presents a quandary for both students and teachers. Clearly the student should not be penalized for not having work from previous years, and it's also important that the student have the opportunity to participate fully in the passage presentation tradition. There are always a few students who have misplaced or never completed their work. These students deserve the opportunity to reflect on and present their growth across the years. For all of these students, it is possible to gather some evidence of academic progress from report cards, interviews with teachers, or other evidence of past academic work.

In addition, athletics, arts, clubs, civic or faith-based organizations, and family members can supply credible evidence of students' growth and learning. For some students, making progress toward becoming an Eagle Scout, starting a garage band, volunteering, or learning a martial art may illustrate growth in knowledge, skills, and character more powerfully than a traditional academic portfolio. The challenges and failures along the way in these non-school arenas are important milestones in a young person's journey to adulthood. Students can be asked to write descriptions of their involvement and reflections about their learning and growth for these type of out-of-school commitments.

You may need to creatively adapt your passage portfolio guidelines for these students. We encourage you to conference with the student and think creatively about what artifacts are available that can be used as evidence to reflect academic and personal growth. Table 7.4 provides some suggestions for artifacts and activities that students could use to create a passage portfolio from scratch.

For students with little academic work, Figure 7.3 provides a reflection tool for identifying significant personal experiences that could be the central topic of a passage presentation.

Table 7.4 Nontraditional passage presentation portfolio components

Artifact	How Students Can Use It
Academic Transcript	Analyze and annotate the transcript to identify trends and reflect on what the grades mean.
Images of or partial components of student work from previous years	Reflect on the part of the work that's available. If no early drafts are available, create a summary that conveys the story of creating the work and what students learned along the way.
Transcripts of interviews with previous teachers (have students email previous teachers if possible)	Summarize the interview and select quotes that comment on what kind of students they were. Respond to the comments (it's their chance to "talk back" respectfully). What did they learn in their previous schooling? What did they learn about themselves as learners?
Clippings from organizational newsletters, the newspaper, or other artifacts of achievement in civic, athletic, or service organizations	Reflect verbally and in writing on these "scrap book" announcements or accolades. Describe their involvement and reflect on their learning. How did their experience shape their growth as a people and as a learners?
A performance or demonstration of a skill or special ability	Present a live or filmed performance or demonstration of a skill (e.g., athletic, musical, job-related). Write a reflection on why this skill matters for their futures.
The story of a personal challenge or adversity that required grit and resilience (e.g. a health crisis or family loss)	Tell the story and reflect on the personal qualities that helped them overcome the challenge. How did the experience change them? Strengthen their resolve about the future? Help them set goals or commit to their community?

Figure 7.3 Exploring my personal growth outside of school
SOURCE: This document is available in the online toolbox at http://www.wiley.com/go/lotolcompanion.

Complete the table below as a way of brainstorming key outside-of-school experiences that have shaped you as a person. Then choose ONE activity or experience to tell a more detailed story about for your extracurricular/personal passage presentation artifact.

Informal activities I've been involved in (e.g., arts, hobbies, informal athletic activities)	
Formal groups I've been involved with (e.g., scouts, youth group, church choir, dance troupe)	
Sports I've been involved with	
Jobs I've worked in	
Family responsibilities I assume (e.g., babysitting siblings, taking care of grandmother)	
Volunteer work I do regularly	
Something really hard that I've learned to do through study, practice, and effort	

Dig deeper into the ONE experience you've chosen from the table. Respond to the following questions to help you prepare to tell the story of your growth and learning.

1. Identify the beginning of the story. When did you commit to this activity or group? Was there an initiation or moment when you knew you wanted to be "in" this activity? Were you stepping up to be of service to your family or community?
2. Who are the main characters of the story (family members, teammates, coaches, mentors, teachers, etc.)? What impact have they had on you?
3. What are the highlights of your experience, the moments that are like photos in your brain? If you have real photos, plan to include them in your portfolio!
4. What specific challenges have you had to overcome along the way? What evidence do you have of these challenges – journal entries, notes, photos, or failed products that could be part of your portfolio?
5. What successes and breakthroughs mark the path of your journey? What evidence or artifacts (e.g., awards, trophies, news clips, etc.) could be part of your portfolio?
6. What have you learned about yourself through this journey?
7. What have you learned about what you contribute to the community around you, and what you receive from others?
8. What have you learned about learning hard things and overcoming challenge?
9. How will this experience help you succeed in the future?

 Challenge #6: My students are focused on what they can do now. They have difficulty seeing their growth over multiple years.

TRY THIS: PROVIDE TOOLS THAT HELP STUDENTS FOCUS AND REFLECT ON SPECIFIC KNOWLEDGE AND SKILLS

If your students have been doing student-led conferences, they are used to sampling their work throughout a course or term. They are likely accustomed to routines for reflecting as they go at the end of each major project. But selecting and reflecting on just a few pieces of work to represent growth and achievement over multiple years can be overwhelming. Students are often stymied by how to choose just a few pieces from among so many choices. They will benefit from tools that help them reflect on and identify

Figure 7.4 Protocol for selecting passage portfolio work
SOURCE: This document is available in the online toolbox at http://www.wiley.com/go/lotolcompanion.

This protocol can be done alone or in collaboration with a partner. If done with a partner, build in pauses for each student to explain her choices and to receive feedback from a partner about which pieces to include and why.
Note: This protocol requires that students have prior portfolios to work with, often from past student-led conferences.

Procedure
1. Pull the tables of contents from previous portfolios since the last passage presentation (usually two or three years).
2. Briefly review all of the work in all of the portfolios to remind yourself of all that you've done and learned over these years.
3. Now, highlight or use a sticky note to mark those pieces of work or reflections that have something special to offer to a multi-year portfolio.
   - Highlight an entry that represents the best work you've ever done
   - Highlight an entry that represents an area of growth for you – a skill or subject area in which you have improved over the years.
   - Highlight an entry that represents the most challenging work you've ever done
   - Highlight an entry that reflects a topic you're still passionate about today
   - Highlight an entry that reflects a work habit that you've really had to work on over the years
   - Highlight an entry that improved the most from start to finish
   - Highlight an entry that says the most about your unique personality or authentic self
   - Highlight the most sincere and deep reflection in your portfolios

important themes or intersections in their work over the years, topics or skills they are passionate about, or work that represents a transformational moment that helps them tell a *particular* story, rather than their *entire* story. Figure 7.4 is a protocol to help students do this kind of culling. (Note: Figure 7.3 could also be used to help students focus in this way.)

Another exercise for helping students compare work across grade levels is to simply ask them to observe how their skills have grown within one subject area. Table 7.5 provides a simple tool for helping students compare their work from one grade to another in each subject area. We have filled it in with a sampling of how a student might use it.

Once students have compared key features of their work in different years within a single subject, use the reflection tool in Figure 7.5 to help them think about the trajectory of their learning and growth across multiple years and what it means for their future.

Table 7.5 What I notice in my work: past and present

Example: English Past	English Present
I notice that I used bad grammar in many of my sentences, I notice that I did not use enough evidence to support my ideas.	I notice that I now pay more attention to grammar and spelling. I capitalize properly and use the correct tense. I think my writing has improved. I have learned more vocabulary that helps me to analyze what I read.
Example: Social Studies Past	**Social Studies Present**
I notice that my work in sixth grade was not always thoughtful. I didn't follow directions well and I made many mistakes. I also see that when I was younger, I did not make many connections from history to my own life.	In eighth grade, I think the quality of my work has improved. I read directions carefully and more than once. I connect my life to history and I ask more questions about why things happen rather than just recording facts and dates.

Figure 7.5 "Big learning" reflection tool

SOURCE: This document is available in the online toolbox at http://www.wiley.com/go/lotolcompanion.

Instructions: Choose one piece of work from each school year that represents "Big Learning." You can think of this as "really hard lessons" or "really important lessons" or even "lessons that I'm really proud of."

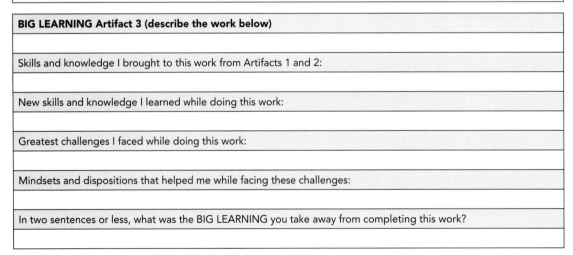

BIG LEARNING Artifact 1 (describe the work here; this should be the earliest piece of work in your portfolio)
Skills and knowledge I brought to this work from previous learning:
New skills and knowledge I learned while doing this work:
Greatest challenges I faced while doing this work:
Mindsets and dispositions that helped me while facing these challenges:
In two sentences or less, what was the BIG LEARNING you take away from completing this work?

BIG LEARNING Artifact 2 (describe the work below).
Skills and knowledge I brought to this work from Artifact 1:
New skills and knowledge I learned while doing this work:
Greatest challenges I faced while doing this work:
Mindsets and dispositions that helped me while facing these challenges:
In two sentences or less, what was the BIG LEARNING you take away from completing this work?

BIG LEARNING Artifact 3 (describe the work below)
Skills and knowledge I brought to this work from Artifacts 1 and 2:
New skills and knowledge I learned while doing this work:
Greatest challenges I faced while doing this work:
Mindsets and dispositions that helped me while facing these challenges:
In two sentences or less, what was the BIG LEARNING you take away from completing this work?

When you reflect on the trends and patterns in your learning across this set of projects, what is the BIG BIG lesson you take with you as you move up to the next grade level?

TRY THIS: PROVIDE STUDENTS WITH TOOLS THAT HELP THEM REFLECT DEEPLY AND MULTI-DIMENSIONALLY

Reflecting on the big picture of their learning and who they are becoming as students and as people is often the greatest challenge for students. At Harborside Academy in Kenosha, Wisconsin, eighth-grade teachers take a comprehensive approach to reflection over multiple years. They frame the selection of passage portfolio pieces as "telling the story" of a student's middle school years and "imagining the story" of the high school years. Identifying or creating the portfolio pieces that tell these stories takes most of a school year. Students do this work in their eighth-grade Crews (advisory groups).

Figure 7.6 walks Harborside students through a process of reflecting on their work aligned with passage presentation learning targets. As you review the Learning Story outline in Figure 7.6 consider text coding each item for the category of reflection it represents:

1. Items that require reflection on academic progress or products

2. Items that require reflection on mindsets and "how you learn"

3. Items that require reflection on future goals and interests

4. Items that require reflection on non-academic traits or experiences

TRY THIS: ZOOM IN ON WORK HABITS EVIDENCED IN STUDENT WORK

It's important that we ask students to reflect not just on their growth in reading and math and other academic subjects, but also on their growth in work habits, such as meeting deadlines and revising their work. These are some of the mindsets that will matter most in college and careers, yet we rarely gather evidence of progress in these areas. Students are not always keen to examine their work habits, but evidence and persistent questions can help them reflect deeply on how work habits support their academic and personal learning. Video Spotlight 7.5 features a student rehearsing for his passage presentation at The Odyssey School of Denver. Passage presentations at Odyssey are explicitly structured to focus on the work habits behind individual pieces of student work.

Video Spotlight 7.5: Reflecting on Work Habits Fosters Growth
https://vimeo.com/313899543

This video features an eighth-grade student, Seamus, sharing data to support a claim about the work habit responsibility. Seamus reflects on the quality of his work, his homework completion, and how his increasing responsibility has benefited him as a student. This video was produced by an EL Education coach, using a phone, so the production quality is not great, however, the content of Seamus's reflections make it 100 percent worthwhile.

Video Reflection Questions
1. How does Seamus use data to support his conclusions about his growth?
2. How does Seamus's reflection on his growing habit of responsibility lead him to set appropriate goals for the future?

Figure 7.6 Learning story outline from Harborside Academy in Kenosha, Wisconsin
SOURCE: This document is available in the online toolbox at http://www.wiley.com/go/lotolcompanion.

Tell Me Your Story: Eighth-Grade Passage Presentations
Learning Target 1: I can explain who I am and who and what has influenced me.
Product: Personal Statement

- *Should include*: Description of yourself and background (short biography)
- Who and what has influenced you and impacted who you are now?
- What did they do/what occurred in your life to influence who you have become? Why is this important to you?
- This section would be the place for photos or other kinds of media that describe you (include hobbies, family, goals)
- Letter to ninth-grade teacher (learning style, success, failures, fears, hopes, dreams for high school, fears about high school)

Learning Target 2: I can define and explain the six Habits of Success (HOS) traits and analyze my own success through those traits.
Product: Habits of Success Statement

- Definitions of the Habits of Success traits in your own words
- Reflection on your Habits of Success traits
  - What HOS traits do you display strongly? Give evidence and anecdotes to support your statements
  - What HOS trait do you feel is your greatest challenge? Give evidence and anecdotes to support your statements
- Why are Habits of Success important to your growth as a student and person?

Learning Target 3: I can explain my academic progress through my test scores (MAPS and ACT Practice) and how they connect to and impact the classes I will take in the future.
Product: MAPS Results and Reflection

- NWEA MAPS Student Progress Report
- Reflection on MAPS scores that identifies your strengths and weaknesses
- Include a specific plan for improvement citing evidence from your scores and address what classes you will take in the future based on this reflection (could be preferences or ACT Practice Scores

Learning Target 4: I can explore my interests and explain how they influence my potential career choices.
Product: Career Cruising Profile and Reflection

- Complete the Career Cruising Match Maker, My Skills and Learning Style Inventory
- Include the print-out of the Career Cruising Match Maker and My Skills
- Reflect upon the results and explain if this is an accurate assessment of you citing evidence from your life to explain why or why not
- List of careers from Career Cruising that interest you
- List of any other careers you are interested in
- What classes do you plan on taking and/or will you need to take in high school to prepare yourself?
- What postsecondary training will you need for that/those career(s)?
- Where specifically can you obtain this postsecondary training (e.g., college, technical school, university, military, internship, etc.) and what are the requirements for admission?

Learning Target 5: I can reflect on my personal and academic growth and my educational environment.
Product: EL Education Reflection

- What is "EL" Learning?
- What design principles do you identify most strongly with?
- How has attending an EL school like Harborside impacted you as a student and person? Why do you think that is?

Product: Crew Reflection

- Describe what Crew is and what it means to you.
- Include camp reflections.

Product: Service Log and Reflection

- What is service and why is it important?
- Explain what service experience had the greatest impact on you and why.

Product: Learning Expedition Reflection and Coursework

- Identify and summarize each learning expedition for each year.
- For each learning expedition include a summative assessment for each academic course, or a summative assessment that covers multiple academic courses.
- For each summative assessment explain what you learned and how you learned it reflecting on your successes and struggles.

Product: Math and Elective (if not covered in Learning Expedition) Reflection and Coursework

- For each summative assessment explain what you learned and how you learned it reflecting on your successes and struggles.

What data could your students include in their passage portfolios to demonstrate their character growth and readiness for the future? Attendance data and homework completion are often used to assess work habits. In addition, other sources of information about a student's character (e.g., commitment to excellence, perseverance, ethic of service) may come from published writing or art (e.g., school literary magazine, newspaper, gallery); awards or news pertaining to sports, community service, or other accolades; or letters, notes, or communications from employers, mentors, or coaches.

Particularly as students get older, more of their accolades and achievements may come from non-academic pursuits. Including a piece of published writing in a passage portfolio, for example, is an opportunity for the student to discuss how academic writing assignments in school created a foundation for success with writing outside of school. Similarly, a student might reflect on how she developed a great work ethic in sports or a challenging class. Encourage your students to tell the story of change in their habits and accomplishments over time.

Learning Target 3: I can ensure that students are prepared to lead passage presentations with professionalism.

Challenge #7: My Students have strong portfolios, but their presentation skills are weak.

TRY THIS: ESTABLISH GUIDELINES FOR DRESS AND INTRODUCTIONS

First impressions count! Several years ago, Carlos, a teenage victim of gun violence, sat in the back row of his high school English class and passionately researched the arguments for gun control. As part of his research, he landed an interview with the mayor of his town, but a few days before the interview he paused at the end of class to ask his teacher, "What should I wear? I can't show up in the mayor's office in my jeans!" With the teacher's help, Carlos acquired a used suit and tie. He showed up nervous, but also more confident, on the day of the interview. Among the most important lessons he learned during that project was that when facing an authentic and unfamiliar audience, especially if you're nervous, dressing professionally matters. For many students setting the bar high with explicit guidance for how to dress – and how to introduce yourself with a handshake – is a positive first step toward success.[1]

Helping students dress and interact with professionalism during their passage presentations will boost their confidence and pride.

Photo Credit: EL Education

---

[1] The National Association of Colleges and Employers offers gender-inclusive, visual guidelines for professional dress (https://s3.amazonaws .com/higherlogicdownload/NACEWEB/UploadedImages/NOYdKcQ2m43ItXCYx0Pw_dress-for-success.png).

To help students get ready to dress for success, consider holding a clothing swap a few weeks before passage presentations. Invite parents and older siblings to clean out their closets and contribute. This could also be a fun opportunity to boost students' enthusiasm for getting dressed up and putting their best foot forward.

In addition to clothing, explicit lessons in how to lead an introduction with a handshake and a "nice to meet you" will bolster students' confidence for presenting professionally. As with all things, practice makes permanent; there's no substitute for repetition. Design a critique lesson in which you and your students develop the criteria for a great introduction with a handshake. Then follow the critique lesson with practice in which students introduce themselves to each other and assess each other based on those criteria.

If there are students for whom the physical contact of a handshake is forbidden due to faith traditions, or for whom direct eye contact is considered culturally impolite, this should be addressed directly and respectfully. It is much better for a student to practice saying, "Excuse me, but my faith does not permit me to shake hands," than for the issue to be awkward and unspoken. Similarly, even with coaching to adjust to typical school and business norms, a student who has grown up learning that direct eye contact with adults is rude will have a difficult time keeping eye contact regularly. It is helpful for that student to say, "Excuse me, but in my culture I was raised that direct eye contact with adults is not polite. I will do my best to address that, but please forgive me if I do not succeed all the time in this." Discussing "the rules" for business handshakes *and* appropriate exceptions is a productive exercise for students, one that deepens understanding and gives equal access to all students.

TRY THIS: USE MODELS TO ESTABLISH EXPECTATIONS FOR TONE, DICTION, AND VISUALS

Some version of "speak loudly and clearly" shows up on almost every presentation skills rubric. But sounding authoritative and personable has to do with more than just volume. Students also need to know how to convey their expertise with "personable confidence," use the appropriate vocabulary, and integrate technology or visuals into their presentation.

These considerations, while more subtle than volume and eye contact, will be familiar to many students once we bring them up. After all, they have watched dozens of YouTube videos, spoken-word performances, Ted Talks, and other presentations to a variety of audiences. Modeling strong presentation skills in the form of a critique lesson is a productive way to help students understand the nuances of strong presentations. The models in the Video Spotlights at the beginning of this chapter are all good examples of presentation skills that can be shown to students. Design a critique lesson for your own students that invites them to notice the techniques these students use to captivate and communicate to the audience. Then create a rubric with your students that will guide them as they prepare for their own passage presentations.

If you require students to have a technology-driven visual presentation that accompanies their oral presentation, provide guidance for the content of the visuals and for what makes a strong visual presentation. Figure 7.7 is an example of very specific guidance that will help students overcome common presentation pitfalls.

Figure 7.7 Guidelines for presentations from Evergreen Community Charter School in Asheville, North Carolina

SOURCE: This document is available in the online toolbox at http://www.wiley.com/go/lotolcompanion.

Required Slide Content (You can have more than 11 slides if you choose, but these must be included).

Slide	Content
1–Title slide	Student Name, School Name, Visual(s)
2–Overview of Portfolio & Presentation	Preview of presentation • What would you like the judges to learn by watching your presentation? • Should align with main points from intro letter
3–Self	Introduce the evidence that you included in the Self section of your Portfolio.
4–Self	Explain why you chose these pieces of evidence to describe yourself. • Be specific about at least one or two pieces of evidence in this section. • **Prompt judges for questions after this slide.**
5–Academics	Introduce the evidence that you included in the Academic section.
6–Academics	Explain why you chose these pieces of evidence to describe your academics. • Discuss strengths, challenges, and evidence of growth. • Relate to one or more Habit of Scholars. • Be specific about at least one or two pieces of evidence in this section. • **Prompt judges for questions after this slide**
7–Evergreen Community	Introduce the evidence that you included in the Evergreen Community section of your portfolio.
8–Evergreen Community	Explain why you chose these pieces of evidence to describe your role in the Evergreen Community. • Relate to one or more Habit of Scholar. • Be specific about at least one or two pieces of evidence in this section. • **Prompt judges for questions after this slide**
9–Beyond Evergreen	Introduce the evidence that you included in the Beyond Evergreen section of your portfolio.
10–Beyond Evergreen	Explain why you chose these pieces of evidence to describe your role in the community Beyond Evergreen. • Be specific about at least one or two pieces of evidence in this section. • Relate to one or more Habit of Scholar.
11–Conclusion	Closing slide–Thanks and prompt for questions

Eighth-Grade Passage Presentation Slide Guidelines:
- Can use PowerPoint, Google slides, Prezi, other presentation programs
- Expected presentation length: 12–15 minutes, with an additional 10 minutes for judges' questions
- *Minimum of 11 slides*, but can have more
- Slides should be main points and visuals; you will verbally explain your evidence. DO NOT READ FROM SLIDES. The slides are a tool to assist you.
- Presentation must follow the order of your portfolio.
- Include at least two Habit of Scholars in your presentation; explain how specific pieces of evidence prove you have developed a specific habit or habits.
- Be sure to add color and photographs or videos of evidence or of your process; this makes it interesting and brings it life!
- Be sure fonts are large enough to easily read and pictures are high quality.
- PROOFREAD! PROOFREAD! PROOFREAD! There should be NO spelling or grammar errors.
- Presentations <u>MUST</u> be brought in on a flash drive. Do not expect the wireless connection to be working. Windows-based computer and projector will be available for students.
- Refer to Grad Panel Description packet for more info on presentation and the judges' rubric.

TRY THIS: PROVIDE ADDITIONAL OR DIFFERENT SUPPORT FOR STUDENTS WHO NEED IT

All students can be successful with passage presentations when given the right support. Work with the specialists at your school to develop the tools and the time that individual students may need to feel confident and prepared to present their work. Table 7.6 provides strategies suggested by specialists at Evergreen Community Charter School in Asheville, North Carolina, and Capital City Public Charter School in Washington, DC, to address some common challenges of special populations in their schools.

Table 7.6 Strategies for students who need additional support

If the portfolio and presentation requirements are overwhelming
<ul><li>Maintain the portfolio learning targets, but reduce the volume of work that needs to be presented (e.g., if the expectation is three products in three content areas, require two products in two content areas).</li><li>Allow the student to present a PowerPoint or Prezi with the same content instead of a written product.</li><li>Provide additional scaffolding for writing reflections (e.g., sentence starters, graphic organizers).</li><li>Minimize homework and assignment expectations in the days leading up to passage presentations.</li><li>Work with a librarian or support person to curate resources and support the research process for capstone projects or individual research topics.</li><li>For students with modifications specified in an Individualized Education Program (IEP), provide a modified rubric for the portfolio and/or the presentation. Have a specialist participate on the panel and explain the modifications to the panelists before they score the rubric (but after the student has presented).</li></ul>

If the student needs more time to organize materials and compile a portfolio
<ul><li>Use part of a resource class to frontload organizational skills and work on portfolios.</li><li>Create an additional "pull-out" advisory time when some students work on portfolios.</li><li>Start early! Introduce these students to portfolio requirements early in the school year and make a tight plan for gathering student work and reflections. Provide due dates prior to the due dates.</li><li>Allow the student to re-present their work or reflections used previously in a student-led conference.</li></ul>

If the student experiences severe anxiety at the thought of presenting
<ul><li>Ensure that at least one panelist is a familiar and friendly face for the student presenting.</li><li>Allow the student to have a peer presentation partner to support him or her with rehearsals and at the passage event itself.</li><li>Reduce the time expected for presenting.</li><li>Allow the student to present to a camera, then replay the video for the panel at the passage presentation.</li><li>Invite older students with the same challenge who have done a passage presentation to share how it felt during and after their presentation.</li><li>Provide reassurance before and time to debrief after rehearsals.</li></ul>

If the student has difficulty responding to questions
<ul><li>Rehearse the question and answer session, and provide kind, specific, helpful feedback on body language and the content of answers.</li><li>Provide some scripted questions to the student and panelists in advance.</li></ul>

If the student is an English language learner and needs language support
<ul><li>Provide graphic organizers with picture words and/or bold vocabulary.</li><li>Pre-teach expectations and the vocabulary of passage presentation documents.</li><li>Rehearse, rehearse, rehearse; provide kind, specific, and helpful feedback on clarity of articulation.</li><li>Allow the student to do part of the presentation in their native language (especially if some members of the panel can understand it).</li><li>Provide prewritten questions to the panel and the student.</li></ul>

TRY THIS: REHEARSE WITH A VARIETY OF AUDIENCES

The big day for passage presentations always arrives surprisingly quickly. When planning for the event, be sure to build in plenty of time for rehearsal with a variety of audiences. Once students have their portfolios completed, begin to rehearse with a low-stakes audience of peers. Students should practice first with others who are familiar with the criteria for a high-quality presentation, and who are vulnerable themselves because they are also presenting. Use a peer critique protocol like those in Chapter 4 to make this lesson productive.

Figure 7.8 Question and sentence stems to guide feedback for passage presentations
SOURCE: This document is available in the online toolbox at http://www.wiley.com/go/lotolcompanion.

Be Kind
- The most memorable artifact in your presentation was . . .
- You were exceptionally engaging when . . .
- I was especially impressed with your reflection on . . . because
- The greatest strength of your presentation was . . .
- You really convinced me that you are ready for next year when you said . . .
- I felt I got to know the real you when you talked about/showed . . .

Be Specific
- When you talked about. . . I wondered . . .
- I learned a lot about how you've grown as a learner when you spoke about/showed . . .
- The most convincing data that you showed was . . .
- You need a little more evidence to support your claim that . . .
- You really hooked me in with your story about . . .
- I got a little distracted when you . . .
- My attention drifted a little when you . . .
- The part that confused me was . . .

Be Helpful
- I'd really like to hear more about . . .
- You might consider providing more/different evidence about . . .
- I wonder why you spent so much/so little time on . . .
- If I could give one piece of advice about your presentation, it would be . . .
- Your presentation left me wondering . . .
- If you were to present . . . again, try focusing more on . . .

Figure 7.9 Seven gauges for a snappy presentation
SOURCE: This document is available in the online toolbox at http://www.wiley.com/go/lotolcompanion.

1. Voice Speed		
Slow mo	Confident and conversational	Fast forward
2. Expression		
Sleepwalking	Respectful and authoritative	Over the top
3. Movement and Gestures		
Statue	Conversationalist	Whirlwind
4. Eye Contact		
Evasive	Friendly	Staring uncomfortably
5. Pacing and Chunking		
Random	Logical and flowing	Rigidly scripted
6. Integration of Media and Visuals		
Disjointed	Seamless	Formulaic
7. Responding to Questions		
Evasive	Helpful	Too much information

Next, look for other, more authentic audiences for students to practice with. Students who are one grade younger or one grade older are often a good choice. Finally, consider bringing in parents and community members to rehearse with students. Parents should not critique their own child, but can be helpful coaches to other students, coaching for poise, movement, expression, eye-contact, pacing, and the integration of technology or visuals. Figures 7.8 and 7.9 may be used as handouts for practice panelists to help them ask probing questions that support students to reflect on and be prepared to answer questions about growth, motivation, and readiness for the future.

Passage presentations are high-stakes events for students, and they will need plenty of opportunities to rehearse and prepare.

Photo Credit: EL Education

 Challenge #8: My students falter when they have to think on their feet.

TRY THIS: OFFER STUDENTS CONCRETE TIPS AND PRACTICE FOR RESPONDING TO QUESTIONS

Perhaps the most nerve-wracking aspect of delivering a talk for any presenter is the question and answer period at the end. Thinking on your feet and responding to questions that you haven't anticipated with answers that you haven't rehearsed is a hurdle for most people. But there are tips you can offer students. Here are a few to get them started:

- Listen attentively to the panel member's question. If you don't understand it, ask him or her to repeat or explain the question before you respond. It's always appropriate to say "I am not sure I understand the question."

- Don't rush. It's fine to think quietly for a minute before you respond.

- Use your portfolio or visuals to elaborate on what you have said earlier in your presentation. Return to your evidence to answer new inquiries or share additional information.

- If you don't know the answer, say so. Then add what next step you would take to find out the answer. For example, "That's an interesting question. I don't know the answer, but if I researched _____, I might be able to find out."

- After you have answered a question, be sure to check in with the panelist to see whether your answer was satisfactory. For example, "Is that helpful?" or "Have I answered your question?" or even "Thank you for asking that question . . ."

As with pacing, movement, and volume, practice answering authentic questions is the key. When students are rehearsing – with any audience – encourage those who are offering feedback to also ask unscripted questions.

Watch the video in Video Spotlight 7.6 in which a sixth-grade student, Ajala, rehearses for her passage presentation by presenting evidence of her ability to collaborate and lead. Notice how the practice panelist asks probing questions. With this video, because it is quite long, we have listed specific time stamps to go along with the questions so that you can skip ahead to specific locations should you wish.

Video Spotlight 7.6: Prompting Students to Reflect during Passage Presentations
https://vimeo.com/313894664

Ajala, a sixth-grade student at The Odyssey School of Denver, shows evidence of her growth and achievement on the work habits Collaboration and Leadership. She uses data from her scientific investigation of water quality in a local stream to defend her claims about working productively in an academic team. This video was produced by an EL Education coach so the film quality is not professional, but the content of the video makes it worth watching.

Video Reflection Questions
- At 2.09, The interviewer starts her question with the phrase, "Can you say a little bit more about . . .?" How does this help Ajala focus in on an extended example to answer the question?
- At 4.27, Ajala expands on her answer to the question, "How did you get better at collaboration and leadership through this project?" What do you think about her humble reflection in this response?
- At 6.00, the interviewer asks, "What does being good at collaboration and leadership have to do with your academic achievement in science? Does it matter?" What other questions could you ask to help a student connect her work habits to academic skills and knowledge?
- At 7:35, the interviewer asks, "How did you end up doing on this project in terms of your academic achievement?" Ajala uses evidence and explanation to support her answer. How does this support her claim about her "deep understanding"?
- At 9:58, Ajala responds to the interviewer's question about transferring her work habits to topics "beyond science." Does Ajala's answer convince you that she's ready for seventh grade and beyond?

And Finally, Figure 7.10 features a checklist that students can use to make sure they are ready to present. Revise or customize this checklist from The Franklin School of Innovation in Asheville, North Carolina, to fit the format and requirements of your passage presentations.

Figure 7.10 Passage presentation preparation checklist from The Franklin School of Innovation in Asheville, North Carolina

SOURCE: This document is available in the online toolbox at http://www.wiley.com/go/lotolcompanion.

Check off each item as you complete it:

- ❏ I filled in my Presentation Script document **using specific evidence** from my reflection essays.
- ❏ I read, and annotated, the Passage Rubric. I know what my panelists will be looking for from my presentation.
- ❏ I wrote my script on index cards using notes/bullet points NOT complete sentences.
- ❏ I rehearsed my presentation in front of my Crew, myself in the mirror, and someone else.
- ❏ I rehearsed using my portfolio and technology.
- ❏ I know how I will adapt if technology fails me.
- ❏ I decided on an appropriate professional outfit to wear to my presentation.
- ❏ I have MEMORIZED the date and time of my Passage Presentation time slot.

Learning Target 4: I can prepare families and community members for the important roles they play in passage presentations.

Challenge #9: I am not sure how to build the panels for passages and what the role of panelists should be.

TRY THIS: CONSIDER YOUR SCHOOL AND COMMUNITY – AND YOUR PRIMARY PURPOSES FOR PASSAGE PRESENTATIONS – AND CREATE PANELS THAT FIT YOUR NEEDS

Creating the Panel Structure

There is no one right way to think about who should be on a panel and what their role should be; it depends on the grade of the students, the culture of the school, and your primary purposes for the passage event. As you think about the purposes of passage presentations for your students, consider whom students should be presenting to and whether the panelists' role is to evaluate the presentation or simply to listen and celebrate as an audience.

In elementary grades, passage presentations often have an audience rather than an evaluative panel, or a panel that does not formally grade the presentation. In secondary grades, the student's family members are sometimes in the audience, but there is typically a panel of community members (e.g., community friends, leaders, and partners; school board members) and educators (e.g., district staff, teachers from the school or the students' future school, and other interested educators) who evaluate the students' presentations.

Panels typically range in size from two or three members to about 6–8 members; the size should reflect what is feasible and best for your school. You need to decide how many presentations a panel will see: in some schools, every passage presentation has a unique panel assembled for that one student; in others, a single panel will sit through hours of presentations by multiple students. Determining the composition of the panel and the different roles of panelists and audience members is an early and important decision when structuring passage presentations. Remember that you can make adjustments every year as you learn more about what works best for you.

If the panel has power to decide if a student "passes" his or her presentation, then it puts more pressure on you at the school to make sure that panelists are well informed and well prepared for their roles, and may affect whom you choose to invite (i.e., last minute additions can be difficult). You may choose to make panel recruitment and preparation easier by having community members be active members of the panel – giving feedback to the student presenters and giving thoughts to the panel itself – but having the teachers from the school on the panel be the only ones who make the designation of "pass" or "not yet."

Recruiting Panelists

If you are new to implementing passage presentations, it can seem daunting to recruit enough panelists to make it work. This gets easier over time, because panelists typically enjoy the opportunity, want to return, and will often be willing to recruit others. When the event becomes a valued tradition, it takes less active recruiting.

Schools typically invite adults who already have connections to the school. The list of panelists can include board members, community members who have come to speak or share expertise in classrooms, and representatives of partner organizations (e.g., groups the school has done fundraising for or with; local colleges, organizations, or businesses who have supported the school with expertise).

Also consider inviting parents – those of students currently doing their passage presentations and those of younger students at the school to serve as panelists (parents do not typically serve as a panelist for their own child's presentation). Parents of younger students will find it powerful to see where their second-grader or fourth-grader is headed in just a few years. Once people have served on a passage panel, especially if the students are well prepared and inspiring, they often become fans of the school and the process. Many schools ask panelists to recruit one other person they know to become a panelist for upcoming passage presentations later in the year or next year. This request can almost double your list of potential panelists.

In many EL Education network schools, older students (such as high school seniors) from the school or from a sister school serve on passage presentation panels. Interestingly, where that is the case, we have found that the presenting students are often more nervous about impressing older student panelists than the adults on the panel (even when those panels have included school and community leaders). Including older students as panelists has multiple benefits for enriching the school community, creating a powerful learning experience for both presenters and panelists.

In some EL Education secondary schools where each passage has a unique panel, students are required to recruit one or more panelists from outside of school who are relevant to that student's life (e.g., a coach, pastor, internship supervisor, dance instructor).

Figure 7.11 lists some of the people you should consider inviting to serve as panelists for passage presentations. Complete the middle and right-hand columns. Then get started reaching out to your community!

Figure 7.11   Individuals to invite to serve as passage presentation panelists
SOURCE: This document is available in the online toolbox at http://www.wiley.com/go/lotolcompanion.

Role	Name	Contact Info
Parents (not on their own child's panel)	(see separate list)	
Grandparents (not on their own grandchild's panel)	(see separate list)	
Older students from your school or a "sister" school		
Community experts who have visited our class		
Local politicians		
School board members		
Local business owners		
School partner organizations or donors		
School custodial staff		
School office staff		
School coaching staff		
After-school or club leaders		
Feeder school teachers or leaders		
Other school volunteers		

Challenge #10: Family and community members don't understand their roles in passage presentations.

TRY THIS: EXPLAIN THE DIFFERENCE BETWEEN EVALUATORS AND AUDIENCE MEMBERS

Like students, family and community members need to clearly understand their role in a passage presentation. In many schools, students invite their families to passage presentations. Families are there to support, honor, and celebrate their child, but not typically to judge the passage presentation, ask questions, or offer feedback. This is a big change for families accustomed to student-led conferences, so it's important that when students or teachers invite families, they also clarify this role and go out of their way to make families feel welcome and comfortable.

Other adults – teachers, community members, and sometimes parents of other students – may serve as judges on the passage presentation panel. Typically panelists provide feedback to student presenters, ask questions, and sometimes evaluate the presentation on a rubric. It's important to make clear that while community members evaluating presentations using a rubric may indicate that a student didn't meet the expectations of their presentation, the final decision about consequences for placement or promotion in the next grade should be made by school personnel who are deeply familiar with grade-level standards, graduation requirements, and district protocols. A student who doesn't pass on the first go may be required to redo all or part of a passage presentation so that it meets graduation standards. Figure 7.12 is an example from The Franklin School of Innovation in Asheville, North Carolina, of a letter to panelists explaining their role.

TRY THIS: INVITE AND INFORM PANELISTS EARLY

Passage presentations are strengthened by healthy community-school partnerships. When schools have good relationships with individuals and organizations in the community, who want to know more about your school and are eager to contribute their expertise and time, you will likely have a more willing pool of candidates eager to be effective passage presentation panelists. Once you have identified an adequate number of panelists to serve your needs, invite them – leaving ample time to find replacements for those who decline or are unavailable. An invitation should also inform panelists about to expect. Further, a brief training session will ensure that panelists feel welcome and confident in playing their role. (See Challenge #11 for more on how to prepare panelists.)

 Challenge #11: Panelists listen to students but don't give meaningful feedback.

TRY THIS: TEACH PANELISTS TO GIVE KIND, SPECIFIC, AND HELPFUL FEEDBACK

Panelists, just like students, may be inclined to provide feedback that is either too harsh or so general that it isn't meaningful to students. At The Odyssey School of Denver, Colorado, the panelist training actually includes a lesson in which panelists critique a model feedback form completed by a former passage presentation panelist. You can see the model in Figure 7.13. The best feedback is super specific,

Figure 7.12 Letter to passage presentation panelists from The Franklin School of Innovation in Asheville, North Carolina

SOURCE: This document is available in the online toolbox at http://www.wiley.com/go/lotolcompanion.

Thank you for volunteering to be a part of Franklin's first-ever Passage Portfolio Presentations! You are providing an authentic audience as our students begin to develop organizational and presentation skills that will be essential in succeeding at any college, or any career, they choose.

Your job is important, but also fairly straightforward. You'll simply use the rubric (see below) to evaluate each presenter during their 5-minute presentation time. We'll have copies waiting for you in each classroom.

Your panel will be made up of you, a Franklin faculty member and a Franklin student. The Franklin faculty member will make sure the presentation starts on time and will move the presenter and group into each segment of the presentation.

There are 20 minutes set aside for each presentation.

<u>**Passage Portfolio Presentation Agenda**</u>
- 1 minute: Student welcome/introduction
- 5 minutes: Presentation
- 5 minutes: Questions/Answers
- 5 minutes: Student steps out, panel completes rubrics / selects highlights and documents feedback
- 4 minutes: Student returns to room to receive feedback

What do I wear?

You may dress casually or professionally. Our students have been encouraged to dress professionally, though presenter appearance is not directly referenced in the scoring rubric.

What kind of questions am I supposed to ask the presenters?

Anything that you want to know more about is OK! Remember, the purpose of the presentation is supposed to be centered around each student's academic and character growth. Students are basically being asked to *prove*, using supporting evidence, that they are deserving of moving on to the next grade. They have selected a metaphor to represent this growth. Any questions along those lines are encouraged and appropriate, though anything that interests you during the presentation is fair game.

How will my evaluation impact the presenter's grade?

The students have received a separate grade on their portfolio from their Crew Leader. That grade will be averaged with the presentation scores they'll receive from you and the Franklin faculty member on your panel. All of those scores together will comprise each student's Habits of Scholarship grade for the fourth quarter.

	Exemplary (4)	Accomplished (3)	Developing (2)	Beginning (1)
Learning Reflections Reflections are thoughtful and address the process of learning and the experience. Reflections are supported with evidence from early and recent work.	Reflections are thoughtful and reflect on the process of learning. Reflections are thoroughly supported with evidence from early and recent work.	Most reflections are thoughtful and reflect on the process of learning. Reflections are supported with evidence from early and recent work.	Some reflections are thoughtful and reflect on the process of learning. Reflections are somewhat supported with evidence from early and recent work.	Reflections present do not address the process of learning. Reflections are not clearly supported with evidence from early and recent work.
Presentation Student communicated his/her thinking in a thoughtful, organized way, and with apparent practice and preparation. Student was able to answer questions and explain work presented.	Student presented work in an organized and thoughtful way. Student was able to answer all questions and thoroughly explain the work presented. Student speaks with fluency and expression Student maintains eye contact, referencing notes but not reading directly from script.	Student presented work in an organized and thoughtful manner. Student was able to answer most questions and explain work presented. Student speaks with fluency and expression. Student generally maintains eye contact, referencing notes but not reading directly from script.	Attempt was made to present, although presentation lacked organization. Student was able to answer some questions without explanation of work. Student does not speak with fluency and expression. Student reads from notes throughout presentation, making limited eye contact.	Student did not present portfolio.

Figure 7.13 Model of completed feedback form used to train passage presentation panelists at The Odyssey School of Denver

SOURCE: This document is available in the online toolbox at http://www.wiley.com/go/lotolcompanion.

A short, personal letter that summarizes the panel's overall impression of how well the student is using habits to impact their academics.

Dear

Thank you for presenting your current thinking about how the Habits of Learner have helped you at Odyssey. The level of reflection you demonstrated was strong, and it showed that you have really thought about what helps you find success academically.

Overall, we felt that you were using most of the Habits of a Learner that you presented to support your academic success. For example, you can see in the notes below that you had a significant amount of evidence that shows that you value quality questions and that you use questions (both your own and others') to push your thinking deeply. Perspective taking is another habit that we can tell you find great value in, for similar reasons. On the other hand, while you were quite reflective about your struggles in collaboration and leadership, we do feel that you are selling this habit short; it can be valuable in your academic success. We hope that you take some time to consider its importance in your future at high school and in work. How do you see high school students using this habit well? What about your parents or other adults?

We are confident that you have a solid foundation to be successful in high school and beyond. We hope that you continue to grow and leverage Habits of Learning (and work) as you mature. We can see from your academic evidence that you are capable of great, powerful work. Thank you for the depth of your reflection today. You left us with a sense of hope for our collective futures.

Habit of a Learner: inquiry	Stars (Strengths)	Stairs (Suggestions)	Comments and questions help focus the student on next steps or aspects about habits to consider. Students will respond to these in a letter.
1. I can use the inquiry process to investigate a topic or problem			
*Student describes how this habit has impacted his/her learning.	You made a strong case for how inquiry helped you gather facts and synthesize your learning in the Weimar Germany project. The use of inquiry resulted in you achieving Exemplary on this assignment!	We were curious about your response to the difference between inquiry in math and humanities. We disagree that math has a more limited scope in which to inquire.	
*Student cites evidence of how this habit has impacted her/his learning.	The enthusiasm and clarity you demonstrated in response to our questions helped us appreciate your broader understanding of how inquiry has helped you academically.	Some boxes may remain empty.	
*Student's description of his/her successes and struggles with this habit	We noticed that many of your strategies in inquiry came off of the habits one pager. We can tell that you used many of the strategies to support you as a student and inquirer.		

relating to one artifact the student presented. Being both kind and specific enables students to hear the feedback, even if it means they need to redo their passage presentation for another audience. It's important to let panelists know how and when their written feedback will be shared with students and if their names will be attached to it. This guidance holds both the panelist and the student accountable for taking the feedback seriously.

A rubric that describes the features and qualities of a good panel presentation can be particularly helpful to panelists. Panelists can simply circle the statements that describe the presentation they have watched. (The passage presentation guides in our online toolbox include rubrics.) Figure 7.13 is an example of the form provided to panelists at The Odyssey School of Denver. The rubric criteria for the presentation appear under each Habit of a Learner in the left-hand column. Panelists then have space to write Stars (strengths) and Stairs (suggestions) for the student presenters.

TRY THIS: PREPARE PANELISTS TO ASK GOOD QUESTIONS

Giving feedback is one thing, but asking probing questions that challenge students to amplify, elaborate on, or illustrate points they have made in the passage presentation is even more difficult. Just as students should be prepared to think on their feet and respond to questions, panelists may need some support to ask the kinds of questions that will most benefit students. Here are some questions to have available to panelists, and to explore with students as well.

- How do you make good decisions about . . .?

- What do you do when you feel like you're really struggling with . . .?

- What evidence can you point to that illustrates . . .?

- How have you grown with respect to . . .?

- When you think about high school (or college, or next year), how will you apply the habits or knowledge you've described in your portfolio?

- How do your habits of learning help you to be a better student?

- Is there a relationship between those habits and the evidence of your achievement?

- What strategies do you use to improve the quality of your work?

- How do you feel about your academic achievement in _____?

- What do you think you contribute to your learning community? What do you think you receive from your learning community?

- If you had to identify one moment or snapshot from this experience that really predicts your future, what would it be and why?

- As you prepare to enter the next grade level, what topics or subjects are you most interested in? What questions are you excited to explore?

- How can you build on the strengths you have shared from your hobbies or non-academic pursuits to improve as a student?

Leaders play a big part in helping teachers implement successful passage presentations. Because passage presentations are typically a schoolwide practice, implemented at critical grade-level transitions, it's crucial that leaders facilitate conversations between grade levels to determine consistent systems, practices, and supporting documents.

The most important role that school leaders play with passage presentations is to lead a positive narrative for staff and students about the power, potential, and value of this structure in promoting student learning. For staff and students, launching student passage presentations could feel like just another thing added to their plate, and a very big one at that. In the worst case scenario, the effort could fuel skepticism, resentment, and private complaining. School leaders can keep the narrative positive by explicitly acting as a booster for this structure:

- Messaging regularly throughout the school community how important it is for students to present their own learning and growth to an authentic audience

- Acknowledging regularly with staff that passage presentations are a lot of work but teachers will be fully supported to do that work

- Carving out ample time for the staff for planning, rehearsing, and hosting passage presentations

- Digging in with staff in the planning and critiquing process of presentation specifics

- Supporting logistics for the event

- Showing up at a wide range of student passage presentations as a panelist or audience member

School leaders can also leverage passage presentations to build allegiance and support for the school in the community. There may be no better experience to win over a community VIP – such as a school district leader or board member, or a local political, faith, or business leader – than having them participate in an inspiring student passage presentation. The most powerful presentations to invite leaders to may not always align with top-performing students. It can be just as inspiring to see the presentation of a student who has overcome significant challenges and has put his or her full heart into becoming a better student and person. Following are a few tips for offering teachers effective support. Table 7.7 summarizes the key action steps for teachers and students that will lead to successful passage presentations with portfolios.

Top Tips

- Facilitate schoolwide conversations and professional development to support all teachers in developing and implementing systems for maintaining passage portfolios and supporting students to prepare for passage presentations.

- Communicate information about passage presentations to families and community members through email announcements, robo-calls, social media, handbooks, and the school website.

- Support teachers in debriefing passage presentations with grade-alike colleagues. Then create an opportunity for the same teachers to share what they learned, and what they need, with teachers of earlier grade levels.

- Support teachers or a task force of teacher leaders to create and/or revise the documents and tools used to prepare for passage presentations.

- Build strong community partnerships and invite community partners to serve as passage presentation panelists. Use passage presentation panels strategically to build allegiance to the school for community and district leaders.

- Celebrate successes publicly! Include photos and/or video from passage presentations in the school newsletter, website, or social media posts.

Table 7.7 Passage presentations with portfolios: Steps to success

What Should Teachers Do?
Clearly explain the purpose and audience of passage presentations.
Clearly explain the roles and expectations for passage presentations.
Support students to create portfolios that show growth and readiness, and that highlight their unique voices and personal accomplishments.
Provide a clear system for evaluating passage presentations. Communicate that system to panelists, students, and families.
Give students many opportunities to rehearse, revise, and polish their presentations.
Celebrate students' success in public ways that include families.
What Should Students Do?
Reflect and document academic and personal growth with evidence.
Prepare multi-year portfolios that are unique, deep, and demonstrate growth and readiness.
Rehearse, revise, and polish their presentations.
Prepare to answer questions about growth and learning.
Be accountable for the content and presentation of their portfolio. Redo the passage presentation if necessary to meet expectations.

As you have read Chapter 7, maybe you have had an opportunity to try some of these strategies and techniques along the way. If not, come back to this post-assessment after you have had a chance to do so. Give yourself whatever time you need to address the learning targets and challenges in a meaningful way. Then take a moment to check your progress in Table 7.8, which is the exact same Learning Target Tracker that appeared at the beginning of this chapter.

Circle or place an X along the continuum from Beginning to Exceeding: **How would you rate your progress toward each learning target** *at this point in time?* Use the space provided to make notes regarding any remaining challenges you may be having or ideas for new and different strategies you want to try.

Table 7.8   Chapter 7 learning target tracker

Learning Target 1: *I can communicate the purpose and audience for passage presentations, and how they are different from student-led conferences.*   Beginning--------------------------------Developing--------------------------------------Meeting------------------------------------Exceeding   Notes:
Learning Target 2: *I can support students to create multi-year portfolios with reflections.*   Beginning--------------------------------Developing--------------------------------------Meeting------------------------------------Exceeding   Notes:
Learning Target 3: *I can ensure that students are prepared to lead passage presentations with professionalism.*   Beginning--------------------------------Developing--------------------------------------Meeting------------------------------------Exceeding   Notes:
Learning Target 4: *I can prepare families and community members for the important roles they play in passage presentations.*   Beginning--------------------------------Developing--------------------------------------Meeting------------------------------------Exceeding   Notes:

Standards-Based Grading

Checking for Understanding during Daily Lessons

Using Data with Students

Learning Targets

Models, Critique, and Descriptive Feedback

STUDENT-
ENGAGED ASSESSMENT

Student-engaged assessment is a system of interrelated practices that positions students as leaders of their own learning.

Standards-Based Grading

Student-Led Conferences

Passage Presentations with Portfolios

Celebrations of Learning

What Is Standards-Based Grading?

The primary purpose of standards-based grading is to communicate about student achievement toward well-defined learning targets. Work habits (often referred to by schools as Habits of Scholarship, or Habits of Work and Learning) are graded separately from academic content, and student engagement is key to the grading process.

Standards-based grading (also called mastery-based, proficiency-based, or competency-based learning) communicates what a student knows and can do at a given point in time. Unlike most traditional grading structures, which combine factors like attendance, behavior, homework assignments, and the mean of test scores into one grade that attempts to capture an "average," for an entire term, standards-based grades focus sharply on what skills, understanding, and content knowledge students can demonstrate by the end of the term. Standards-based grades measure progress toward well-defined learning targets aligned with standards and are given for each separate target. Work habits are assessed and reported separately from academic content and skills. The grading process engages students in regular self-assessment, reflection, and tracking their own progress toward meeting standards.

The deficiencies of traditional grading are profound. When Ariana's parents see that she got a C in Algebra, what does that mean? It may mean that she aced all of her tests and knows the material perfectly, but was inconsistent with her homework and attendance. It may mean that she almost failed all of her tests and does not understand the material at all, but was polite and always prompt with her homework. It may mean that she failed her tests for the first half of the term, and then fully grasped the concepts and got A's for the second half. It may even, to some unclear extent, reflect how well Ariana gets along with her teacher.

Standards-based grading is a transformative practice for students. It gives them a deep sense of ownership over their progress and enables them and their families to understand clearly what they know and can do relative to required academic standards. Standards-based grading can also clarify the correlation between the work habits students need to learn effectively (e.g., doing homework, persevering through challenge, collaborating) and academic accomplishments, so that students can focus on improvements that will have the most impact. As Susan McCray's adjacent statement makes clear, what's important is mastering bike riding, not averaging in all of one's first attempts and inevitable falls.

The old system may be deficient, but that does not mean that adopting a new paradigm of grading will be an easy shift. Changing hundreds of years of tradition – including rituals of schooling that almost all teachers and parents perceive as normal and right – is not an easy enterprise. The transition from traditional to standards-based grading, and the mechanics of gathering accurate data and synthesizing it into grades that are consistent across faculty and subject areas in a school, are huge challenges for teachers and leaders. These challenges require thoughtful systems for making the transition within a schoolwide community, and thoughtful tools for implementing standards-based grading with students in your own classroom.

In this chapter, we build on the strategies offered in Chapter 8 of *Leaders of Their Own Learning* to help you meet three learning targets. Along the way, we provide examples and tools to help you address the common challenges many teachers and leaders face when implementing standards-based grading.

> When you're learning how to ride a bike, you're going to fall off the bike 16,000 times. And then you start putting your foot out, and then popping wheelies. If I average in every time you fell off the bike, you would fail bike riding.
>
> —*Susan McCray, teacher, Casco Bay High School, Portland, Maine*

Learning Targets for Chapter 8

1. I can help families and students understand the "why" behind standards-based grading.
2. I can effectively implement standards-based grading in my classroom, school, or district.
3. I can assess my students' work habits.

Pre-Assessment: Track Your Progress: Chapter 8

Before we dive in, take a moment to assess yourself on each of the learning targets for this chapter. In Table 8.1, circle or place an X along the continuum from Beginning to Exceeding: **How would you rate your progress toward each learning target** *at this point in time?*

We'll give you a chance to assess yourself again at the end of the chapter.

Table 8.1   Chapter 8 learning target tracker

Learning Target 1: *I can help families and students understand the "why" behind standards-based grading.*   Beginning---------------------Developing----------------------Meeting--------------------Exceeding   Notes:
Learning Target 2: *I can effectively implement standards-based grading in my classroom, school, or district.*   Beginning---------------------Developing----------------------Meeting--------------------Exceeding   Notes:
Learning Target 3: *I can assess my students' work habits.*   Beginning--------------------Developing----------------------Meeting-------------------Exceeding   Notes:

Learning Target 1: I can help families and students understand the "why" behind standards-based grading.

Challenge #1: How will I explain standards-based grading to students and families if I don't fully understand it myself?

TRY THIS: BUILD YOUR KNOWLEDGE ABOUT THE PRINCIPLES OF STANDARDS-BASED GRADING AND THE BENEFITS TO STUDENTS

Standards-based grading is grounded in principles and beliefs about grading that differ from traditional grading. These principles and beliefs are often deeply ingrained – the product of our own schooling and learning experiences, rather than a coherent, consciously developed philosophy of assessment. Before you examine the theory behind standards-based grading, take a moment to reflect on your current grading practices and beliefs by checking the statements that are true for you in Table 8.2.

The principles and practices of standards-based grading present a major shift in thinking for many teachers. Count the number of checks you have in each column of Table 8.2. If you have significantly more checks in Column 1, representing more traditional grading practices, the shift is likely to be more challenging for you. If you have more checks in Column 2, representing standards-based grading practices, the shift may come more easily.

Table 8.2 How difficult will it be for you to shift to standards-based grading?

Check the statements that are true for you	
Column 1	**Column 2**
❏ I include one of more of the following in grades: effort, participation, tardiness, attendance, and/or adherence to rules.	❏ I grade a student's academic work independently from her work habits.
❏ I reduce marks on work submitted late.	❏ I grade late work for full credit as long as the student has negotiated an extension. Lateness may impact the student's work habits grade, but not his academic grade.
❏ I assign grades based on a student's achievement as compared to other students.	❏ I assign grades based on the student's achievement relative to the standard or learning target.
❏ I grade everything students turn in.	❏ I believe students learn from their mistakes. I grade select assignments after they have had time to practice.
❏ I average together scored assignments when calculating grades.	❏ I weight more recent assignments more heavily than earlier assignments/assessments. I look to see if the student's scores are trending up or down.
❏ I include zeros for missing work when determining grades.	❏ I give incompletes, then score the work when the student completes it.
❏ I believe there should be a limit to the number of students who receive an A.	❏ I believe that all students can meet standards with the right support and opportunities.
# of checks in Column 1:	# of checks in this Column 2:

Casco Bay High School in Portland, Maine, which has been using standards-based grading for many years, articulates some of the principles of standards-based grading as follows in its family grading guide:

1. Grades should clearly communicate what students know and are able to do in each class.

2. Learning cannot be averaged; students need time to practice and learn from mistakes.

3. Students should have multiple opportunities to show what they know and can do.

4. Schools should support students in acquiring *all* of the essential knowledge and skills in a course, not just a portion of it.

5. If students are working hard to meet standards, they deserve more time and support to learn the material and opportunities to retake assessments.

6. All students should have the opportunity to excel.

Some of these principles may challenge your current thinking about grades. To learn more about the research behind these principles, consider reading Ken O'Connor's *A Repair Kit for Grading: Fifteen Fixes for Broken Grades* (Pearson: 2010) and discuss what you learn with a colleague or study group. There is an overview available online[1] that provides an excellent distillation of the text, with "questions to ponder" and videos to view and discuss. We don't agree with everything in O'Connor's book and you may not either. A study group is a great place to examine controversial practices and determine what fits for your school and what doesn't. The 15 fixes are very accessible and provide great provocation for a fruitful discussion with colleagues. Here are some additional options for study group reading:

- Guskey T. and Brookhart S. (2019), *What We Know about Grading: What Works, What Doesn't, and What's Next*.

- *Standards-Based Grading Activities, Strategies, and Professional Development Resources for K–12 Teachers,* a grab-bag of challenges, solutions, and debates offered by and for teachers, available online at https://creditsforteachers.com/K12-Standard-Based-Grading-Resources

- Townsley, M. and Buckmiller, Tom (2016). *What Does the Research Say about Standards-Based Grading?* Available online at http://www.eastland308.com/UserFiles/Servers/Server_3095463/File/District_Information/SBG_Research.pdf

Table 8.3 offers further exploration of the principles of standards-based grading as well as the implications and action steps for teachers and leaders who are putting these principles into practice in their schools.

After exploring and discussing some of the resources in this section, complete the 3-2-1 exit ticket in Figure 8.1, which will help you reflect on your current grading practices before you explore the rest of the challenges in this chapter.

---

[1] http://www.smore.com/n4pgh-15-fixes-for-broken-grades

Table 8.3 Standards-based grading: principles, implications, and actions

Implications	Actions for Teachers and Leaders
Principle: Grades must accurately describe a student's progress and current level of achievement.	
Assessments must precisely reflect the degree to which a student is meeting a learning target or standard. Grades and credits must similarly reflect a compilation of assessments. Consequently, standards, learning targets, and assessments must be carefully aligned for each course or subject area within a grade level. When determining a student's progress toward a single long-term learning target, it is unfair to average his or her scores toward that target over time. Instead, teachers must look holistically at what current assessment results, or the trend in scores, tell them about a student's current mastery of knowledge and skills.	1. Determine long-term learning targets that reflect the essential or prioritized standards. 2. Determine a set of criteria that describe a "quality" assessment. 3. Create or identify multiple high-quality assessments that measure each learning target. 4. Determine how many of the long-term learning targets students must reach to pass and earn credit. 5. Determine whether a student can pass without having made some measurable progress toward each of the long-term learning targets. 6. Determine the method for calculating students' final academic grades per class based on the set of long-term learning targets. 7. Determine the lowest grade that will earn credit. 8. Determine the grading scale and associated language in correlation with action 7. 9. Ensure that the grade book doesn't average across assignments or assessments, but allows teachers to look for trends and weight more recent assessments more heavily than early assessments for the same learning target. 10. Ensure that the grade book calculates final grades using the methods determined in prior decisions.
Principle: Work habits should be assessed and reported separately from academic progress.	
This answers the age-old question, "What does a B mean?" In a traditional grading system, a student who tried hard, participated and turned in homework but never came to understand the outcomes of the course could receive a B. In that same class, a student who showed understanding of the content but came to class late, sporadically turned in homework and was disruptive in class could also receive a B. Schools that use standards-based grading will ideally hold students accountable to both academic learning targets and work habits, but these must be assessed and reported separately. The first student in the previous scenario might receive a C on academics and an A on work habits. The second student might receive an A in academics and a C on work habits.	1. Determine the process that teachers, teams, and the school will use to choose the work habits that will be reported on per term. 2. Communicate the work habits and their importance to students. 3. Communicate the importance of work habits grades to families and other stakeholders (e.g., colleges) 4. Create specific descriptors for the behaviors that can be measured to demonstrate work habits. 5. Determine a system for collecting assessment information about work habits. 6. Determine a method for reporting progress on work habits.
Principle: Grades are for communication, not motivation or punishment.	
Schools should provide documentation and/or training to each stakeholder group (e.g., students, families, other schools, colleges, and universities), so they understand what grades mean and what a grade report or transcript says about student achievement. Teachers should communicate progress toward learning targets frequently and transparently without shame or blame. Teachers should be able to provide "evidence" for grades in the form of assessments and student work assessed with clear standards-based criteria.	1. Design a plan for educating students and families about the grading and reporting policy and procedures. 2. Design a succinct document to accompany student transcripts which explains how a student's grades were derived and what they mean. 3. Select or create an electronic grade book to be used schoolwide. Ensure that it is capable of holding multiple data points for each long-term target and that it allows for standards-based grading (not simple averaging).

(continued)

Table 8.3 Continued

Implications	Actions for Teachers and Leaders
Principle: Student engagement is the key to the grading process.	
Students need to know what they are expected to learn and be able to do in order to take responsibility for their learning and communicate with teachers in the assessment process. If a learning target is important enough to grade, it is important enough to invest in instructionally and assess multiple times in multiple ways. Teachers should track all assessment information and use professional judgment to determine what assessment information is of quality, is most recent, and most representative of what the student currently understands or can do.	1. Use student-engaged assessment practices (i.e., checks for understanding) that allow students to know how they are doing relative to learning targets on a daily basis. 2. Determine consistent schoolwide practices for giving students access to their individual progress toward learning targets (e.g., data tracking forms, reflection journals, progress reports). 3. Implement practices that enable students to communicate their progress toward learning targets (i.e., portfolios, student-led conferences). 4. Give students and families access to ongoing, digital grade reporting systems.

Figure 8.1 3-2-1 exit ticket for study groups or individual reflection
SOURCE: This document is available in the online toolbox at http://www.wiley.com/go/lotolcompanion.

Three implications that challenge or affirm the way I grade students now.
1.

2.

3.

Two standards-based grading practices I have questions about
1.

2.

One principle I strongly support
1.

TRY THIS: TAKE TIME TO EDUCATE YOURSELF, YOUR STAFF, AND YOUR COMMUNITY; IMPLEMENT CHANGE SLOWLY

The shift to standards-based grading is a big change for families and communities, as well as teachers and students. Knowing the research that supports this practice isn't enough; you also need to anticipate the concerns and questions of other stakeholders. When Lexington County School District One in Lexington, South Carolina, opened a new high school in 2013–14, they also put into place a new proficiency-based learning system that reflected a year's worth of study and research amongst school leaders and teachers. Almost immediately, parents, especially more affluent parents with aspirations for their children to attend highly competitive colleges and universities, brought complaints and concerns to the local school board. Parents worried that their child's grade point average would decrease, that homework wouldn't count, and that it was unfair for students who didn't meet standards on the first assessment to be able to retake the test.

A month later, as teachers began to conduct formative assessments and to record summative assessment scores aligned with learning targets, students appeared at a school board meeting to defend the new grading system. They liked all the feedback they were getting from teachers and the opportunity to retake assessments after additional instruction and learning. It was a tumultuous start to the school year, according to the district's chief academic officer Gloria Talley, but the district ultimately weathered the storm by striking some key compromises with parents – for example, allowing homework and formative assessments to "count" for a small percentage of the grade and implementing a penalty for some late work.

Over the next two years, after conducting focus groups and listening sessions with the school board, families, and teachers, Lexington One's leadership refined the grading system. "It took a lot of professional courage to stay the course," Talley says, "but five years in, we're glad we did. What we learned is how important it is to allow teachers and principals ownership and leadership of the implementation, how important it is to deeply educate the community. Identify your key stakeholders early and seek their input, then keep them involved at every step as you learn together how to make the shift. It's not about the grades. It's about learning. It's about what's best for kids."[2]

Challenge #2: Students and families are used to traditional grading. How do I help them understand how standards-based grading supports students?

TRY THIS: INSPIRE FAMILIES BY SHOWING THEM THE BENEFITS OF STANDARDS-BASED GRADING

Now that you have a deeper understanding of the practices you want to refine or implement, you need to communicate them to families in a way that allows them to support their child and understand the components of your assessments and reporting system. Start with some simple, video-based resources like those that follow to help your students' families understand *what* standards-based grading is and *why* it's good for their child. Each of these videos is under five minutes and can be a valuable tool in your toolbox.

- "Letter grades, rubric scores, percentages are nonsense symbols." Rick Wormeli offers a different perspective on implementing grading in your classroom: https://www.youtube.com/watch?v=z4QVcghKsGY

- This teacher-created video helps students and parents at Harlem Middle School understand their standards-based reports: https://www.youtube.com/watch?v=HMf2FvBSi24

- Video Spotlight 8.1 provides a deeper look at the impact of standards-based grading on students, teachers, and families at Casco Bay High School in Portland, Maine.

Video Spotlight 8.1: Why Use a Standards-Based Grading System?
https://vimeo.com/43992307

In this video, a parent, a student, a teacher, and the principal from Casco Bay High School in Portland, Maine, discuss how standards-based grading works at their school and the benefits of the system.

Video Reflection Questions
1. Could you use the bike riding analogy to explain standards-based grading to your students or families? What counterarguments might they offer?
2. How does standards-based grading ensure that all students do quality work and make progress toward meeting standards?

---

[2] A cautionary tale of the backlash against mandatory implementation of standards-based grading in Maine provides additional suggestions. Barnum, M. (2018). Maine went all in on "proficiency-based learning" – then rolled it back. What does that mean for the rest of the country? Chalkbeat. Retrieved online https://www.chalkbeat.org/posts/us/2018/10/18/maine-went-all-in-on-proficiency-based-learning-then-rolled-it-back-what-does-that-mean-for-the-rest-of-the-country.

TRY THIS: CREATE A GRADING GUIDE THAT CLEARLY COMMUNICATES THE WHAT AND WHY OF STANDARDS-BASED GRADING

A carefully crafted classroom, school, or district grading guide is key to helping parents understand the purpose and practice of standards-based grading. When questions or concerns arise, refer back to and unpack this document with families. Following are some sample grading guides with features worth borrowing as you construct your own. Each of these guides can be found in our online toolbox (http://www.wiley.com/go/lotolcompanion):

- Lexington County School District One, Lexington, South Carolina, a comprehensive K–12 school district takes care to explain the district's commitment to research-based practices and the principles behind standards-based grading.

- Metropolitan Expeditionary Learning School, a grades 6–12 charter school in New York City provides parents with a concise guide to its mastery grading reports that responds to frequently asked questions from parents

- Open World Learning Community, a grades 6–12 school in Saint Paul, Minnesota, provides a wealth of information about its standards-based grading practices on its website,[3] including an informative "Do Now" slide show to guide a family information session. Our online toolbox also includes their Staff Grading Guide.

TRY THIS: PROVIDE STUDENTS AND FAMILIES WITH A COMPARISON OF TRADITIONAL AND STANDARDS-BASED GRADING

Because families and students are used to traditional grading practices, showing them a side-by-side comparison of the practices used for traditional grading and standards-based grades is especially useful. It helps people to "see" the difference and anticipate how standards-based grading will impact their own student's report card. Table 8.4 and Figure 8.2 show comparisons of traditional and standards-based

Table 8.4 Comparison of traditional and standards-based grading from Two Rivers Public Charter School in Washington, DC

Traditional Grading	Standards-Based Grading
Final grades are an average of performance, effort, homework completion, and other criteria developed by the teacher. As a result, what final grades communicate are often unclear and vary greatly from teacher to teacher.	Final grades describe a student's progress toward specific course standards (or learning targets). The specificity enables students and families to clearly identify strengths and areas for improvement.
A certain average is required to pass a class and receive credit. Students may not have mastered a large portion of the material but will still receive credit.	To receive credit, students must meet criteria for each and every course standard within a class.
Grades are viewed as rewards or punishments for overall school performance.	Grades are viewed as a tool for communicating student progress toward specific course standards (or learning targets).
Work habits, such as homework completion or on-task behavior, are averaged in with course grades. This practice can raise or lower grades without clarity as to why.	Work habits are reported and graded separately and are evidence and skill-based. They are viewed as equally as important as academic grades.
Grading is something done by teachers to students and is generally NOT well understood by students.	Students play an active role in understanding learning targets, tracking their progress, identifying next steps, and communicating their progress.

---
[3] https://www.spps.org/domain/6451

Figure 8.2 Comparison of traditional and standards-based grade books at Oakhurst Elementary School in Decatur, Georgia

Traditional Grade Book						Final grade
Suzy	84	80	75	85	83	B
Johnnie	91	100	100	82	85	A–
Connie	77	100	70	60	55	C
Victoria	62	59	58	55	66	D–
Elizabeth	87	95	83	92	88	B+
Matthew	0	7	98	100	95	D–
Katie	98	94	89	100	93	A

Standards-Based Grade Book						Final grade
Suzy	3	3	3	4	3	3
Johnnie	4	4	3	3	3	3
Connie	3	4	2	2	2	2
Victoria	3	2	2	2	3	2
Elizabeth	3	4	3	4	3	3
Matthew	1	1	4	4	4	4
Katie	4	4	3	4	4	4

4 = Exceeds   3 = Meets   2 = Approaching   1 = Does Not Meet

grading at two different schools. Table 8.4 describes the differences at one school and Figure 8.2 *shows* how the differences appear in a grade book at another school. In Figure 8.2, notice that while the percentages in the traditional grade book are roughly reflected by the holistic scores in the standards-based grade book, the final grades for some students are quite different. Why do you think Matthew received a D in the traditional grade book but a 4 (exceeds expectations) in the standards-based grade book? (Note: We return to this report card again when talking about "spotting the trend" in Challenge #4.)

TRY THIS: SHOW FAMILIES WHAT A STANDARDS-BASED REPORT CARD LOOKS LIKE SO THEY KNOW WHAT TO EXPECT

A standards-based report card looks quite different from a traditional report card. Because it provides more precise information about what a student knows and can do, it is typically longer and more detailed than a traditional report card. Families will need some coaching to understand just how to read this new report. Sharing examples of the report card in advance of sending the real thing can help families learn what to expect and create an opportunity for them to ask questions. Figures 8.3 and 8.4, from a primary school and a high school, provide parents with guidance about both the format and the content of their child's report card. In the primary report card, notice how the literacy standards are unpacked into measurable learning targets and key vocabulary words to give families a clear indication of just what their child knows and can do. On the high school report card, notice that academic learning targets are reported separately from behavior or work habits. The abbreviation CL means that the student is exhibiting the work habit "consistently." G means that the student is "generally" or sometimes demonstrating the behavior.

Figure 8.3 Sample kindergarten report card from Decatur City Schools, Decatur, Georgia
SOURCE: The complete version of this document is available in the online toolbox at http://www .wiley.com/go/lotolcompanion.

Kindergarten/Year:	Companion Document for Teachers, Parents, and Students					
		9-weeks				
Standard/Strand: Reading Literature	**"I can…" statements"**	1	2	3	4	**Vocabulary**
RL.K.1. With prompting and support, ask and answer questions about key details in a text	When someone helps me:					Complete sentences
	I can answer questions about key details in a text.					Details
	I can ask questions about key details in a text.					
	I can share important information about a text.					
1a. Make predictions to determine main idea and anticipate an ending. (Alabama standard)	I can make a prediction about what will happen next in the story.					Prediction
	I can make a prediction about how a story will end.					Main Idea
RL.K.2. With prompting and support, retell familiar stories, including key details.	When someone helps me:					
	I can retell the beginning of the story.					Beginning
	I can retell the middle of the story.					Middle
	I can retell the end of the story.					End
	I can retell the beginning, middle, and end of the story.					Retell
RL.K.3. With prompting and support, identify characters, settings, and major events in a story.	When someone helps me:					
	I can name the characters in a story.					Character
	I can name the setting in a story.					Setting
	I can name the important parts in a story.					Event
	I can name the characters, settings, and important parts in a story.					
RL.K.4. Ask and answer questions about unknown words in a text.	I can ask questions about words I don't know in a story.					Clarification
	I can answer questions about words I don't know in a story.					
RL.K.5. Recognize common types of texts (e.g. storybooks, poem).	I can tell when words are a poem.					Fiction/narrative
	I can tell when words are a story.					Nursery rhymes
	I can tell when words are a fairy tale.					Poetry
	I can tell when words are a nursery rhyme.					Fairy tales
						Fantasy
RL.K.6. With prompting and support, name the author and illustrator of a story and define the role of each in telling the story.	When someone helps me:					Author
	I can name the author and what he/she does.					Illustrator
	I can name the illustrator and what he/she does.					
RL.K.7. With prompting and support, describe the relationship between illustrations and the story in which they appear (e.g., what moment in a story an illustration depicts.	When someone helps me:					Illustration
	I can tell what a story will be about by looking at the pictures on the front cover and the pictures in the book.					Text
						Relationship
RL.K.9. With prompting and support, compare and contrast the adventures and experiences of characters in familiar stories.	When someone helps me:					Character
	I can tell how two characters are alike in stories.					Alike/ Compare
	I can tell how two characters are different in stories.					Different/ Contrast
	I can tell how characters are alike and different in stories.					Story
RL.K.10. Actively engage in group reading activities with purpose and understanding. [RL.K.10]	I can share in fiction reading activities.					Fiction
Standard/Strand: Reading Informational Text	**"I can…" statements"**	1	2	3	4	**Vocabulary**
RI.K.1. With prompting and support, ask and answer questions about key details in a text.	When someone helps me:					Question
	I can ask questions after listening to nonfiction.					Nonfiction
	I can answer questions after listening to nonfiction.					Details

(cont. online)

Figure 8.4 Sample high school report card from Beaverton School District, Beaverton, Oregon
SOURCE: This document is available in the online toolbox at http://www.wiley.com/go/lotolcompanion.

Student Name:		Beaverton School District	School Name:
		Report Card Standards	School Address:
Grade:	Homeroom Teacher:		School Phone Number:

High School End-of-Semester Report Card
This report card incorporates the Common Core State Standards and Oregon State Standards. It provides information on your child's progress in key areas within each subject, as well as academic behaviors. Each column represents a grading period and, with each additional column, shows growth over time. Only two courses are listed on this sample report card—IB English HL I and Alg/Geo/Stats III.

ACADEMIC Learning Targets
Each subject area will list the Academic Learning Targets aligned to the Common Core and/or Oregon State Standards. The teacher will provide feedback on your child's progress with a Summary Judgment and may include comments. Given that Academic Learning Targets are part of the year-long plan for the course, many students may still be Developing or Nearing Proficient early in the learning of the new targets. All students need to be proficient by the end of the year to be fully prepared for the next grade level. Note: An * means that this target was not assessed during this grading period.

Summary Judgments represent a collection of evidence (assignments and assessments) on each Academic Learning Target. All high schools, except MYP schools (ISB and Mountainside), use a 1-4 scale for Summary Judgments. MYP schools use a 1-8 scale for Summary Judgments.

To find out more information, visit your school's website.

Course: IB English HL I Period 1

Teacher:	Sept5-Nov2	Sept5-Feb1
Class Attendance		
Absences	3	6
Tardies	2	4
BEHAVIOR Learning Targets		
Manages responsibilities as a student	G	CI
Self directs learning	CI	CI
Effectively communicates and works effectively within a team or group	G	CI
Recognizes the rights, responsibilities and opportunities of living, learning, and working in an interconnected digital world and acts in ways that are safe, legal, and ethical	G	G
ACADEMIC Learning Targets		
Presents information effectively	*	4
Demonstrates knowledge and understanding of literary texts	2	3
Demonstrates an appreciation of literary features	3	3
Demonstrates appropriate organization and development	3	4
Corrects language in writing	3	3
Reflects on work to improve writing and oral presentations	1	2
Academic Mark	C	B
Comments:		

Course: Alg/Geo/Stats III Period 2

Teacher:	Sept5-Nov2	Sept5-Feb1
Class Attendance		
Absences	4	12
Tardies	0	1
BEHAVIOR Learning Targets		
Manages responsibilities as a student	CI	CI
Self directs learning	G	CI
Effectively communicates and works effectively within a team or group	G	G
Recognizes the rights, responsibilities and opportunities of living, learning, and working in an interconnected digital world and acts in ways that are safe, legal, and ethical	G	CI
ACADEMIC Learning Targets		
Understands and applies the characteristics of a function	2	4
Identifies, uses and solves for variables	1	3
Uses and applies geometric properties of mathematics	*	3
Uses and applies statistics and probability to mathematics	2	2
Communicates clearly and explains reasoning so others can follow how a problem is solves	1	3
Reasons mathematically to solve problems in real-life context	2	2
Recognizes patterns and describes them as relationships or general rules	2	3
Current Progress Indicator	-	=
Academic Mark	D	B
Comments:		

BEHAVIOR Learning Targets
The Behavior Progress section allows the teacher to provide feedback on your child's progress in the Behavior Learning Targets. These are the skills necessary for your child to be a successful learner.

Academic Mark
Letter grades appear at each grading period, and is calculated by averaging the summary judgments. See school's website for grade conversion.

Current Progress Indicator
Each subject area could include its own progress measure that indicates whether the student is learning at a significant (+), steady (=) or minimal (–) rate.

TRY THIS: PROVIDE FAMILIES WITH A TIMELINE FOR IMPLEMENTATION

To ensure that faculty, families, and students are on-board with standards-based grading, we recommend a very slow timeline for implementation. Revisit the previous section, *Try This: Take Time to Educate Yourself, Your Staff, and Your Community; Implement Change Slowly.* Map out the barriers and bridges for implementation in your own community. Plan ahead for the time it takes to educate and garner support within your community before starting this practice. The Beaverton School District in Beaverton, Oregon, which includes Health and Sciences High School (an EL Education network school that piloted these practices for the district's high schools), began exploring standards-based grading in 2004. Over the next 13 years, they gradually developed the policies, reporting structures, training for teachers, documents, and parent buy-in to implement these practices successfully at every grade level, in every school, for every student. You can read the full history and the steps they took to cultivate both confidence and competence in all stakeholders on their website.[4]

Among the comprehensive guidance documents about standards-based grading that the district provides on its website is the Frequently Asked Questions document in Figure 8.5, which also answers questions about how standards-based grading impacts special populations like students with disabilities and English language learners. Explore this document and the website. How could you use this information to facilitate conversations with your students and families about standards-based grading?

Figure 8.5 Frequently asked questions from the Beaverton School District, Beaverton, Oregon
SOURCE: This document is available in the online toolbox at http://www.wiley.com/go/lotolcompanion.

General Questions	Response
What is standards-based learning?	Standards-based learning is a series of instructional, assessment and reporting practices built around standards. Well defined standards identify specific knowledge and skills a student should master in each subject area at each grade level. They should describe what a student should know and be able to do as a result of instruction and experiences in school. Proficiency levels describe how well a student is advancing towards meeting the standard. If a student is proficient for a standard, they have met all the criteria for that standard. (See the "Why standards-based learning?" page on the BSD website.)
Why is the BSD implementing a standards-based learning system (SBLS), including changing report cards?	In an effort to support the district's goal of ensuring that all students graduate college and career ready, a standards-based learning system is being implemented across the district. A standards-based learning system teaches and assesses student learning based on common learning targets. The learning targets are part of a K–12 learning progression of learning leading to college and career readiness. The goal of a standards-based system is to provide clear, effective feedback about student learning. Our goal is for marks used on our reports to support and promote learning, so we must be sure they provide information about student achievement toward the learning targets that have been assessed.
How does a standards-based learning system impact special student populations (English language learners, talented and gifted students, and special education students)?	English Language Learners (ELL) We have seen evidence that more ELLs are engaged and motivated in classrooms where standards-based learning is a focus. Because teachers are targeting instruction, they are able to diagnose exactly what students have learned and what they still need to learn while using a variety of strategies to ensure learning of concepts. With the constant feedback, practice, and opportunities to demonstrate their understanding in a variety of ways, students are engaged in their own learning. This helps them persevere in a system that can be challenging to navigate, resulting in greater student success.

---

[4] https://www.beaverton.k12.or.us/depts/tchlrn/Pages/SBL_History.aspx

General Questions	Response
	<u>Talented and Gifted</u> Within a standards-based classroom, gifted and talented students who show early mastery of fundamental skills and concepts can move forward with their learning, engaging with the curriculum at a higher level and focusing on deeper, more challenging coursework. <u>Special Education Students</u> A standards based learning system ensures that all students, regardless of ability or disability, have the opportunity to work in some way towards learning targets. For most students receiving Special Education support, only minor accommodations are needed within the general classroom setting in order for the students to achieve success and make progress toward targets. A standards-based learning system allows all students, including those with individual education plans, to be assessed on what they know and can produce.
How do I see the learning targets and rubrics being used by my student's teacher?	Use the "Learning Target" or "Scoring Guides/Rubrics" links within BSD website. You can select the subject area and then the grade level along the left-hand side of the Learning Target/Rubric page. You can then expand each learning target to see the rubric and Supporting Learning Targets (details within each Learning Target).
If a teacher offers multiple opportunities, won't kids stop trying the first time?	Multiple opportunities allow students to show their growth and/or consistency on each learning target. They also provide the teacher with sufficient evidence to determine the student's current level of proficiency. That said, teachers may choose to determine the number of opportunities they will provide and communicate this early on in the course. Teachers can also establish the number of pieces of evidence (opportunities completed) that will be required to have sufficient evidence to determine the student's current level of proficiency. In addition, a teacher determines the number of opportunities needed to discern an individual student's level of proficiency.
Does a teacher have to give retakes?	Retaking an assessment is one of many ways to provide multiple opportunities. Other solutions include building an instructional plan that has multiple tasks addressing each learning target, having students produce predetermined additional evidence, or observation of/conversation with the student.
Isn't the work of creating district learning targets and rubrics already finished?	The work of developing BSD learning targets and rubrics ranges from some in their third year of revision to some that have yet to be created. Regardless, we will continue to refine targets and rubrics based on teacher feedback.

Secondary Questions	Response
Isn't it harder to earn an A in a standards-based system?	Many of our students have historically demonstrated a high level of achievement and this will continue regardless of how it is reported. In a standards-based system, rubrics describe Highly Proficient achievement in terms of consistency, precision, application, and independence. The same descriptors we have always used to describe the level of rigor historically required to earn an "A." A standards-based system does require a level of proficiency across all of the major concepts and skills taught. The intent of a standards-based classroom is to encourage student success with all instruction, assessment, and reporting tied to clearly defined learning targets. If we make a deliberate effort to base grades on proficiency levels within the stated learning targets and the result is a shift in the distribution of grades, we should have a larger discussion around what the letter grade has been communicating and what we want it to communicate.
Doesn't the electronic grade book assign the students' grades?	The electronic grade book uses established criteria to consider all evidence around each learning target to make a letter grade recommendation to the teacher. Teachers will ensure the letter grade accurately represents each student's demonstrated learning and change it if necessary.

Learning Target 2: I can effectively implement standards-based grading in my classroom, school, or district.

 Challenge #3: I have so many standards and learning targets. Which ones should count toward grades?

TRY THIS: COLLABORATE WITH YOUR TEAM TO PRIORITIZE YOUR STANDARDS AND LEARNING TARGETS

When we ask teachers what they hope students will learn in a semester, their response is often something like this: "The first half of the textbook..." But we all know that students don't actually learn *everything* in the first half of their history or algebra text. Nor do they really need to: much of the content is accessible instantly on their phones. However, there are key concepts in history and algebra that if students do not grasp clearly, their understanding of the field and ability to do work effectively in that discipline has no foundation. A useful question may be this: What are the six things that if your students did not know, or could not do, by the end of this term, you would feel that you failed as a teacher (e.g., effectively contrast two ancient civilizations, graph linear equations). Those things should be long-term learning targets, and the basis for course credit and grades.

It's not easy to decide on that list of long-term learning targets. Paring down is painful. We have seen history departments and math departments in heated arguments over narrowing down those key standards or skills. But these are great discussions – some of the most important discussions teachers can have: What is most important that our students learn in this discipline? You can try to do this independently as a history teacher, or as a second grade teacher, but those discussions are much more effective and deep if they take place with colleagues in a team meeting.

The first thing schools need to do is determine which standards have priority for grades and how to bundle them into priority learning targets that will appear on report cards. Articulating the 4 to 10 learning targets that represent an entire term's worth of learning for a given subject is a process of deliberation that demands collaborative attention from grade level and subject area teams *before* the full implementation of standards-based grading. The process of focused decision making and consensus building, usually spearheaded by instructional and teacher leaders, may take months or even a full year.

Larry Ainsworth suggests four criteria for determining which standards should rise to the level of "priority standards" and be the basis for learning targets that appear on a standards-based report card:[5]

- Endurance (lasting beyond one grade or course; concepts and skills needed in life)

- Leverage (crossover applications within the content area and to other content areas; i.e., interdisciplinary connections)

- Readiness for next level of learning (prerequisite concepts and skills students need to enter a new grade level or course of study)

- External exam requirements (national, state, provincial, college, and career)

---

[5] Retrieved from: https://www.larryainsworth.com/prioritizing-the-common-core-power-standards.

Evaluating your standards against these criteria is challenging cognitive work connected to the steps we described in Chapter 1, Figures 1.7 and 1.8, for unpacking and bundling standards into learning targets. But it is essential work that must be completed before identifying which assessments will measure students' progress toward long-term targets and, therefore, what assignments will make up the list of grades in your grade book.

 Challenge #4: I'm still not sure how to set up my grade book or how to calculate grades.

TRY THIS: SET UP YOUR GRADE BOOK WITH SUMMATIVE ASSESSMENTS THAT MATCH PRIORITY LEARNING TARGETS. ASSESS OTHER LEARNING TARGETS FORMATIVELY

Once you have your priority learning targets determined, identify the assessments that will allow you to measure whether students are meeting those targets. Each priority target should have more than one summative assessment, so that students have multiple opportunities to demonstrate their mastery of the target. When you are grading, the trend in a student's summative assessments related to a single standard will provide the measure of the student's achievement on that standard.

How many assessments you have for a particular standard depends on how "priority" the standard is. For example, some learning targets need to be assessed multiple times over the course of a term or school year because they are part of a broad, enduring skill or understanding (e.g., literacy skills, foundational math concepts). Others may only be assessed once or twice as part of a discrete unit of study (e.g., knowledge related to a narrow topic or a skill related to a particular product or format). Many non-priority learning targets are building blocks for big umbrella priority standards. These building blocks can be assessed formatively so that students receive feedback along the way to meeting the priority standard. For example, the following learning targets from a second-grade study of insects are all building blocks to priority literacy standards. Can you guess what the literacy standards are that overarch these learning targets?

- I can research facts about my topic in an informational text.

- I can identify the parts of my insect's life cycle.

- I can use scientific words to write the story of an insect's life.

- I can create a detailed and realistic diagram of an insect life cycle.

The teacher who taught this unit assessed each of these "building blocks" formatively, giving students feedback on their research, science content understanding, and writing drafts. Students didn't receive grades for these parts of the project, but they did get the feedback they needed to improve their work and for the teacher to know that they were on track to reach the long-term target.

At the end of the unit, her students wrote realistic stories about the insect they had researched, and illustrated their stories with a life-cycle diagram. The teacher assessed the final drafts as a first summative assessment for two priority standards: *I can conduct a short research project and demonstrate understanding of my subject* and *I can write an informative text that conveys information clearly and accurately.* In the course of the year, she would assess these two standards again using other assessments involving research and informational writing.

How you set up your grade book to accommodate both formative and summative grades depends on whether you are using an online program or an old-fashioned paper grade book. Watch the video in Video Spotlight 8.2 to see how one high school teacher balances formative and summative assessments so that priority standards truly receive priority.

Video Spotlight 8.2: Understanding Grades in a Standards-Based System
https://vimeo.com/43990524

In this video, an eleventh-grade humanities teacher from Casco Bay High School in Portland, Maine, explains how she sets up her grade book for standards-based grading.

Video Reflection Questions
1. How do the "assignments" teacher Susan McCray uses to assess her standards align with the skills required by each standard?
2. McCray notes that she often matches the same assessment to multiple standards. What long-term tasks are your students doing that could be used to assess more than one of your standards?
3. Why is it important to have multiple assessments for each standard?

TRY THIS: FOR STANDARDS THAT ARE ASSESSED MULTIPLE TIMES, CHOOSE A GRADE CALCULATION METHOD THAT FITS YOUR NEEDS

It is a rare student who masters the art of writing an argument on the first try. Like many academic skills, writing a persuasive argument involves many incremental skills that students can learn and practice individually before they compose a full-blown argument. In standards, these incremental skills are often listed as the "objectives" or "performance indicators" of a larger umbrella standard. When you set up your grade book, consider two valuable ways of calculating a grade for a priority standard that is assessed in pieces over time.

When you have multiple assessments related to a single standard that add up to a final summative assessment (e.g., an argument paper), **spotting the trend** across these assessments is often the best approach. This is sometimes called the "power law" calculation method. So for the assessments in Table 8.5, for example, the trend is up, and the student earns a final score of 3 based on that trend.

You can see another example in the grade-book comparison in Figure 8.2, which was introduced in Learning Target 1 earlier in this chapter. Connie's score of 2 reflects not an average of high and low scores on this standard over time, but consistently low scores on multiple assessments at the end of the course. Similarly, Matthew's final grade of 4, also from Figure 8.2, reflects that while he performed poorly on the

Table 8.5 Spotting the trend across incremental assessments

Analyzing primary sources	2
Citing evidence	2
Writing a claim	2
Organizing an argument	4
Using evidence to support an argument	3
Argument paper	3
Final Score	3

first two assessments of the standard, he demonstrated that he exceeded mastery in the last four assessments of the standard. To determine final course grades (Connie's score of 2 and Matthew's score of 4), the teacher has looked at the trend of their assessments and landed on a score that represents their level of mastery at a point in time at the end of the course.

Another approach that is particularly useful when you have multiple similar assignments that assess the same exact skills (e.g., journal entries, weekly quizzes, book club discussions) is the **decaying average** approach. A decaying average means that more recent assessments of a standard will be weighted more heavily than the initial assessments of that standard, but initial assessments still count for something. The decaying average approach may seem at first to violate the principle that grades must accurately describe a student's progress and *current* level of achievement. But it may be a good option for teachers or districts that are transitioning from traditional grading to standards-based grading. It can make the transition feel less abrupt for students and families. In a grade determined through decaying average, what students know and can do at the end of the term or course counts more than what they were able to do at the beginning. The results accurately describe the student's progress over time, and because students know that every assessment matters, they also feel that their time and efforts are honored.

Table 8.6 shows the final grade determined using a traditional averaging approach, the trend spotting approach, and a decaying average approach.

Table 8.6   Three approaches to grading similar assignments over time

Standard: Document and analyze data to support claims and conclusions.			
Assessment	Traditional Straight Average	Spotting the Trend	Decaying Average Rate 65%
Science notebook 1	2	2	2
Science notebook 2	3	3	3
Science notebook 3	4	4	4
Final Score	3	4	3.53

Online grading software programs make standards-based grading more efficient and manageable. Two that we've found to be especially well-designed for standards-based grading are JumpRope and PowerSchool. (In PowerSchool, the default decaying average rate is 65%, but you can enter other decaying average percentages if you choose.)

 Challenge #5: How do I empower ALL students to track their progress toward standards-based grades?

TRY THIS: FOCUS STUDENTS ON THE STANDARD AND WHAT IT WILL TAKE TO MEET IT

When students truly understand the standard they are trying to meet and have access to the skills or knowledge to do so, the doorway to success is wide open. Unpacking the learning target in a lesson (described in Chapter 1) is one way to make the standard more transparent for students. Another way is to design your lessons specifically to address the skills or knowledge that will bridge the gap between not meeting and meeting the standard. Video Spotlight 8.3 features an eleventh-grade teacher from Casco Bay High School in Portland, Maine, providing feedback just when students need it, and in time for them to make progress toward meeting their writing learning targets. On students' first drafts, teacher Susan McCray highlights criteria on the rubric that students are not meeting. She then offers focused mini-lessons in those areas. Students can choose to work independently, or to attend the mini-lesson before they work on their next draft.

Video Spotlight 8.3: Descriptive Feedback Helps All Students Reach Proficiency
https://vimeo.com/43992570

In this video, high school juniors explain how the teacher's descriptive feedback and a rubric related to specific writing standards helps them know exactly what to do to meet the standard.

Video Reflection Questions
1. What strategies does this teacher use to help the students make revision decisions that will get them to the learning targets?
2. Based on what you see in your own students' work, what mini-lessons might you develop to make the pathway to meeting standards more transparent for students in your own classroom?

TRY THIS: ENGAGE STUDENTS IN TRACKING THEIR OWN ASSESSMENTS

The secret sauce of standards-based grading is *student-engaged* assessment. Chapter 3 provides a number of tracking tools students can use to gather evidence of their learning. Your students can also record and analyze their assessment results so that they see the connection between their mastery of standards and their grades. The "I can" in every learning target the student meets becomes a declaration of their newly demonstrated knowledge and skills. A form like that shown in Figure 8.6 enables students to connect the dots between the standard, the learning targets, the questions on your assessment, and their own results. Figure 8.7 provides another example, in Spanish. Note that the World Language standards are listed at the bottom of the tracker and the daily learning targets are aligned to those standards. Finally, Figure 8.8 shows how one teacher had students record their own assessment scores for learning targets in a science unit. At the end of the unit, students looked for trends in their scores and gave themselves a final score. Students then reflected on their growth or failure to grow relative to specific targets.

It's likely that none of the trackers we have shown you will perfectly meet your needs, but there are probably aspects of each that would be a good fit. Using what you know so far, design a tracker that meets the needs of your classroom, and be sure to include an opportunity for students to reflect on their progress.

TRY THIS: GIVE STUDENTS OPPORTUNITIES TO RETAKE ASSESSMENTS

One of the common challenges of instituting standards-based grading is implementing a retake policy and practice that empowers students to learn from their mistakes (failing first, and then succeeding). The notion that students can retake an assessment goes against the grain of traditional grading and is a practice of standards-based grading you will likely need to explain and defend at first. When students are competing against each other rather than against a standard, then a do-over feels like an unfair advantage. But when students are competing *against a standard,* then everyone has multiple opportunities to succeed and it's okay if everyone does succeed in the end.

Figure 8.6 Algebra assessment tracker from Irving A. Robbins Middle School in Farmington, Connecticut

SOURCE: This document is available in the online toolbox at http://www.wiley.com/go/lotolcompanion.

Algebra (Ch. 3 Algebraic Linear Equations)

Name _____

Assessment of Learning & Student Reflection

Date _____ Per. ____

Content Area Standard: Create and Reason with Equations and Inequalities

E (exceed) M (meets) N (needs improvement) B (below standard)

Performance Indicators & Learning Targets	Questions	Points/ EMNB	Student Analysis & Reflection
Analyze and solve problems using linear equations and inequalities with one variable, using algebraic methods		_____/pts. E M N B	
I can use algebra to solve linear equations with one variable.	1,2,3,4		• I have demonstrated total mastery of these learning targets. • I have mostly demonstrated these learning targets but made small errors. • I have not demonstrated mastery of these learning targets yet.
I can use algebra to solve, check, and graph linear inequalities.	6		
I can identify and classify a linear equation based on its number of solutions.	7		
I can use algebra to solve real-world problems involving linear equations with one variable.	9,10		
Create equations that describe 2-variable linear relationships and use them to solve problems		_____ /pts. E M N B	
I can represent a linear relationship between two variables in multiple ways.	8a,8b		• I have demonstrated total mastery of these learning targets. • I have mostly demonstrated these learning targets but made small errors. • I have not demonstrated mastery of these learning targets yet.
I can use algebra solve real-world problems involving linear relationships between two variables.	8c,8d		
I can solve for a variable in a two-variable equation.	5		

Next Step:

- I'm ready to move on! Focus on the next standard.
- Seek additional tutoring to learn these skills.
- Practice and study, then retake the assessment and improve my score.

Created by the math department, Irving A. Robbins Middle School

Figure 8.7 World language assessment tracker from Irving A. Robbins Middle School in Farmington, Connecticut
SOURCE: The complete version of this document is available in the online toolbox at http://www.wiley.com/go/lotolcompanion.

Nombre: _____ Apellido: _____

Learning Targets: Puedo. . .self-evaluate against the learning targets.
        Puedo. . .set goals with action plans for areas of improvement

Daily Learning Target Puedo. . .	Still need to master	Mastered, but need to review	Completely mastered
comunicar mis necesidades de la clase (Oral Proficiency, Circumlocution)			
identificar objetos de la clase (tarea, pizarra, libro, lápiz, etc.)			
expresar la fecha (el _____ de _____ = el dos de mayo)			
leer un calendario en un país español (lunes 1st day of the week on calendar)			
usar artículos indefinidos y definidos (el, la, los, las, un, una, unos, unas)			
expresar mi horario de la escuela (la clase de ciencias, etc.)			
hacer y contestar una pregunta en una frase completa (ask & answer question in complete sentence – & question words)			
usar pronombres personales (yo, tú, él, ella. . .)			
identificar lugares en la comunidad (parque, banco, biblioteca, casa, tienda, etc.)			
conjugar y usar verbos en el tiempo presente (o, as, a, amos, áis, an, o, es, e, emos. . .etc.)			
conjugar y usar el verbo irregular "ir = to go" con un sustantivo (lugar) y un verbo (acción) (voy al restaurante; voy a comer)			
expresar la hora y a qué hora (son las tres/es la una; a las tres/a la una)			
usar preposiciones con el verbo 'estar' (estoy cerca del banco)			

(cont. online)

Figure 8.8 Year-long target tracker from King Middle School in Portland, Maine

Name _____   Sequence: 5

Year-Long Target Tracker: Final Reflection

Target	Trend of Grades	Overall Grade
sample	2, 2, 2+, 3, 2	2.5
I can use the scientific method to investigate	3, 3, 3, 3	3
I can use mathematics to organize, present, and explain data	2+, 3, 3, 3, 3	3
I can analyze my own and other's scientific work	3, 4, 3, 3, 3	3.1
I can support a claim using experimental data and scientific knowledge	4, 3, 3, 3	3.1
I can summarize the main ideas in a non-fiction text or other media resource	2+, 4	3

1. Identify one target where you showed **growth**. What habits, behaviors, or actions do you think helped you to grow in this area? I can summarize the main ideas in a non-fiction or other media resources I studied the thing I was writing about and then also tried the exceeds option.

2. Identify one target where you did **not** show growth. What were some obstacles that prevented you from growing in this area? I can use the scientific method to investigate. I didn't try the exceed options.

Revisit Video Spotlight 3.4, in Chapter 3, which features menu math, to see an example of students working and working on a standard until they get it – competing only against themselves. The practice of allowing students to retake assessments, with some parameters that make it logistically manageable and ensure that students take responsibility for *learning* from their mistakes, is an essential element of standards-based grading.[6]

To ensure that students are not taking advantage of the time it takes teachers to create and administer retakes, world language teachers at Irving A. Robbins Middle School in Farmington, Connecticut, created the form in Figure 8.9. This form requires students to take responsibility for scheduling a retake and planning, with their families, for taking action that will lead to a different result on the retake. Analyze this form and then make your own list of actions students could take prior to retaking an assessment in your class.

TRY THIS: ELIMINATE THE ZERO AND PROVIDE AMPLE SUPPORT FOR MEETING STANDARDS

Sooner or later, every teacher faces the challenge of attempting to grade a student who simply hasn't turned in enough work to demonstrate mastery. In the past you may have scored all of Annabelle's missed assignments as zeros, and a string of zeros in your grade book means Annabelle is failing your course even though she may in fact be capable of demonstrating mastery of some or all of the material. What can you do to grade Annabelle's work fairly and meet your deadline for turning in grades?

To support students like Annabelle who are missing assignments, an assignment contract like the one in Figure 8.10 is a good place to begin. Put the contract in place as soon as the student has missed an assignment; don't wait until the end of the grading term. If students are also adding finished work to their portfolios along the way, the missing assignment contract should be added to the portfolio as a placeholder for the work that will be made up according to the terms of the contract.

If the student breaches the contract and still doesn't turn in the work, consider these options.

- Assign an incomplete rather than a final grade; withhold the grade until the student completes the work. Provide a new deadline for completion.

- Assign a 1 for the missing assignment. Grade the other work that has been completed for this standard (perhaps using a decaying average formula).

- If the student is able to demonstrate mastery by means other than this assignment, you should still assign a 0 or 1 for work habits. This way the missing work "counts," against the student's work habits grade, but not against his academic achievement. Grading all of the building blocks of a major project will help to avoid the problem of having no gradable evidence.

TRY THIS: PARTNER WITH SPECIALISTS TO HELP ALL STUDENTS MEET STANDARDS

In addition to Annabelle, you may have another student, Collin, who struggles to make progress toward standards. Collin has a learning disability and is diagnosed with Attention Deficit Disorder. He needs a different set of supports so that he can make steady progress toward learning targets and,

---

[6] Assessment expert Rick Wormeli (2016) offers some excellent guidance about the parameters that make "redos" less demanding on teachers and more helpful to students in "The Right Way to Do Redos." Middleweb, retrieved from https://www.middleweb.com/31398/rick-wormeli-the-right-way-to-do-redos.

Figure 8.9 World language retake form from Irving A. Robbins Middle School, Farmington, Connecticut

SOURCE: This document is available in the online toolbox at http://www.wiley.com/go/lotolcompanion.

---

1. This form must be completed and signed by the teacher to agree on the retake date.
2. The retake must be taken within two weeks of receiving feedback, but not during the final week of the trimester.
3. Retakes may be given in a different format than the original assessment.
4. PowerSchool will reflect the higher score.

Part I: Student Information

Name: Period:

Part II: Reflection in a Growth Mindset

Assessment Name:

Standard Score on 1st attempt:

Learning Target/Performance Indicators:

Why do you think that you are not yet meeting or exceeding standard on this concept?

What <u>specific</u> class content do you still need to master in preparation to retake this assessment?

When are you available to retake the assessment? (two dates please)   ____/____ ____/____

*no more than two weeks after you received feedback

Part III: Learning Activities

Choose **at least 3** learning activities that will help you learn or continue to practice the content before you retake the assessment. You may want to make an appointment with your teacher to determine which activities will be the most helpful. **You must show the teacher evidence that these were completed.**

- ❏ Make corrections on the original assessment.
- ❏ Study with a family member.   (Signature: _____)
- ❏ Study with a classmate/friend.   (Signature: _____)
- ❏ Teacher tutoring session.   (Signature: _____)
- ❏ Complete or redo homework and/or classwork.
- ❏ Make your own practice assessment with an answer key.
- ❏ Make flashcards.
- ❏ Use quizlet.com to make flashcards and practice vocabulary.
- ❏ Draw the vocabulary words.
- ❏ Create note cards with the verb conjugation charts using your notes/website/Google Classroom.
- ❏ Take the verb conjugation quizzes on the website/the internet.
- ❏ Watch verb conjugation videos on the website/the internet.
- ❏ Record yourself using your cell phone or a funny app.
- ❏ Get creative (write a song, create a mnemonic device, make a poster, create a flyer).
- ❏ Other: _____

Part IV: Signatures (All 3 are required)

Student Signature: _____

Parent/Guardian Signature: _____

Teacher Signature: _____

Retake Score: _____ **(teacher will record following retake)**

Figure 8.10 Missing assignment contract

SOURCE: This document is available in the online toolbox at http://www.wiley.com/go/lotolcompanion.

Name _____

Teacher _____ Date _____

Assignment of Concern _____

Learning targets this assignment was designed to assess:

Why didn't you turn in the assignment?

Are there other ways that you can provide evidence of meeting these targets? Explain . . .

What support do you need to meet these targets?

- ❑ Reteaching/tutoring
- ❑ Practice
- ❑ Time (after school, before school, Saturday school, recess)
- ❑ Retake the assessment
- ❑ Other: _____

When will you turn in the assignment if granted an extension?

Student signature _____

Parent signature _____

Teacher signature_____

ultimately, standards. The vast majority of students with disabilities, and those with Individual Education Programs (IEPs), will be working toward the same standards as every other student in their grade. Learning targets should never be changed and students should not work toward standards that are not at their grade level unless this modification is specifically called for by an IEP. Instead, students should be provided with the scaffolding and support they need to access their learning and reach the same standards as their peers. Collaboration between general education and special education teachers is critical from the outset. Working together, differentiated instruction and additional scaffolding can support all students to meet the same learning targets and grade-level standards.

The same principle holds true for English language learners. These students deserve access to the same rich and rigorous curriculum as every other student and learning targets should not be changed as an accommodation for them. Instead, scaffolds should be put in place that ensure their progress. Video Spotlight 2.4, in Chapter 2, provides an excellent example of a general education science teacher and an English as a Second Language teacher working together to support English language learners to meet challenging eighth-grade science learning targets. Also, refer back to Challenge #5 in Chapter 1 for guidance on unpacking learning targets with English language learners to ensure they understand where they are headed with their learning at the start of and throughout lessons.

Learning Target 3: I can assess my students' work habits.

Challenge #6: How do I measure learning behaviors that develop slowly over time?

TRY THIS: IDENTIFY OBSERVABLE OR QUANTIFIABLE EVIDENCE OF WORK HABITS

Learning behaviors, like academic skills, are measured at a given point in time. Some, like attendance and turning in homework, are easy to quantify. Others, like perseverance and initiative, are harder to measure. Lay the groundwork for measuring work habits by translating your classroom or school work habits (often referred to as Habits of Scholarship, Habits of Work, or Habits of Effective Learners) into character learning targets that describe the concrete behaviors that embody the habit. These character learning targets should be as visible and alive in your classroom as academic learning targets. They can be assessed multiple times over the course of a term so that students receive credit for both their growth and their achievement in strong work habits.

Many schools within the EL Education network develop a progression of character learning targets for the school's common work habits that steps up through the grade levels so that, for example, students and families are able to see how "persistence" in sixth-grade looks different than it does in eleventh-grade (see Figures 8.11 and 8.12 for excerpts from two examples).

Challenge #7: I don't have time to assess work habits regularly and consistently.

TRY THIS: ENGAGE STUDENTS IN ASSESSING THEIR OWN WORK HABITS

Teachers often feel overwhelmed by the task of assessing and entering multiple or daily grades for work habits. One way to reduce the pressure to grade, grade, grade, and to give students themselves more ownership of their learning, is to record only summary grades based on regular student reflection.

At the Metropolitan Expeditionary Learning School in New York City, teachers and leaders created a rubric for the school's Habits of Work and Learning (HOWLS). Students use this rubric – frequently zeroing in on one row at a time – to self assess habits related to a particular assignment or classroom task (Figure 8.13). Students provide evidence for their scores on exit tickets, and teachers then give a summary grade in the grade book based on a number of exit tickets throughout a unit of study. This self-assessment approach is especially effective if students reflect immediately following an assignment or assessment and then leverage the process to set a S.M.A.R.T. goal for improving their habits.

TRY THIS: THERE'S AN APP FOR THAT!

Just as there are high-quality online grading programs for academic grades, there are apps and programs that can make assessing work habits less time consuming. These apps will also summarize calculations

Technology is a tool that both teachers and students can leverage to track work habits regularly and consistently.

Photo Credit: EL Education

for you and even communicate the results to another faculty member (e.g., advisor, Crew leader, home-room teacher) who may be doing the summary grade reporting for that student. The best application we know of, used by dozens of EL Education network schools, is JumpRope. JumpRope and other programs (such as PowerSchool) allow teachers to enter grades for character learning targets, just as you would enter grades for academic learning targets.

Once you have determined character learning targets, simply enter them in your online grade book. For example, perhaps one of your work habits is "collaboration," and the associated character learning target is "I can listen actively and contribute ideas during group work." You could assess this character learning target either by strategic listening during regular small group work in your classroom or by gathering evidence from students' self-assessments. By the end of the term, you will have multiple grades entered related to this work habit and will be able to calculate a final score that is a fair assessment of the student's mastery.

TRY THIS: BUNDLE AND PRIORITIZE ONE OR TWO WORK HABITS FOR EACH UNIT OF STUDY OR ACADEMIC TERM

Another strategic way to manage what can feel like a double workload of grading both character learning targets and academic learning targets is to chunk the work habits by term or assignment. So, for example,

Figure 8.11 Excerpt from the habits of scholarship continuum at the Franklin School of Innovation in Asheville, North Carolina

	8th grade	9th grade	10th grade
Persistence	• I use the resources I'm provided or the support of my peers before seeking help from a teacher. • I grapple with challenging texts, tasks, and projects in class and outside of class • I revise my work in response to feedback to create a complex, authentic, and well-crafted product.	• I use the resources I'm provided or the support of my peers before seeking help from a teacher. • I plan and manage my time on projects that require multiple sessions in and outside of class. • I evaluate feedback from peers and teacher, and then I revise to improve my work.	• I seek out challenges in class and in my community; I use what I've learned to make the world a better place. • I manage my time on individual and group projects, especially those conducted largely outside of class. • I problem-solve effectively when obstacles arise. • I evaluate feedback from peers and teachers and revise my work as many times as necessary for best quality outcomes.
Collaboration	• I help facilitate various group work protocols to maximize engagement. • I share my ideas and listen respectfully to others. • I seek multiple perspectives in group work and discussion • I give constructive peer feedback in the form of kind, helpful, and specific suggestions and/or questions.	• I lead various group work protocols to maximize engagement and productivity. • I share my ideas, listen respectfully, and actively include all members of my community. • I work to resolve conflict and find the common ground between multiple perspectives in group work and discussion. • I use kind, helpful and specific questions and critical feedback to improve the quality of our work.	• I adapt and lead various group work protocols to maximize engagement and productivity. • I use accountable talk to build on others' ideas and energize the group's critical thinking. • I respectfully evaluate multiple perspectives and help my group identify the best strategy for solving problems and accomplishing a task. • I approach tasks in the spirit of inquiry, inviting and contributing kind, helpful, and specific feedback that improves the quality of our work.

although a long-term project may leverage collaboration, initiative, and responsibility for meeting deadlines, you could decide to *grade* only the work habit responsibility for that project. Then on the next major project, or the next term, grade the work habits initiative or collaboration. This approach gives students time to practice and reflect on some work habits while they are being assessed on another. And it means your grading can be more focused and less overwhelming in terms of the number of grades to be recorded.

Consider the following questions as you plan strategically for which habits to assess and when.

1. What tasks am I asking students to do in the next term?

2. What work habits will they most need to accomplish those tasks?

3. What character learning targets match those work habits and when will I share them with students?

4. Which character learning targets am I prepared to assess? Are they measurable? Can I measure them multiple times without feeling overwhelmed?

Figure 8.12   Work habits progression from The Odyssey School of Denver

1. Responsibility	
I can begin to advocate for myself. I can maintain focus in class. I can complete quality work on time.	
2-3	1. I can complete quality homework on time. 2. I can maintain my focus in class. 3. I can identify which crew courtesies are easy for me to hold up and which challenge me.
4-5	1. I can explain how I use targets to support myself as a learner. 2. I can use my planner to support myself as a learner. 3. I can complete quality first draft work. 4. I can consistently demonstrate focus and participation in class.
6-8	1. I can demonstrate consistent use of strategies (e.g. my own notes, participation in class, before and after school help sessions, RTD, etc.) to fully engage in my learning. 2. I can complete quality class work on time. 3. I can act as an intentional up-stander.
2. Revision	
I can use critical feedback to improve my work.	
2-3	1. I can make changes to improve the quality of my work based on the areas I identified when comparing my work to the rubric/criteria list. 2. I can use feedback from teachers and/or peers to improve the quality of my work. 3. I can describe several tools/strategies I use to edit my work. 4. I can describe the difference between editing and revising.
4-5	1. I can use a rubric or criteria list to improve the quality of my work. 2. I can describe how I decide which feedback to use to improve the quality of my work and which to ignore. 3. I use one or more effective tools/strategies to eliminate all editing errors in my final draft.
6-8	1. I can demonstrate how I know my final draft is my "best work". 2. I can demonstrate a consistent use of revision strategies. 3. I can create a final product that meets my purpose with my audience in mind.
3. Inquiry	
I can use the practices, tools and skills of an academic discipline to investigate, evaluate, form and test theories. I use those skills to understand specific situations and make sense of big ideas in that discipline.	
2-3	2-3 is responsible for introducing the inquiry process to kids. Students will be able to name the process that learners go through when studying a topic deeply: 1. Develop Questions 2. Find Resources 3. Develop conclusions 4. Report conclusions
4-5	1. I can pose quality questions that help me study a topic deeply. 2. I can find resources that help me confirm or deny my theory. 3. I can interpret the information that I have. 4. I can report and defend my findings to an outside audience.
6-8	1. I can develop deep, probing questions and/or theories based on initial research and background knowledge. 2. I can locate diverse and quality resources that help me answer my questions and deepen my understanding. 3. I can evaluate and synthesize the information/evidence I found. 4. I can report findings in a way that helps my audience access it.

Metropolitan Expeditionary Learning School
A SCHOOL FOR A SUSTAINABLE CITY

The Habits of Work and Learning (HOWLS) for our school are based in the language of our Core Values - Respect, Stewardship, Intellect and Curiosity, Success and Failure, and Advocacy. Our HOWLS demonstrate our ability to put our Core Values into action on a daily basis in all classes.

HOWL	4 *This means that ......*	3 *This means that ......*	2 *This means that ......*	1 *This means that ......*
I AM RESPECTFUL TO MEMBERS OF OUR COMMUNITY. CORE VALUE: • Respect	• I carefully select my words, adjusting my language to audience and purpose. • I am polite and my body language conveys this. • My words are kind and respectful. I never use my words to hurt others. • I show others the respect that I deserve. I respect the voice, ideas, and work of others and know that I can learn from others. • My feedback is generally specific, constructive, and kind. • I work to share the airtime and am genuinely interested in what others are saying.	• I carefully select my words, adjusting my language to audience and purpose. • I make an effort to be polite and most of the time, my body language conveys this as well. • My words are kind and respectful. I never use my words to hurt others. • I often show others the respect that I deserve. I could be more gentle with my spoken and written responses. • My feedback is sometimes vague. • I often share the airtime fairly. I show interest in what others are saying.	• I carefully select my words, adjusting my language to audience and purpose. • I make an effort to be polite and most of the time, my body language conveys this as well. • My words are generally kind and respectful, but I slip up every once in a while. • I sometimes show others the respect that I deserve. • My feedback has lacked some specifics and helpfulness, and feels unkind. • I need to work harder to share the airtime and don't always seem interested in what others are saying.	• I rarely adjust my language to audience and purpose. • I must be more aware of my body language and the message that it sends. • My words are sometimes kind and respectful. I occasionally curse or use my words to hurt others. • I do not often show others the respect that I deserve. • I need to be gentle with my spoken and written responses. My feedback is mostly general, not helpful and is unkind. • I either don't share or take too much of the airtime. I seldom seem interested in what others are saying.

Challenge #8: What are my options for communicating grades for work habits on a report card so that they mean something and don't make the report card too long?

TRY THIS: DESIGN YOUR REPORT CARD TO DELIVER THE INFORMATION PARENTS NEED

Designing a report card that accommodates grades for both work habits and academics requires a careful balance between too much information and not enough. Separate grades for each work habit in every course at a secondary school will make the report card a very long document that many families will find overwhelming or confusing. Averaging all the work habits grades into a single number for all work habits and all courses can make it hard for a parent to know which habit the student needs to work on and in which setting (e.g., a student may score well in persistence in language arts, but lack persistence in math). Figures 8.14 and 8.15 show two different ways of reporting work habits.

At The Franklin School of Innovation in Asheville, North Carolina (Figure 8.14), work habits are averaged together and reported as a single score for all classes in each grading term. The score for each of the three habits is recorded as a comment for the current grading term. The Odyssey School of Denver (Figure 8.15) reports work habits by grade-level specific character learning targets. You saw other examples earlier in this chapter in Figures 8.3 and 8.4.

Figure 8.14   Habits of scholarship on report card from the Franklin School of Innovation in Asheville, North Carolina

	First Quarter	Second Quarter	Third Quarter	Fourth Quarter	Final Habits of Scholarship Grade
ELA Grade 7 Course absences = 0		87%	90%		
Habits of Scholarship Grade 7 Course Absences = 8		3.7	3.7	3.8	Action 3.6 Persistence 3.8 Collaboration 3.8
Literacy Lab Course Absences = 0	Exceeds Standards	Meets Standards	Exceeds Standards		
Math Grade 7 Course Absences = 4	83%	91%	87%	81%	
Physical Education Grade 7 Course Absences = 0	Exceeds Standards	Exceeds Standards			

Figure 8.15   Eighth-grade habits of learning report card from The Odyssey School of Denver

1. Habits of a Learner		100
Habits of a Learner		100
Overall Habits of a Learner Mastery		100
- Collaboration and Leadership: I can contribution to a common goal through my words and actions.		EX
- Collaboration and Leadership: I can effectively implement leadership strategies.		AC
- Inquiry: I can use the inquiry process to investigate a topic.		EX
- Perspective Taking: I can use multiple perspective to help me understand events and issues.		EX
- Responsibility: I can complete quality work on time.		EX
- Responsibility: I can consistently use strategies to engage in my learning.		AC
- Revision: I can use revision strategies to improve my work and actions.		EX

Challenge #9: Our required report card format doesn't include work habits. What are other ways I can use to communicate a work habits grade to students and families?

TRY THIS: CREATE OPPORTUNITIES FOR STUDENTS TO REFLECT ON AND DISCUSS THEIR WORK HABITS WITH FAMILIES

For reasons of compliance or because they want to underscore the importance of work habits in narrative rather than numerical ways, many schools choose not to put work habit grades on report cards at all. Instead (or in addition) these schools communicate progress on their work habits through reflection and conversation at student-led conferences and passage presentations. Figure 8.16 illustrates a reflection tool students use to prepare for student-led conferences. Students self-assess each of their work habits on the rubric and then write in the evidence they will show in their student-led conference to support the score they have given themselves.

Passage presentations are another structure in which students and families can reflect on and discuss the correlation between a student's work habits and her academic progress. Video Spotlights 7.5 and 7.6 in Chapter 7, featuring students Seamus and Ajala from The Odyssey School of Denver, are good examples of students "reporting" on their habits through passage presentations.

At The Franklin School of Innovation, teachers took the following innovative approach to communicating progress on work habits, which they call Habits of Scholarship. Habits of Scholarship grades were compiled by students in their Crews (advisory groups). After teachers had confirmed the accuracy of the grades, students themselves emailed the report to their parents, along with a reflection on the evidence that generated the grades. The email was accompanied by the following note from the student's Crew leader.

Dear _____,

Below you will find an email from your child and an attachment that includes scores for our Habits of Scholarship: Action, Collaboration, Inquiry, and Persistence. As an EL Education school, we believe that while test scores are important for showing what a student knows at the end of the school year, students' success in the classroom and in life is ultimately defined by the quality of their work and the quality of their character.

To foster conversation and reflection with students, teachers developed learning targets that describe what scholarly habits look and sound like in action at each grade level. You'll see these targets in the target tracker completed by students.

This semester teachers scored these targets based on evidence, such as turning in work, revising drafts, asking questions, and collaborating productively with peers. Students then reviewed the scores and share their reflection with you in the email below.

While the habits scores are separate from your child's academic grade and GPA, research shows that over the course of a student's schooling, strong habits of scholarship reinforce a student's academic success, and poor habits of scholarship ultimately make it difficult for a student to manage the workload, challenge, and independence expected of students in college and careers. Supported by teachers and parents, students are responsible for their own learning, and mistakes are an opportunity for growth and new learning.

Please talk with your child about their Habits of Scholarship scores to get a more complete picture of what these habits mean to them. Celebrate your child's growth over the course of the school year and from one grade level to the next. Help your child to set actionable goals for improving their habits for the remainder of this year and in preparation for the next grade level.

Finally, if you have questions about these scores or your child's habits, please contact me. It's been a pleasure to have your child in my crew; I am happy to continue this conversation in support of your child's success at Franklin.

Figure 8.16 Work habits reflection tool from Capital City Public Charter School in Washington, DC

Step 2. Core Values Mastery: *Respect for Democracy: I participate in class discussion for the benefit of the classroom community.*

Overall Core Value Mastery:	

B. Learning Target Reflection:
Strengths: put a star next to at least 2 bullet points you think you do well
Areas for improvement: Circle at least 2 bullet points you think can improve on

4	3	2	1
• I always respect the class norms for a healthy learning environment we established at the beginning of the semester • I never use electronics in class • I volunteer my ideas often in class discussion • I am a leader when doing group work	• I almost always respect the class norms for a healthy learning environment we established at the beginning of the semester • I almost never use electronics in class • I volunteer my ideas in class discussion • I am an active participant in doing group work	• I sometimes respect the class norms for a healthy learning environment we established at the beginning of the semester • I use electronics in class • I rarely volunteer my ideas in class discussion • I sometimes participate in group work	• I rarely respect the class norms for a healthy learning environment we established at the beginning of the semester • I regularly use electronics in class • I do not volunteer my ideas often in class discussion • I am not an active participant in doing group work

Created by Wanda Gregory

Challenge #10: Families and students discount work habit grades because they don't "count" on official transcripts.

TRY THIS: BRING IN COLLEGE ADMISSIONS COUNSELORS TO TALK ABOUT THE IMPACT OF WORK HABITS ON COLLEGE SUCCESS

Many schools are bound by state or district mandates for what can be included on an official transcript. Sometimes this means that standards-based academic grades must be converted into percentages or letter grades on transcripts that are sent to colleges or employers. Figure 8.17 shows one such conversion formula. Unfortunately, the grades for work habits that appear on the school-created report card or as part of a student-led conference agenda may not appear on students' official transcripts. Some families may conclude that work habits don't really matter to colleges because they aren't on the transcript, but college admissions officers and employers know differently. Indeed, these habits are the secret to succeeding and graduating from college or to growing in a career.

Figure 8.17 Grade conversion chart from Capital City Public Charter School in Washington, DC

Standards Based Range	Traditional Grading Scale	Letter Grade Equivalent	GPA Quality Points
4.0	95-100	A	4.0
3.75	90-94	A-	3.75
3.5	87-89	B+	3.5
3.25			3.25
3.0	82-86	B	3.0
2.75	79-81	B-	2.75
2.5	76-78	C+	2.5
2.25			2.25
2.0	70-75	C	2.0
1.75	65-69	D	No Credit
1.5	60-64	D-	No Credit
1.25	55-59	F	No Credit
1.0	0-54	F	No Credit

4 = Mastered Standards, 3 = Proficient in Standards, 2 = Met Standards, 1 = Did Not Meet Standard
created by Belicia Reaves and Dr. Katryna Andrusik

Michael Stefanowicz, Assistant Director of Admissions at Saint Michael's College, and the President of the Consortium of Vermont Colleges, wrote in a blog[7] for JumpRope: "Habits of work are still important. Assessing students based on their ultimate academic achievement in light of approved standards is a pillar of standards-based learning, and that's what should constitute a student's final grade in a high school course. However, habits of work are important to colleges. Students have more freedom in college and are expected to take charge of homework completion, study habits, time management, and the seeking out of academic support. Habits of work should be reported somewhere on the transcript or narratively in the school counselor's recommendation letter. Ideally, high schools should articulate standards for habits of work and devise a system to assess them objectively, based on evidence."

To allay families concerns about what's on and what's not on the transcript, consider inviting a student alum who is now in college or, better still, a college admissions counselor to talk about the importance of effective work habits.

TRY THIS: MAKE THEM COUNT, BUT DO IT CAREFULLY

The practice of standards-based grading requires us to separate work habits and character from academic achievement—for good reason—but sometimes this creates problems when districts or transcripts require a single, final grade. If work habits and character are not a part of that single grade, then students, families, and teachers may not take these skills seriously. It's possible to use a compromise solution: create a report card for students and their families that includes learning targets for academics, work habits, and character, so that these are separate and accountable areas that each require a successful score. And, additionally, use a formula to combine these areas into a single grade, when that is required.

The Springfield Renaissance School in Springfield, Massachusetts, for example, has found that students and parents take work habits much more seriously when they are included in the overall course grade the

---

[7] "Navigating the College Application Process with Your Standards-Based Transcript" Jan 4, 2016.

district compels them to report. At Renaissance, academic learning target grades count for 80% of a student's final grade and Habits of Work grades count for 20% of the final grade. The Renaissance Habits of Work are:

1. I come to class ready to learn.

2. I actively and collaboratively participate in class.

3. I assess and revise my work.

4. I complete daily homework.

Also at Renaissance, the Honor Roll is entirely based on Habits of Work scores, and the Renaissance Scholars Program (which comes with school privileges of expanded choice and autonomy) uses Habits of Work scores in its requirements for induction.

Most teachers agree that *how* students learn matters at least as much as *what* they learn. By giving students ample opportunity to reflect on those work habits, score them against a clear and specific rubric, and share their self-assessment with teachers and families, you reinforce this value. Before you finish this chapter, take a critical look at the report card you are currently using and reflect on how you can revise or supplement it to clarify and underscore students' work habits grade.

A transition to standards-based grading will only succeed if there is true understanding and buy-in from faculty, students, and families. This is the vital role of school leadership. There is no student-engaged assessment shift that has the potential to generate more controversy and opposition. If it feels to the faculty or community like a top-down mandate being done *to* them, rather than an initiative they are supporting and helping to shape, it has little chance of success. School leadership must build a movement in the faculty and community to embrace the change, through clear, respectful communication, frequent meetings, and shared leadership of the substantial work that this entails. The roll-out may need to be gradual.

School leaders can also provide essential support in coordinating all the work. An individual teacher can assess students' work habits and academic progress toward standards using the tools and techniques in this chapter, but those grades must be communicated to families as part of a schoolwide (or district-wide) reporting system. Thus it makes sense for teachers and leaders to collaborate in redesigning and making consistent a schoolwide grading system that is standards-based. Following are a few tips to guide leaders in supporting the work of implementing a standards-based grading system. Table 8.7 then summarizes the key action steps for teachers and students that will lead to success.

Top Tips

- Foster an inquiry-based dialogue with teachers and families. Listen to community concerns and learn together about the practices and implications of using a standards-based grading system in your school community.

- Build a toolbox for standards-based grading well in advance. This includes choosing an online grading program, creating evidence-gathering and reflection tools, and ensuring that teachers' grade books are compatible with grade calculation and reporting tools.

- Provide ample and early professional development for teachers and leaders so that teachers learn how to set up their grade books and gather evidence of progress toward both academic and character (work habits) learning targets, well before grades are due at the end of a term.

- Be patient and open to new ideas, and anticipate challenges. Standards-based grading is a big shift for many teachers. Provide supports such as grading buddies and extra tutorials for teachers who struggle with the theory or implementation of standards-based grading. Lift up innovative ideas from teachers and be willing to change "the system" to improve the result.

Table 8.7 Standards-based grading: Steps to success

What Should Teachers Do?
Learn the research behind standards-based grading and its implications for grading practices and routines.
Educate families and students about what to expect and how standards-based grading is different from traditional grading.
Engage students in tracking their progress toward meeting standards and demonstrating their work habits.
Collaborate with specialists to support students with disabilities and English language learners to succeed within a standards-based grading system.
Assess and report academic progress and work habits separately.
Use online grade books and other tools for entering and calculating standards-based grades efficiently and accurately.
What Should Students Do?
Reflect on and track their progress toward meeting standards and demonstrating their work habits.
Explain the correlation between their academic progress and their habits.
Compile and present evidence of their learning relative to standards-based learning targets.
Set goals and create action plans for improving standards-based grades.

As you have read Chapter 8, maybe you have had an opportunity to try some of these strategies and techniques along the way. If not, come back to this post-assessment after you have had a chance to do so. Give yourself whatever time you need to address the learning targets and challenges in a meaningful way. Then take a moment to check your progress in Table 8.8, which is the exact same Learning Target Tracker that appeared at the beginning of this chapter.

Circle or place an X along the continuum from Beginning to Exceeding: **How would you rate your progress toward each learning target *at this point in time?*** Use the space provided to make notes regarding any remaining challenges you may be having or ideas for new and different strategies you want to try next.

Table 8.8   Chapter 8 learning target tracker

Learning Target 1: *I can help families and students understand the "why" behind standards-based grading.*
Beginning---------------------Developing-----------------------Meeting--------------------Exceeding
Notes:

Learning Target 2: *I can effectively implement standards-based grading in my classroom, school, or district.*
Beginning---------------------Developing-----------------------Meeting--------------------Exceeding
Notes:

Learning Target 3: *I can assess my students' work habits.*
Beginning--------------------Developing-----------------------Meeting--------------------Exceeding
Notes:

What's in the Online Toolbox?

These files can be downloaded from the Online Toolbox that supports *Leaders of Their Own Learning Companion,* at http://www.wiley.com/go/lotolcompanion.

"Check Yourself" Checklists

Chapter 1: Crafting High-Quality Learning Targets Checklist

Chapter 1: Using Learning Targets throughout a Lesson Checklist

Chapter 2: Creating a Positive Classroom Culture for Checking for Understanding Checklist

Chapter 2: The "Don't Forget the Debrief" Checklist

Chapter 3: Creating Effective Systems for Data Collection Checklist

Chapter 4: Choosing a Model Checklist

Chapter 4: Peer Critique Checklist

Chapter 4: Planning for Quality Work Checklist

Chapter 5: Student-Led Conference Agenda/Portfolio Contents Checklist

Chapter 6: Preparing High-Quality Work for Public Display Checklist

Online-Only Files

Chapter 3

Presentation slides to accompany Close Up: Setting S.M.A.R.T. Goals with Second-Graders at Noah Wallace School in Farmington, Connecticut

Chapter 5

Presentation slides to accompany Figure 5.6: Second-Grade Student-Led Conference Script from Noah Wallace School in Farmington, Connecticut

Chapter 7 Portfolio Guides

Third, Fifth, and Eighth Grade Passage Presentation Guide from Odyssey School of Denver

Eighth Grade Passage Portfolio Guide from Evergreen Community Charter School in Asheville, North Carolina.

Tenth Grade Portfolio Passage Guide from Capital City Charter School in Washington, DC

Twelfth Grade Senior Seminar Expedition Curriculum Map from Capital City Charter School in Washington, DC

Chapter 8 Grading Guides

Faculty Grading Guide from Open World Learning Community in St. Paul, Minnesota

Grading Practices Guide from Lexington County School District One in Lexington, South Carolina

Standards-Based Grading Mastery Reports FAQs from Metropolitan Expeditionary Learning School in New York City

Copies of Figures from the Book

Chapter 1

Figure 1.1: Test Yourself: Assessing Learning Targets for Precise and Helpful Verbs

Figure 1.3: Map Your Own Learning Targets onto the Knowledge, Reasoning, and Skills Framework + Bloom's Revised Taxonomy

Figure 1.7: Key Steps for Unpacking Standards

Figure 1.8: Key Steps for Bundling Standards

Chapter 2

Figure 2.1: Sample Form for Observing Students Upholding Classroom Norms

Figure 2.2: Back-to-Back and Face-to-Face Protocol

Figure 2.3: Lesson Plan with Opportunities to Check for Understanding Pre-Identified

Figure 2.4: Strategic Observation Tracker to Accompany the Lesson Plan in Figure 2.3

Figure 2.5: Test Yourself: Match Checking for Understanding Techniques to Your Needs

Figure 2.6: Small-Group Discussion Tracker

Figure 2.7: Problem-Solving Strategy Tracker

Figure 2.8: Contribution/Collaboration Matrix

Figure 2.11: Preplanned Questions and Teacher Reflections from Genesee Community Charter School in Rochester, New York

Figure 2.12: Questioning Observation Note-Catcher

Chapter 3

Figure 3.1: Sample FAQs for Families

Figure 3.2: Lesson Plan for Exploring the Value of Data

Figure 3.6: Collaborative Exit Ticket Data Sort Protocol

Figure 3.7: Independent Reading Tracker

Figure 3.8: Number Sense Tracker

Figure 3.9: Math Quiz Tracker from The Noah Wallace School in Farmington, Connecticut

Figure 3.10: Growth Mindset Target Tracker

Figure 3.11: Math Test Error Self-Analysis

Figure 3.12: Written Work Error Self-Analysis

Figure 3.13: Sample Statistics Lesson

Figure 3.15: Goal Setting Worksheet for Literacy

Figure 3.16: Goal Setting Tool for Argument Writing from Irving A. Robbins Middle School in Farmington, Connecticut

Figure 3.17: Math Goal- Setting Tracker from Irving A. Robbins Middle School in Farmington, Connecticut

Figure 3.18: 3-2-1 Exit Ticket

Chapter 4

Figure 4.1: Student Checklist for Worthy Revision

Figure 4.2: Questions to Ask Yourself When Test Driving a Task

Figure 4.3: Attributes of High-Quality Student Work

Figure 4.4: The Quality Work Protocol

Figure 4.6: Revolutionary Rum

Figure 4.7: A Weak Model of Student Work: Survey Data Conclusion Statement

Figure 4.8: Social Activism PSA Criteria List with Learning Targets from Irving A. Robbins Middle School in Farmington, Connecticut

Figure 4.9: The Praise, Question, Suggestion Protocol

Figure 4.10: Peer Feedback Protocol for Pairs

Figure 4.11: Poster Mock-up Feedback Note-Catcher

Figure 4.12: How Rock-Solid is My Argument Note-Catcher

Figure 4.13: 3-2-1 Revision Action Plan

Figure 4.14: Rubric Row for Reflecting on Revision of Work

Chapter 5

Figure 5.1: Student-led conference logistics checklist from Washington Heights Expeditionary Learning School in New York City and The Franklin School of Innovation in Asheville, North Carolina

Figure 5.2: High School Portfolio Requirements for Student-Led Conferences from Metropolitan Expeditionary Learning School in New York City

Figure 5.3: Accountability Tracking Sheet by Learning Target

Figure 5.4: Writing Reflection Form for Student-Led Conferences from Two Rivers Public Charter School in Washington, DC

Figure 5.5: Sample Student-Led Conference Preparation Calendar from the Franklin School of Innovation in Asheville, North Carolina

Figure 5.6: Primary Student-Led Conference Script from The Noah Wallace School in Farmington, Connecticut

Figure 5.7: Middle School Student-Led Conference Script from Two Rivers Public Charter School in Washington, DC

Figure 5.8: High School Student-Led Conference Agenda from Gilbert High School in Gilbert, South Carolina

Figure 5.9: Lesson Plan: Student-Led Conference Preparation Critique

Figure 5.10: Letter to Families from Two Rivers Public Charter School in Washington, DC

Figure 5.11: Student-Led Conference Parent Survey Adapted from The Franklin School of Innovation in Asheville, North Carolina

Figure 5.12: Student-Led Conference Parent Survey from Oakhurst Elementary School in Decatur, Georgia

Chapter 6

Figure 6.1: Celebration of Learning Planner from Kuumba Academy Charter School in Wilmington, Delaware

Figure 6.4: Documentation Panel and Student Work Note-Catcher

Figure 6.5: Student Script for Presenting Work at a Celebration of Learning

Figure 6.7: Gallery Walk Protocol for Noticing Changes in Drafts

Figure 6.8: Snake Song Performance Rubric from Conservatory Lab Charter School in Boston

Chapter 7

Figure 7.1: Triple-A Visioning Tool for Seniors

Figure 7.2: Letter to Families from Metropolitan Expeditionary Learning School in New York City

Figure 7.3: Exploring My Personal Growth Outside of School

Figure 7.4: Protocol for Selecting Passage Portfolio Work

Figure 7.5: "Big Learning" Reflection Tool

Figure 7.6: Learning Story Outline from Harborside Academy in Kenosha, Wisconsin

Figure 7.7: Guidelines for Powerpoint Presentations from Evergreen Community Charter School in Asheville, North Carolina

Figure 7.8: Question and Sentence Stems to Guide Feedback for Passage Presentations

Figure 7.9: Seven Gauges for A Snappy Presentation

Figure 7.10: Passage Presentation Preparation Checklist from The Franklin School of Innovation in Asheville, North Carolina

Figure 7.11: Individuals to Invite to Serve as Passage Presentation Panelists

Figure 7.12: Letter to Passage Presentation Panelists from The Franklin School of Innovation in Asheville, North Carolina

Figure 7.13: Model of Completed Feedback Form Used to Train Passage Presentation Panelists at the Odyssey School of Denver

Chapter 8

Figure 8.1: 3-2-1 Exit Ticket for Study Groups or Individual Reflection

Figure 8.3: Sample Kindergarten Report Card from Decatur City Schools, Decatur, Georgia

Figure 8.4: Sample High School Report Card from Beaverton School District, Beaverton, Oregon

Figure 8.5: Frequently Asked Questions from the Beaverton School District, Beaverton, Oregon

Figure 8.6: Algebra Assessment Tracker from Irving A. Robbins Middle School in Farmington, Connecticut

Figure 8.7: World Language Assessment Tracker from Irving A. Robbins Middle School in Farmington, Connecticut

Figure 8.9: World Language Retake Form from Irving A. Robbins Middle School, Farmington, Connecticut

Figure 8.10: Missing Assignment Contract

Figure 8.13: Habits of Work and Learning Rubric from Metropolitan Expeditionary Learning School in New York City

References

Ainsworth, L. (n.d.) Larry talks about priority standards. Retrieved from: https://www.larryainsworth.com/prioritizing-the-common-core-power-standards

Berger, R., Rugen, L., and Woodfin, L. (2014a). *Leaders of their own learning: Transforming schools through student-engaged assessment*. San Francisco, CA: Jossey-Bass.

Berger, R., Woodfin, L., Plaut, S., and Dobbertin, C. (2014b). *Transformational literacy: Making the common core shift with work that matters*. San Francisco, CA: Jossey-Bass.

Berger, R., Strasser, D., and Woodfin, L. (2015). *Management in the active classroom*. New York, NY: EL Education.

Berger, R., Woodfin, L., and Vilen, A. (2016). *Learning that lasts: Challenging, engaging, and empowering students with deeper instruction*. San Francisco, CA: Jossey-Bass.

Hess, Karin K. (2009, updated 2013). Linking research with practice: A local assessment toolkit to guide school leaders. Retrieved from https://www.karin-hess.com/cognitive-rigor-and-dok

Klein, J. (2015). Say "Wrong answer" while encouraging growth mindsets. Retrieved from: http://motionmath-games.com/say-wrong-answer-while-encouraging-growth-mindsets

Michaels, S., and O'Connor, C. (2012). *Talk science primer*. Cambridge, MA: TERC. http://inquiryproject.terc.edu/shared/pd/TalkScience_Primer.pdf. Based on Chapin, S., O'Connor, C., and Anderson, N. (2009). *Classroom discussions: Using math talk to help students learn, grades K–6 (2nd ed.)*. Sausalito, CA: Math Solutions Publications.

Stefanowicz, M., (2016). Navigating the college application process with your standards-based transcript. Retrieved from: https://www.jumpro.pe/single-post/2017/02/14/Navigating-the-College-Application-Process-with-Your-Standards-Based-Transcript

Stiggins, R., Arter, J., Chappuis, J., and Chappuis, S. (2006). *Classroom assessment for student learning: Doing it right – using it well*. Portland, OR: Assessment Training Institute.

Vogler, K. (2008). Asking good questions. *Educational Leadership* 65 (9).

Zinsser, W. (2012). *The writer who stayed*. Philadelphia, PA: Paul Dry Books.

Index

A

Ainsworth, Larry, 286
Algebra: assessment tracker, 291; introducing learning targets in, 19–20
Anchor charts, 59
Apps, for grading work habits, 297–298
Archiving, portfolio, 242–244
Argument writing: goal setting tool for, 110; poster mock-up feedback for, 148
Arter, J., 14
Assessment: classroom norms, 50; frequent, 41; Mathematics Assessment Project, 134–135; standards-targets document on, 40; video on end-of-cycle, 112; work habits, 297–302; written work error self-analysis, 100–101. *See also* Post-assessment; Pre-assessment; Student-engaged assessment
Assignments: missing, 170, 294; revision, 121–124, 149–150
Attire, passage presentation, 254–255
Attributes of High-Quality Work, 126–127, 152
Audiences: authentic, 159; interaction with, 225
Authenticity, quality work and, 126

B

Background knowledge, questions requiring, 75
Back-to-Back and Face-to-Face, 30; classroom norms protocol, 51, 55; for collaboration improvement, 54, 55; procedure and variations, 55
Big learning reflection tool, 250
Bloom's Revised Taxonomy, 14; Depth-of-Knowledge levels and, 15, 18; Hess Cognitive Rigor Matrix and, 18; Knowledge, Reasoning, and Skills Framework and, 16; question stems based on, 70–71
Brookhart, S., 276
Buckmiller, Tom, 276

C

Calendars, presentation rehearsal, 172–173
Capital City Public Charter School, 246; grade conversion chart, 305; passage presentation variations, 239–240; work habits reflection tool, 304
Casco Bay High School, 273; standards-based grading at, 273, 276, 288; videos, 279

Case studies: on enlisting experts to improve student work, 142–143; learning target for Algebra II Class, 19–20. *See also* Close Up

Catch and release strategy: for critique lessons, 136; for learning targets, 27–28

Celebrations of learning: audience interaction in, 225; community involvement in, 199; community members as VIPs in, 225–226; definition and overview, 196; documentation panels for, 198–204; exhibit pre-identifying for, 223; families and, 199, 223–224; growth focus of, 217–218; look-fors and questions for parents attending, 224; planning, 197, 198–200; post-assessment, 229; pre-assessment, 196; presentation formats for, 223; public displays and, 205–214; quality work in, 204; rehearsing for, 220; schoolwide, 198; script for presenting work in, 217; snake song performance sample rubric for, 221–222; steps to success, 228; student reflections on learning in, 215–217; student role and activities during, 218–220; template use challenge, 203–204; top tips for, 227; as tradition, 201; uniqueness highlighted in, 203–204

Chappuis, J., 14

Character learning targets, 33–35

Checking for understanding, 47; checklist, 58; classroom norms and, 50–52; debriefing as priority for, 79–81; definition of, 47; ELLs and, 57; growth-oriented statements in, 51–52; lack of techniques challenge in, 60–66; learning targets for teachers in, 48, 58; post-assessment, 84; practice as necessary, 82; pre-assessment, 48–49; protocols for, 53–54, 61–63, 66, 67; quick-check techniques for, 61–63; steps to success, 83; teacher shortcuts problem, 82; technique selection and, 62–63; top tips for, 82–83; tracking forms, 67–70

Checklists: checking understanding, 58, 79; for choosing a model, 135; crafting learning targets, 17, 35; data use with students, 106; debriefing, 80–81; passage presentation, 261; peer critique, 151; portfolio contents, 171; revision-worthy assignments, 122

Close Up: data analysis using other students' process, 93–95; on student-led conferences, 159–160

Codman Academy, 237–238

Cognitive Rigor Matrix (CRM), 17, 18

Cognitive skills: ELLs and, 25–26; learning targets with varying, 14; playful learning targets with, 17; questions to develop, 70–71

Collaboration, student: with community experts, 142; Contribution/collaboration matrix, 70; data use, 96; protocols to increase, 53–60; public learning for increasing, 56

The College School, 202

Communities: celebrations of learning and, 199; passage presentations and, 264; VIP treatment of members of, 225–226

Complexity, quality work and, 126

Concept Map/Interactive Word Wall, 62

Conservatory Lab Charter School, 201; second-graders celebration of learning, 201, 204, 221–222; snake song performance rubric from, 221–222

Contextualizing, learning target, 13

Contract, missing assignment, 296

Contribution/collaboration matrix, 70

Conversation cues, for ELLs, 56–57

Conway Elementary, 161

Craftsmanship, quality work and, 126

Criteria List: critique lessons and, 138–139; social activism PSA, 139

Critique lessons, models and, 107; beginning, 131; bringing experts into, 142–143; catch and release strategy for, 141; conferences and, 140–141; criteria list and, 138–139; critique and revision timeline, 123–124; definition of, 119; designing, 137; future papers focus in, 141–142; kind, specific, and helpful sentence stems for, 143; ownership and inquiry in, 137–138; peer critique and, 145; post-assessment, 118; poster mock-up feedback note-catcher, 148; pre-assessment, 120; revision planning and, 123; sentence stems for, 137, 144; steps to success, 153. *See also* Descriptive Feedback; Peer feedback

Critiques: gallery, 136; in-depth, 136

CRM. *See* Cognitive Rigor Matrix

Culture: classroom norms and, 50–52, 59; of constructive critique, 152; passage presentations and, 255, 262; quality, 152

D

Darling-Hammond, Linda, 31

Data use, with students: big picture challenge for, 107; building data notebooks, 100–101; checklist, 107; data inquiry conference, 103, 105; discrepant data investigation, 105; elementary grades data trackers, 99; FAQs for families, 91; girls basketball example of, 92–93; goal setting and, 108–112; Improvement plan action steps for, 111; independent tracking and, 103; lack of interest challenge, 91–92, 103; learning targets, 86, 97, 107; overview, 87–89; paper management, 97; primary grades data trackers, 98; protocols, 96; rigid idea of data challenge, 89; routine incorporation of, 95; secondary grades data trackers, 100; statistics introduction, 103–104; steps to success, 114; student collaboration and, 96; student-engaged assessment and, 113; writing analysis comparison for, 93–95

Debriefing: Exit Tickets for, 80–81; learning targets and, 29–31; student-led conference, 188

Decaying average approach, to grading, 289, 294

Depth-of-Knowledge levels, 15, 18

Descriptive Feedback: improving future work in, 141–142; learning targets for, 120–121, 136; planning for revision and critique, 123–124; pre-assessment, 120; quality work and, 119, 126–127; standards-based grading and, 290

Digital portfolios, 244

Documentation panels: for celebrations of learning, 198–204; for collaboration, 59; note-catcher, 214

E

English language learners (ELLs): conversation cues for, 56–57; Interpreters for, at student-led conferences, 164; learning targets for, 26–27, 296; student-led conferences and, 164

Evergreen Community Charter School: celebration of learning in, 200; kindergarten celebration of learning, 225; model use by middle-school students of, 145; passage presentations in, 240–241

Exhibition of learning. *See* Celebrations of learning

Exit Tickets, 31, 67; data sort note-catcher, 96; for data use collaboration, 94; for debriefing, 80–81; in goal setting, 112; for study groups or reflection, 278

Experts: critique lessons and, 142–143; standards specialists, 294, 296; video on kindergarteners as, 219

F

Families: celebrations of learning and, 199, 223–224; conference role of, 184; data routines explained to, 92; data use FAQs for, 91; feedback from, 186–187; passage presentations and, 241–242, 264; standards-based grading and, 279–285; student-led conferences and, 163, 181–187, 242; work habits discounted by, 304

Feedback: from families, 186–187; ineffective, 141; from passage portfolio panelists, 264–266; peer, 144; student reflection and evaluation of, 148; on student-led conference, 176; work habits, 300. *See also* Descriptive Feedback; Peer feedback

Fieldwork, student reflections on, 215

Final word presentations, 238

Fishbowl protocol, 51

Fox Creek Elementary, 195, 241

Franklin School of Innovation, 160–161; habits of scholarship continuum from, 302; letter to passage presentation panelists from, 264; parent survey from, 187; passage presentation checklist from, 261; preparation calendars, 172; report card from, 302; self-talk poster, 52; work habits approach of, 303–304

G

Genesee Community Charter School: data use video, 96; documentation panels from, 209; preplanned teacher questions example from, 73–74

Gilbert High School, 188

Goal setting: argument writing tool for, 112; Exit Ticket for, 112; math example of, 111; reading example of, 108; student-led conferences family, 185; worksheet, 109

Grade books, 287–288

Grade conversion chart, 305

Grade-level standards, learning targets in relation to, 36–41

Grading: quantitative and qualitative portfolios and, 168 (*See also* Standards-based grading); comparison of traditional and standards-based, 280–281; decaying average approach to, 289, 294; grade calculation methods, 287–289; guides, 280; for multiple years, 247; spotting the trend method of, 288–289

Group presentations, sample script for, 217

Growth mindset, 152; target tracker, 99

Growth-oriented statements, 51–52

Guskey, T., 276

H

Habits of Scholarship, 273; continuum, 302. *See also* Work habits

Habits of Work at Renaissance, 104

Handbooks, family, 181

Harborside Academy, 214, 251

Health and Science School, 240

Hess, Karin K., 18

Human Bar Graph, 31, 67

I

I do/We do/You do, lesson structure as, 20

IEPs. *See* Individual Education Programs

Improvement plan action steps, data use and goal setting, 111

Index Card Protocol, 90

Individual Education Programs (IEPs), 257, 285, 296

Inquiry, inviting student, 71

Interactive Word Wall, 62

Interdistrict School for Arts and Communication (ISAAC), video on immigrants, experts working with, 142

Irving A. Robbins Middle School, 109, 110, 119, 139; Algebra assessment tracker from, 291

ISAAC. *See* Interdistrict School for Arts and Communication

J

JumpRope, 289, 298, 305

K

King Middle School: checking for understanding video from, 66; class norms video, 50; Index Card Protocol video, 90; Scaffolding Research-Based Writing video, 140; year-long target tracker from, 293

King Philip Middle School, student-led conferences and, 181

Knowledge: Bloom's Revised Taxonomy and, 16; learning targets application of, 16; Reading, and Skills Framework, 14–15

Kuumba Academy, schoolwide celebration of learning, 198–199

L

Learning displays, **213–214**

Learning targets, 23; accountability for, 43; Algebra II Class case study in, 19–20; breaking lesson into multiple, 11; catch and release strategy, 27–28; celebrations of learning, 216; character, 33–35;

Learning targets (*continued*)
character with academic, 35; for
checking understanding, 48, 59, 79;
checklists for crafting, 17, 35;
clay bird beak example of, 9–10;
cognitive skill levels and, 14;
contextualizing, 13; for data use with
students, 86, 97, 107; debriefing and,
29–31; definition of, 7; Depth-of-
Knowledge levels and, 15, 18; for
descriptive feedback, 120–121, 136;
ELL, 25–26, 296; first-grade criteria
for, 14–15; introducing, 19–20;
in Knowledge, Reasoning, and
Skills Framework, 14–15; learning-
not-doing focus of, 11–12; lesson
structure and, 21–22, 27–28; long-
term, 39, 277; nested, 38; passage
presentations, 234, 252; planning
ahead for, 19; playful, 17; post-
assessment tracker for, 43–44; as
puzzles, 24; reflection questions and,
216; report cards and, 283; sentence
starters for progress toward,
179–180; standards and, 36–41; for
standards-based grading, 274; steps
to success, 43; strategic unpacking
of, 22–27; student experience of
using, 7; for student-led conferences,
157–158; third-grade math example,
79–80; top tips for, 43; tracking
forms, 28; tracking systems for,
169–170; verbs for writing, 15–16,
40–41; writing on everything, 31–32.
See also Trackers, learning target
Learning walk, 3
Lesson plans: conference preparation,
178; data value exploration,
92; statistics, 104. *See also*
Critique lessons

Lesson structure: learning targets
and, 21–22, 27–28; for literacy, 21;
for math, 22
Lexington County School
District One, standards-based
grading in, 280
Long-term learning targets,
38–39, 277

M

Mary O. Pottenger Elementary School,
celebration of learning in, 223
Math: Cognitive Rigor Matrix for
science and, 18; goal setting and,
111; learning target for third-grade,
79–80; lesson structure for, 22;
Mathematics Assessment Project,
134–135; Menu, 103; video on
deep engagement with, 134; video
on improving thinking and, 76;
water usage lesson plan in, 65. *See
also* Algebra
Meadow Brook High School, quality
work protocol in, 129
Metropolitan Expeditionary Learning
School, 166, 240, 280; habits of work
learning rubric from, 301; letter to
families, 242
Mindset, growth, 52, 99
Missing assignments, 170;
contract, 296; standards-based
approach to, 296
Models: case study on use of experts
and, 142–143; checklist for
choosing, 135; definition and use of,
119; instructiveness of weak, 132–
133; ISAAC example of professional,
142; literacy workshop, 21; with
multiple perspectives, 134–135;

passage presentation, 234–235, 255–256, 266; post-assessment, 118; pre-assessment, 120; schoolwide bank of, 152; slide presentation, 256; with specific strengths, 130–132; student inspiration from, 130; student-led conference, 173; teacher sharing of, 124. *See also* Critique lessons, models and

Multi-year portfolios, 255

N

Noah Wallace School, 93–95, 108; conference script from, 174

Norms: academics blended with, 51; classroom culture and, 50–52, 59; colleague observation of, 52–53

Note-catchers: data sort, 96; documentation panel, 214; for peer feedback, 146, 148; poster mock-up feedback, 148

Numbered Heads Together protocol, 104

O

Oakhurst Elementary School, 187

Odyssey School, Denver: documentation panel from, 213; eighth-grade report card, 302; Menu Math video, 103; model feedback from for panelists, 266; passage presentation guide from, 246; passage presentations and, 241; student-led conferences, 181, 186; work habits approach of, 300

Open World Learning Community, 280

P

Panelists, passage presentation, 262–263; feedback from, 264–266

Parents: conferences accommodating working, 163; look-fors and questions for, 224; as practice partners, 177; questions to ask children at conference, 184; report cards and, 302; student-led conference formats and, 186; student-led conference survey for, 187

Parent-teacher conferences. *See* Student-led conferences

Passage presentations, with portfolios: agenda sample, 265; archiving issues, 242–244; attire for, 254–255; character growth data in, 251; checklist, 261; communicating importance of, 238–239; content of, 245–246; definition and overview, 233; evaluation chart for panelists, 265; families and, 241–242; gauges for snappy, 258; grade level and, 235; learning story outline for, 252; as milestone and tradition, 237–238; models, 234–235, 255–256; multi-dimensional reflection and, 249–250; nontraditional components for, 247; out-of-school learning content in, 245; panelists for, 262–263; personal vision and, 237–238; post-assessment, 270; PowerPoint presentations in, 256; pre-assessment, 234; professional, 254–255; protocol for work selection, 249; purpose and value of, 234–236; recruiting panelists for, 262–263; rehearsal, 258–259; responding to questions

Passage presentations (*continued*) during, 259–260; senior talk format for, 238; steps to success, 269; student reflection and, 249–250; tone, diction, visuals in, 255; variations, 239–240; work habits evidence in, 251

Peer feedback (critique), 145; art students example of, 145; checklist for teachers on, 151; connecting revision with, 149–150; giving credit for revision process in, 149; note-catchers for, 146, 148; praise, question, suggestion protocol for, 145–146; protocol for student pairs giving, 147; revision action plan and, 149; student reflection and evaluation in, 149–150

Perkins, David, 47

Playful learning targets, 17

Portfolios, student: archiving, 242–244; contents checklist, 171; digital, 244; incomplete, 170; maintenance, 242–244; multi-year, 243; out-of-school learning included in, 245; presenting balanced, 164–165. *See also* Passage presentations, with portfolios

Post-assessment: celebrations of learning, 229; for checking understanding, 84; critique lessons, models, 119; for data use, with students, 115; learning target tracker, 44; passage presentation, 270; standards-based grading, 309; student-led conferences, 191

Praise, Question, Suggestion Protocol, 145–146

Pre-assessment: for celebrations of learning, 196; for checking understanding, 48–49; data use with students, 88; for descriptive feedback, 120; for models, critique, 120; for passage presentations, 234;

for standards-based grading, 274; for student-led conferences, 158

Presentations, 195; rehearsal, 172–173, 177, 258–259; student roles and formats for, 220; student script for celebration of learning, 217. *See also* Passage presentations, with portfolios

Primary grades, learning targets for, 24–25

Priority standards, 286

Protocols: Back-to-Back and Face-to-Face, 30, 51, 55; Bumper Sticker, 62; checking for understanding, 53–54, 61–63, 66, 67; classroom norms, 50; Concept Map/Interactive Word Wall, 62; data use, 94; definition of, 53; Exit Ticket, 31, 67, 80–81, 96, 112, 278; Fishbowl, 51; Flip Check, 63; focusing on few, 60; Gallery Walk, 218; Human Bar Graph, 31, 67; Index Card, 90; Numbered Heads Together, 104; passage portfolio work selection, 249; peer feedback, 145–146; quality work, 128; Rapid Fire Brainstorm, 63; for reflection during learning process, 170–171; Speed Dating, 145; student collaboration, 53–60; student pair feedback, 147; Think-Pair-Share, 30, 60; Thumb-ometer, 51, 61, 62, 67; Whole-Class Learning Target Tracker, 63; Write-Pair-Share, 30

Q

Quality work: attributes, 126–127, 152; celebrations of learning and, 204; checklist, 125; checklist for public display of, 205; improving future work, 141–142; protocol,

128; school culture and, 152; underestimating time needed for, 204–205; video on models, critiques and, 136

Questions: Bloom's Revised Taxonomy-based, 73–74; data use FAQs for families, 91; debriefing, 29; FAQs on standards-based grading, 284–285; generic, 74–75; look-fors and, 224; neutral response to answered, 72–73; for parents to ask children at conference, 184; for passage presentation panelists, 267; preplanned, 73–74; question-asking patterns, 76–78; tips for responding to presentation, 259–260; volleyball style, 71. *See also* Video reflection questions

Quick checks, 47, 61–63; benefit of, 61; factual or brief-response, 61; monitoring confusion or readiness, 61; for probing understanding and reflection, 61; status checks, 61; table of additional, 61–62; Thumb-ometer, 50, 61, 62

R

Reading: independent reading tracker, 98; K-2 foundations skills block, 112; Knowledge, Reading, and Skills Framework, 14–15; second-grader goals for, 108; video on scientific thinking and, 66

Recruiting, passage presentation panelist, 262–263

Reflection, student, 61, 148, 149–150, 170–171; celebrations of learning and, 215–217, 221–222; form for writing and, 171; on mastery and progress, 179–180;

multi-dimensional, 249–250; passage presentations and, 249–250, 260; on performance, 222; questions for stimulating, 216; on specific skills and knowledge, 248; on work habits, 251; work habits discussion and, 303

Rehearsal: calendars, 172–173; for celebrations of learning, 220; passage presentation, 258–259; for student-led conferences, 172–173, 177

Report cards: high school sample, 283; kindergarten sample, 282; standards-based, 280–281; work habits on, 302–304

Revision: connecting feedback to, 149–150; documentation panel, 208; peer feedback and action plan for, 149; student checklist for, 122; student-led conferences and, 176; work categories that deserve, 121–122

River Bluff High School: digital portfolio, 244; student-led conference, 159

Rocky Mountain School of Expeditionary Learning, documentation panel from, 210

Rubrics: for celebrations if learning, 220–221; for work habits, 301

S

St. Louis, Missouri: The College School in, 211

St. Michael School of Clayton, 210

Scaffolding: critique and revision through, 123; research-based writing and, 140

Science, 66, 240; CRM for learning targets in math and, 18

Scripts: for celebrations of learning, 217; group presentation sample, 217; for student-led conferences, 174–175

Self-assessment: student work habits, 297; written work error self-analysis, 100–101

Senior talks, 238

Sentence starters, for progress toward learning targets, 179–180

Sentence stems: in critique lessons, 137, 144; kind, specific, and helpful, 143

S.M.A.R.T. Goals, 107, 108

Socratic Circle, 31

Speed Dating Protocol, 145

Spotting the trend method, of grading, 288–289

Springfield Renaissance School, 19–20, 47, 182, 238; Habits of Work statistics lesson at, 104; out-of-school learning challenge, 246

Standards: learning targets in relation to, 36–41; specialists to help students meet, 296; World Language, 290

Standards-based grading: Ainsworth's priority standards, 286; assessment retakes for students, 290–291; assessment tracking, 290–291; definition and overview, 273–274; descriptive feedback and, 290; families and, 279–285; FAQs on, 284–285; grade calculation, 287–289; implementation timeline, 284; learning targets for, 274; missing assignment contract and, 296; other terms for, 274; post-assessment, 309; pre-assessment, 274; principles of, 276; reading recommendations, 276; report card, 280–282, 302–304; showing families benefits of, 279; steps to success, 308; student focus on standard and requirements, 290; student-engaged assessment in, 290–291; study group for learning about, 276; support provision to students, 294; traditional vs., 273; transitioning to, 275, 276–279; work habits and, 274, 297–302; work habits inclusion in report card, 302–304; year-long target trackers, 293; zero eliminated in, 294

Stiggins, R., 14

Student-led conferences: agency development through, 185; agendas for, 176; debriefing, 188; definition of, 157; facilitation skill teaching for, 182–184; family engagement in, 163, 181–187, 242–244; family role in, 184; format differentiation for, 186; high school examples of, 159–160; learning not doing focus of, 179–180; learning targets for, 157–158; missing assignments and, 170; models, feedback and revision for, 176; models for, 169, 173; multiple, simultaneous, 159, 161; organizing large-school, 159–160; parent survey, 187; portfolio contents checklist, 171; post-assessment, 191; pre-assessment, 158; preparation critique lesson plan, 178; presentation rehearsal before, 172–173, 177; scheduling, 159–160; schoolwide structures for, 189; scripts for, 174–175; sentence starters for learning target progress, 179–180; staff preparedness for, 162–163; staggered, 162; steps to success, 190; student portfolios for, 165–166; student role in, 182–184; teacher role in, 184; test scores and data sharing in, 167–168; tracking systems and,

169–170; traditions created for, 181–182; translators for, 164; writing reflection form and, 171. *See also* Celebrations of learning

Surveys, parent, 187

T

Tahoe Expedition Academy, 236

Think-Pair-Share: anchor chart, 59; Write-Pair-Share and, 30

Thumb-ometer, 51, 61, 62; when to use, 67

Townsley, M., 276

Trackers, learning target, 8, 28, 30; celebrations of learning, 196, 229; checking for understanding, 48–49; for data use with students, 115; for descriptive feedback, models, 122; elementary grades data, 98; growth mindset, 99; math goal setting, 111; passage presentation, 270; personal learning, 63; post-assessment, 44; primary grades data use, 98; Problem-solving strategy, 69; small group discussion, 68; for standards-based grading, 309; Strategic Observation Tracker, 66; for student-led conferences, 158; student-led conferences and, 169–170, 191; whole-class, 61; year-long, 293. *See also* Post-assessment

Traditional grading: standards-based vs., 273; transitioning from, 275, 276–279; transitioning to standards-based from, 276–279

Traditions: celebrations of learning as, 201; passage presentation, 237–238; student-led conferences, 181–182

Two Rivers Public Charter School, 48, 175, 182; comparison of grading systems, 280

W

Washington Heights Expeditionary Learning School (WHEELS), 160–161, 189, 233

Winnona Park Elementary School, celebration of learning at, 200

Wood Hill Middle School, celebration of learning of, 208

Work habits, student: academic progress as separate from, 274, 275, 277; apps for grading, 297–298; building and prioritizing, 297; families and students view of, 303–304; feedback on, 300; passage presentations and, 251; progression, 300; quantifiable evidence of, 297; on report cards, 302–304; rubric, 301; standards-based grading and, 297–302; student self-assessment of, 297; in traditional grading, 280; transcripts and, 305

Workshop Model, 21–22

The World of Inquiry School #58, 212

Wormeli, Rick, 279

Writing: argument, 110, 149; data analysis and, 93–95; error self-analysis, 100–101; on everything, 31–32; learning target, 18–19; reflection form, 171; scaffolding research-based, 140; verbs for learning target, 9–10, 40–41